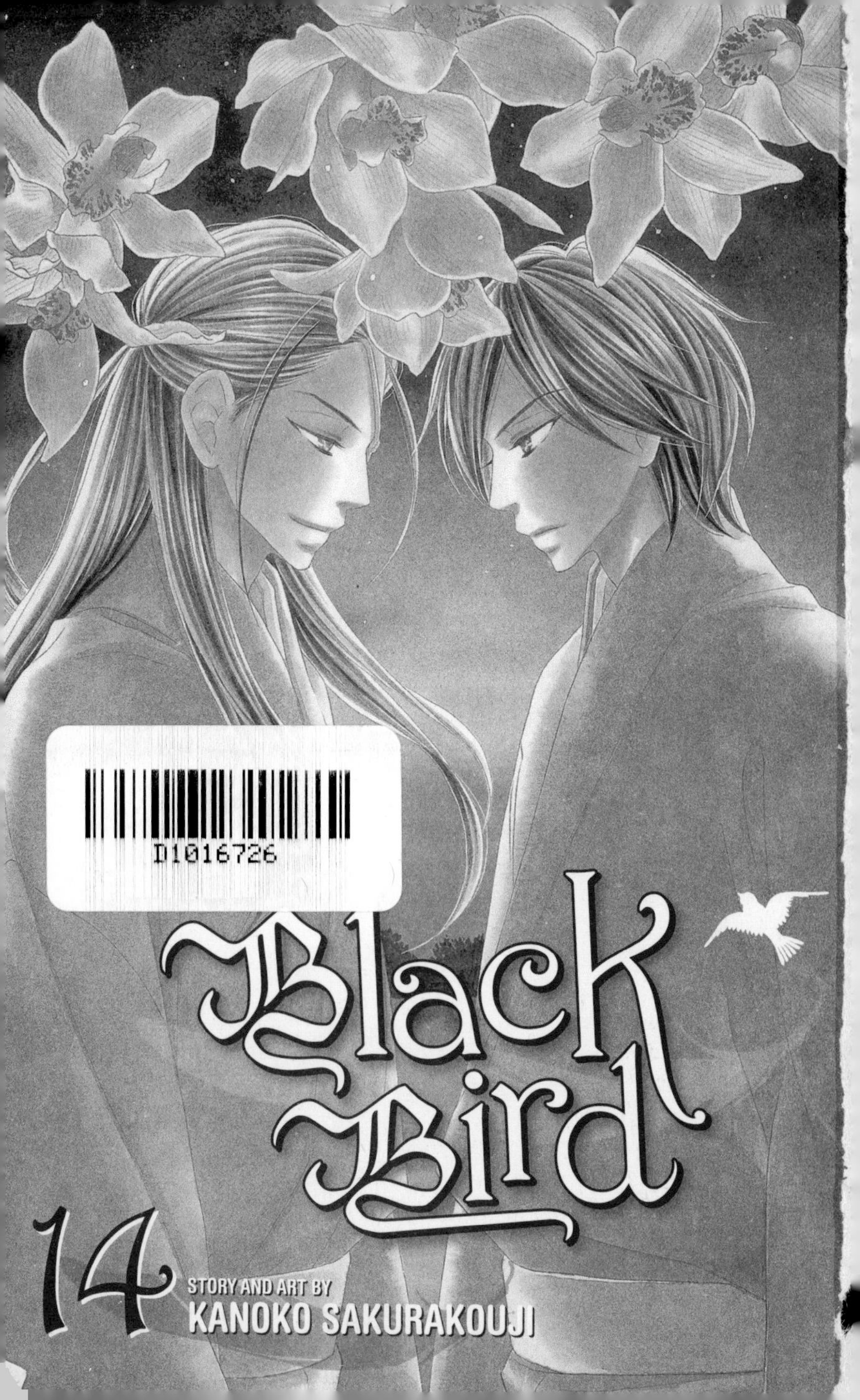
Black Bird
14
STORY AND ART BY
KANOKO SAKURAKOUJI

Black Bird

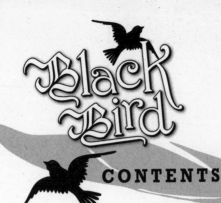

CONTENTS

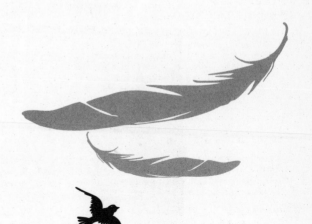

CHARACTERS

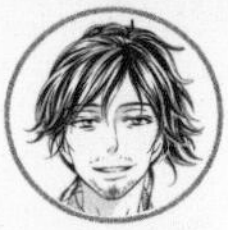

YOH USUI
Father of Kyo and Sho. He was formerly the leader of the tengu clan.

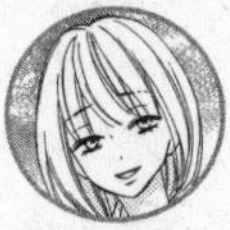

KAEDE
Her father Roh supported Sho's ambitions to seize the clan leadership. She is Sho's attendant.

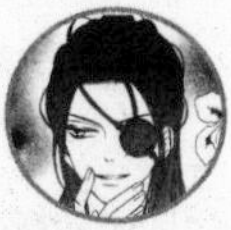

SHO USUI
Kyo's older brother and an ex-member of the Eight Daitengu. He is also known as Sojo. His attempted coup failed and he is currently plotting near the tengu village.

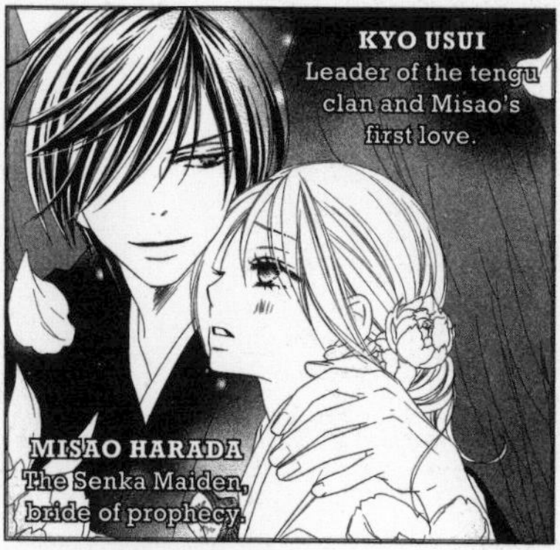
KYO USUI
Leader of the tengu clan and Misao's first love.
MISAO HARADA
The Senka Maiden, bride of prophecy.

THE EIGHT DAITENGU
Kyo's bodyguards. Their names designate their official posts.

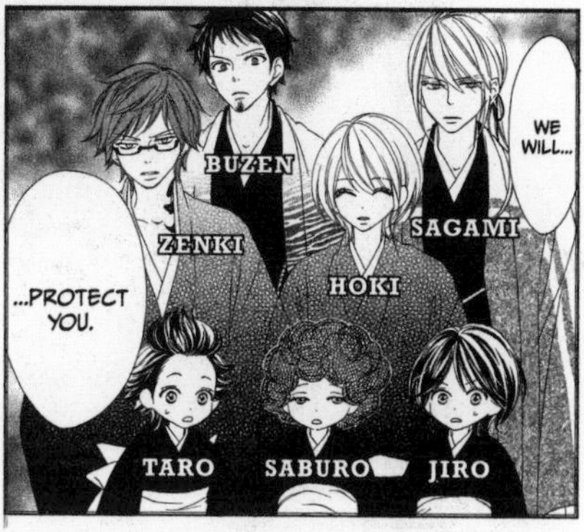
WE WILL...
...PROTECT YOU.
BUZEN
ZENKI
SAGAMI
HOKI
TARO
SABURO
JIRO

STORY THUS FAR
Misao can see spirits and demons, and her childhood sweetheart Kyo has been protecting her since she was little.

"Someday, I'll come for you, I promise."
Kyo reappears the day before Misao's 16th birthday to tell her, "Your 16th birthday marks 'open season' on you." She is the Senka Maiden, and if a demon drinks her blood, he is granted a long life. If he eats her flesh, he gains eternal youth. And if he makes her his bride, his clan will prosper...And Kyo is a *tengu*, a crow demon, with his sights firmly set on her.

Kyo avoided sleeping with Misao because he knew that sex with a demon is somehow dangerous for the Senka Maiden, but when poison nearly killed him, he finally gave in and took Misao.

Now that Kyo's powers have no equal, his older brother Sho, presumed dead, reappears. Sho plans to use the might he obtained through his resurrection, Misao's blood, and his domination of other demon clans to throw the tengu village into confusion and create a world of anarchy.

But something strange is happening to Sho's resurrected body, and to try and halt its progress, Misao gives Sho some of her blood.

Powerful once again, Sho challenges Kyo to battle. In the midst of the fight, someone's arm is lobbed off and lands in front of Misao!

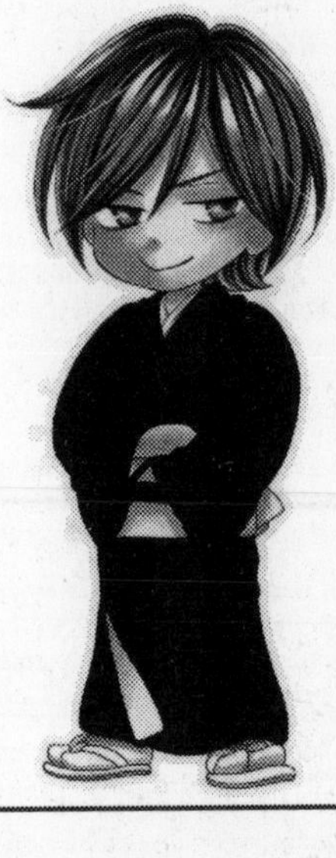

Black Bird

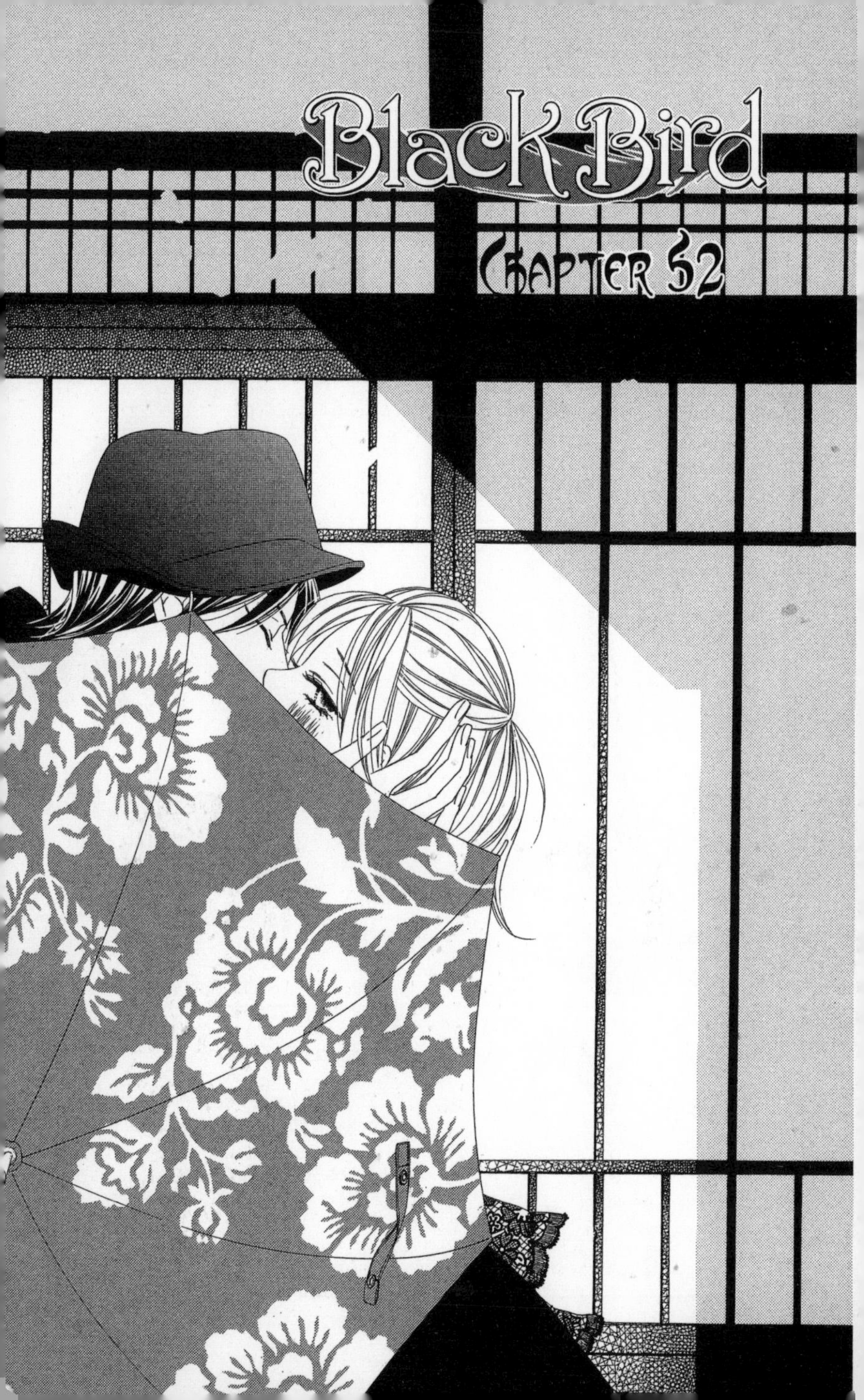
Black Bird
Chapter 52

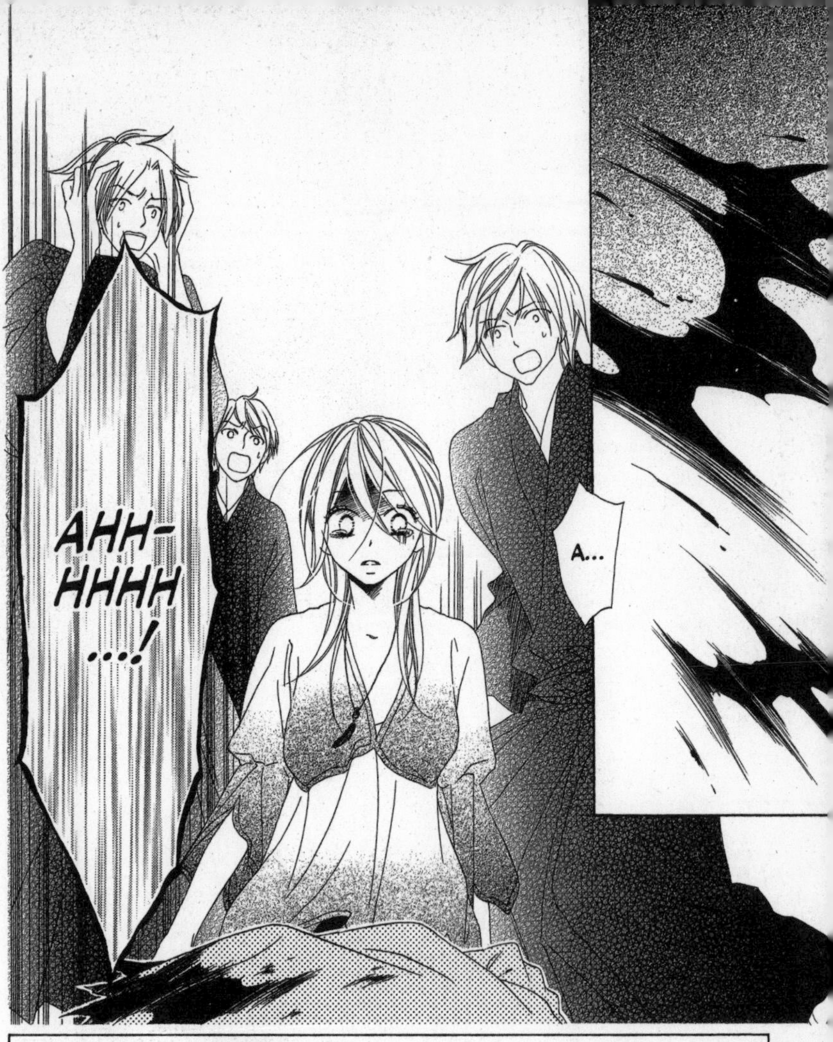
A...
AHH-HHHH...!

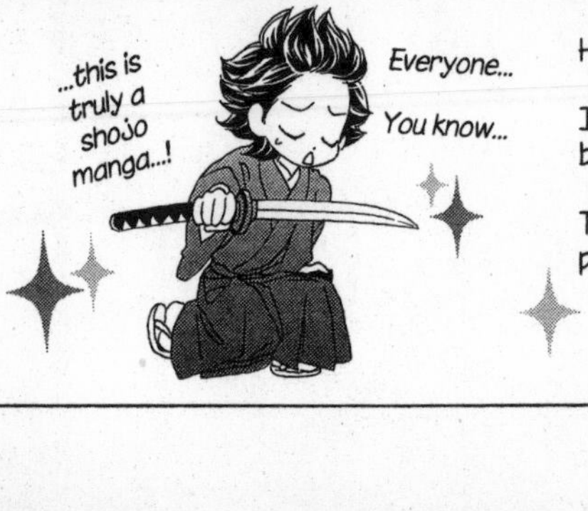
Everyone...
You know...
...this is truly a shojo manga...!

Hello, this is Sakurakouji.

It doesn't seem appropriate below a picture like this ↑ but...

Thank you very much for picking up volume 14!

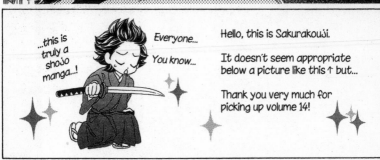

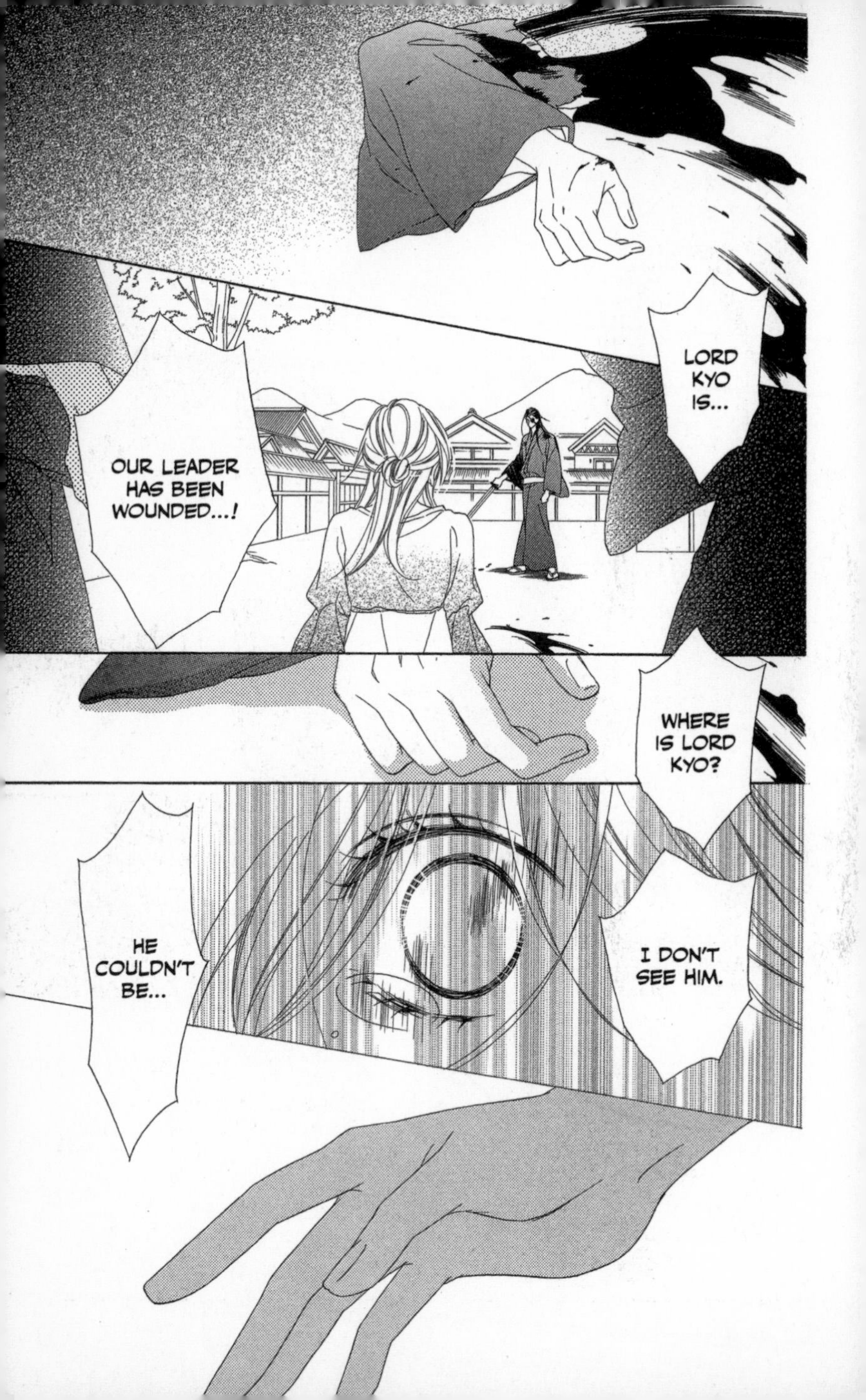
LORD KYO IS...
OUR LEADER HAS BEEN WOUNDED...!
WHERE IS LORD KYO?
I DON'T SEE HIM.
HE COULDN'T BE...

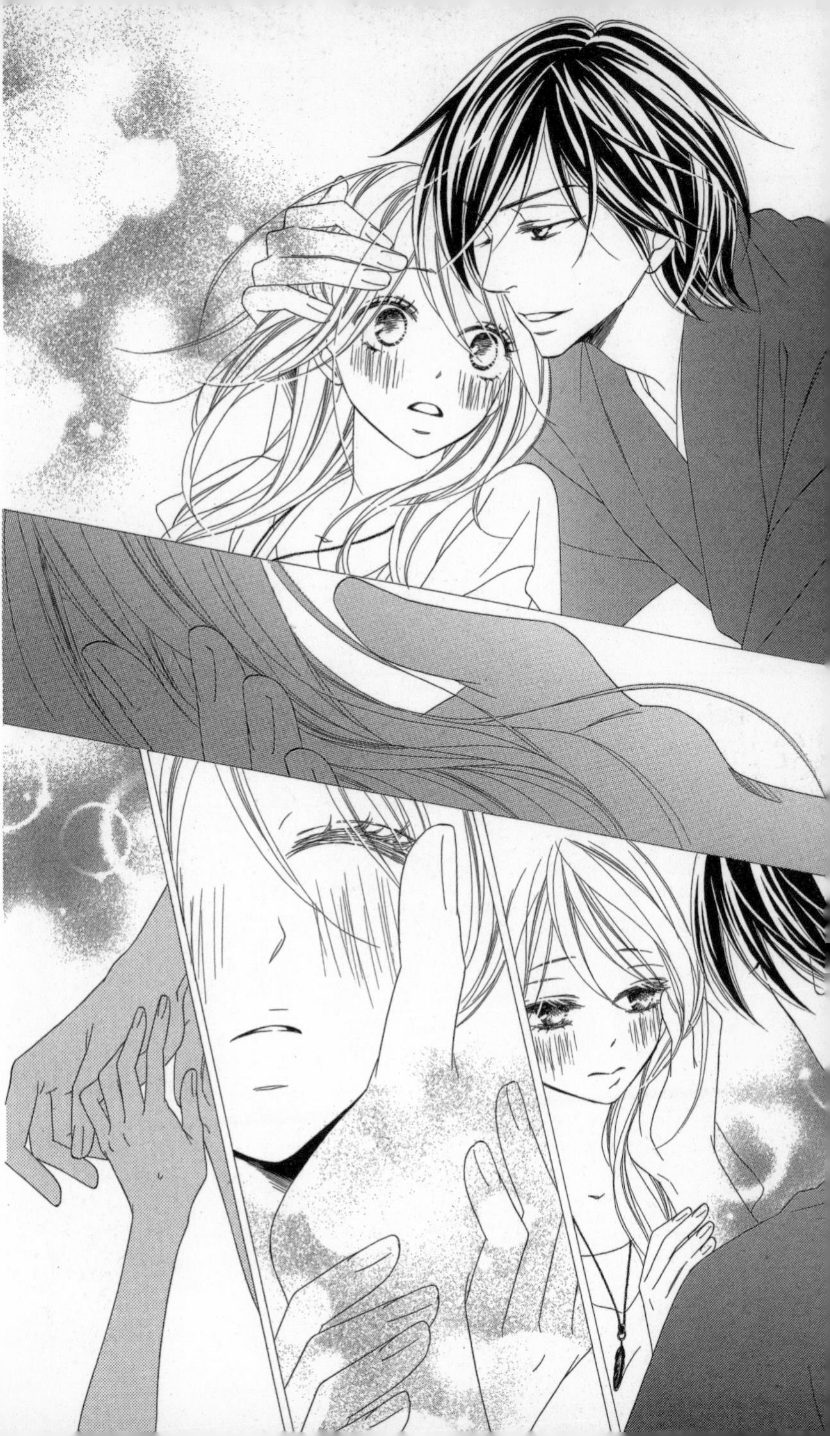

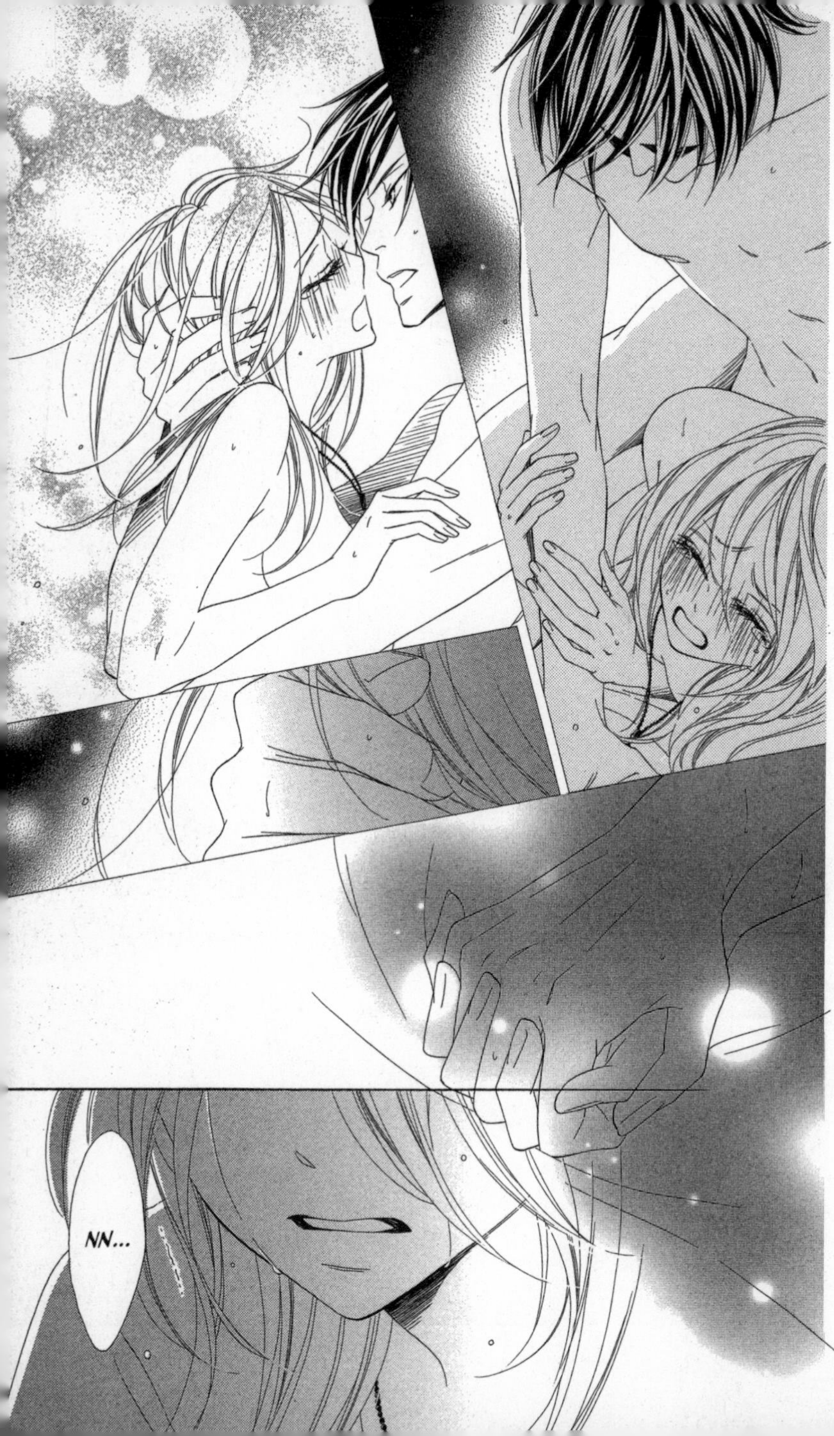
NN...

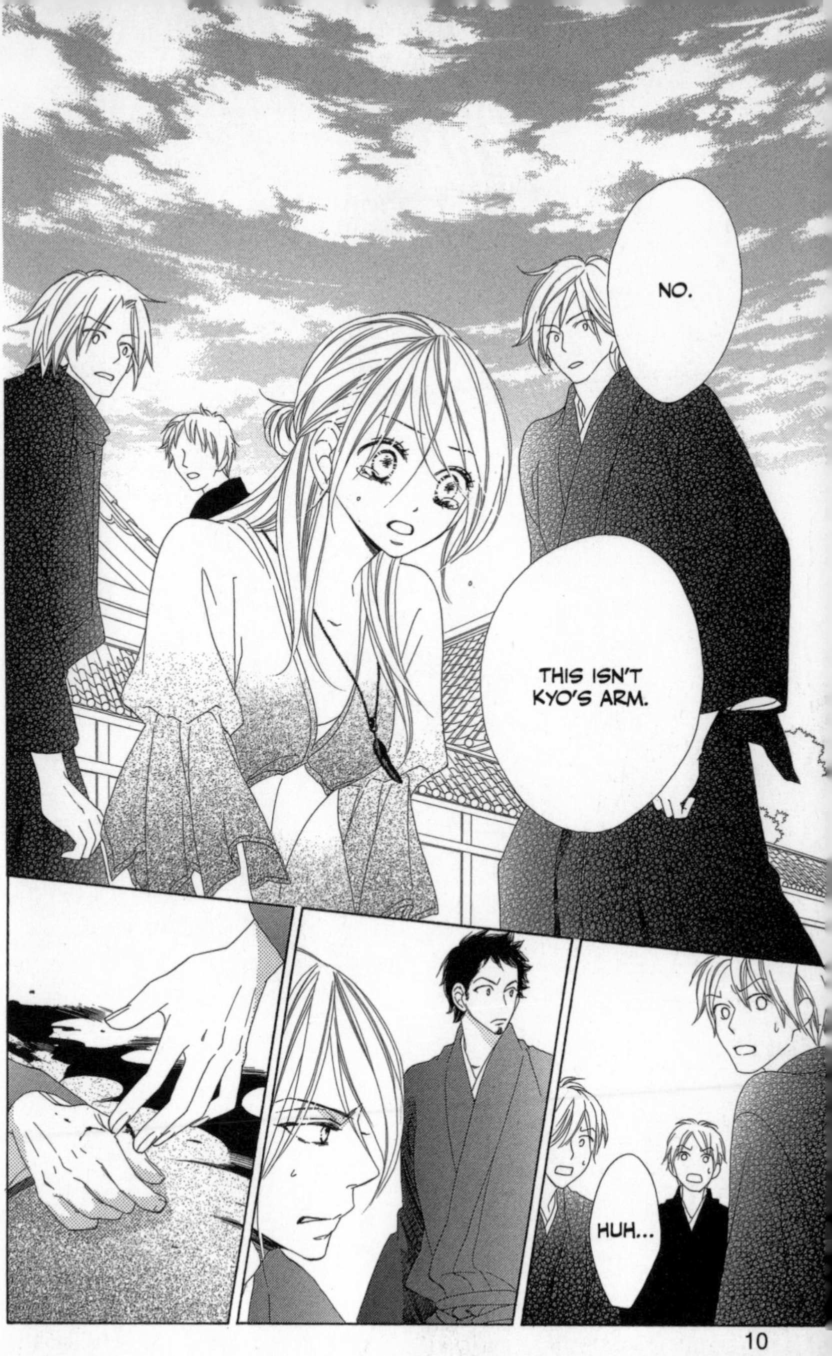
NO.
THIS ISN'T KYO'S ARM.
HUH...

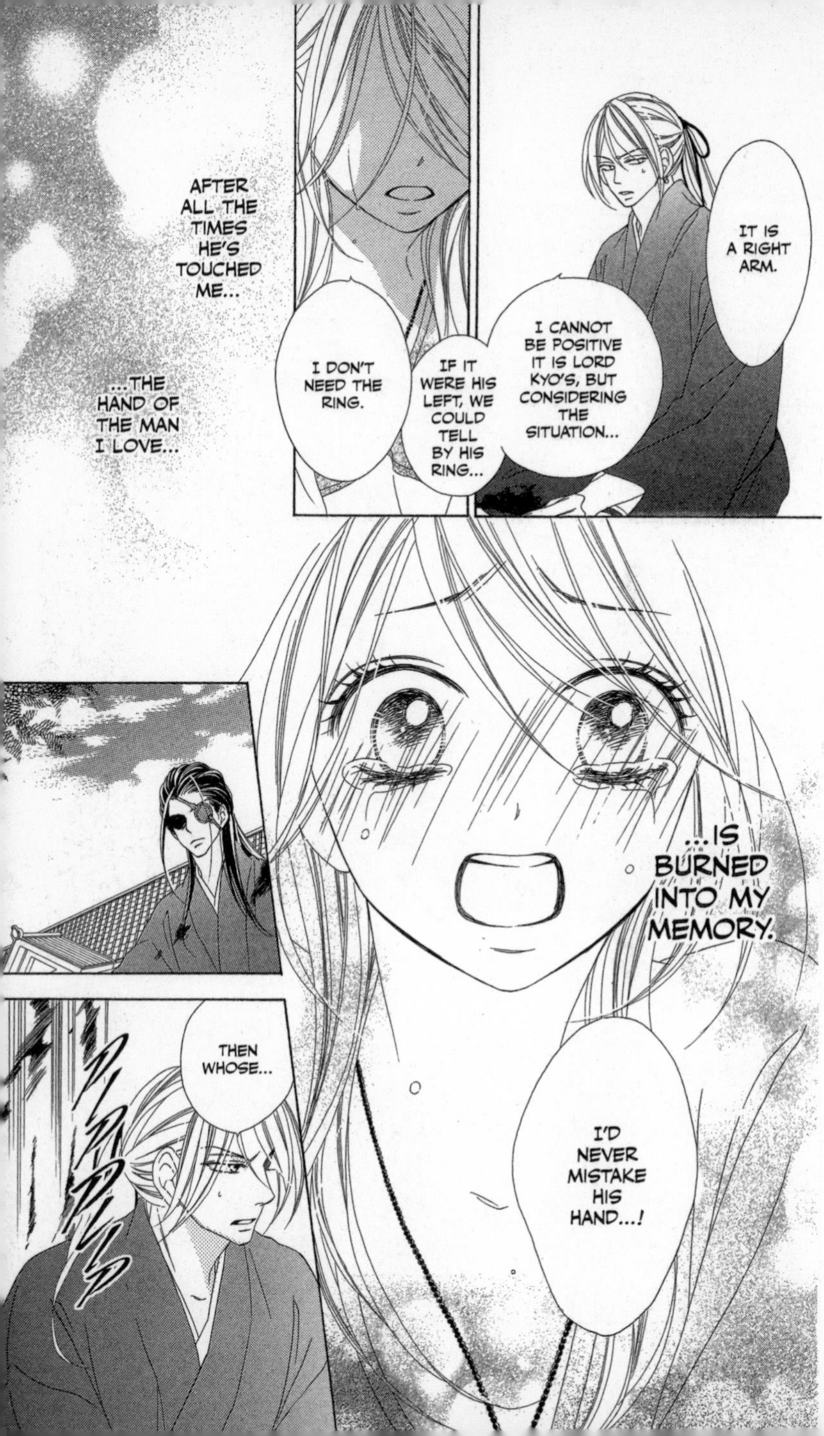
IT IS A RIGHT ARM.
I CANNOT BE POSITIVE IT IS LORD KYO'S, BUT CONSIDERING THE SITUATION...
IF IT WERE HIS LEFT, WE COULD TELL BY HIS RING...
I DON'T NEED THE RING.
AFTER ALL THE TIMES HE'S TOUCHED ME...
...THE HAND OF THE MAN I LOVE...
...IS BURNED INTO MY MEMORY.
I'D NEVER MISTAKE HIS HAND...!
THEN WHOSE...

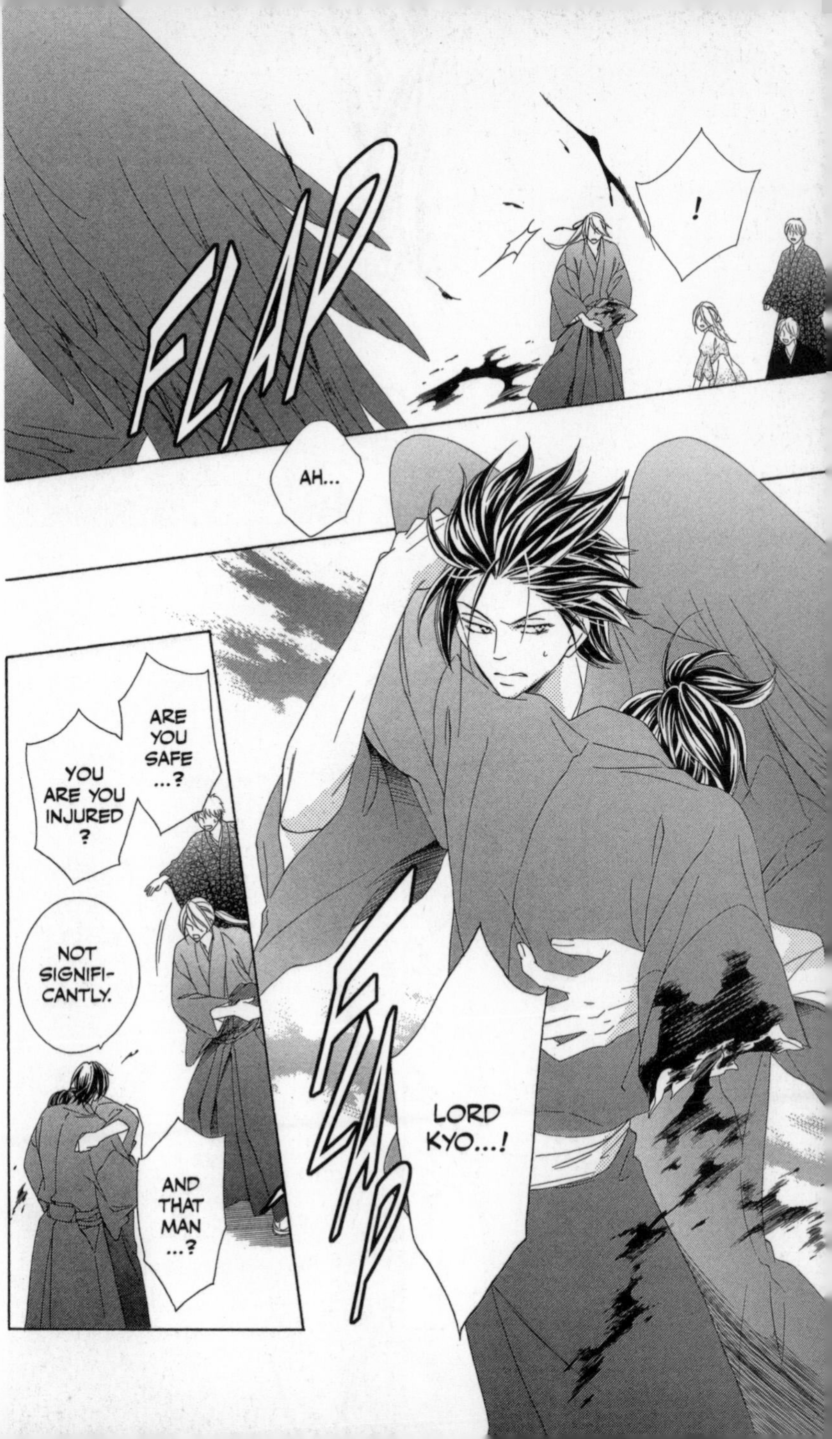
!
FLAP
AH...
LORD KYO...!
FLAP
ARE YOU SAFE ...?
YOU ARE YOU INJURED ?
NOT SIGNIFI-CANTLY.
AND THAT MAN ...?

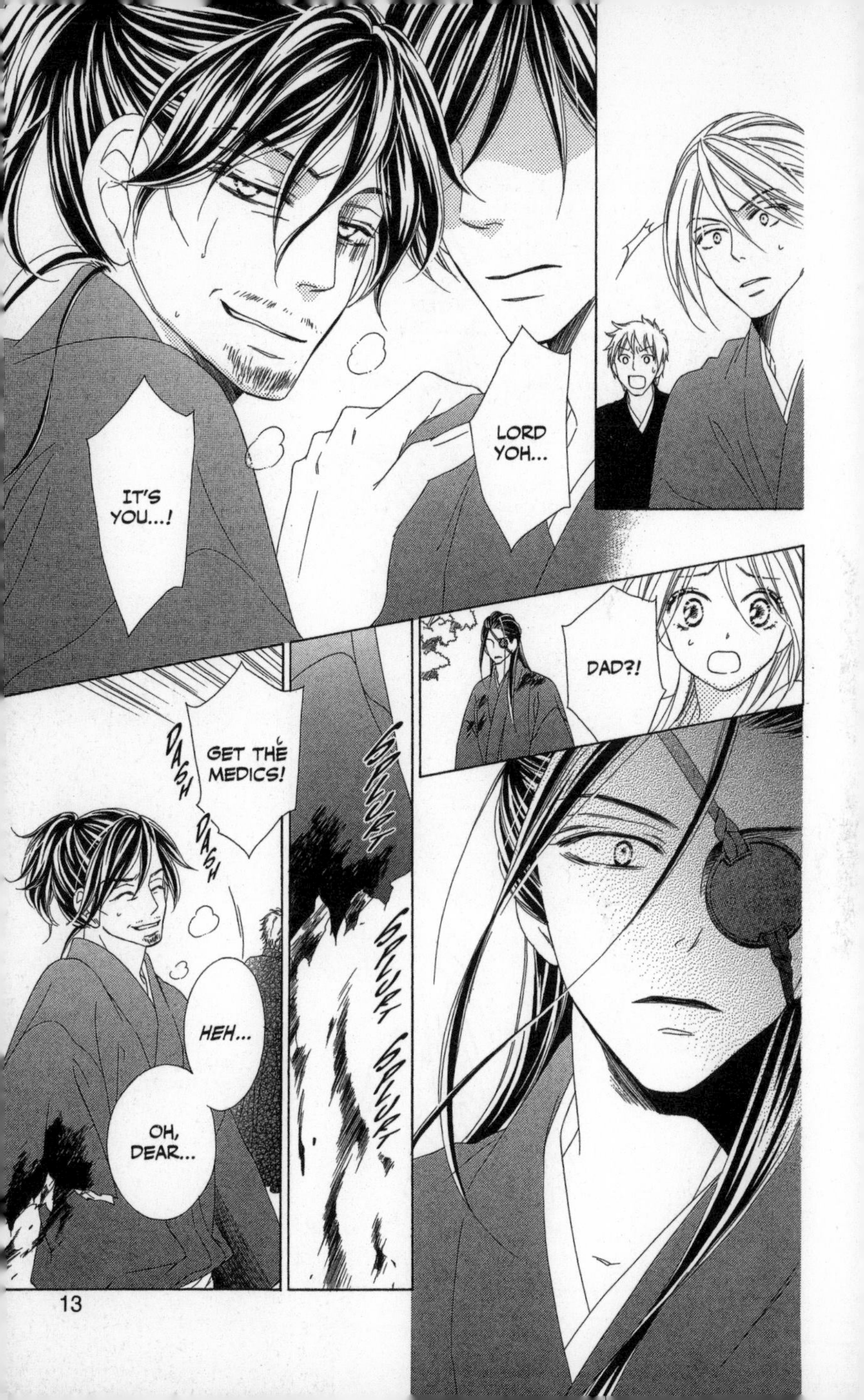
LORD YOH...
IT'S YOU...!
DAD?!
GET THE MEDICS!
DASH
DASH
HEH...
OH, DEAR...

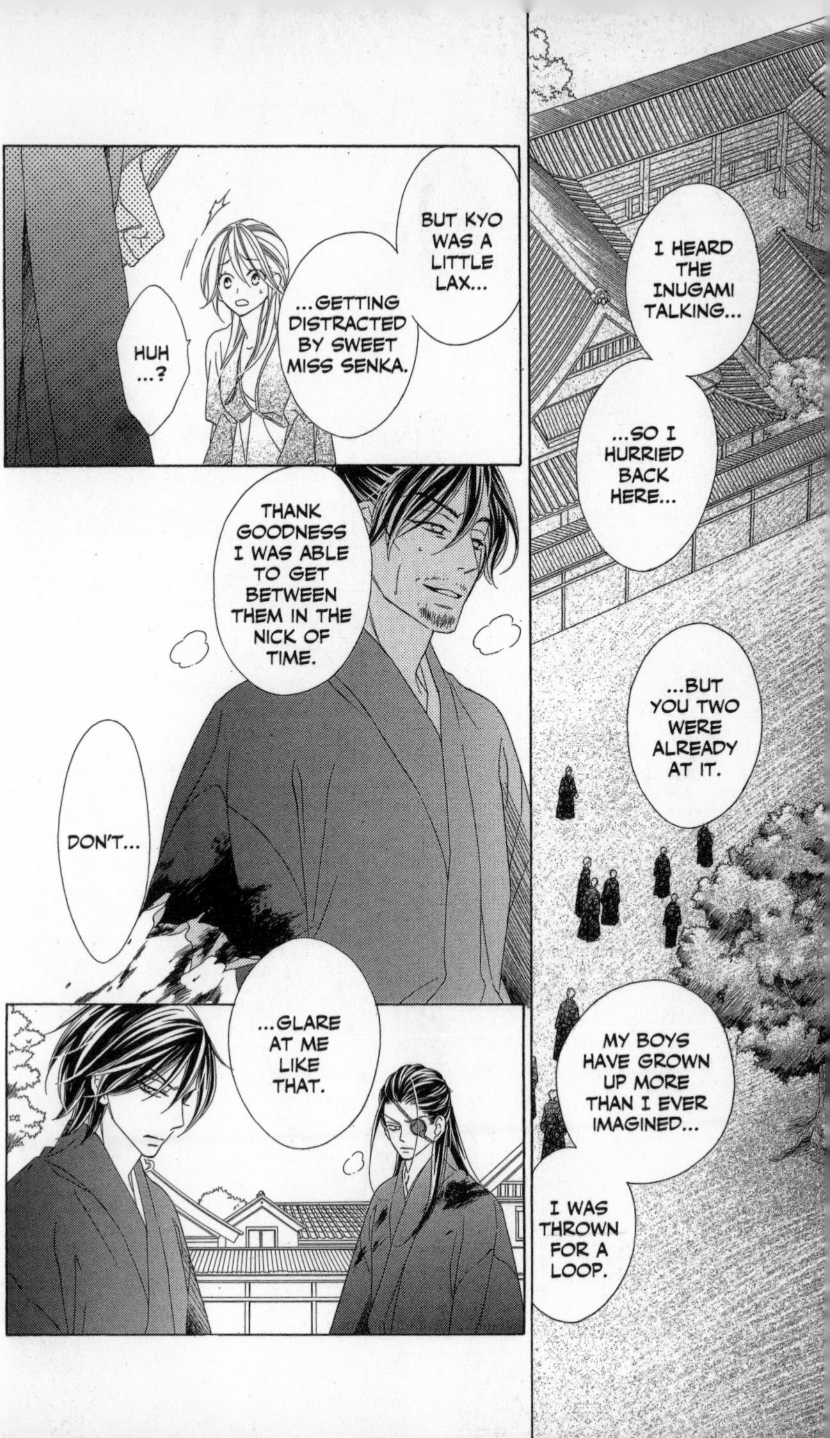
I HEARD THE INUGAMI TALKING...
...SO I HURRIED BACK HERE...
...BUT YOU TWO WERE ALREADY AT IT.
MY BOYS HAVE GROWN UP MORE THAN I EVER IMAGINED...
I WAS THROWN FOR A LOOP.
BUT KYO WAS A LITTLE LAX...
...GETTING DISTRACTED BY SWEET MISS SENKA.
HUH ...?
THANK GOODNESS I WAS ABLE TO GET BETWEEN THEM IN THE NICK OF TIME.
DON'T...
...GLARE AT ME LIKE THAT.

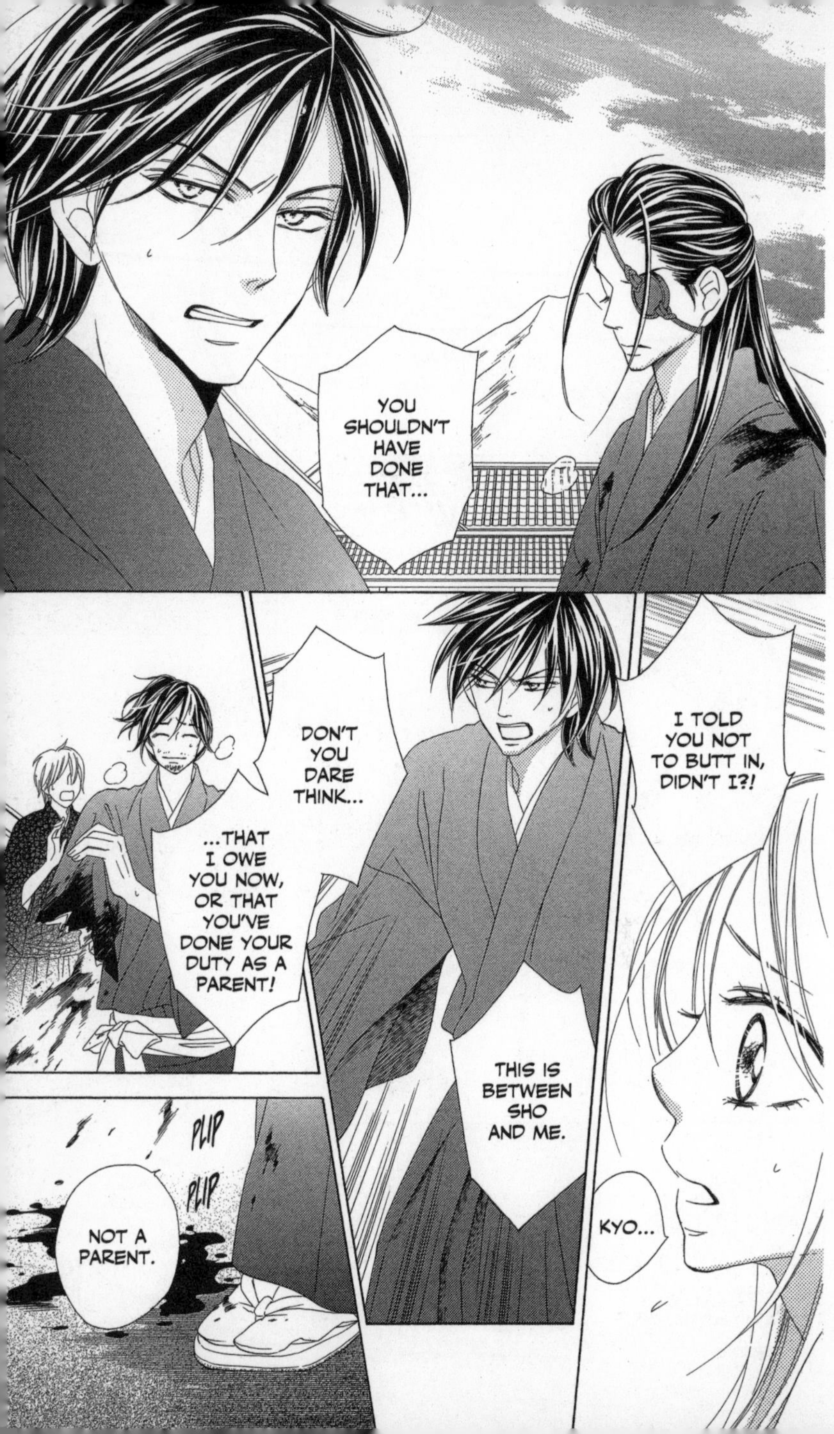
YOU SHOULDN'T HAVE DONE THAT...
I TOLD YOU NOT TO BUTT IN, DIDN'T I?!
THIS IS BETWEEN SHO AND ME.
KYO...
DON'T YOU DARE THINK...
...THAT I OWE YOU NOW, OR THAT YOU'VE DONE YOUR DUTY AS A PARENT!
PLIP
PLIP
NOT A PARENT.

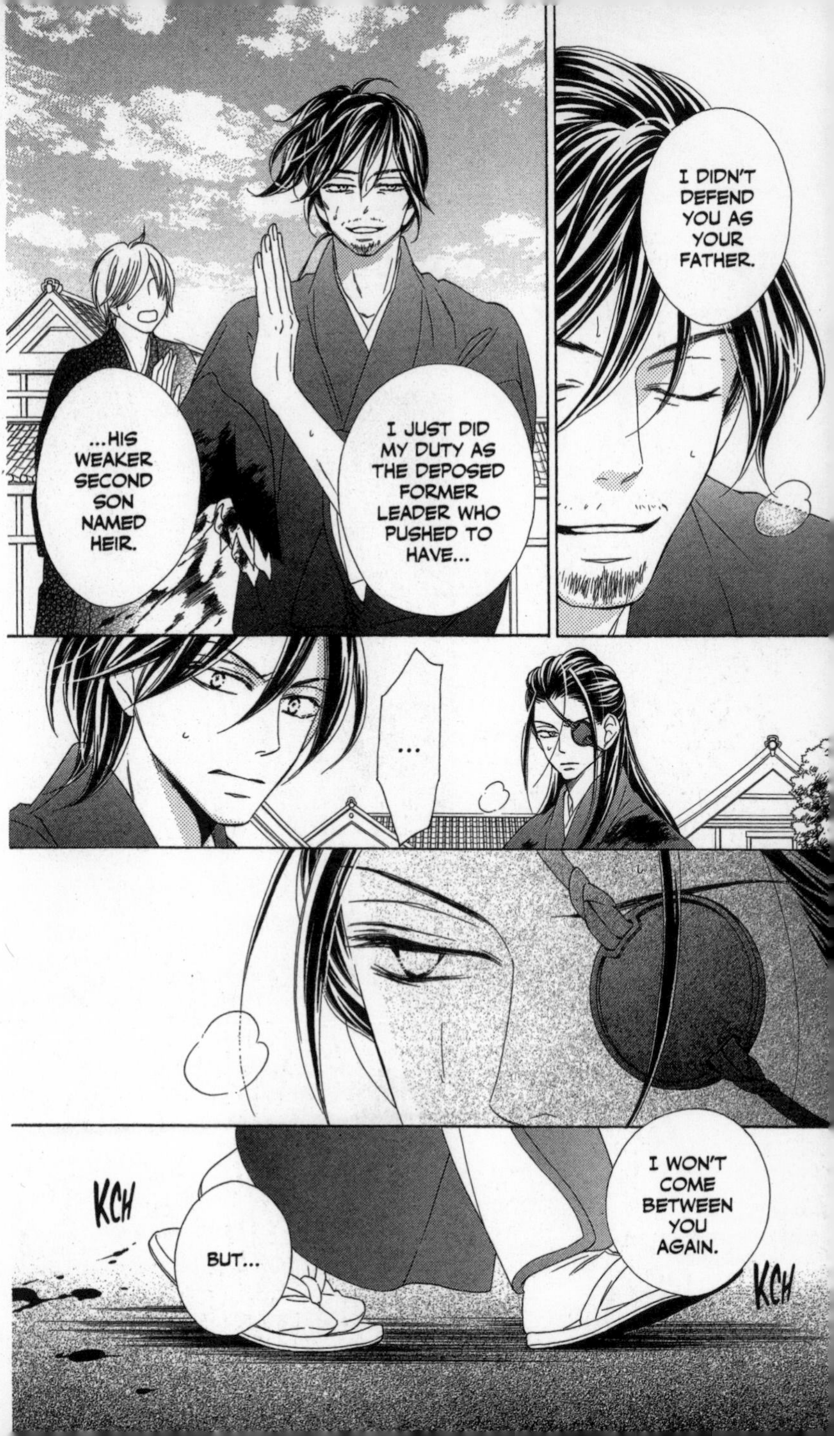
I DIDN'T DEFEND YOU AS YOUR FATHER.
I JUST DID MY DUTY AS THE DEPOSED FORMER LEADER WHO PUSHED TO HAVE...
...HIS WEAKER SECOND SON NAMED HEIR.
...
I WON'T COME BETWEEN YOU AGAIN.
KCH
BUT...
KCH

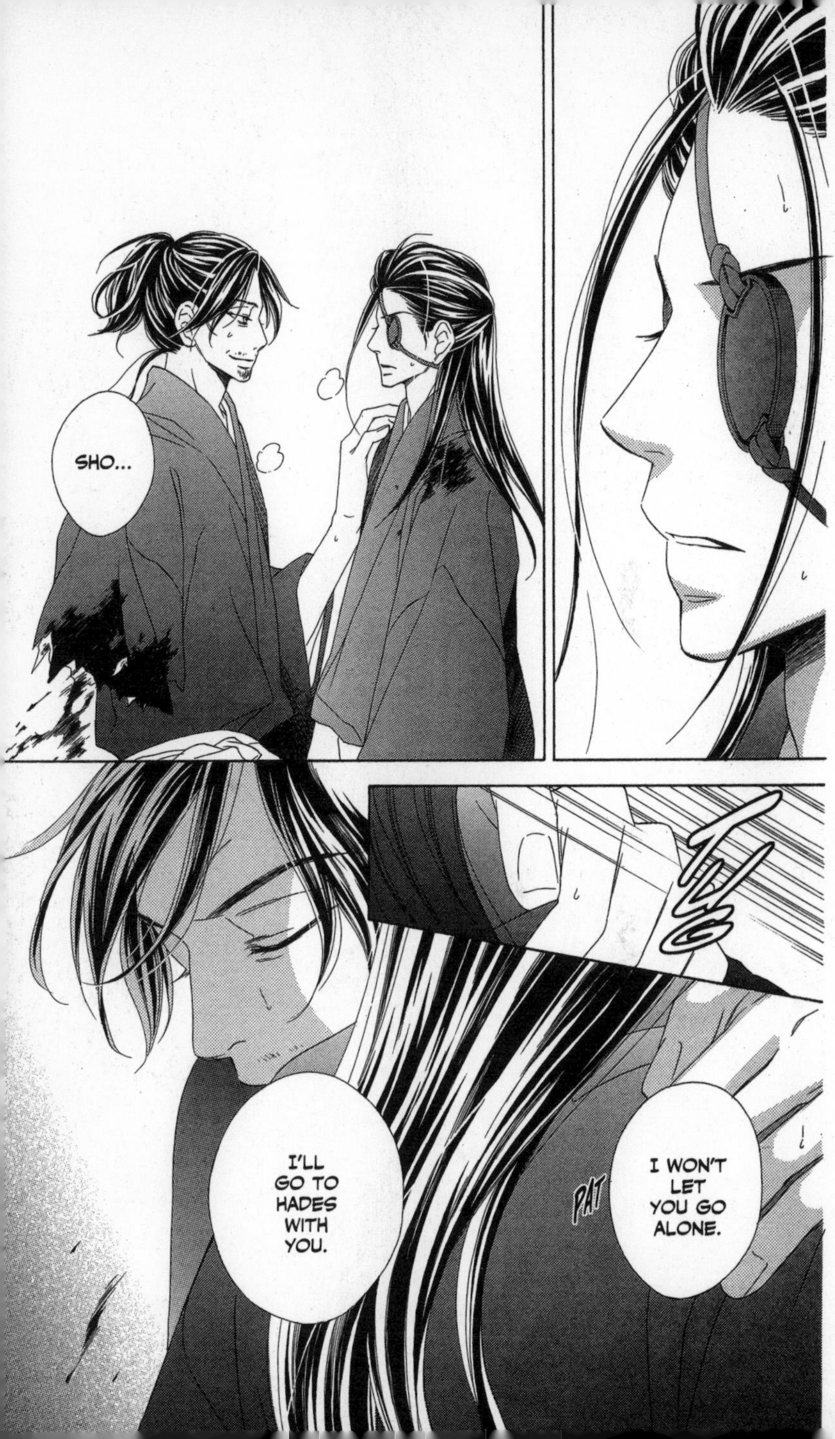
SHO...
TUG
I WON'T LET YOU GO ALONE.
PAT
I'LL GO TO HADES WITH YOU.

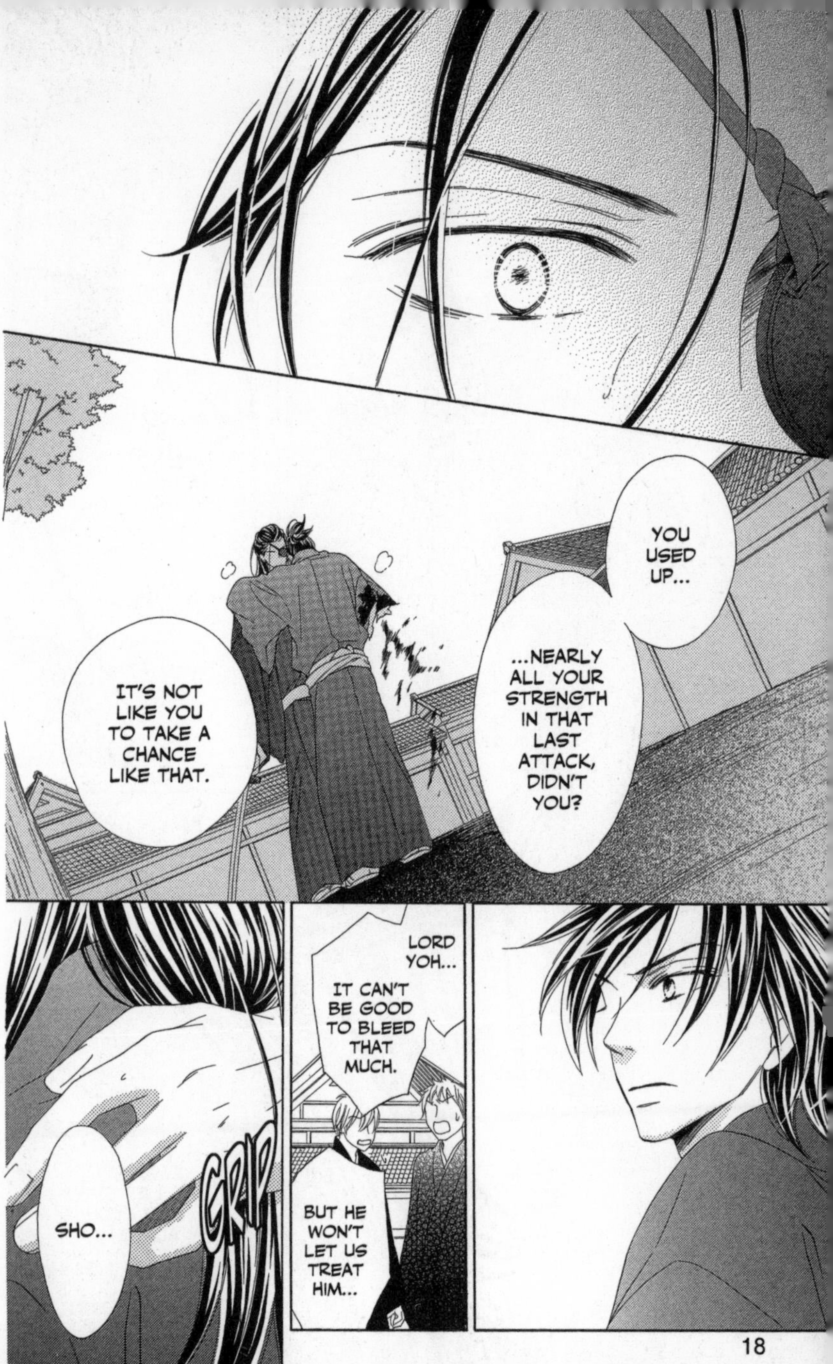
YOU USED UP...
...NEARLY ALL YOUR STRENGTH IN THAT LAST ATTACK, DIDN'T YOU?
IT'S NOT LIKE YOU TO TAKE A CHANCE LIKE THAT.
LORD YOH...
IT CAN'T BE GOOD TO BLEED THAT MUCH.
BUT HE WON'T LET US TREAT HIM...
GRIP
SHO...

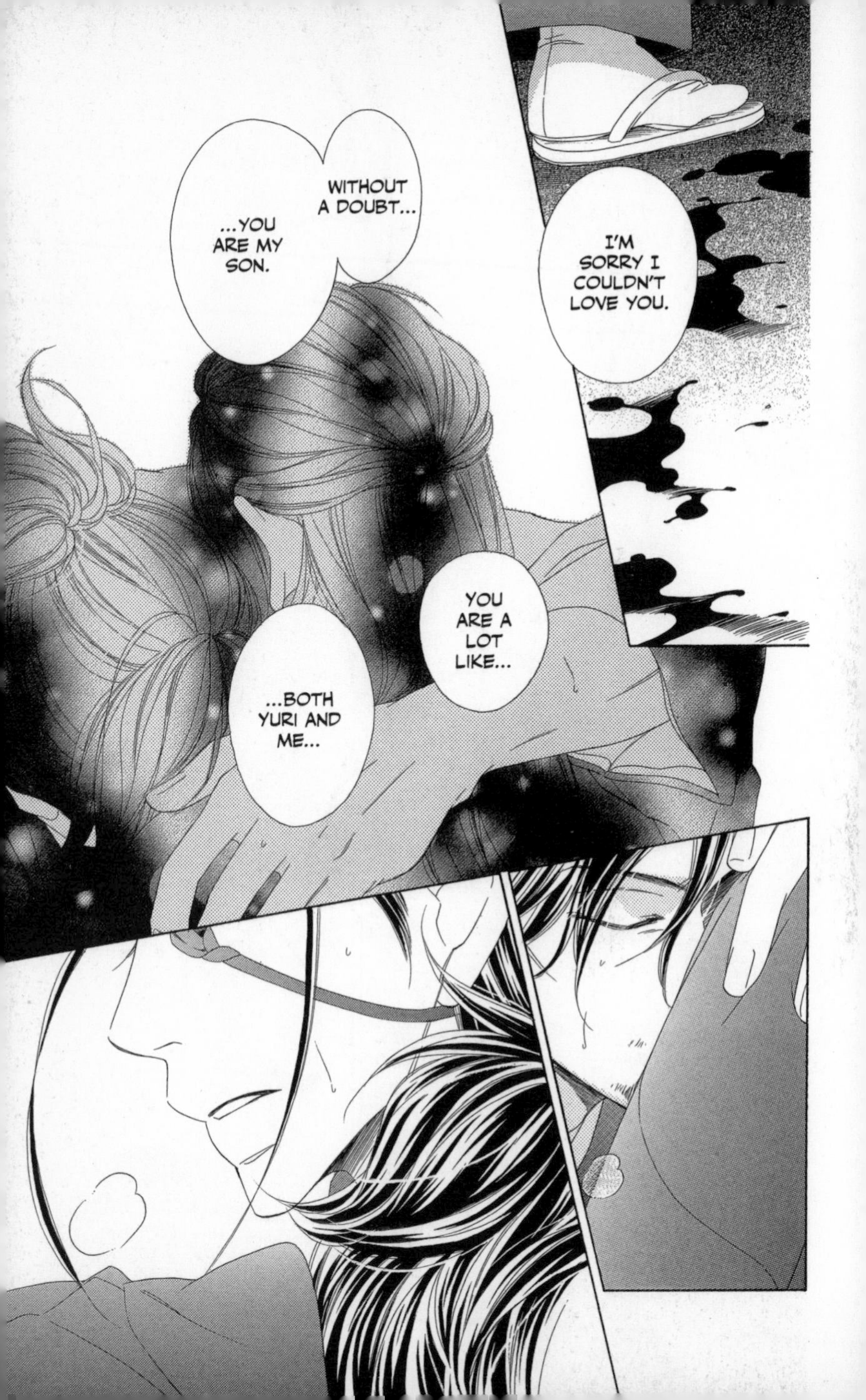
I'M SORRY I COULDN'T LOVE YOU.
WITHOUT A DOUBT...
...YOU ARE MY SON.
YOU ARE A LOT LIKE...
...BOTH YURI AND ME...

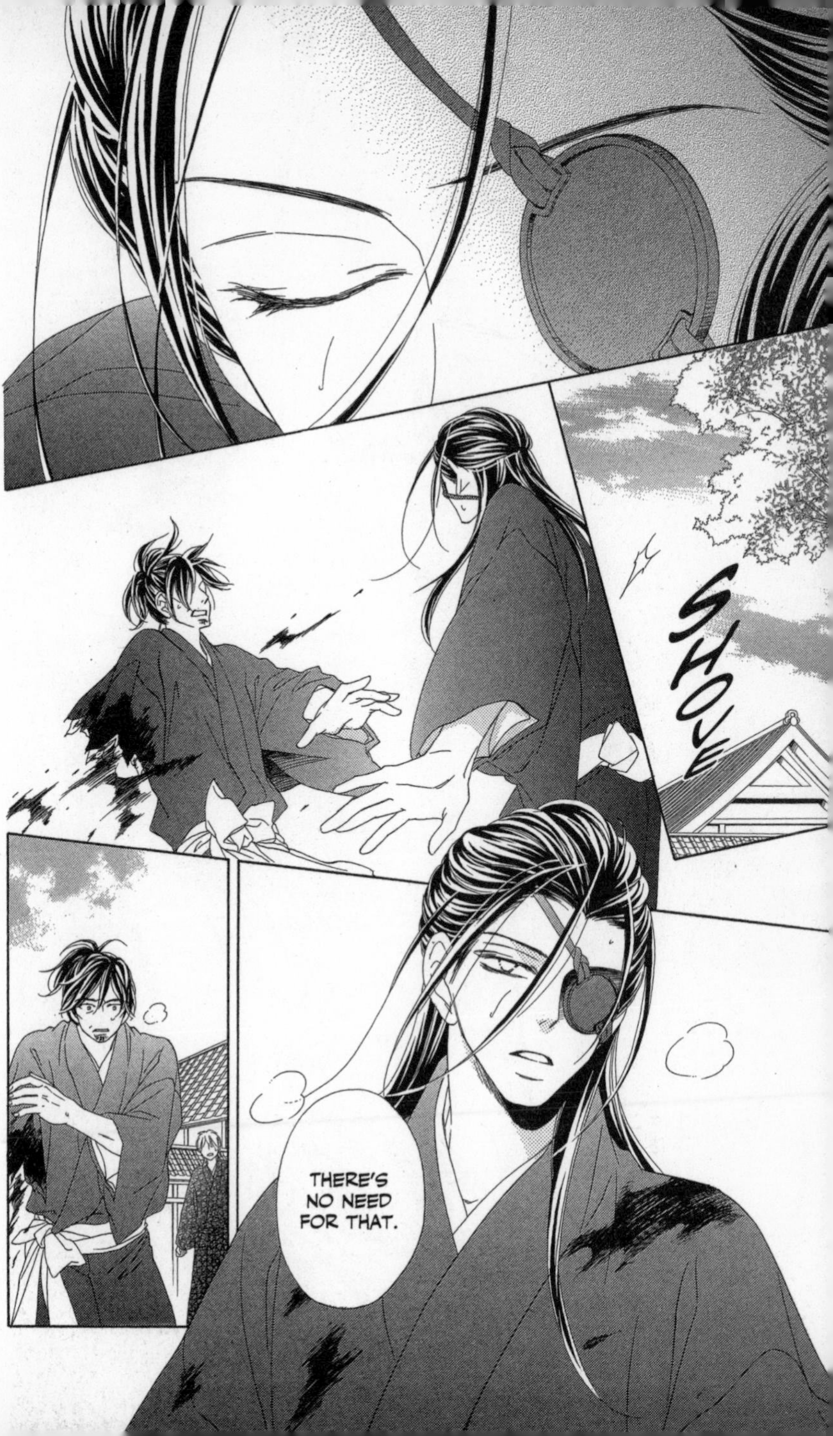
SHOVE
THERE'S NO NEED FOR THAT.

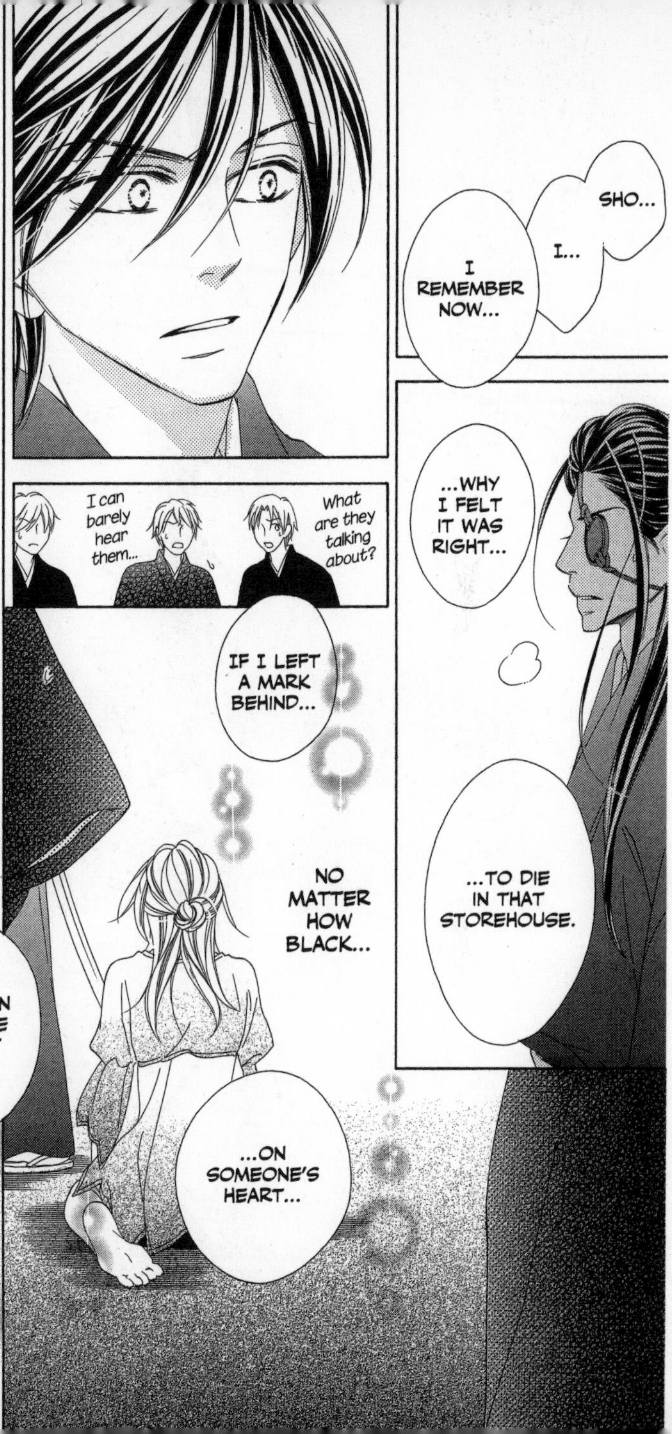
SHO...
I...
I REMEMBER NOW...
...WHY I FELT IT WAS RIGHT...
...TO DIE IN THAT STOREHOUSE.
What are they talking about?
I can barely hear them...
IF I LEFT A MARK BEHIND...
NO MATTER HOW BLACK...
...ON SOMEONE'S HEART...
IF I CAN BELIEVE I LEFT ONE...
"MISAO..."

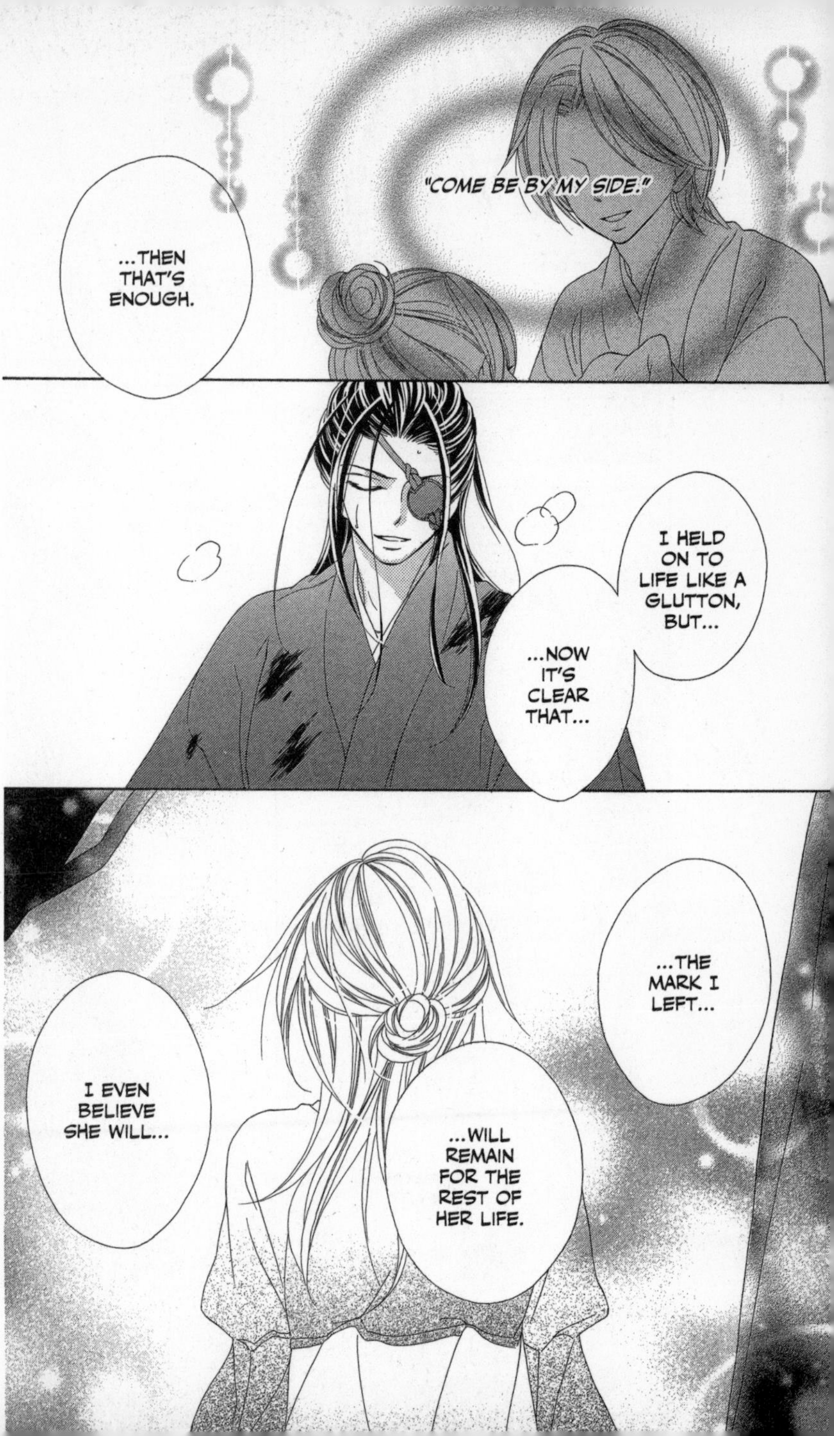
"COME BE BY MY SIDE."
...THEN THAT'S ENOUGH.
I HELD ON TO LIFE LIKE A GLUTTON, BUT...
...NOW IT'S CLEAR THAT...
...THE MARK I LEFT...
...WILL REMAIN FOR THE REST OF HER LIFE.
I EVEN BELIEVE SHE WILL...

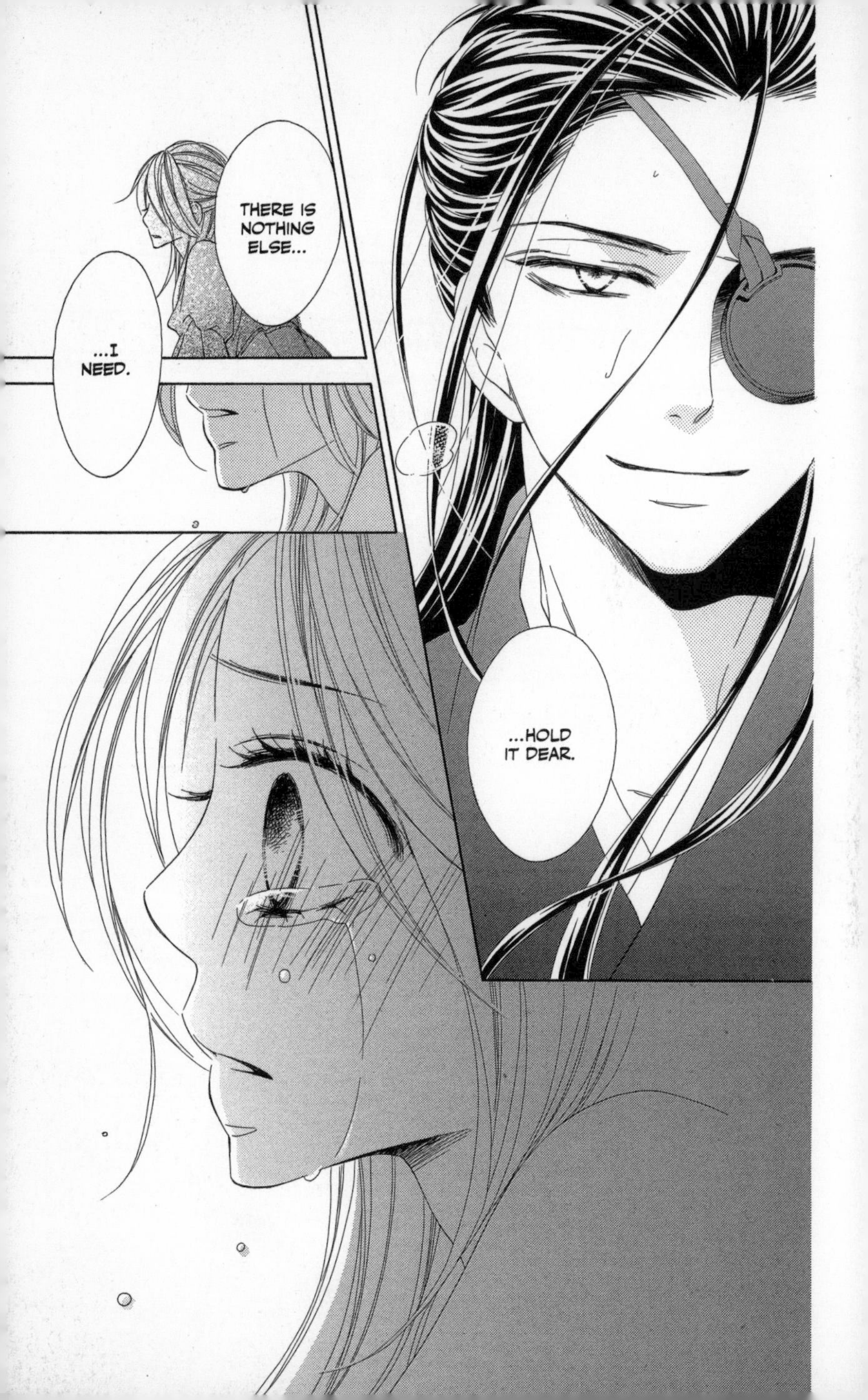
...HOLD IT DEAR.
THERE IS NOTHING ELSE...
...I NEED.

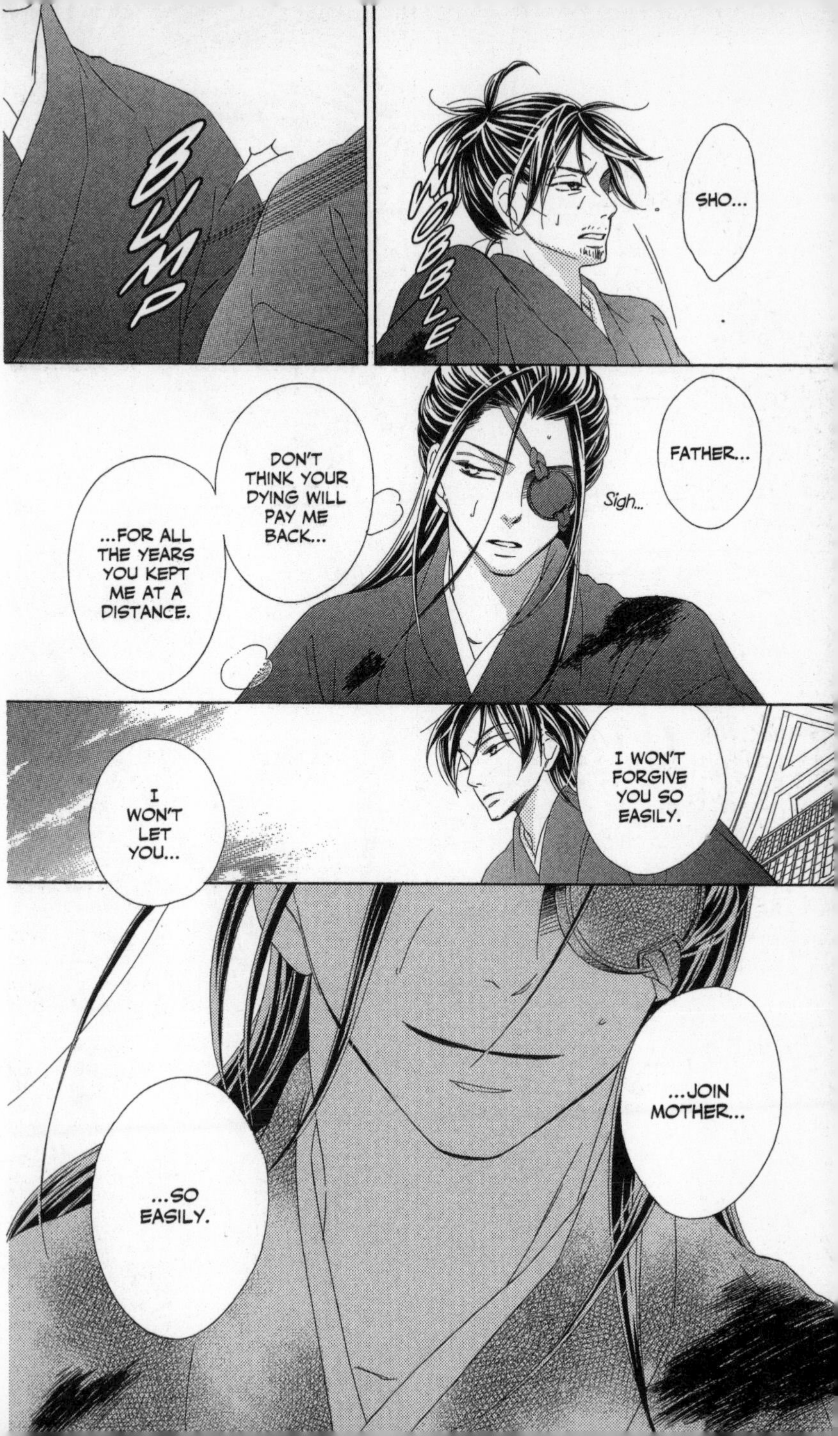
SHO...
WOBBLE
BUMP
FATHER...
Sigh...
DON'T THINK YOUR DYING WILL PAY ME BACK...
...FOR ALL THE YEARS YOU KEPT ME AT A DISTANCE.
I WON'T FORGIVE YOU SO EASILY.
I WON'T LET YOU...
...JOIN MOTHER...
...SO EASILY.

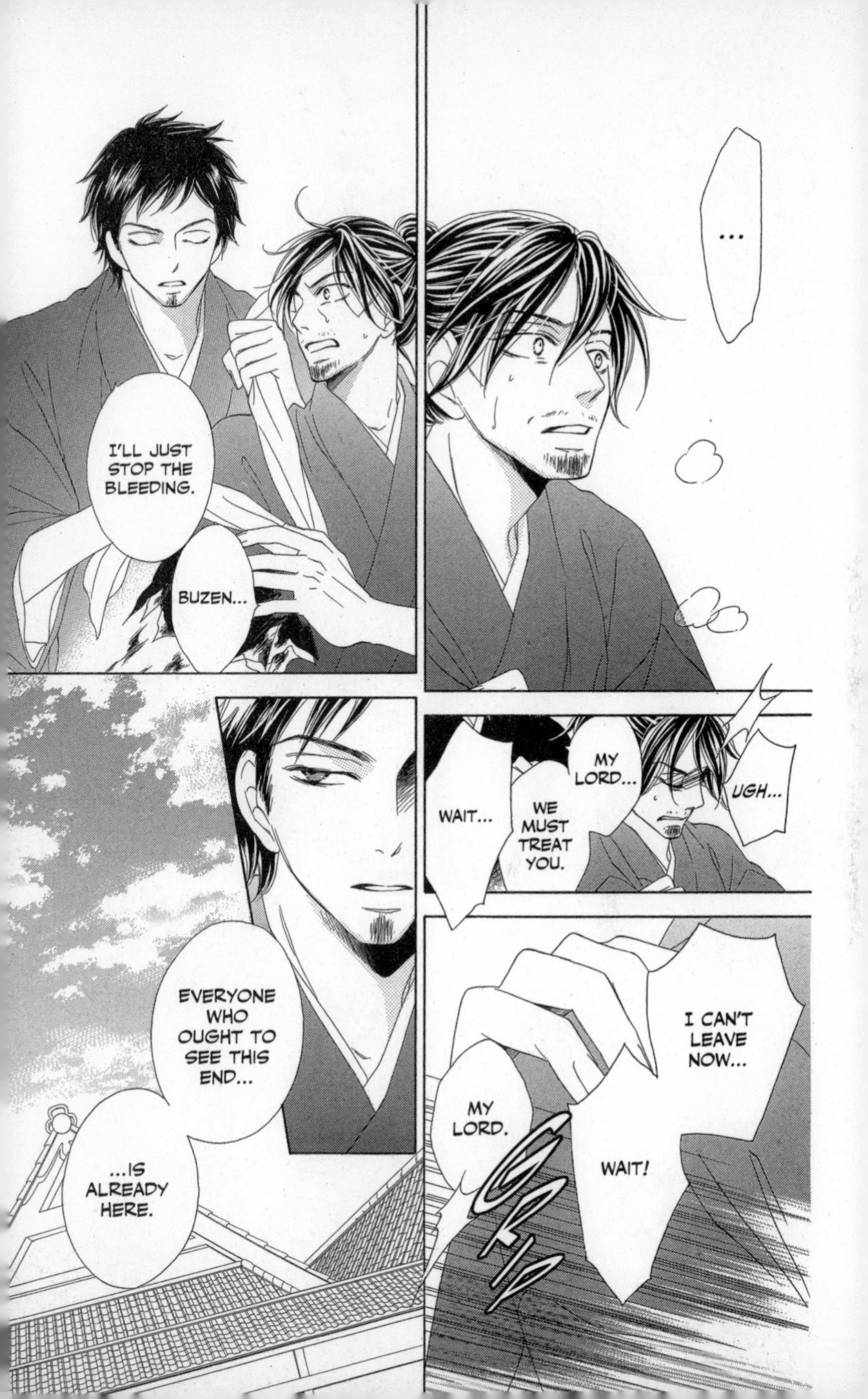
...
I'LL JUST STOP THE BLEEDING.
BUZEN...
UGH...
MY LORD...
WE MUST TREAT YOU.
WAIT...
I CAN'T LEAVE NOW...
WAIT!
MY LORD.
GRIP
EVERYONE WHO OUGHT TO SEE THIS END...
...IS ALREADY HERE.

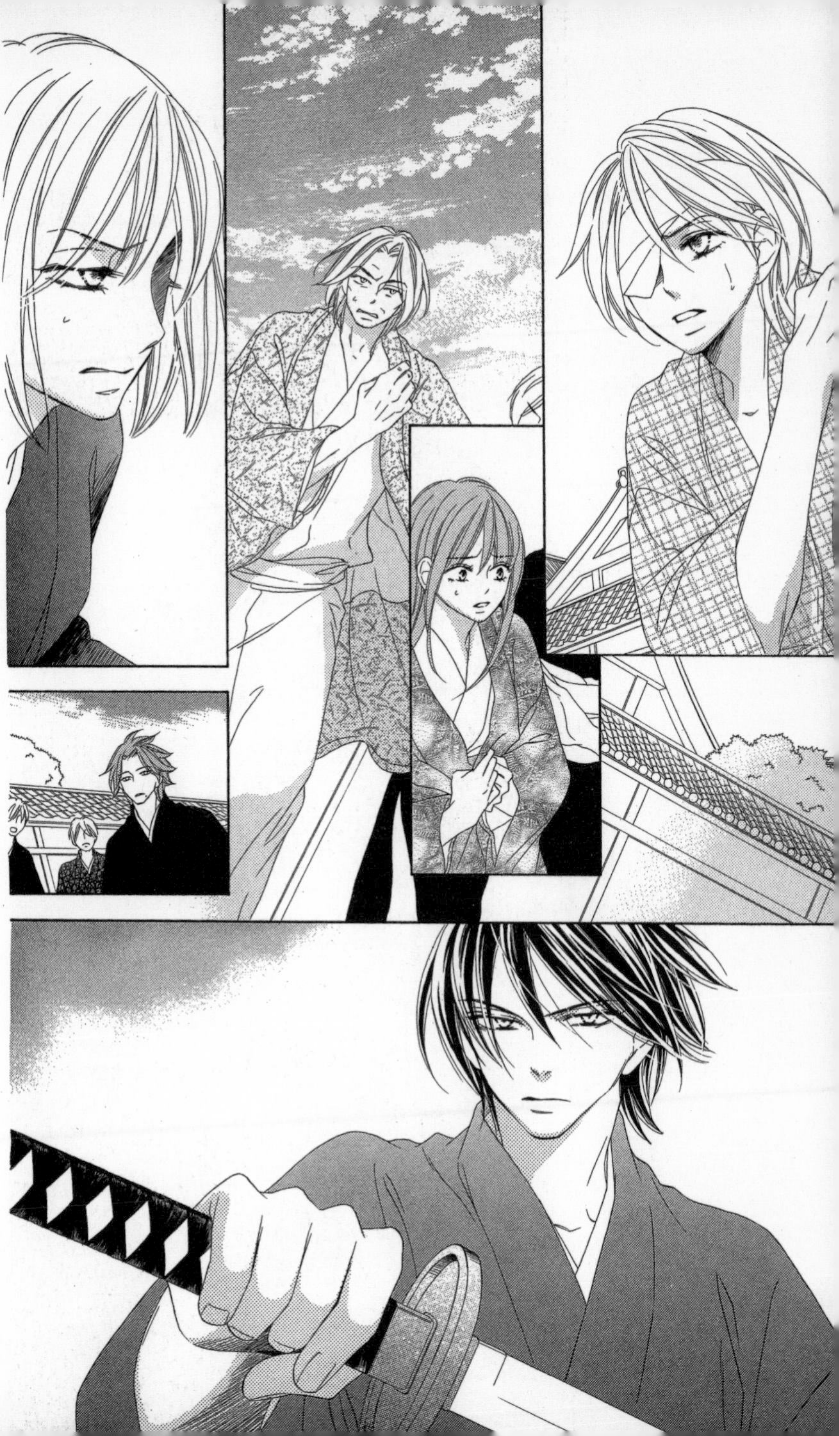

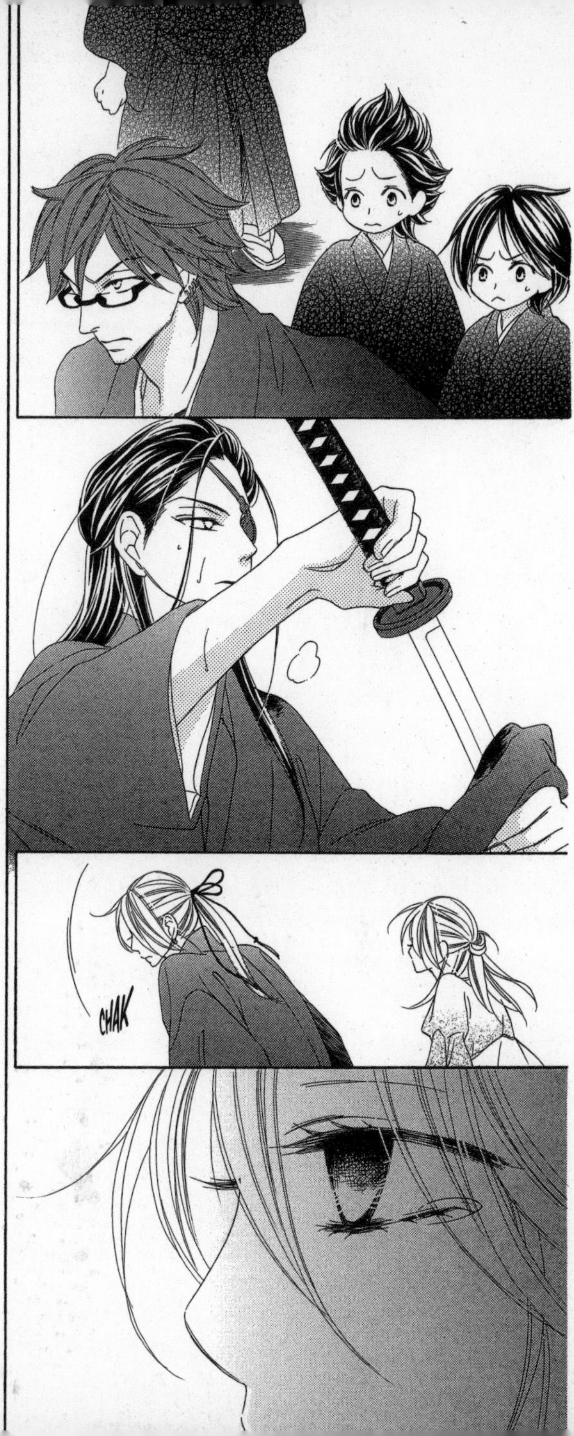
CHAK

I MUST SEE IT THROUGH.

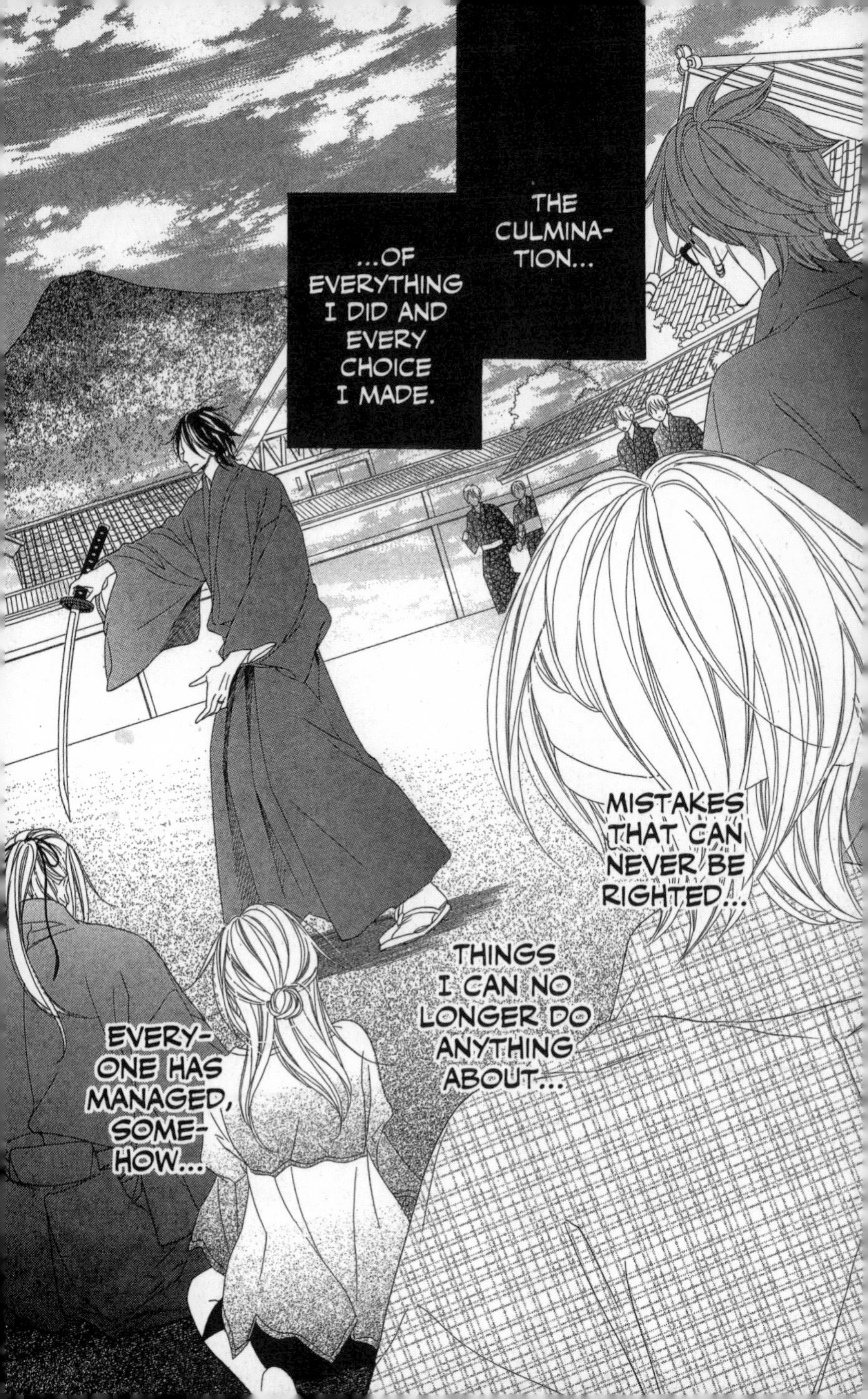
THE CULMINATION...
...OF EVERYTHING I DID AND EVERY CHOICE I MADE.
MISTAKES THAT CAN NEVER BE RIGHTED...
THINGS I CAN NO LONGER DO ANYTHING ABOUT...
EVERYONE HAS MANAGED, SOMEHOW...

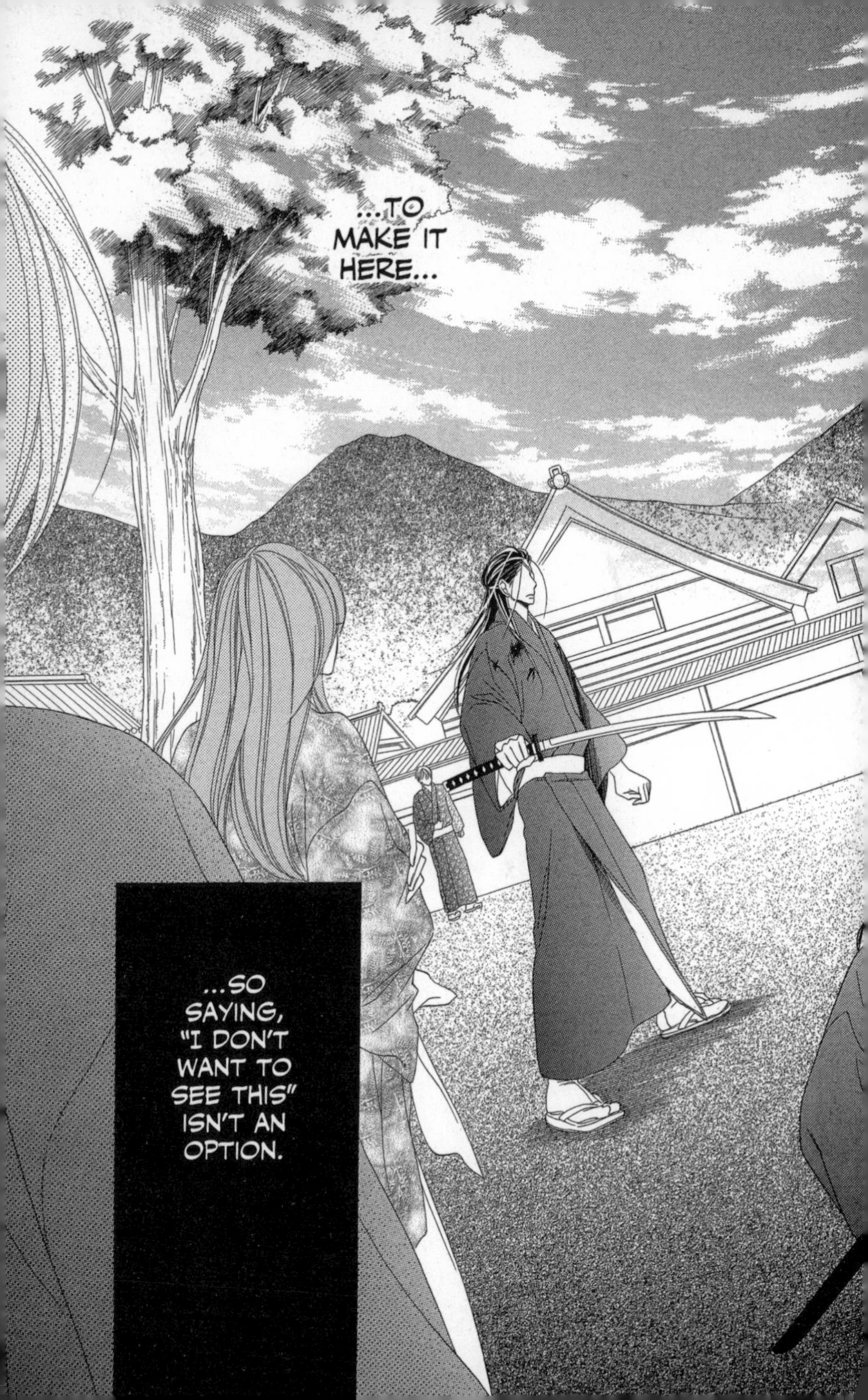
...TO MAKE IT HERE...
...SO SAYING, "I DON'T WANT TO SEE THIS" ISN'T AN OPTION.

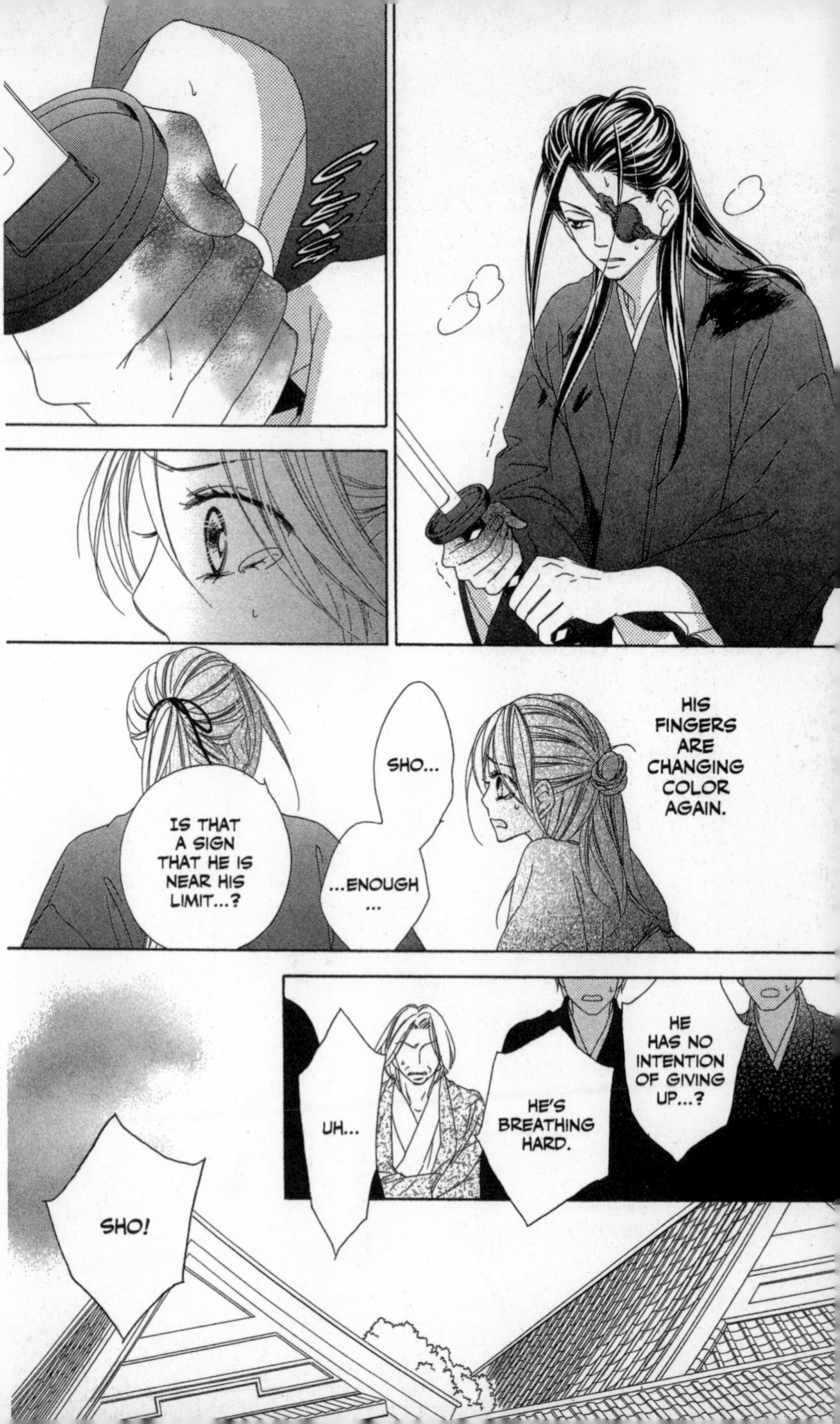
HIS FINGERS ARE CHANGING COLOR AGAIN.
SHO...
...ENOUGH ...
IS THAT A SIGN THAT HE IS NEAR HIS LIMIT...?
HE HAS NO INTENTION OF GIVING UP...?
HE'S BREATHING HARD.
UH...
SHO!

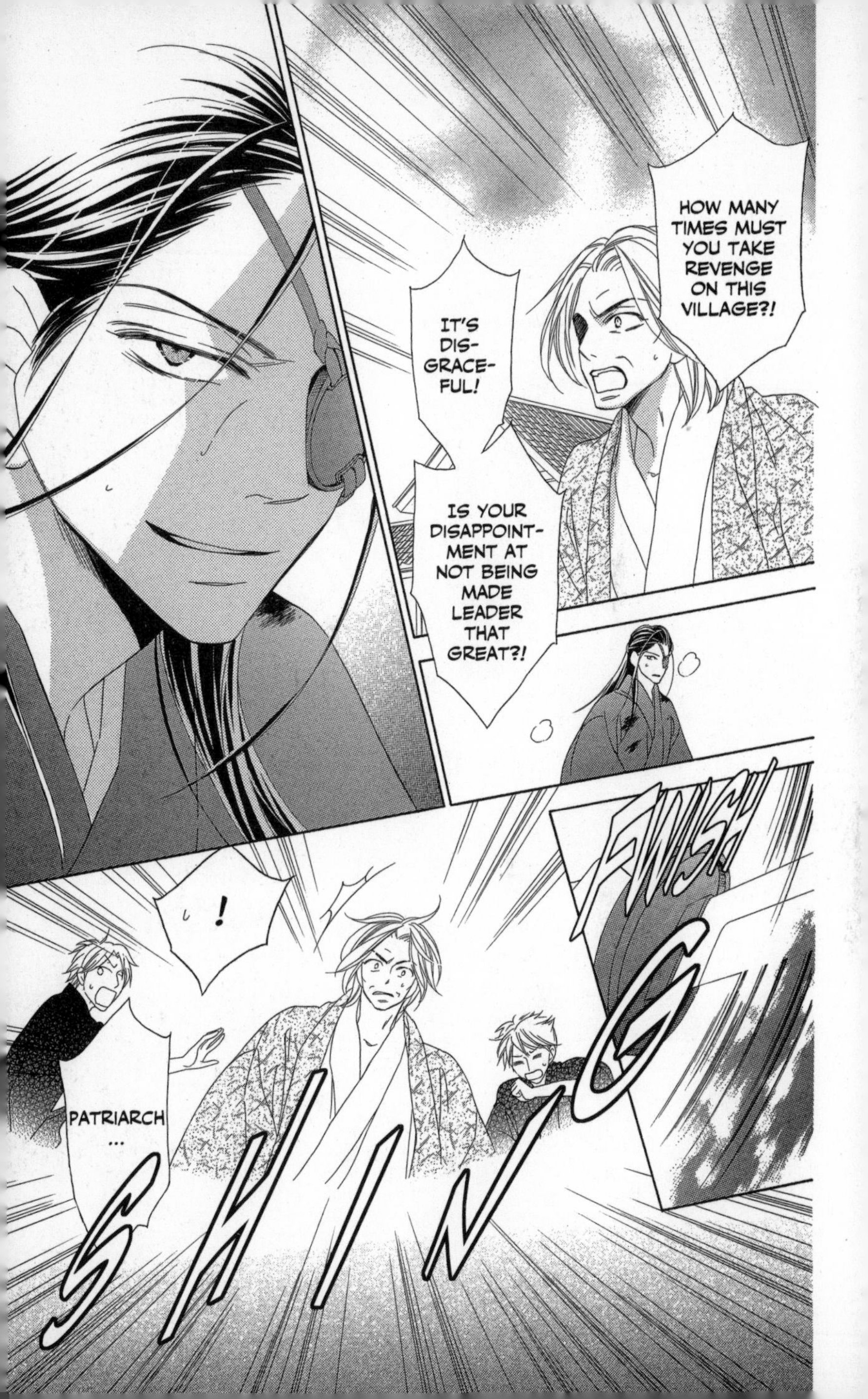
HOW MANY TIMES MUST YOU TAKE REVENGE ON THIS VILLAGE?!
IT'S DIS-GRACE-FUL!
IS YOUR DISAPPOINT-MENT AT NOT BEING MADE LEADER THAT GREAT?!
FWISH
!
PATRIARCH ...
SHING

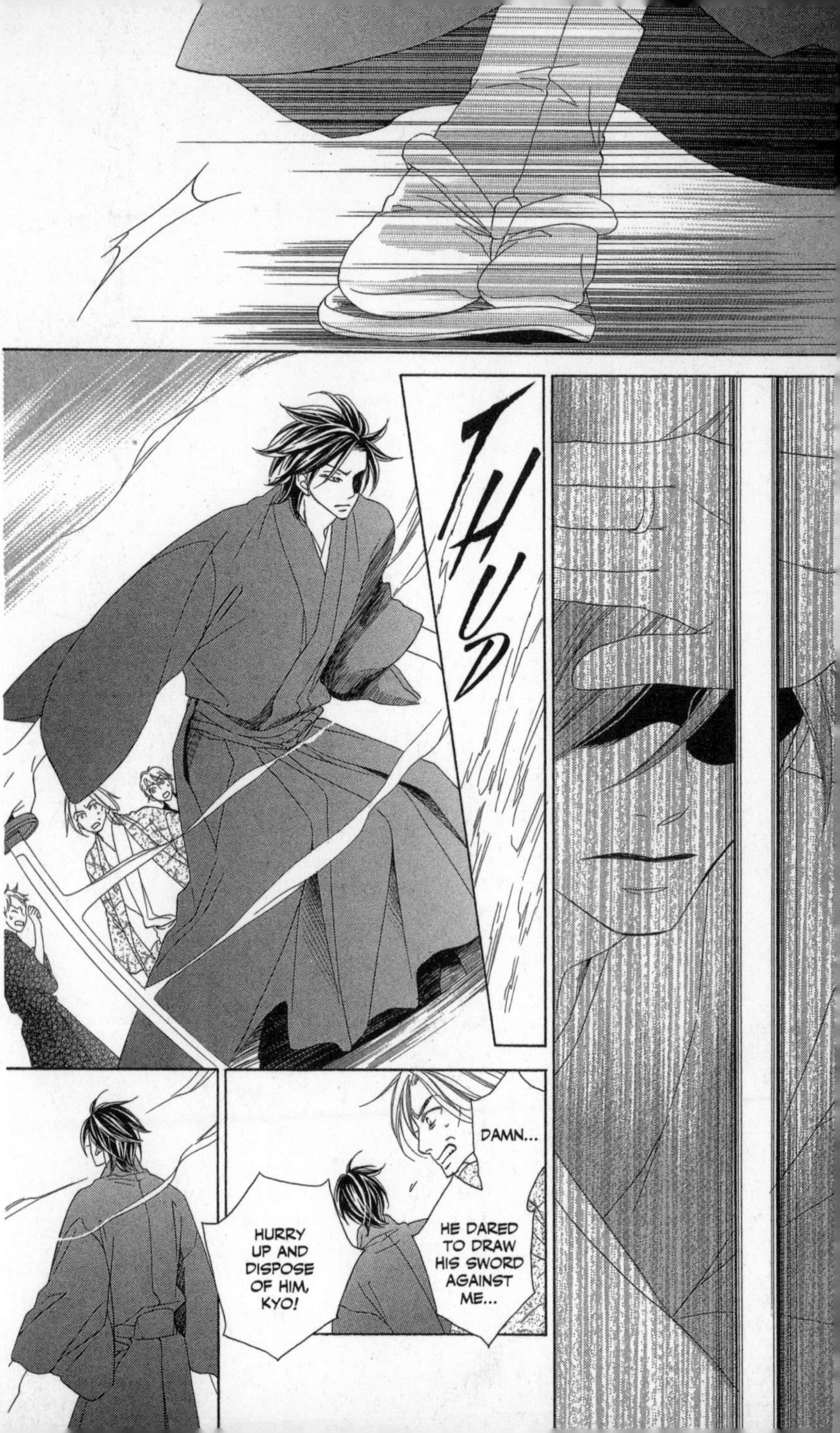
THUD
DAMN...
HE DARED TO DRAW HIS SWORD AGAINST ME...
HURRY UP AND DISPOSE OF HIM, KYO!

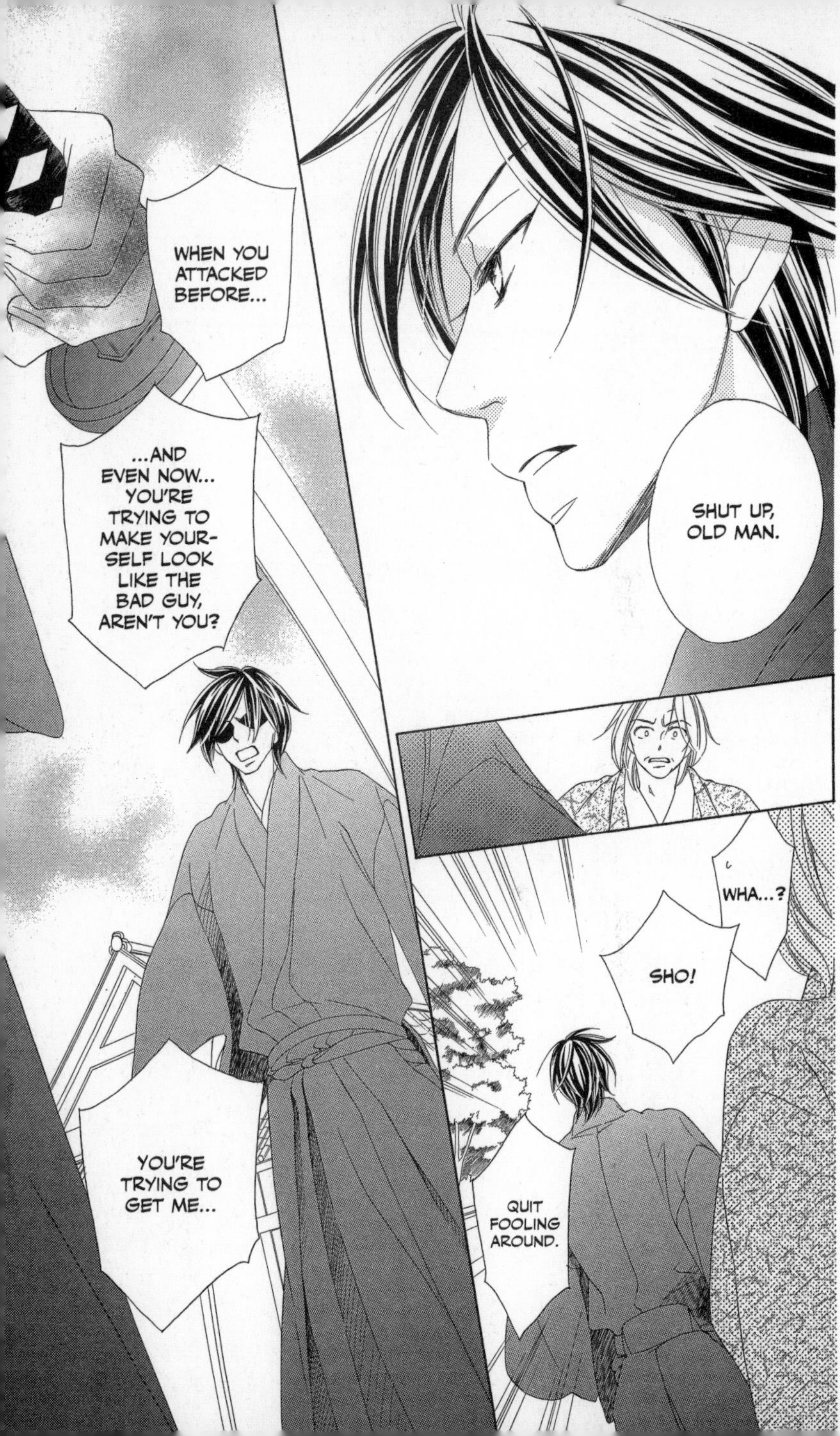
SHUT UP, OLD MAN.
WHA...?
SHO!
QUIT FOOLING AROUND.
WHEN YOU ATTACKED BEFORE...
...AND EVEN NOW... YOU'RE TRYING TO MAKE YOUR-SELF LOOK LIKE THE BAD GUY, AREN'T YOU?
YOU'RE TRYING TO GET ME...

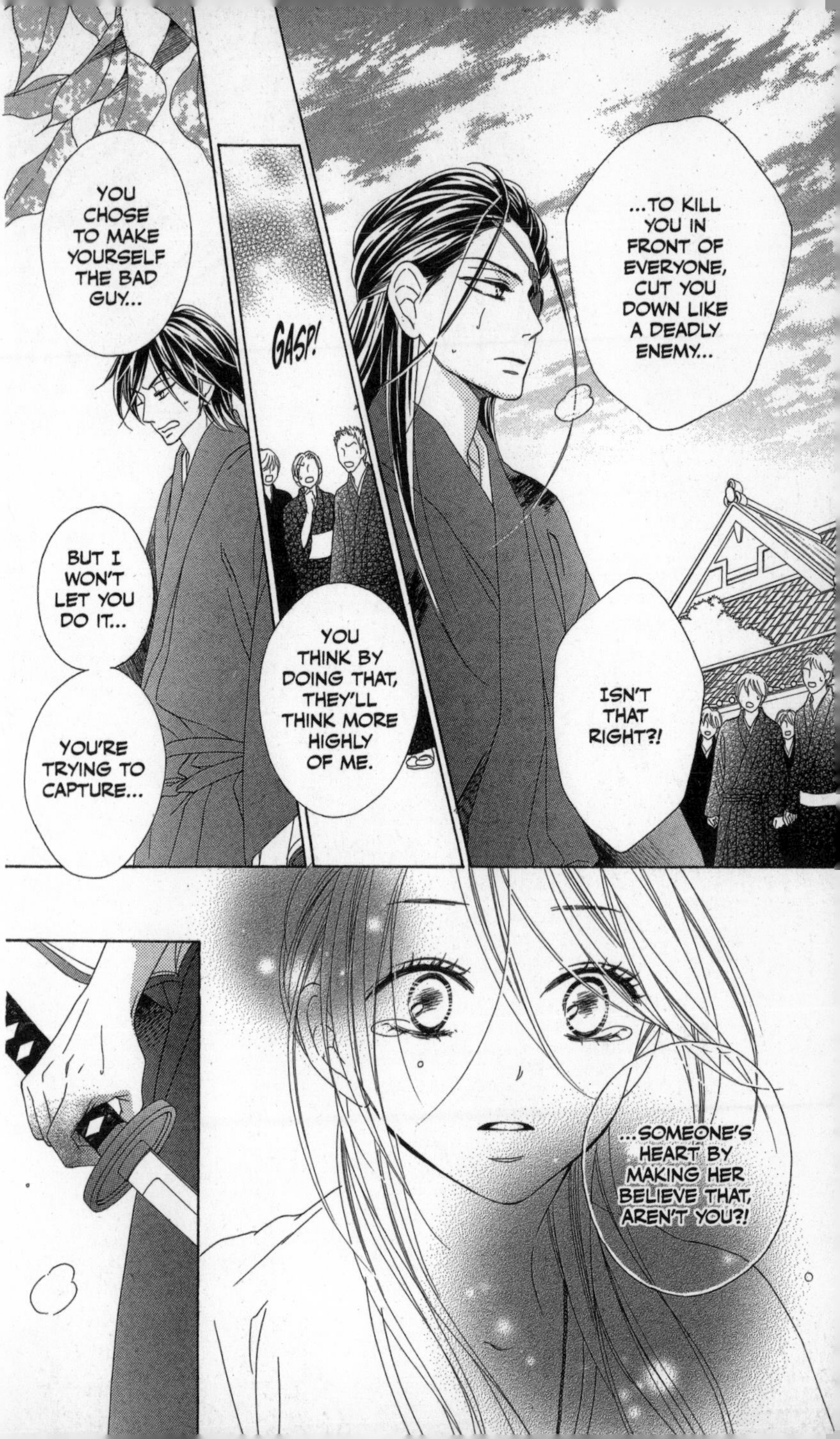
...TO KILL YOU IN FRONT OF EVERYONE, CUT YOU DOWN LIKE A DEADLY ENEMY...
ISN'T THAT RIGHT?!
GASP!
YOU THINK BY DOING THAT, THEY'LL THINK MORE HIGHLY OF ME.
YOU CHOSE TO MAKE YOURSELF THE BAD GUY...
BUT I WON'T LET YOU DO IT...
YOU'RE TRYING TO CAPTURE...
...SOMEONE'S HEART BY MAKING HER BELIEVE THAT, AREN'T YOU?!

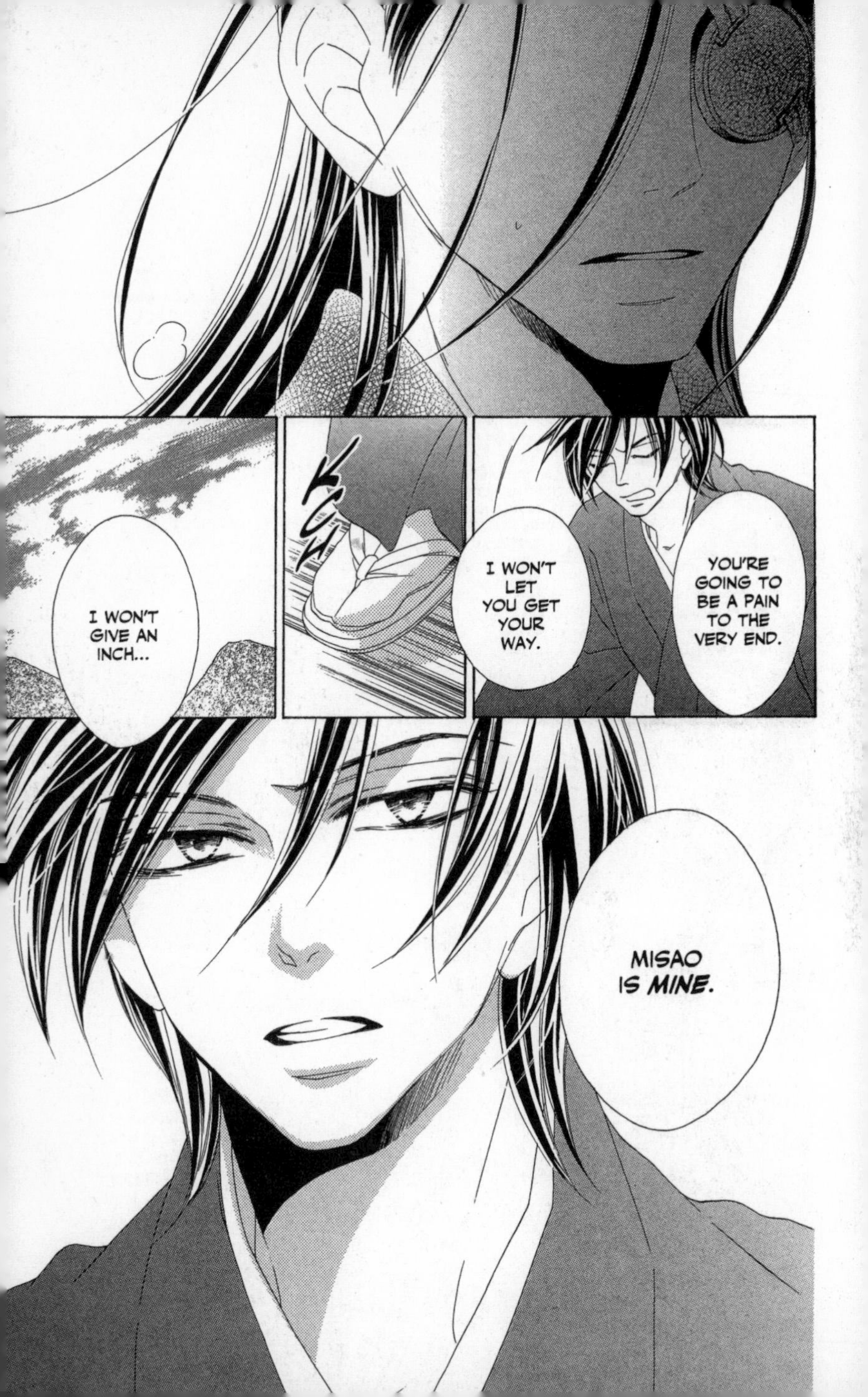
YOU'RE GOING TO BE A PAIN TO THE VERY END.
I WON'T LET YOU GET YOUR WAY.
I WON'T GIVE AN INCH...
MISAO IS *MINE*.

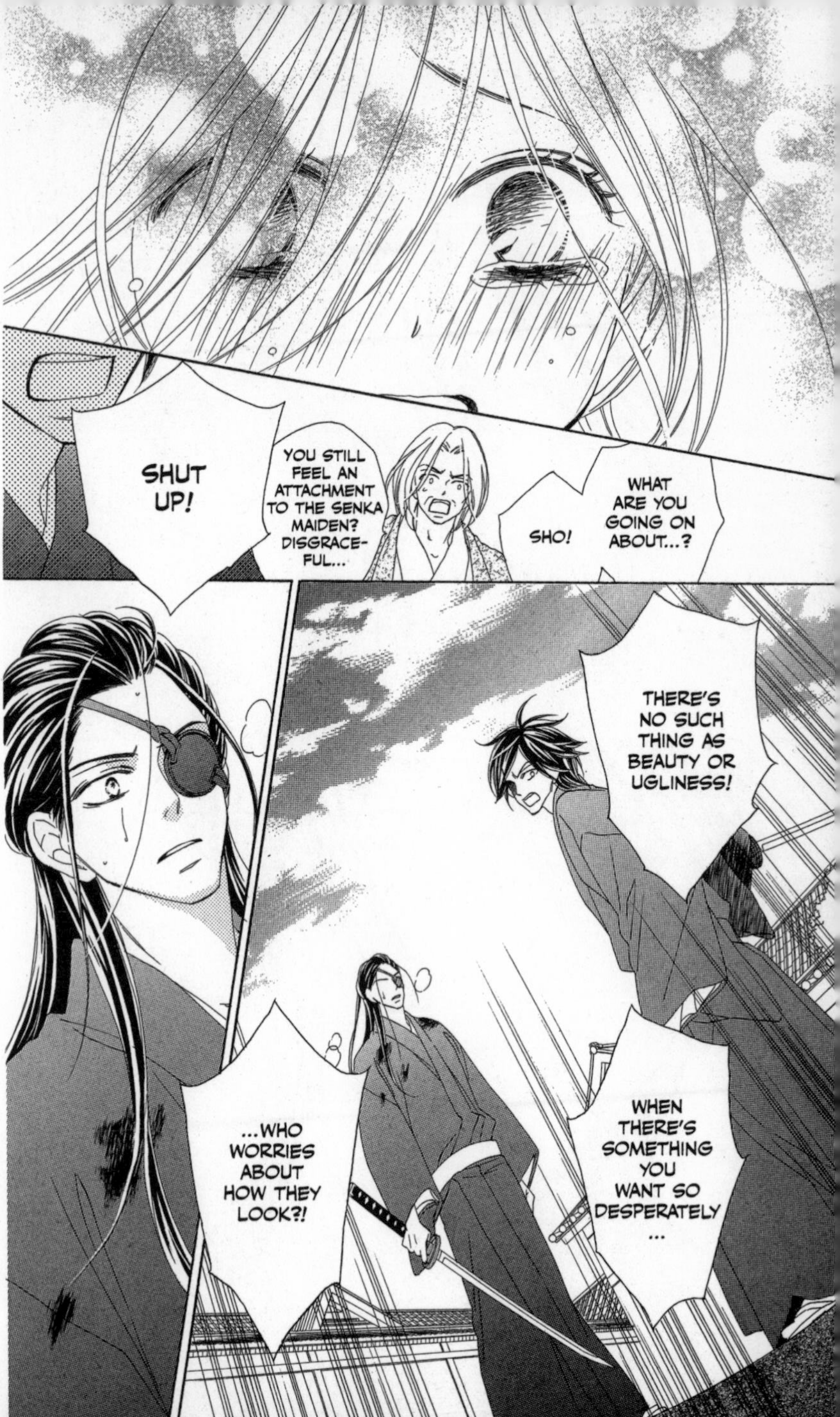
WHAT ARE YOU GOING ON ABOUT...?
SHO!
YOU STILL FEEL AN ATTACHMENT TO THE SENKA MAIDEN? DISGRACEFUL...
SHUT UP!
THERE'S NO SUCH THING AS BEAUTY OR UGLINESS!
WHEN THERE'S SOMETHING YOU WANT SO DESPERATELY ...
...WHO WORRIES ABOUT HOW THEY LOOK?!

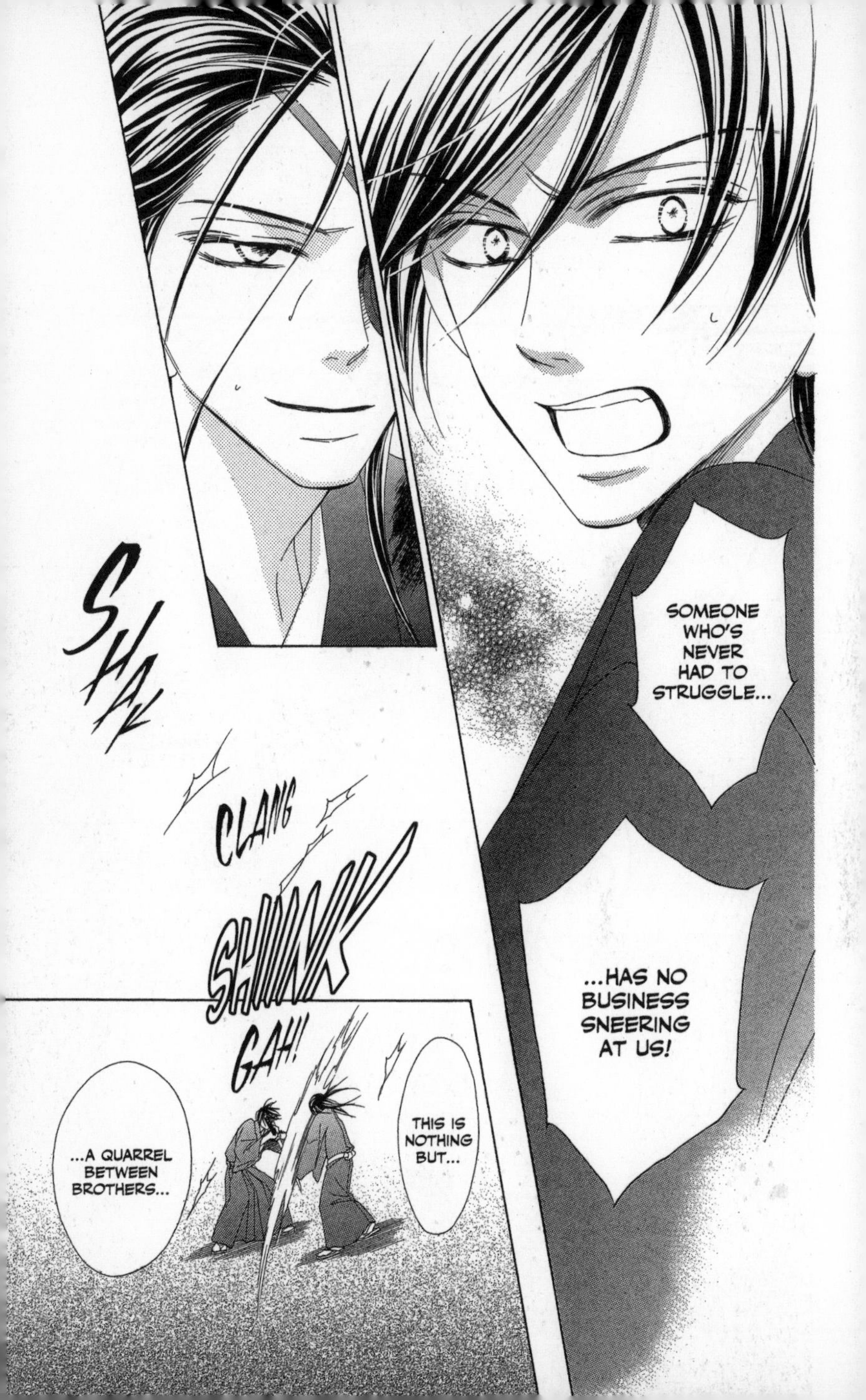
SOMEONE WHO'S NEVER HAD TO STRUGGLE...
...HAS NO BUSINESS SNEERING AT US!
SHAN
CLANG
SHINK
GAH!!
THIS IS NOTHING BUT...
...A QUARREL BETWEEN BROTHERS...

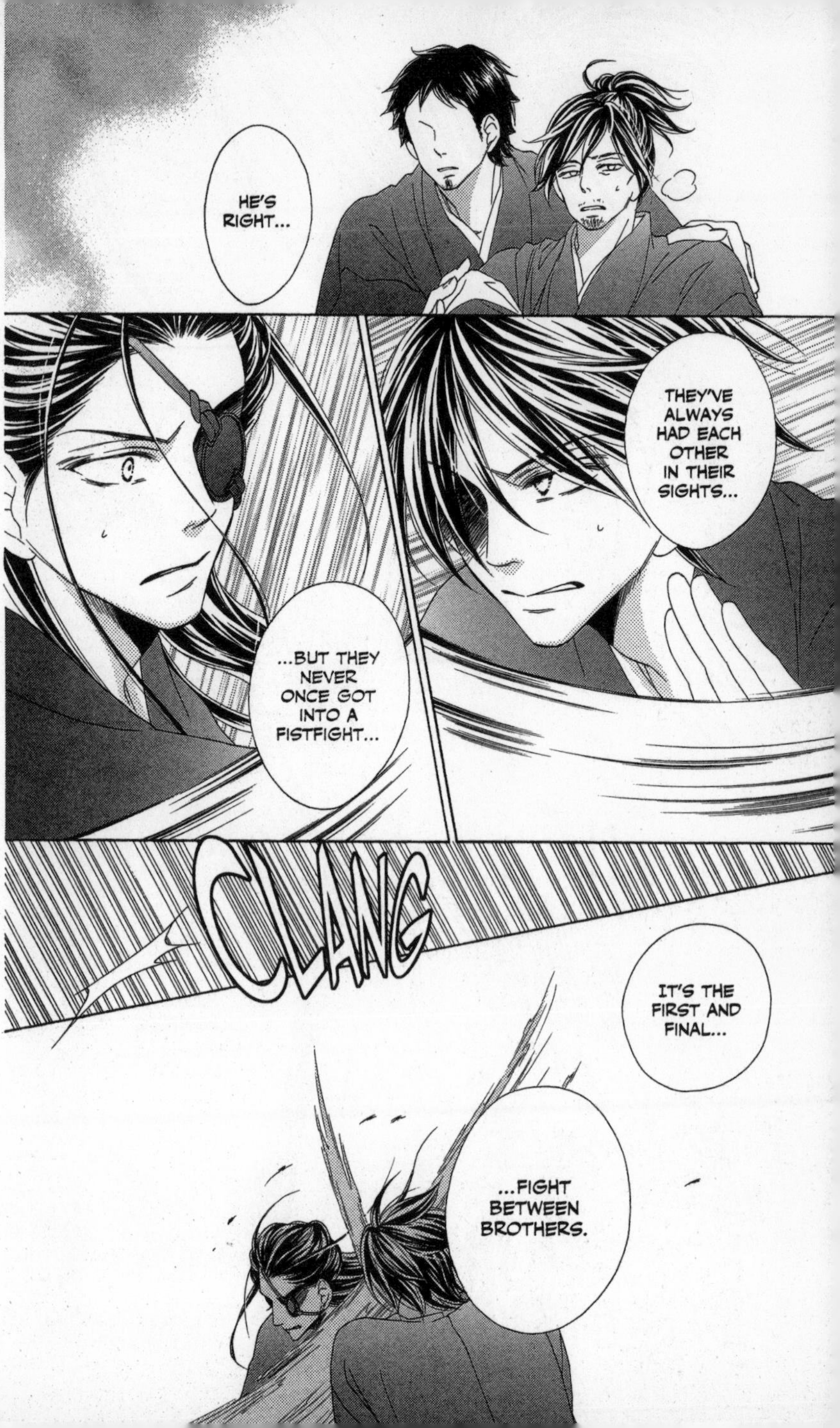
HE'S RIGHT...
THEY'VE ALWAYS HAD EACH OTHER IN THEIR SIGHTS...
...BUT THEY NEVER ONCE GOT INTO A FISTFIGHT...
CLANG
IT'S THE FIRST AND FINAL...
...FIGHT BETWEEN BROTHERS.

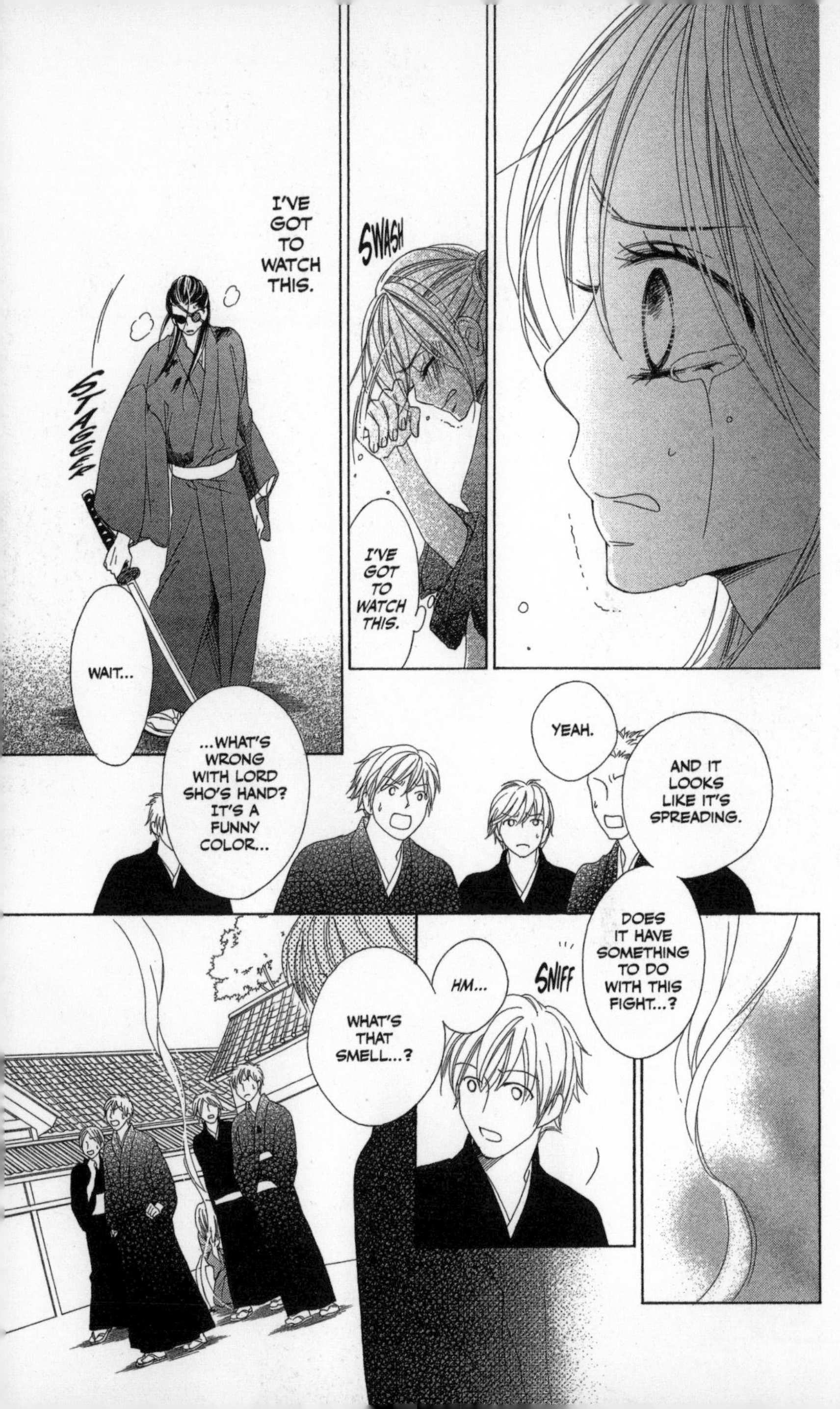
SWASH
I'VE GOT TO WATCH THIS.
I'VE GOT TO WATCH THIS.
STAGGER
WAIT...
...WHAT'S WRONG WITH LORD SHO'S HAND? IT'S A FUNNY COLOR...
YEAH.
AND IT LOOKS LIKE IT'S SPREADING.
DOES IT HAVE SOMETHING TO DO WITH THIS FIGHT...?
SNIFF
HM...
WHAT'S THAT SMELL...?

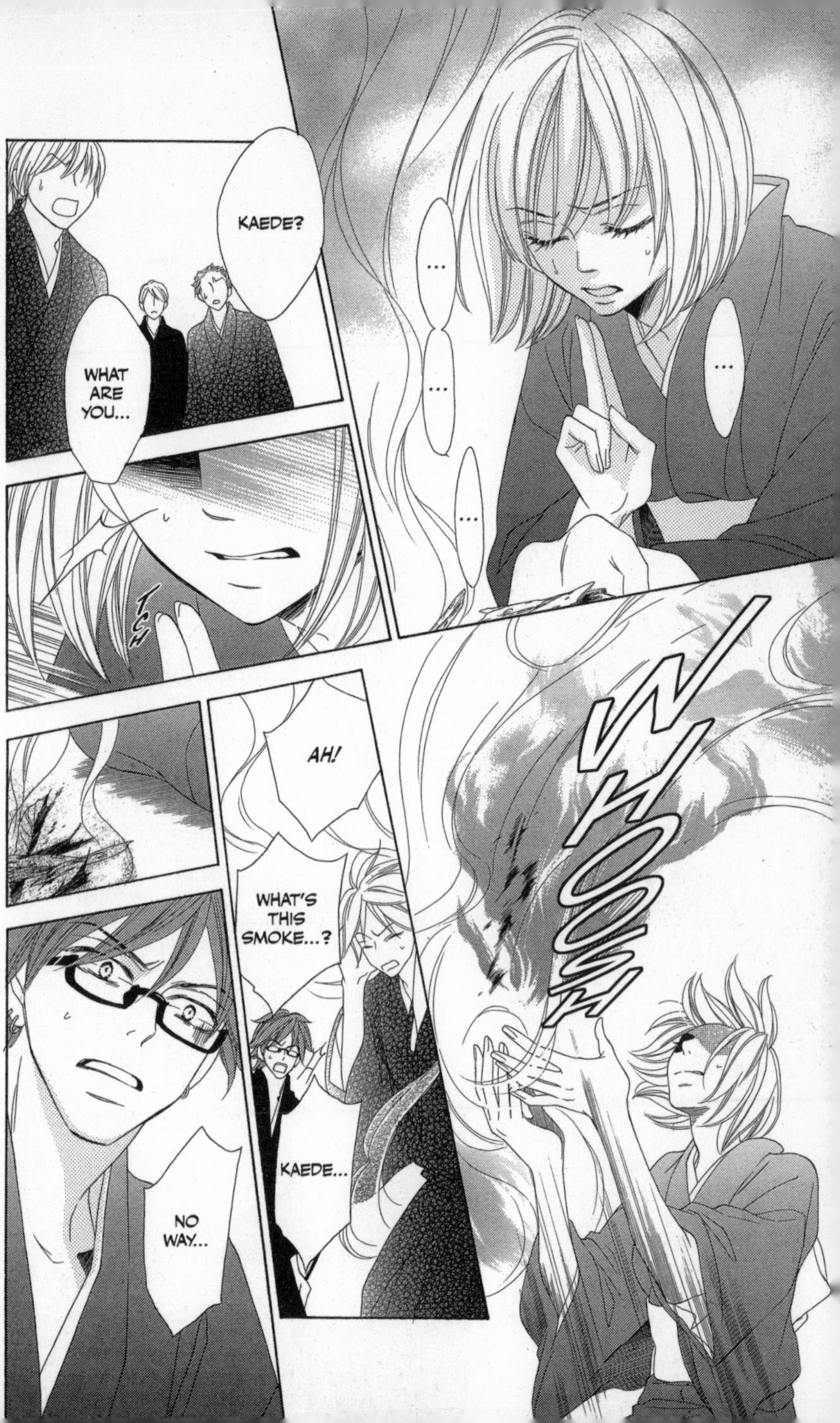
...
...
...
...
KAEDE?
WHAT ARE YOU...
TCH
WHOOSH
AH!
WHAT'S THIS SMOKE...?
KAEDE...
NO WAY...

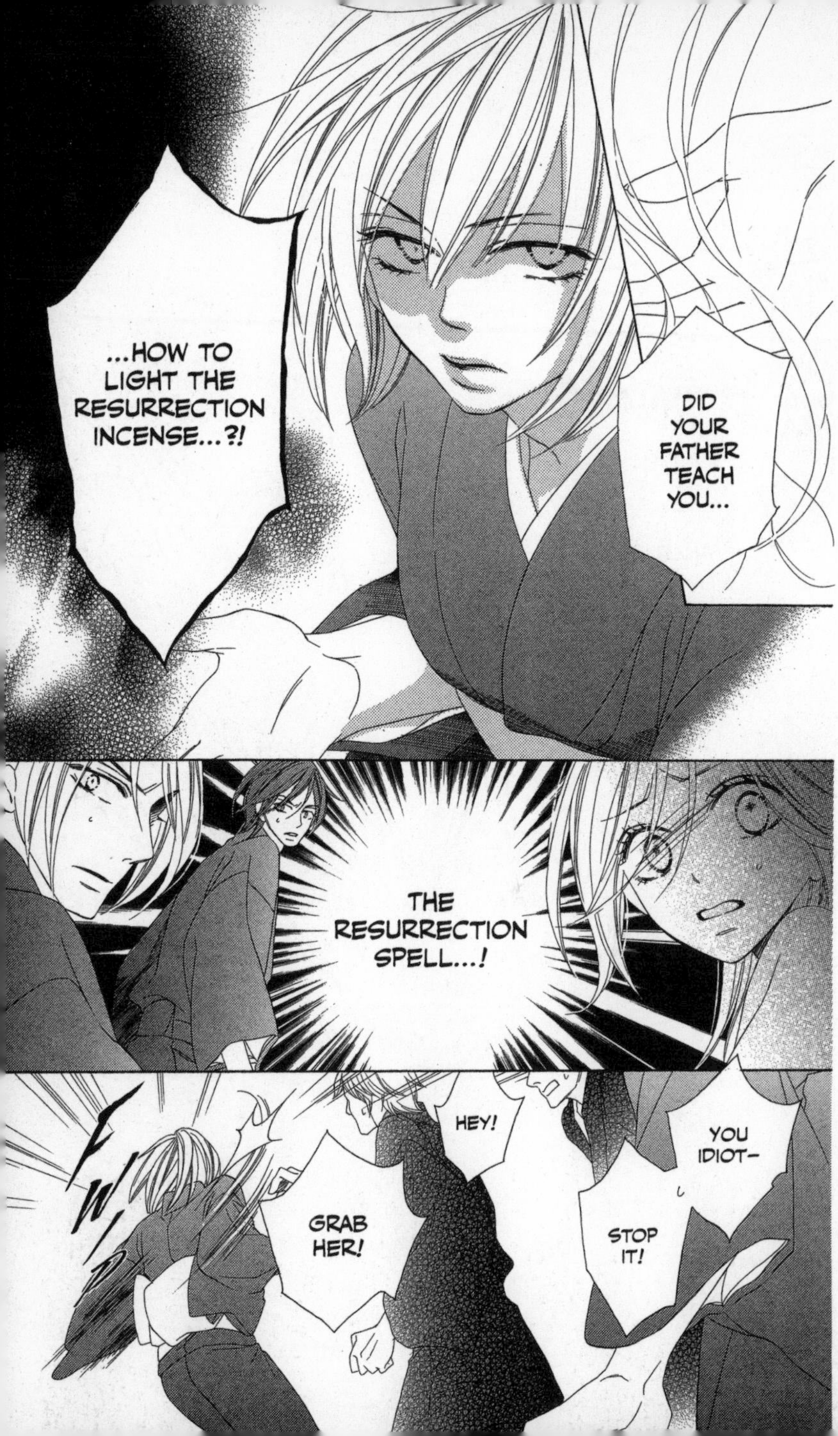
DID YOUR FATHER TEACH YOU...
...HOW TO LIGHT THE RESURRECTION INCENSE...?!
THE RESURRECTION SPELL...!
YOU IDIOT—
HEY!
STOP IT!
GRAB HER!

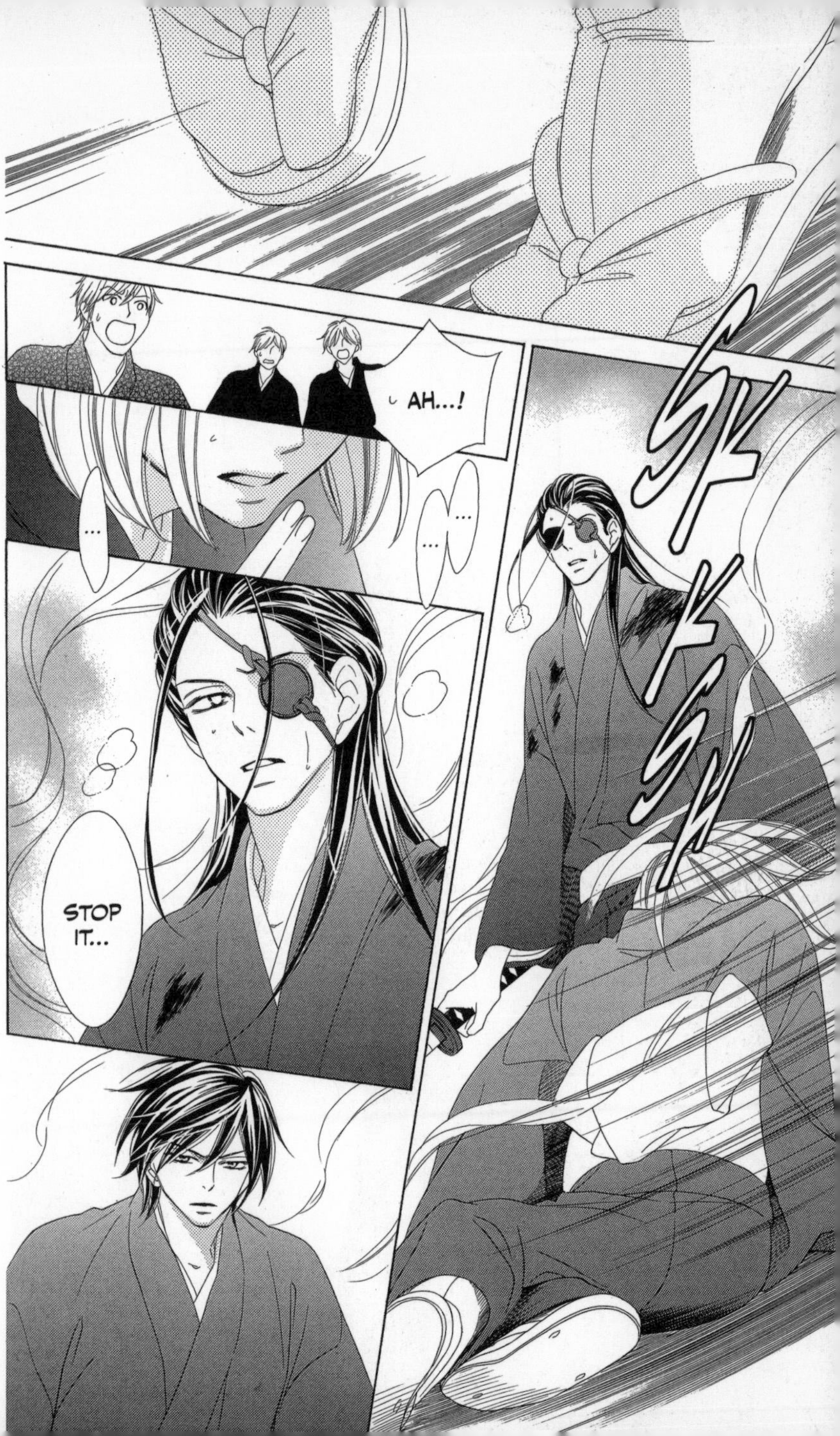
AH...!
...
...
...
STOP IT...

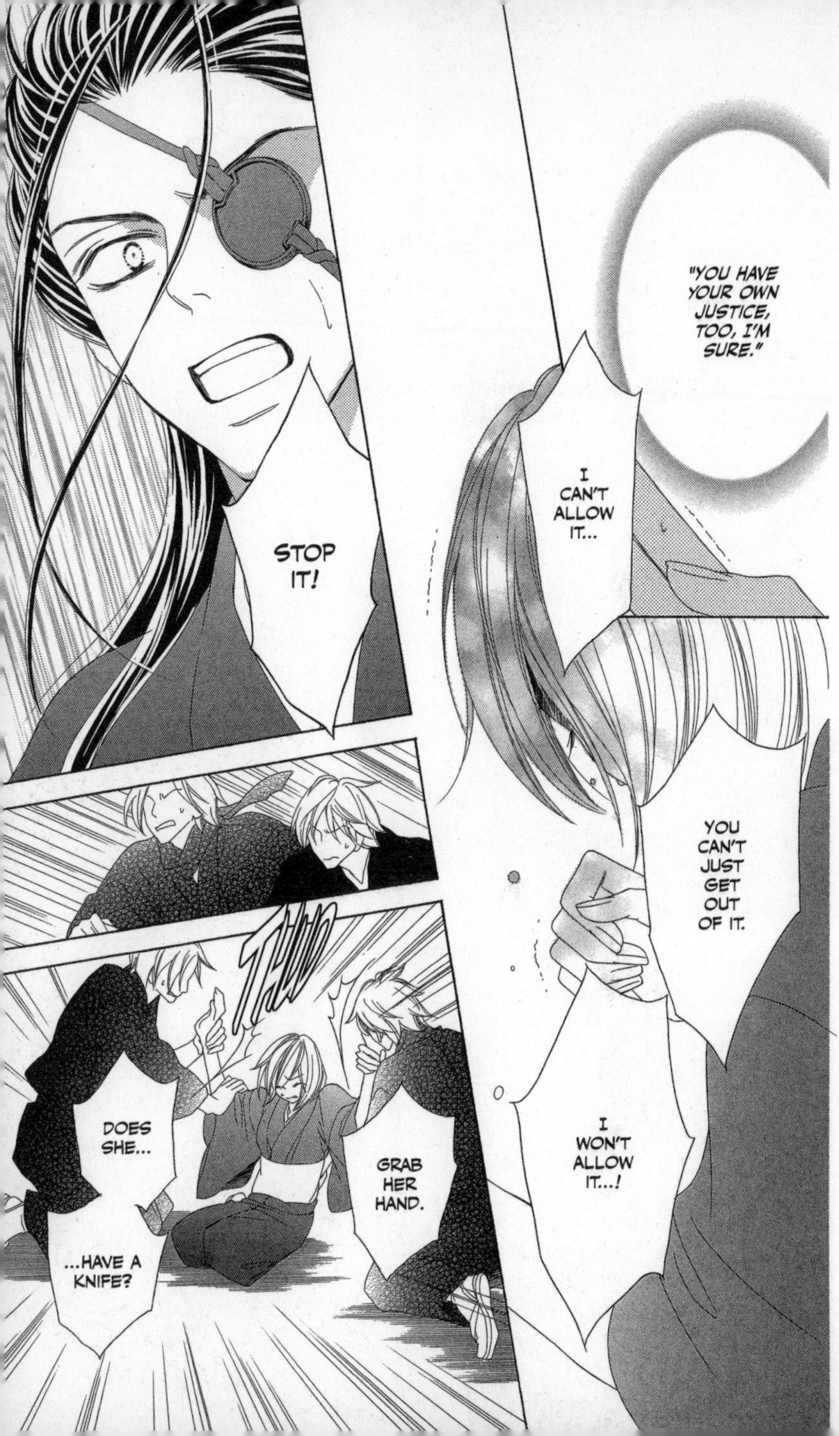
"YOU HAVE YOUR OWN JUSTICE, TOO, I'M SURE."
I CAN'T ALLOW IT...
YOU CAN'T JUST GET OUT OF IT.
I WON'T ALLOW IT...!
STOP IT!
THUD
GRAB HER HAND.
DOES SHE...
...HAVE A KNIFE?

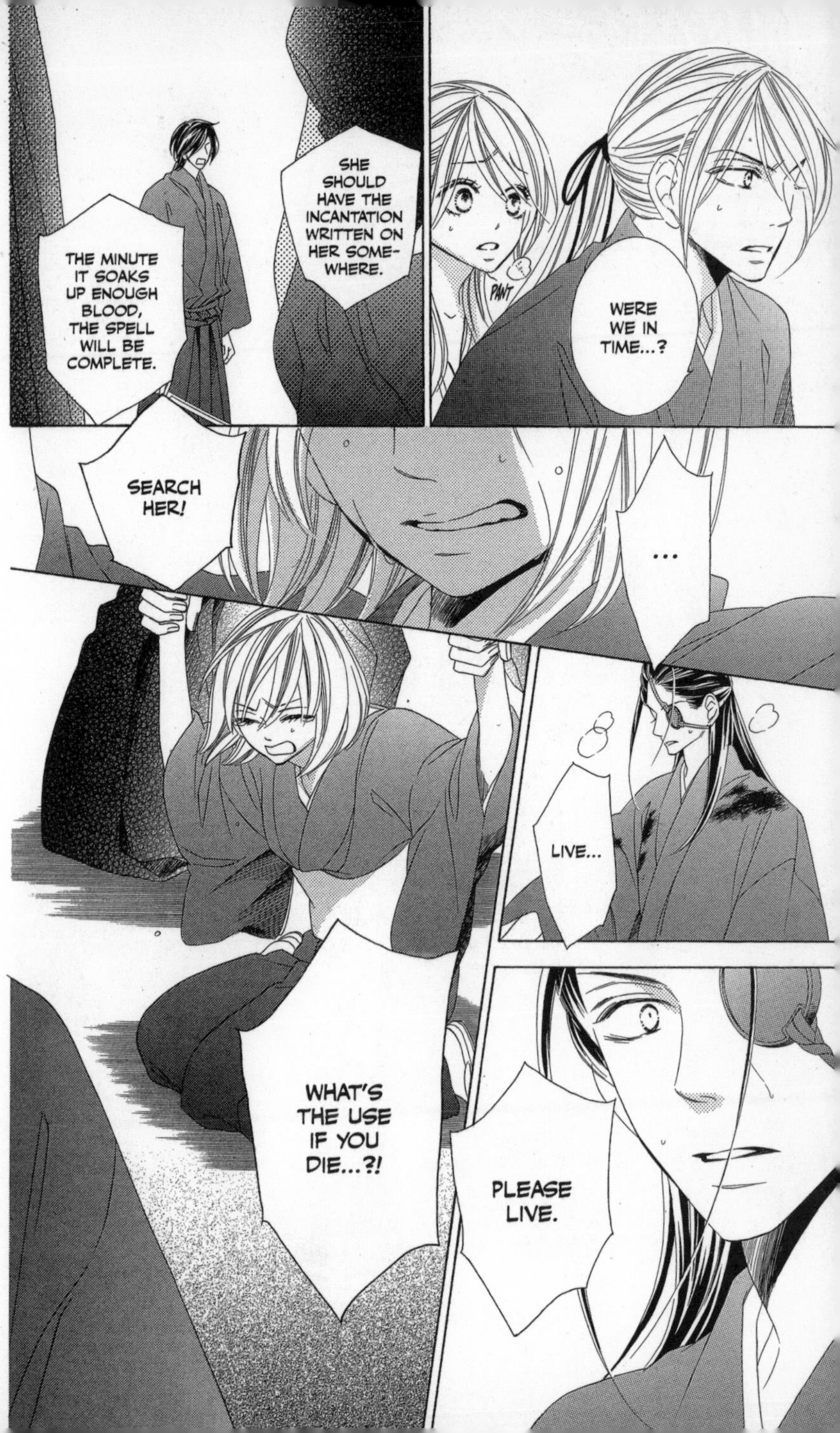
PANT
WERE WE IN TIME...?
SHE SHOULD HAVE THE INCANTATION WRITTEN ON HER SOMEWHERE.
THE MINUTE IT SOAKS UP ENOUGH BLOOD, THE SPELL WILL BE COMPLETE.
...
SEARCH HER!
LIVE...
PLEASE LIVE.
WHAT'S THE USE IF YOU DIE...?!

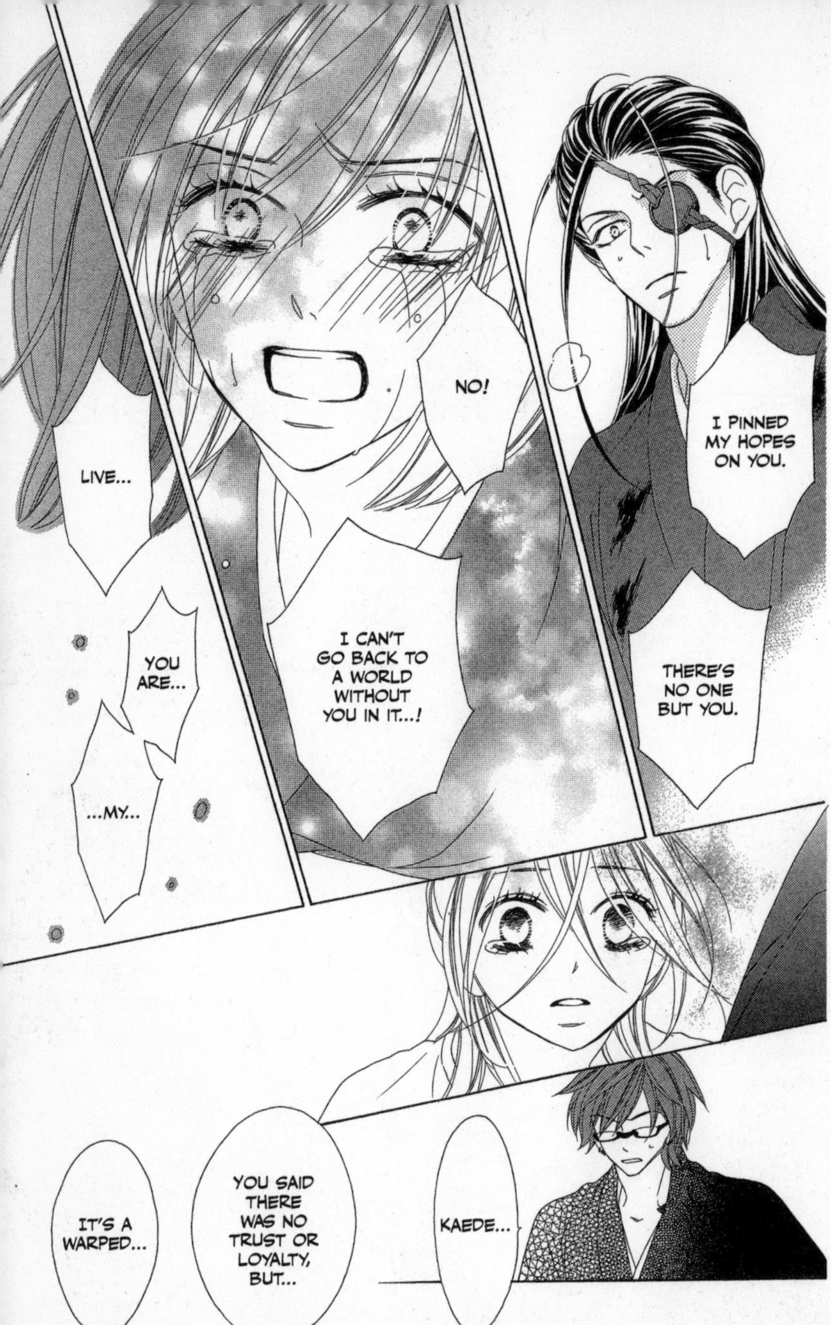
I PINNED MY HOPES ON YOU.
THERE'S NO ONE BUT YOU.
NO!
I CAN'T GO BACK TO A WORLD WITHOUT YOU IN IT...!
LIVE...
YOU ARE...
...MY...
KAEDE...
YOU SAID THERE WAS NO TRUST OR LOYALTY, BUT...
IT'S A WARPED...

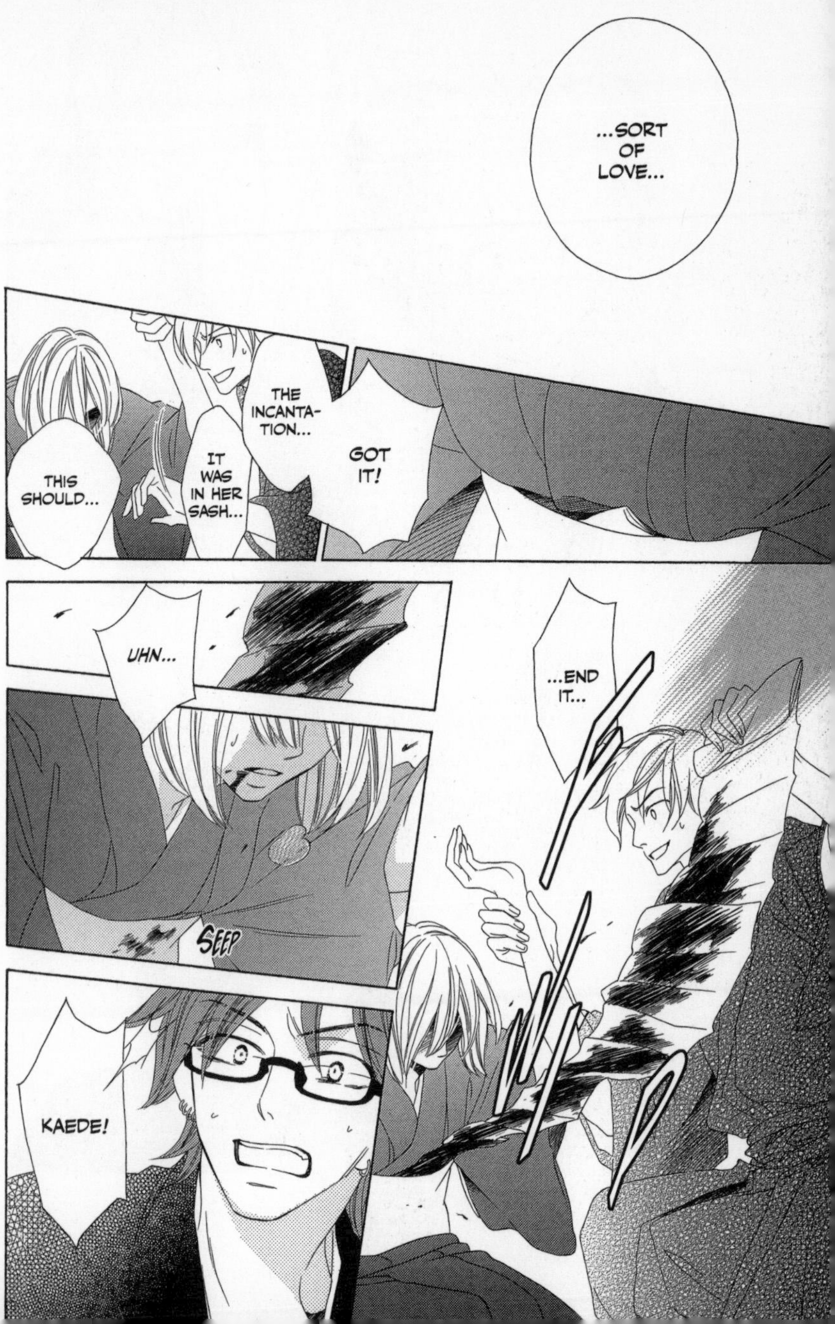
...SORT OF LOVE...
GOT IT!
THE INCANTATION...
IT WAS IN HER SASH...
THIS SHOULD...
...END IT...
UHN...
SEEP
KAEDE!

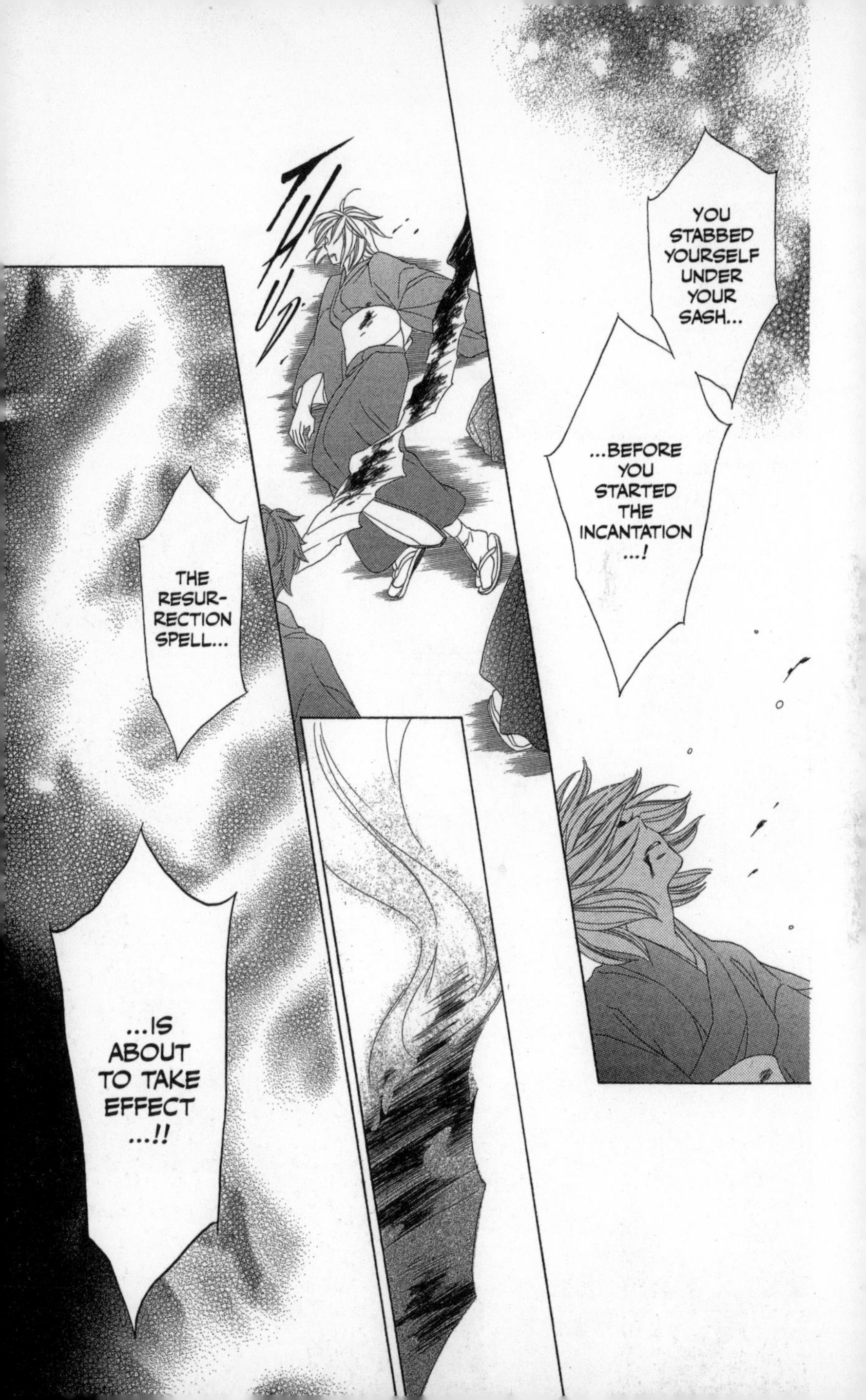
YOU STABBED YOURSELF UNDER YOUR SASH...
...BEFORE YOU STARTED THE INCANTATION ...!
THE RESUR-RECTION SPELL...
...IS ABOUT TO TAKE EFFECT ...!!

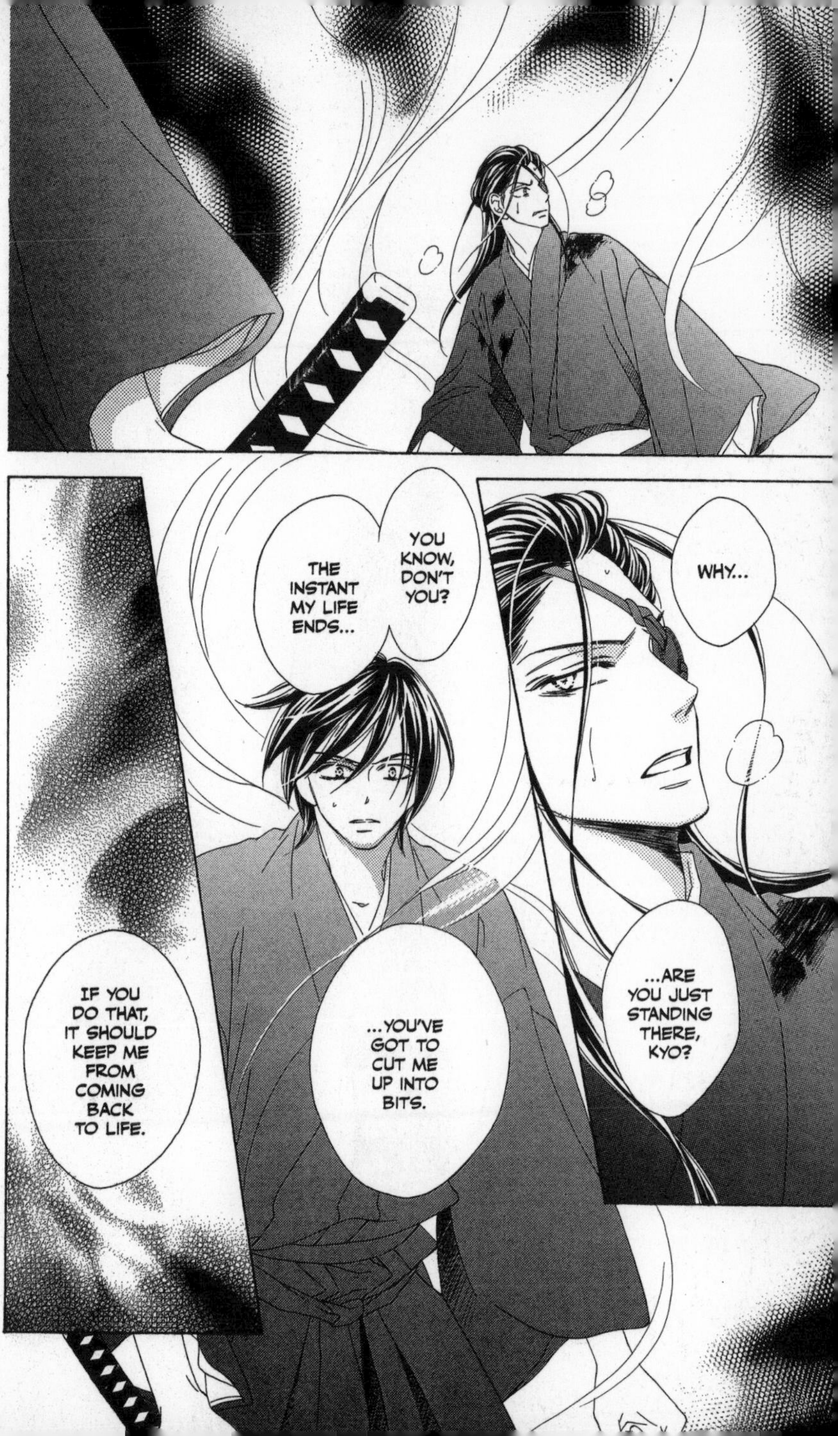
WHY...
...ARE YOU JUST STANDING THERE, KYO?
YOU KNOW, DON'T YOU?
THE INSTANT MY LIFE ENDS...
...YOU'VE GOT TO CUT ME UP INTO BITS.
IF YOU DO THAT, IT SHOULD KEEP ME FROM COMING BACK TO LIFE.

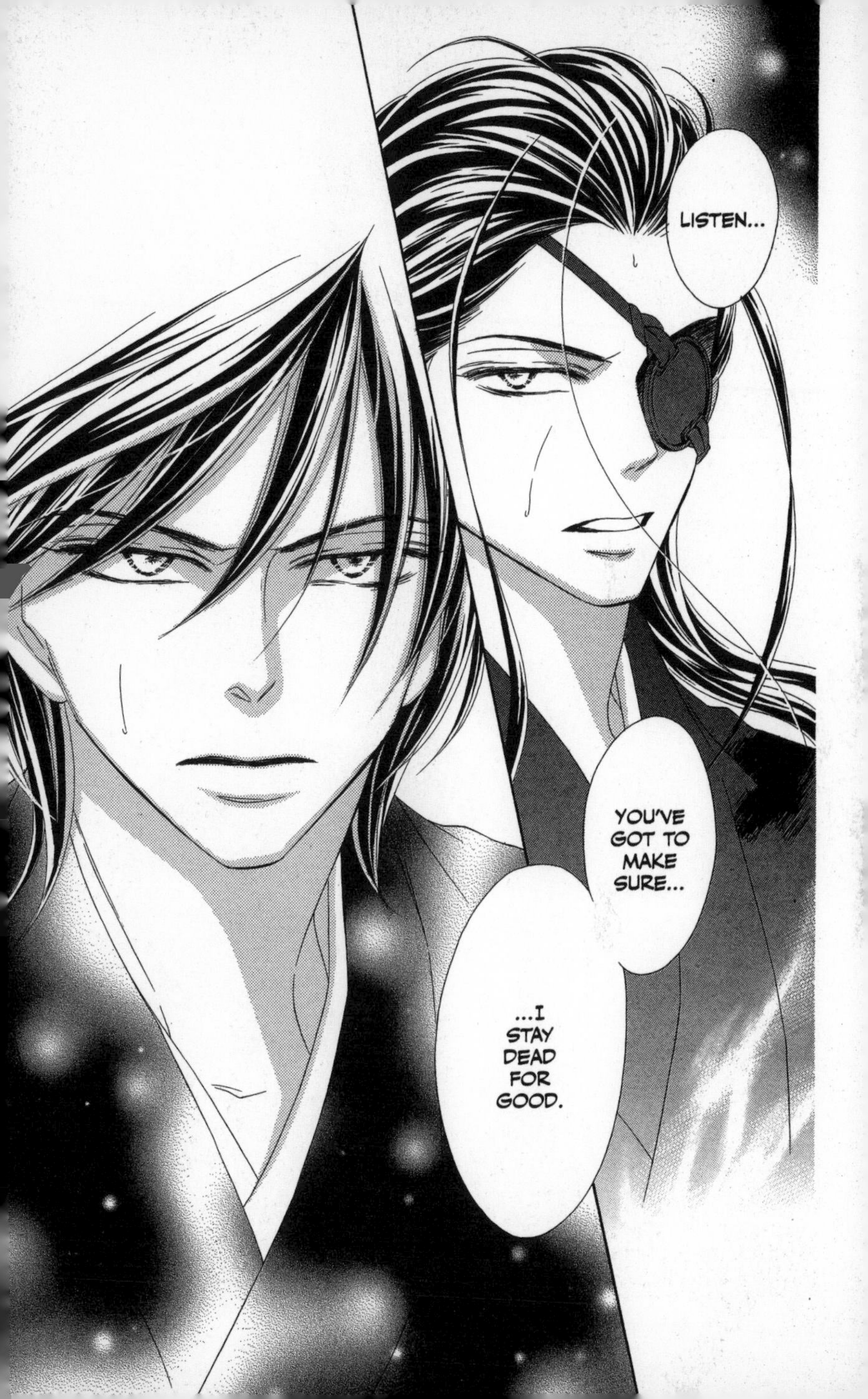
LISTEN...
YOU'VE GOT TO MAKE SURE...
...I STAY DEAD FOR GOOD.

BlackBird

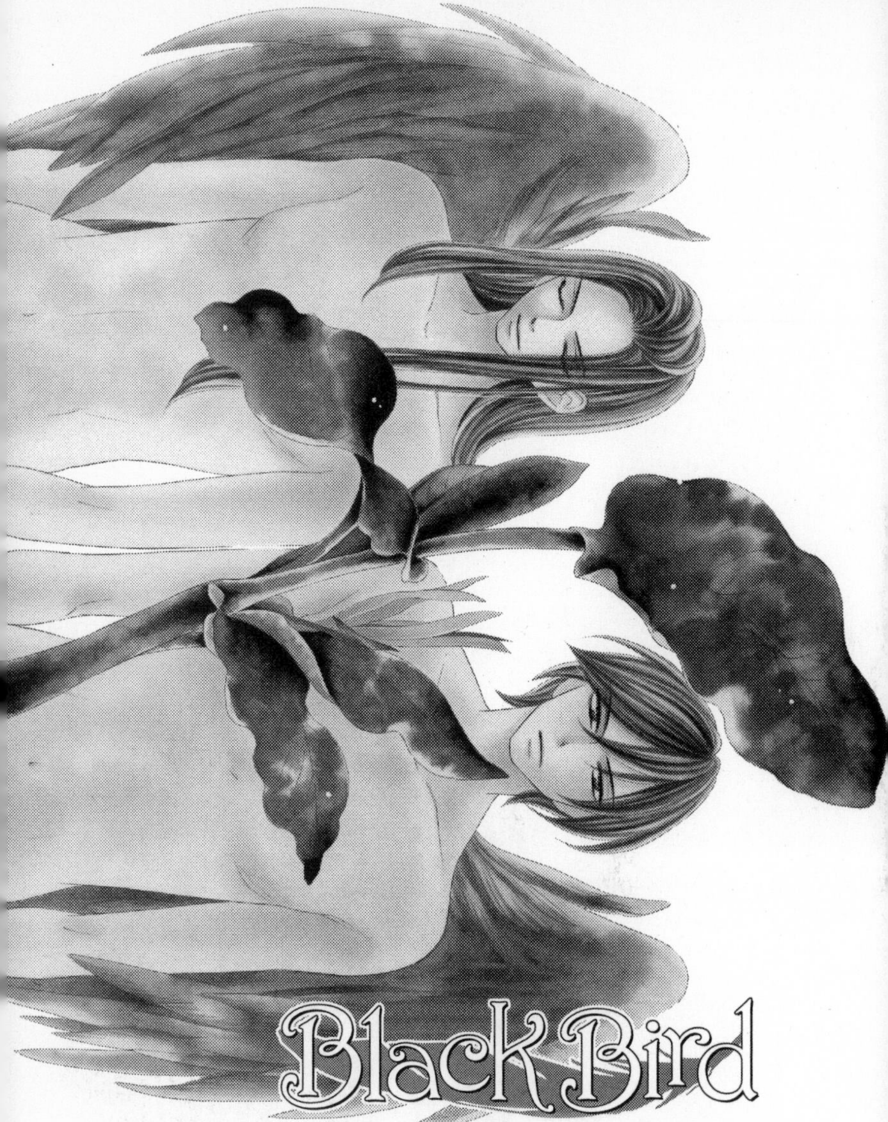

Black Bird

Chapter 53

Black Bird

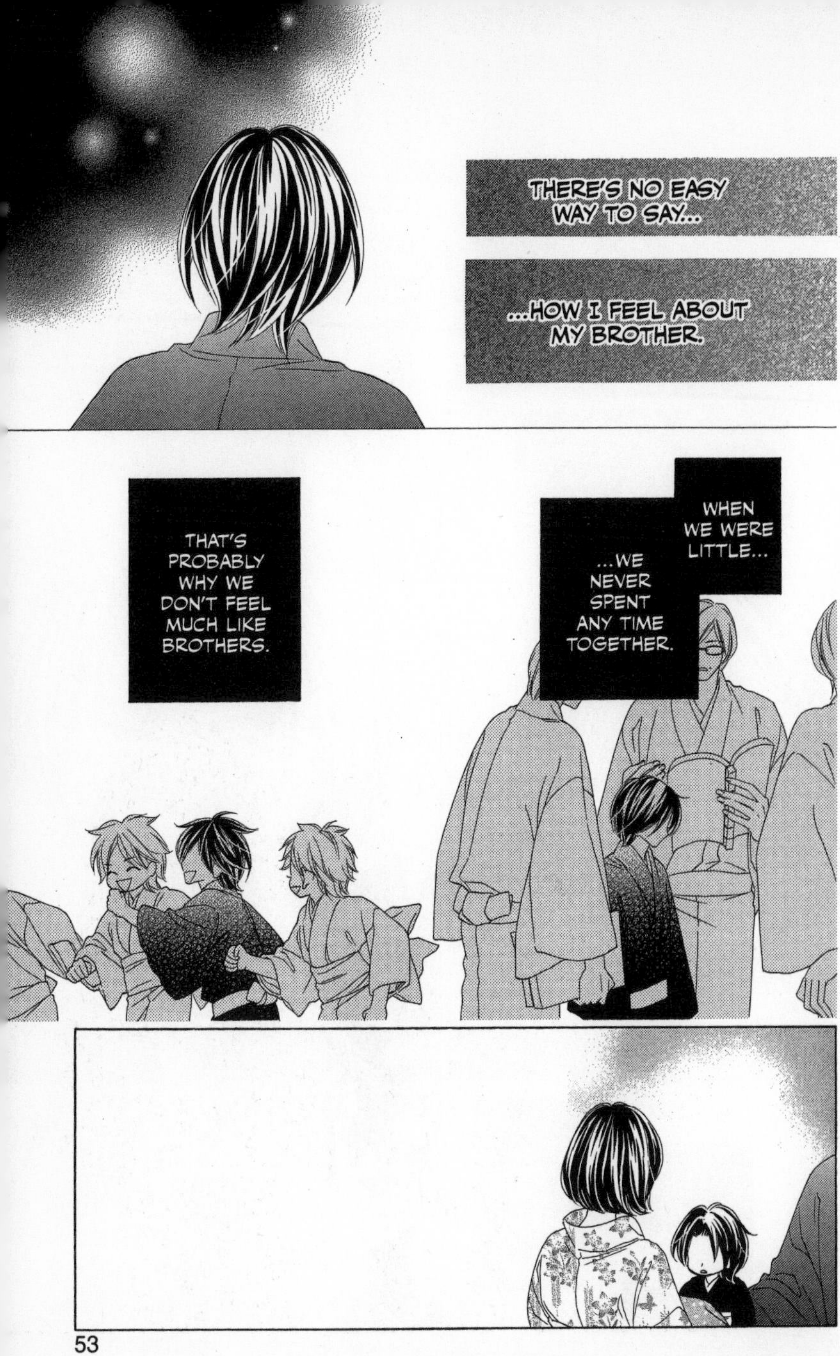
THERE'S NO EASY WAY TO SAY...
...HOW I FEEL ABOUT MY BROTHER.
WHEN WE WERE LITTLE...
...WE NEVER SPENT ANY TIME TOGETHER.
THAT'S PROBABLY WHY WE DON'T FEEL MUCH LIKE BROTHERS.

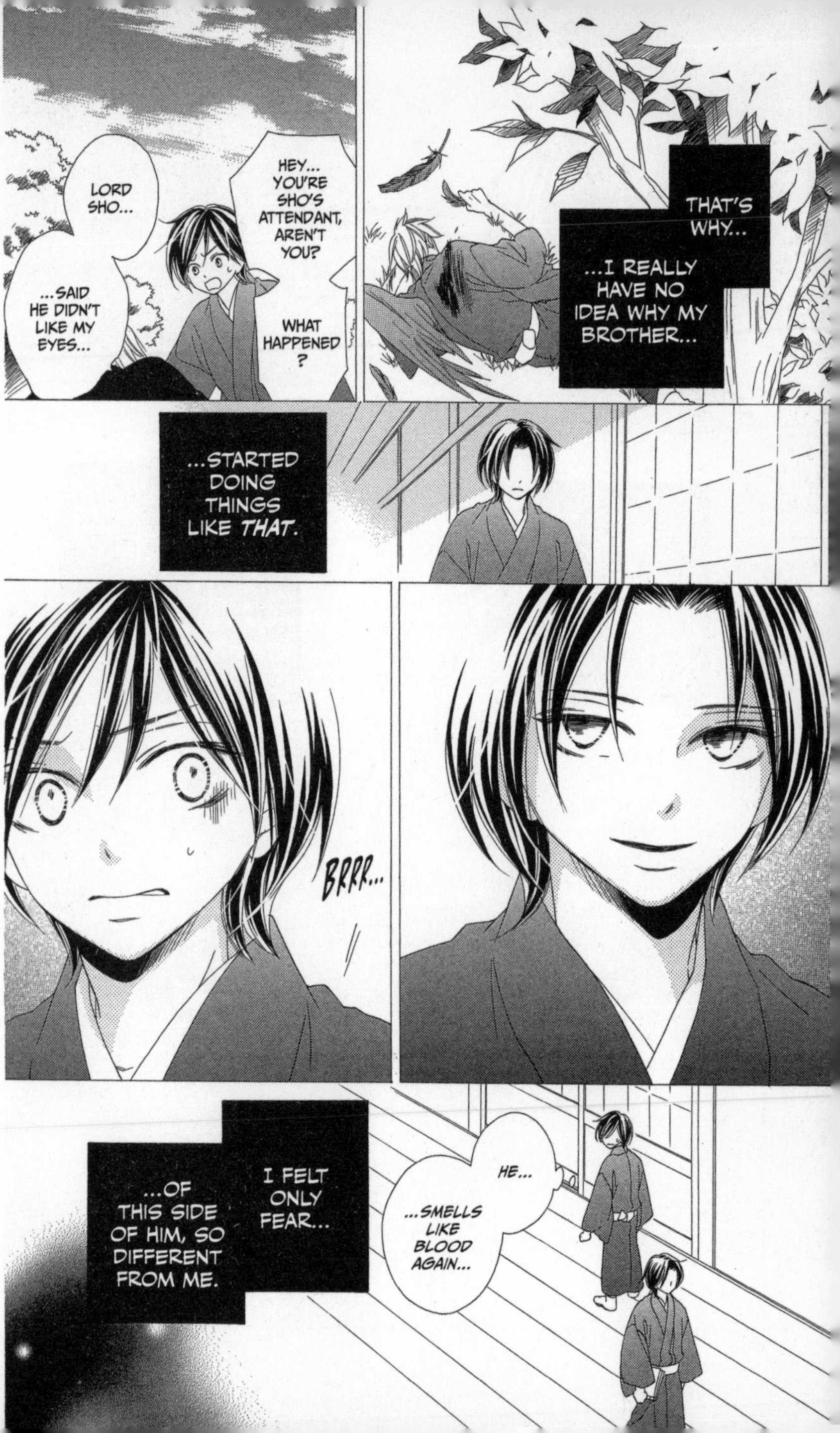
THAT'S WHY...
...I REALLY HAVE NO IDEA WHY MY BROTHER...
HEY... YOU'RE SHO'S ATTENDANT, AREN'T YOU?
WHAT HAPPENED?
LORD SHO...
...SAID HE DIDN'T LIKE MY EYES...
...STARTED DOING THINGS LIKE *THAT*.
BRRR...
HE...
...SMELLS LIKE BLOOD AGAIN...
I FELT ONLY FEAR...
...OF THIS SIDE OF HIM, SO DIFFERENT FROM ME.

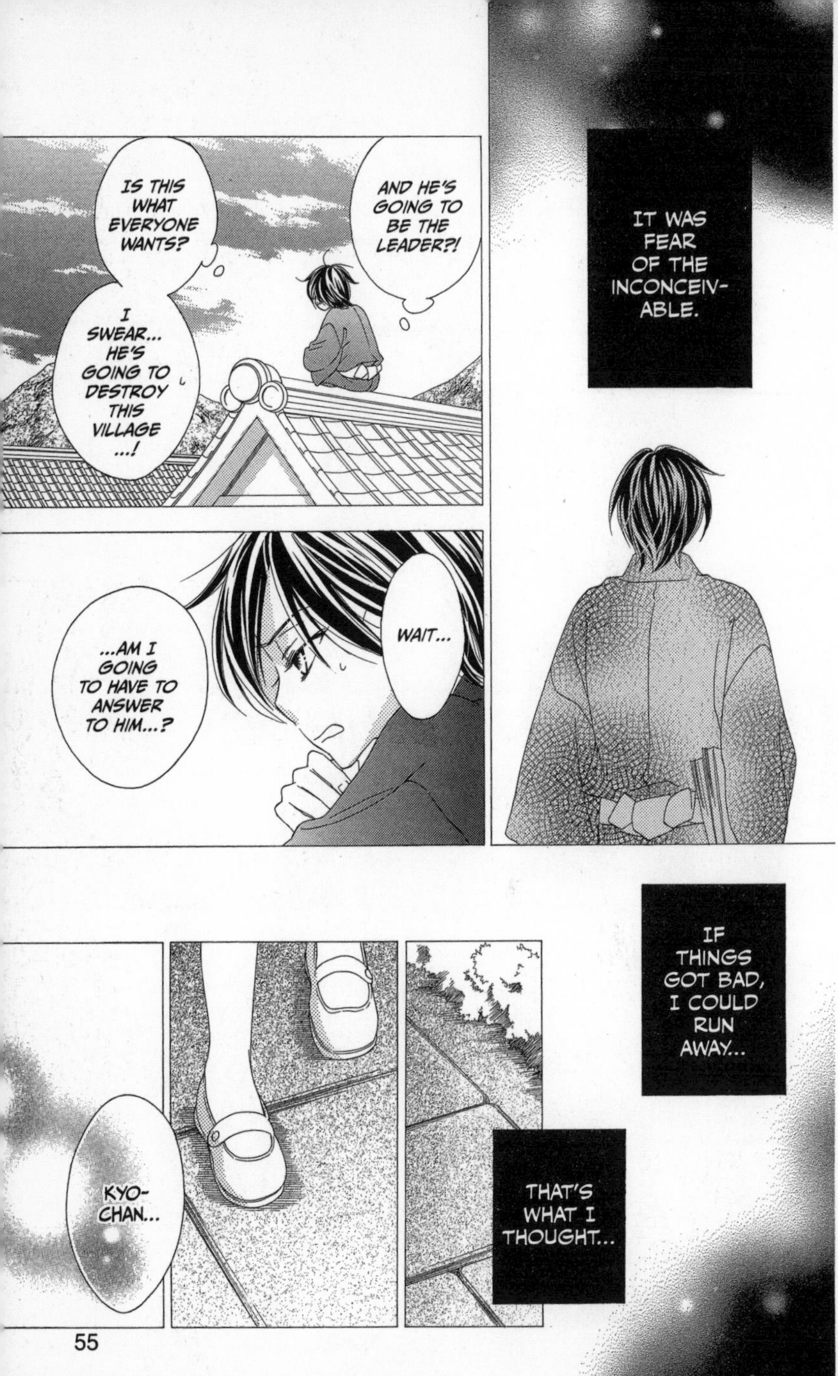
IT WAS FEAR OF THE INCONCEIV-ABLE.
AND HE'S GOING TO BE THE LEADER?!
IS THIS WHAT EVERYONE WANTS?
I SWEAR... HE'S GOING TO DESTROY THIS VILLAGE ...!
WAIT...
...AM I GOING TO HAVE TO ANSWER TO HIM...?
IF THINGS GOT BAD, I COULD RUN AWAY...
THAT'S WHAT I THOUGHT...
KYO-CHAN...

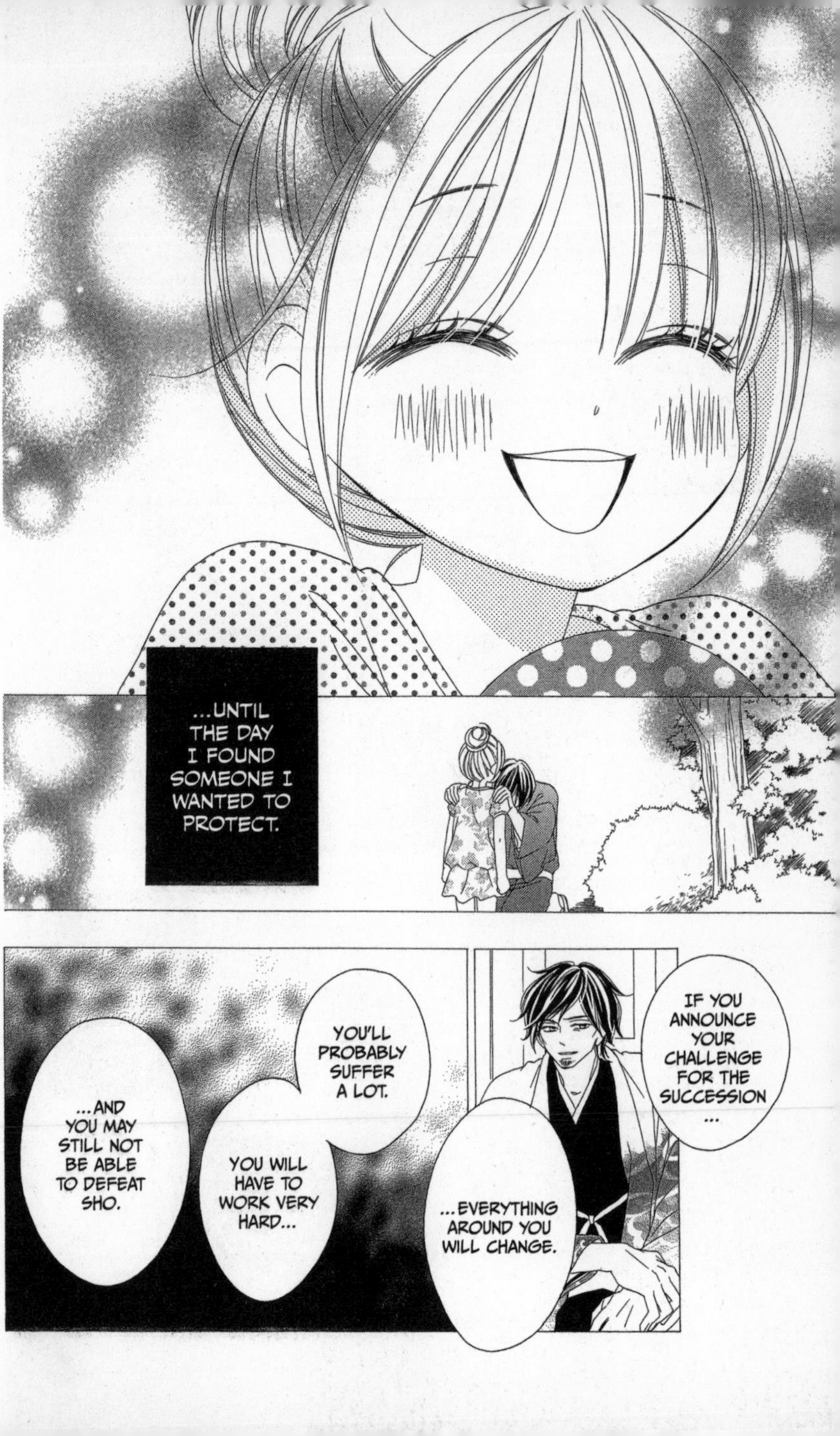
...UNTIL THE DAY I FOUND SOMEONE I WANTED TO PROTECT.
IF YOU ANNOUNCE YOUR CHALLENGE FOR THE SUCCESSION...
...EVERYTHING AROUND YOU WILL CHANGE.
YOU'LL PROBABLY SUFFER A LOT.
YOU WILL HAVE TO WORK VERY HARD...
...AND YOU MAY STILL NOT BE ABLE TO DEFEAT SHO.

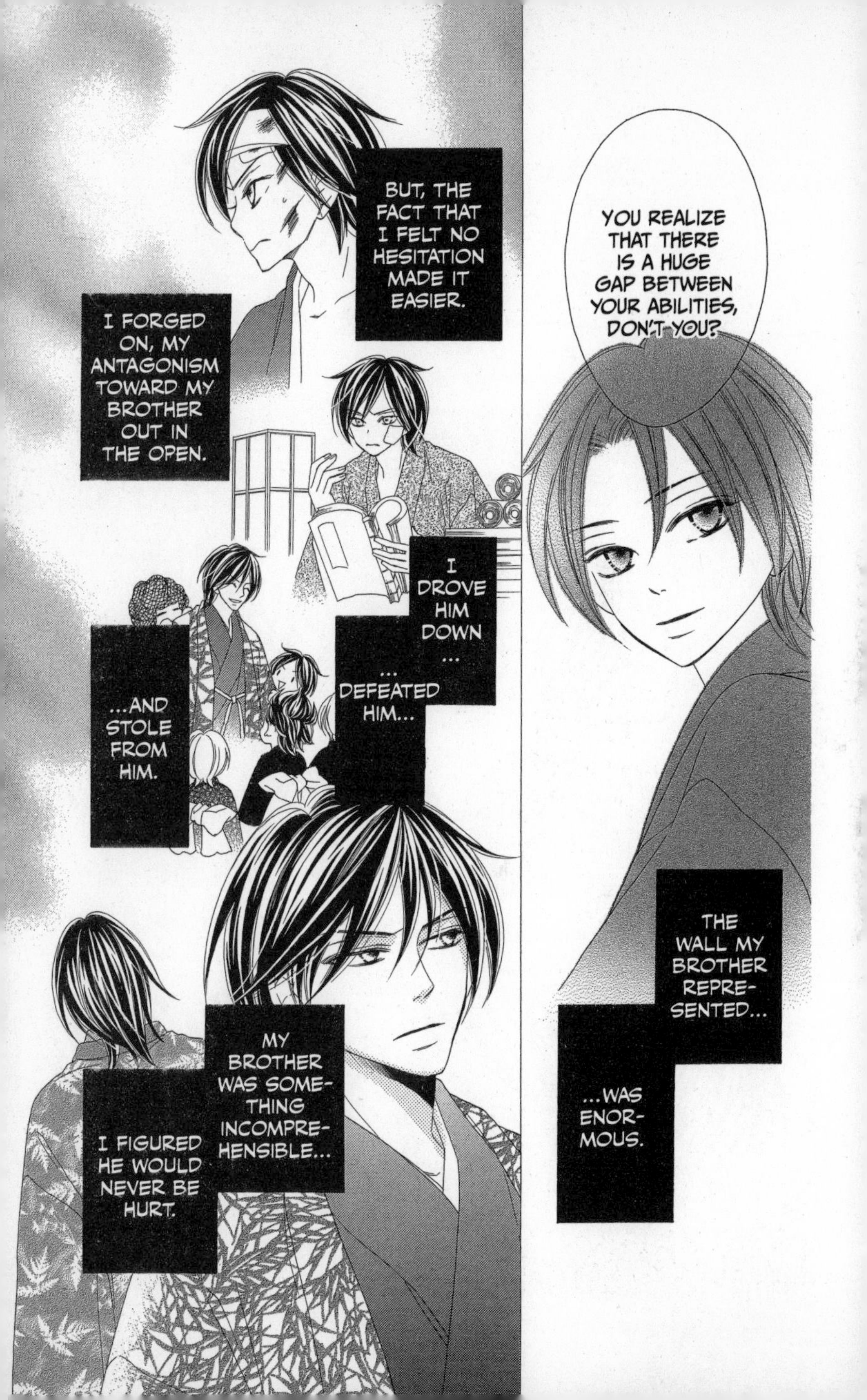
YOU REALIZE THAT THERE IS A HUGE GAP BETWEEN YOUR ABILITIES, DON'T YOU?
THE WALL MY BROTHER REPRESENTED...
...WAS ENORMOUS.
BUT, THE FACT THAT I FELT NO HESITATION MADE IT EASIER.
I FORGED ON, MY ANTAGONISM TOWARD MY BROTHER OUT IN THE OPEN.
I DROVE HIM DOWN...
...DEFEATED HIM...
...AND STOLE FROM HIM.
MY BROTHER WAS SOMETHING INCOMPREHENSIBLE...
I FIGURED HE WOULD NEVER BE HURT.

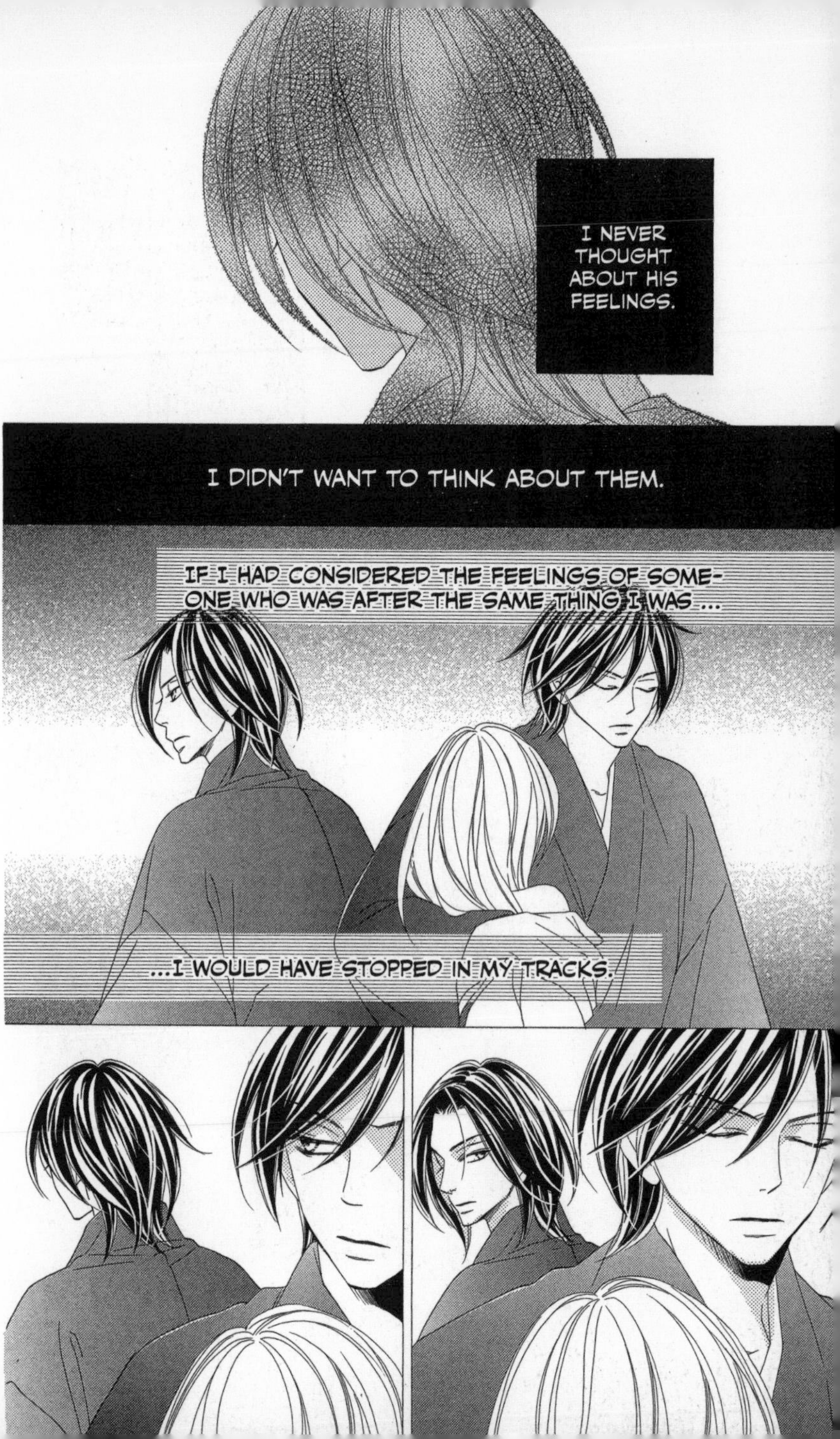
I NEVER THOUGHT ABOUT HIS FEELINGS.
I DIDN'T WANT TO THINK ABOUT THEM.
IF I HAD CONSIDERED THE FEELINGS OF SOME-ONE WHO WAS AFTER THE SAME THING I WAS ...
...I WOULD HAVE STOPPED IN MY TRACKS.

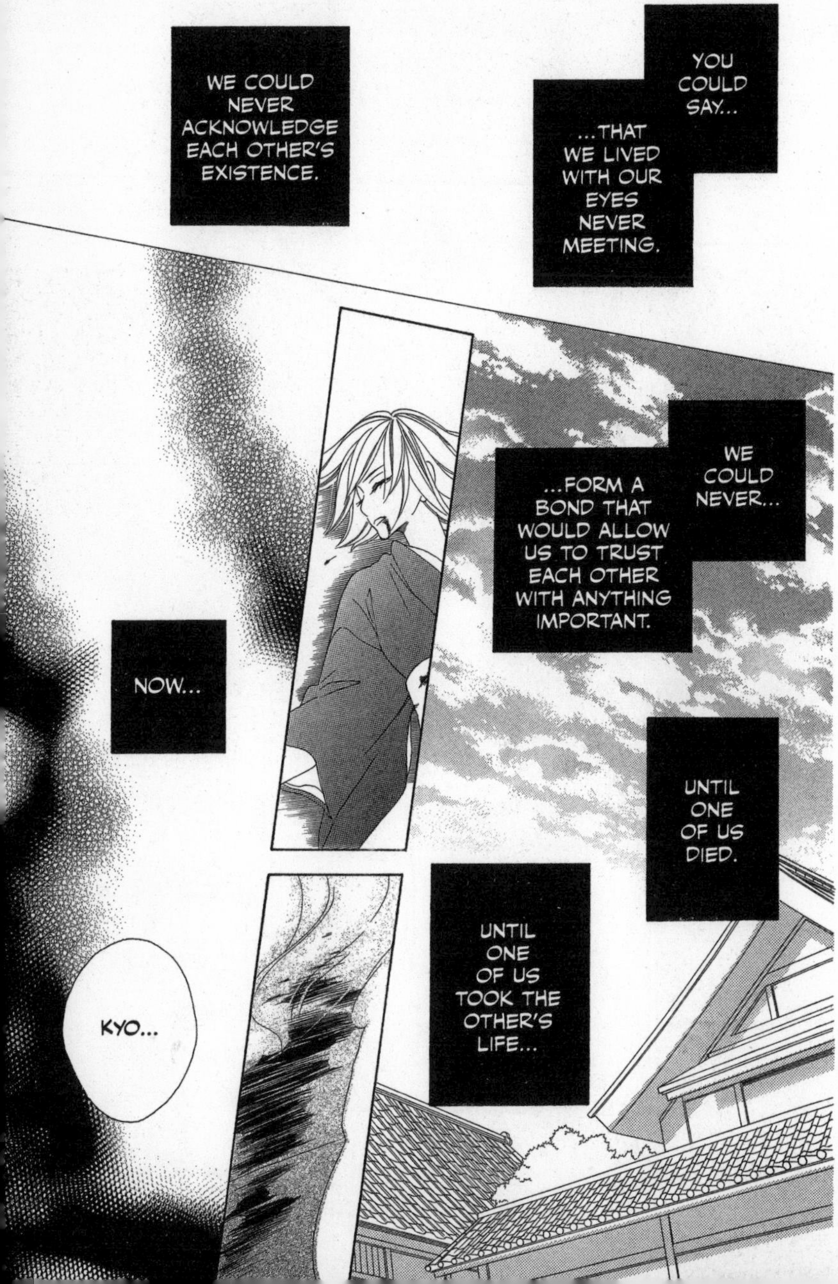
YOU COULD SAY...
...THAT WE LIVED WITH OUR EYES NEVER MEETING.
WE COULD NEVER ACKNOWLEDGE EACH OTHER'S EXISTENCE.
WE COULD NEVER...
...FORM A BOND THAT WOULD ALLOW US TO TRUST EACH OTHER WITH ANYTHING IMPORTANT.
UNTIL ONE OF US DIED.
UNTIL ONE OF US TOOK THE OTHER'S LIFE...
NOW...
KYO...

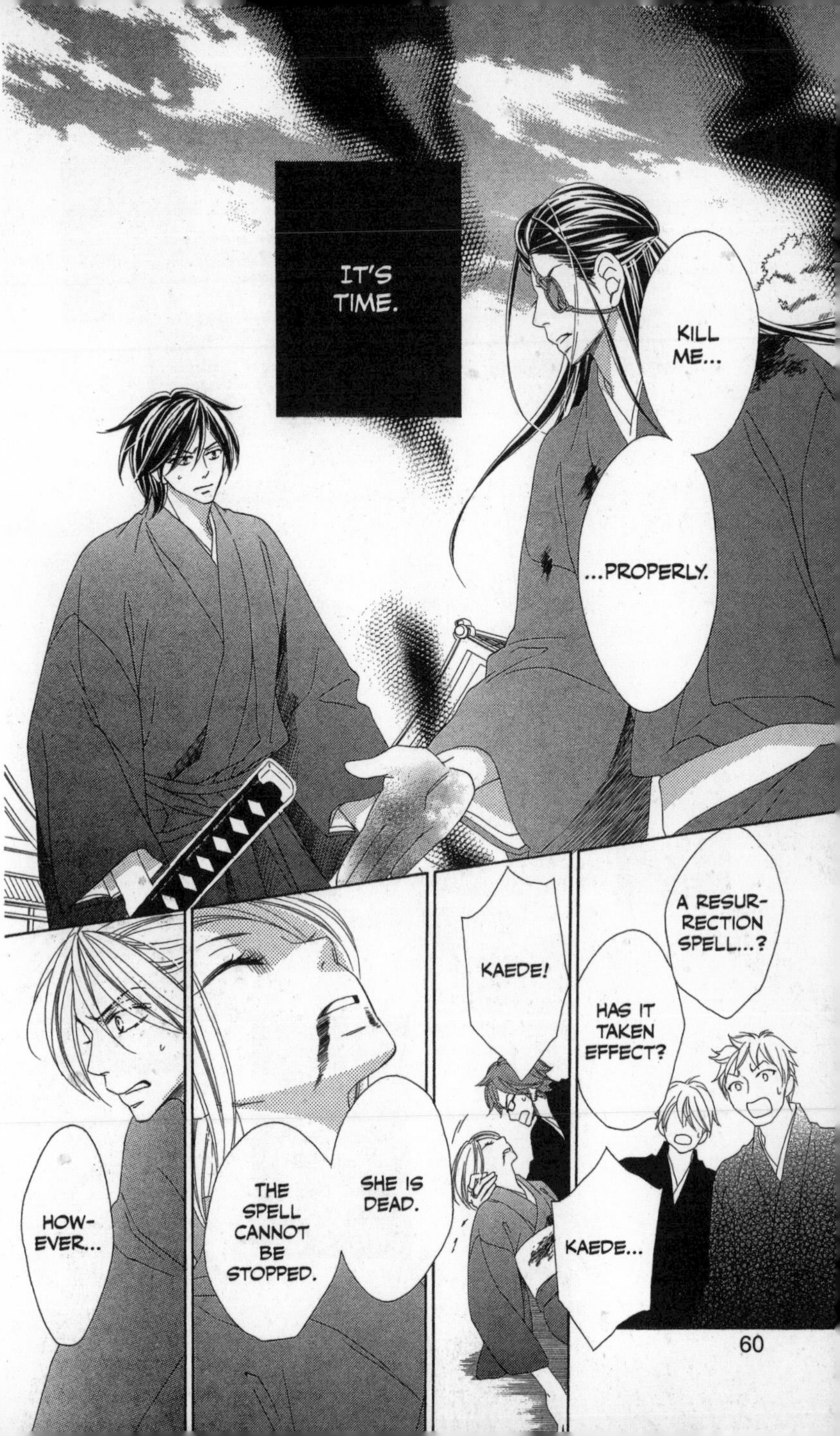
KILL ME...
...PROPERLY.
IT'S TIME.
A RESUR-RECTION SPELL...?
HAS IT TAKEN EFFECT?
KAEDE...
KAEDE!
SHE IS DEAD.
THE SPELL CANNOT BE STOPPED.
HOW-EVER...

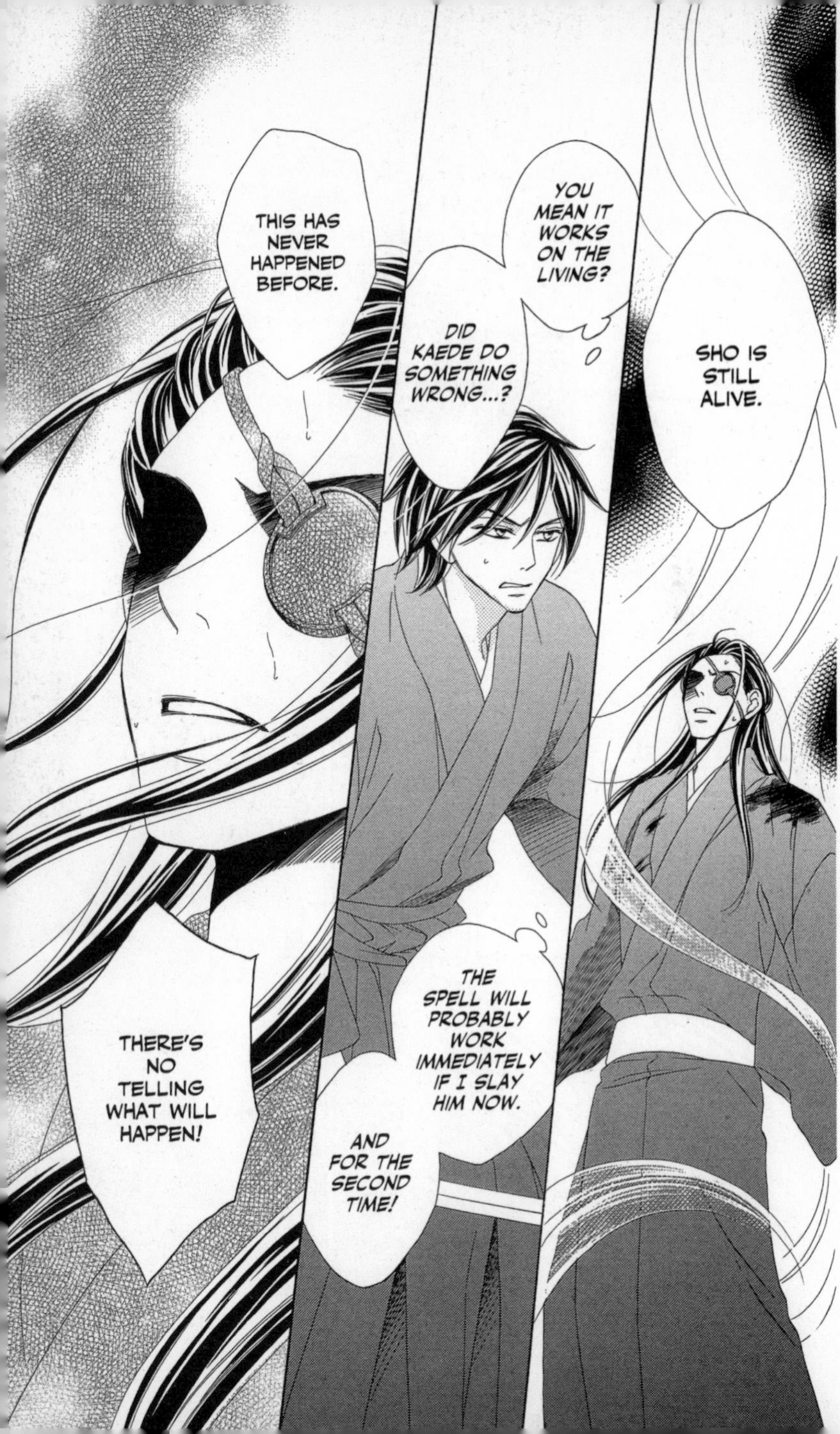
SHO IS STILL ALIVE.
YOU MEAN IT WORKS ON THE LIVING?
DID KAEDE DO SOMETHING WRONG...?
THE SPELL WILL PROBABLY WORK IMMEDIATELY IF I SLAY HIM NOW.
AND FOR THE SECOND TIME!
THIS HAS NEVER HAPPENED BEFORE.
THERE'S NO TELLING WHAT WILL HAPPEN!

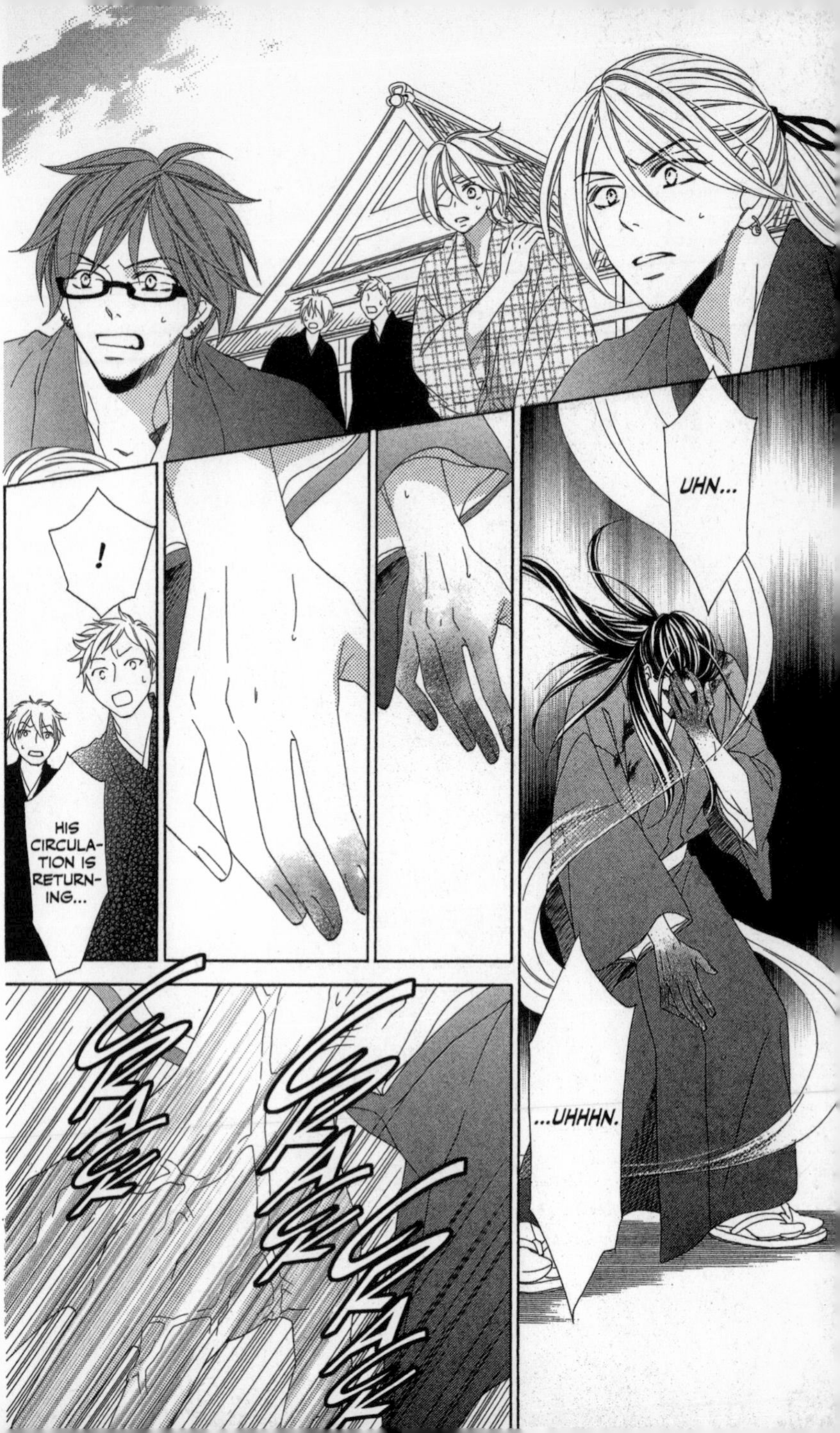
UHN...
...UHHHN.
!
HIS CIRCULATION IS RETURNING...

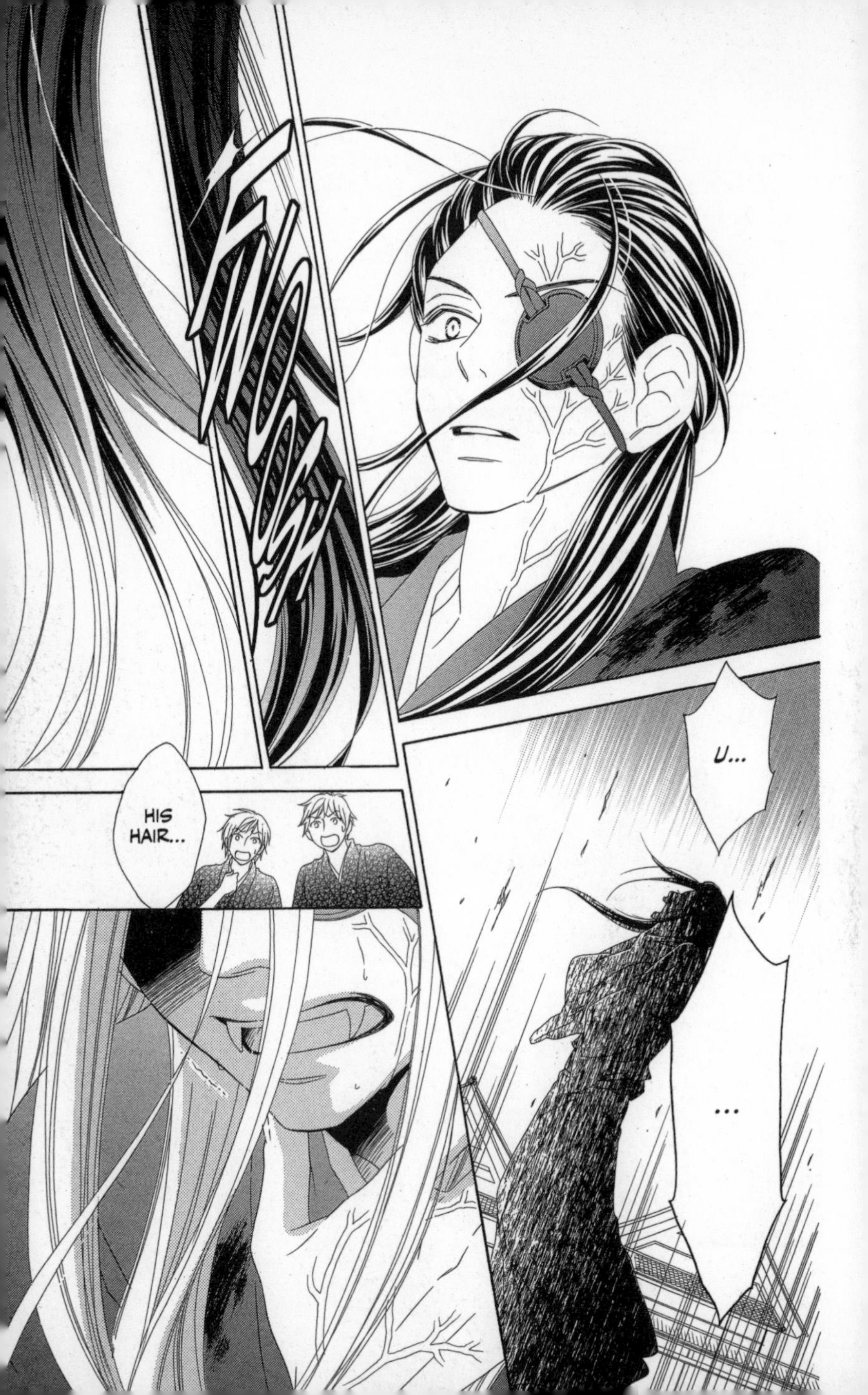
FWOSH
U...
...
HIS HAIR...

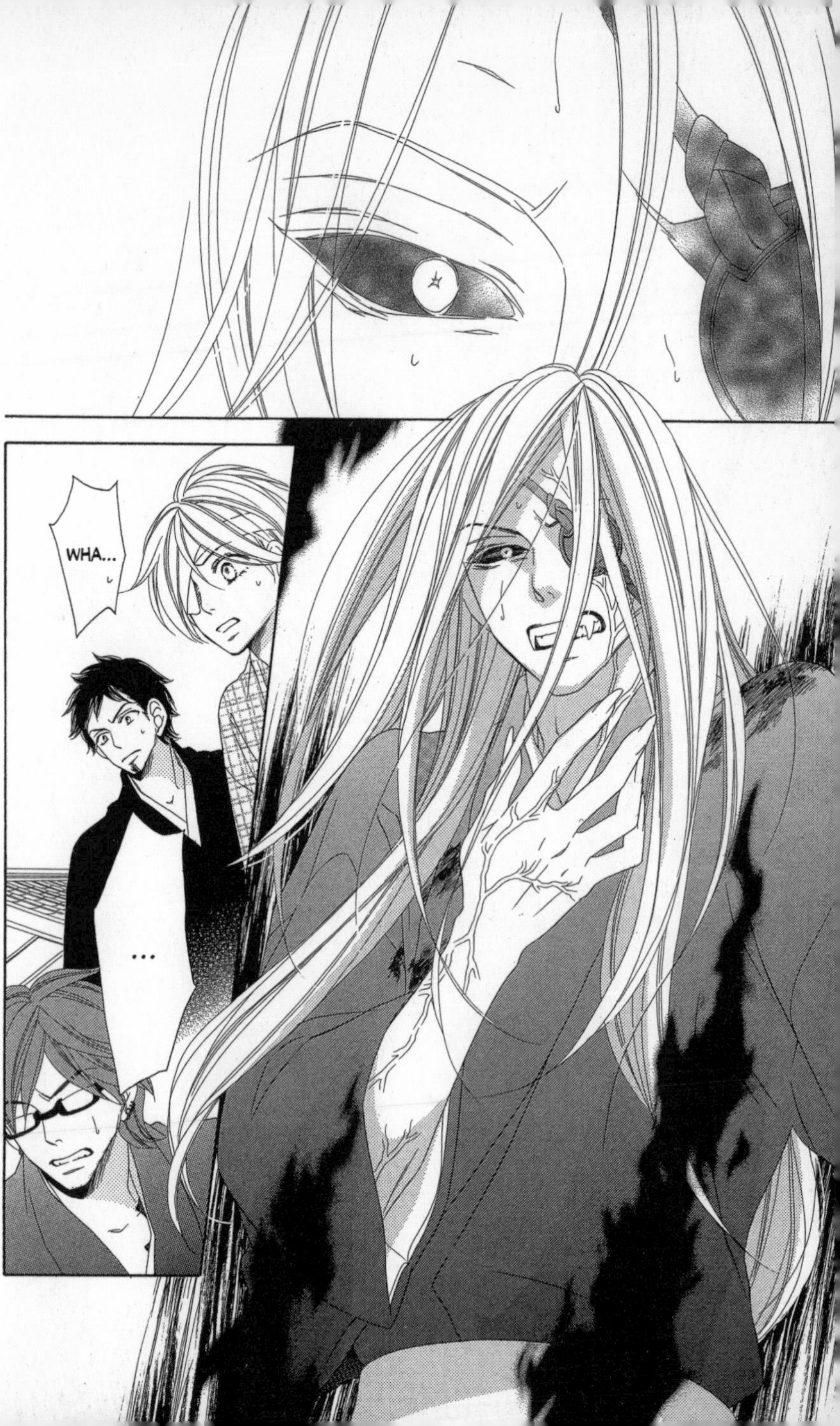
WHA...
...

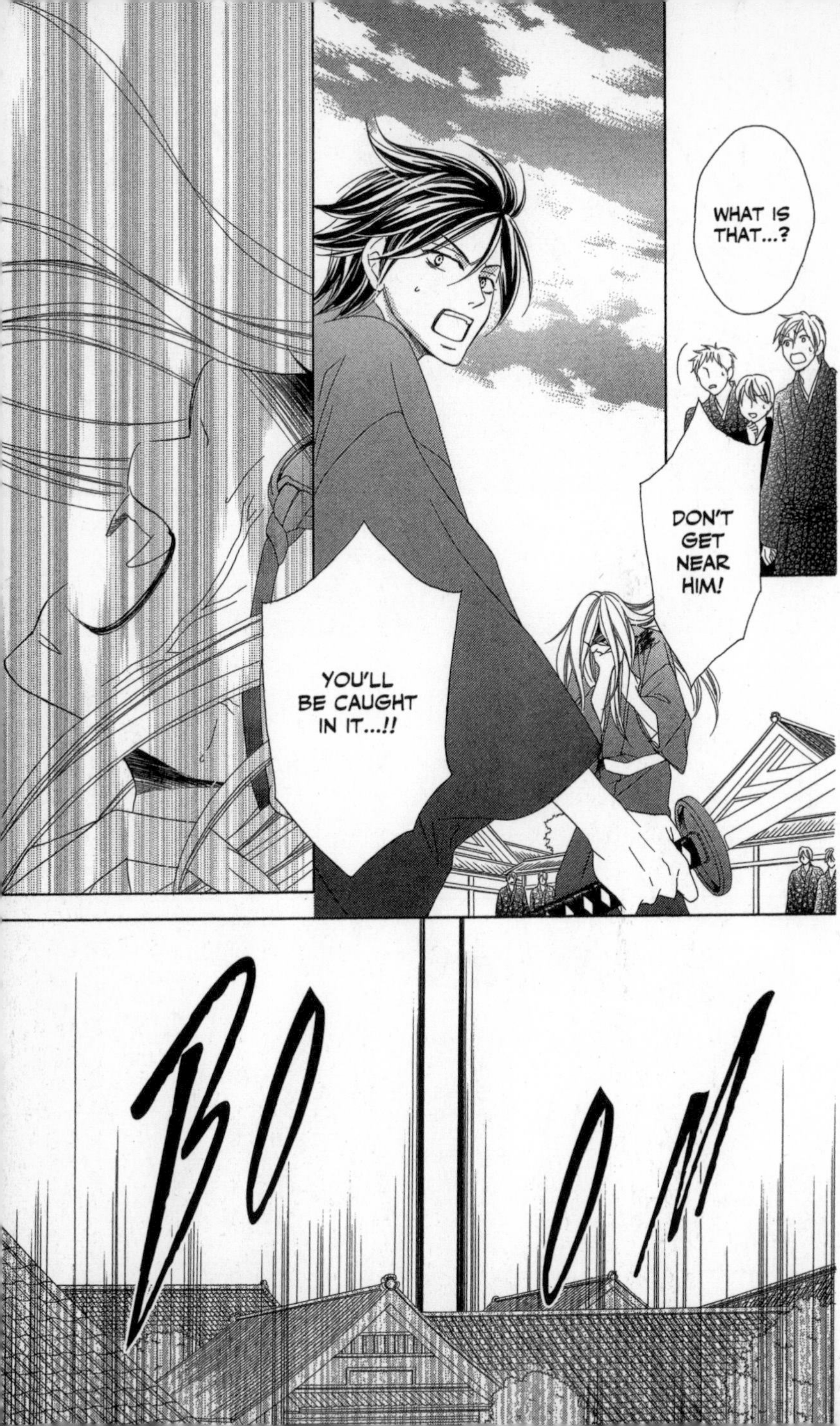
WHAT IS THAT...?
DON'T GET NEAR HIM!
YOU'LL BE CAUGHT IN IT...!!
BOOM

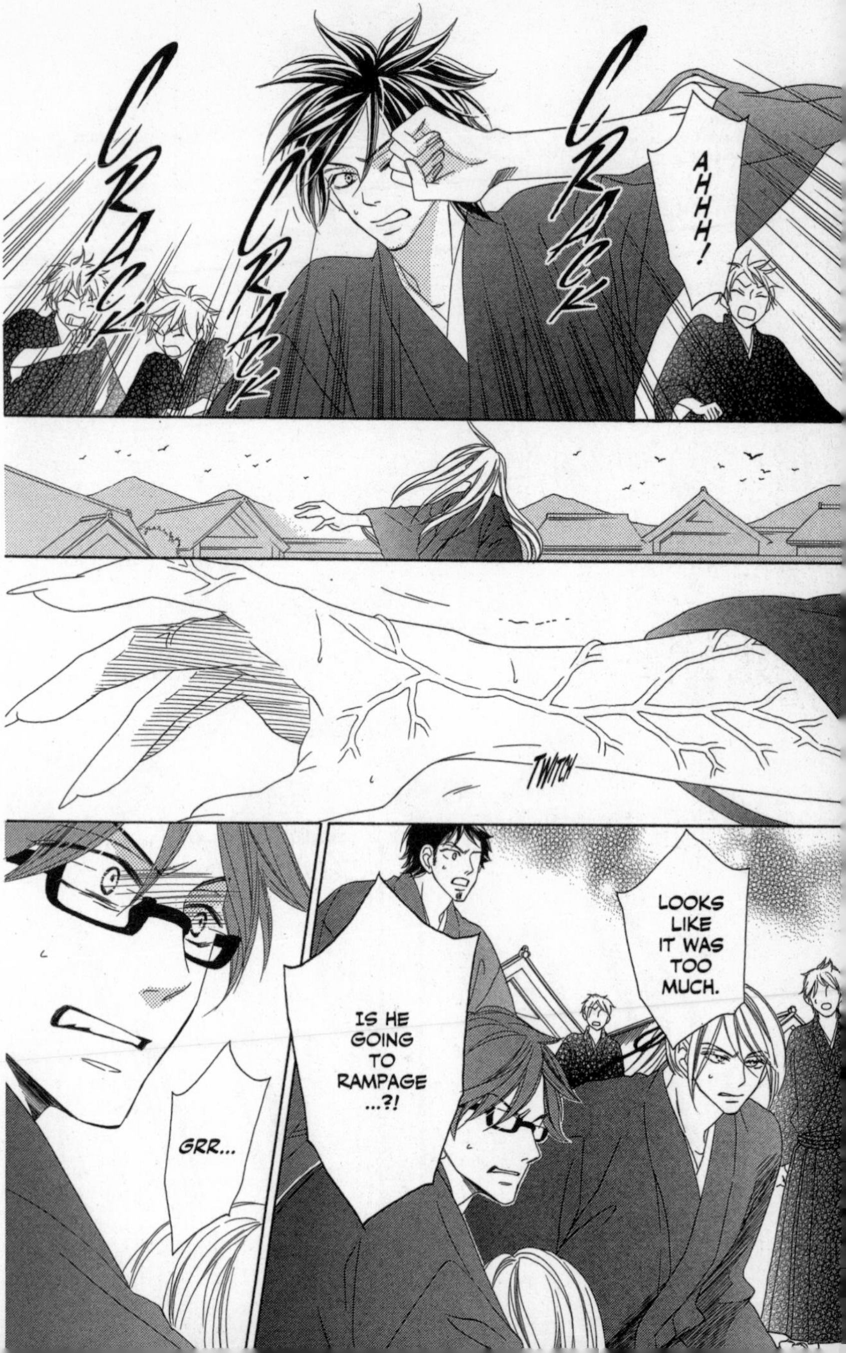
CRACK
AHHH!
CRACK
CRACK
TWITCH
LOOKS LIKE IT WAS TOO MUCH.
IS HE GOING TO RAMPAGE ...?!
GRR...

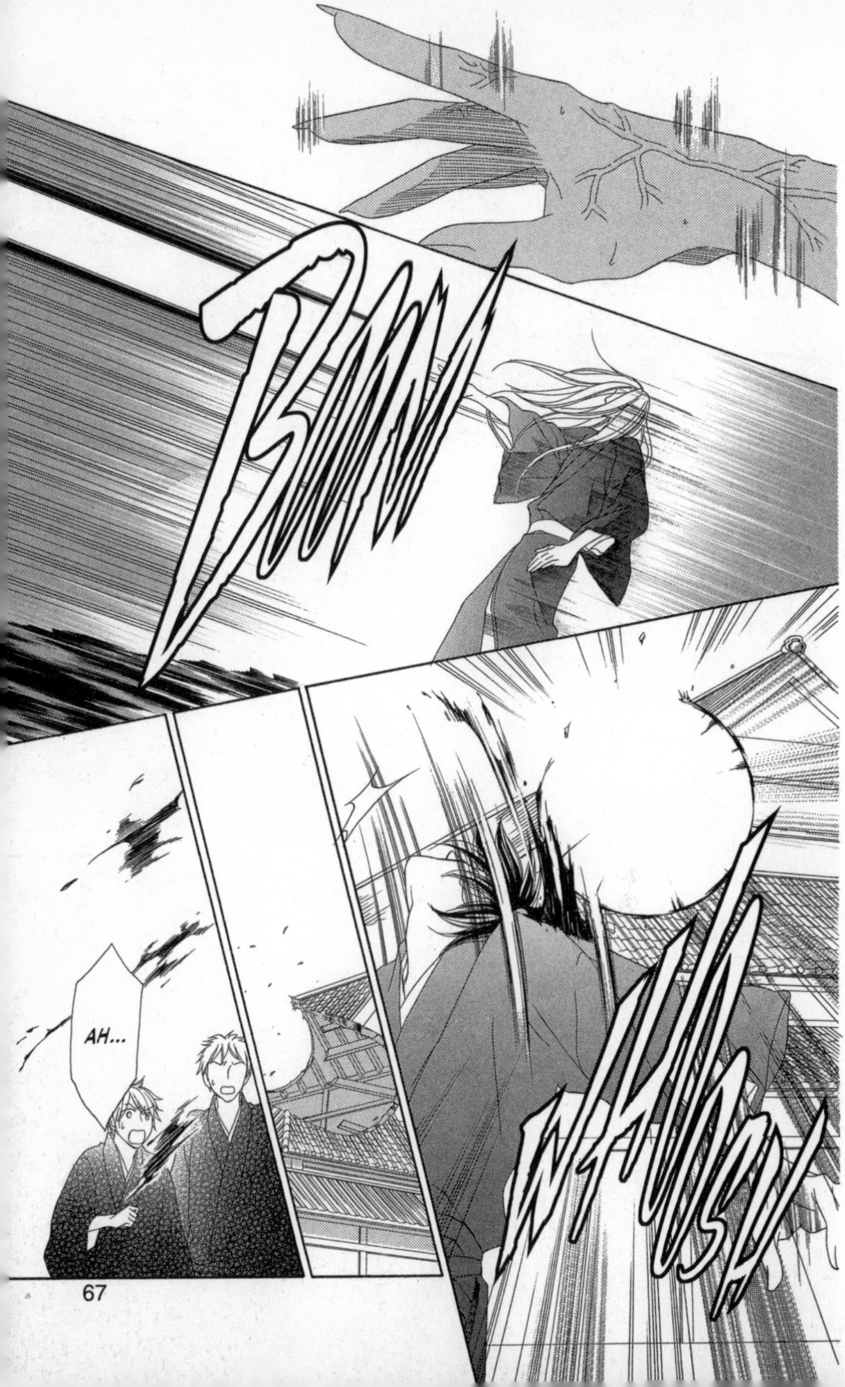
BAM
WHOOSH
AH...

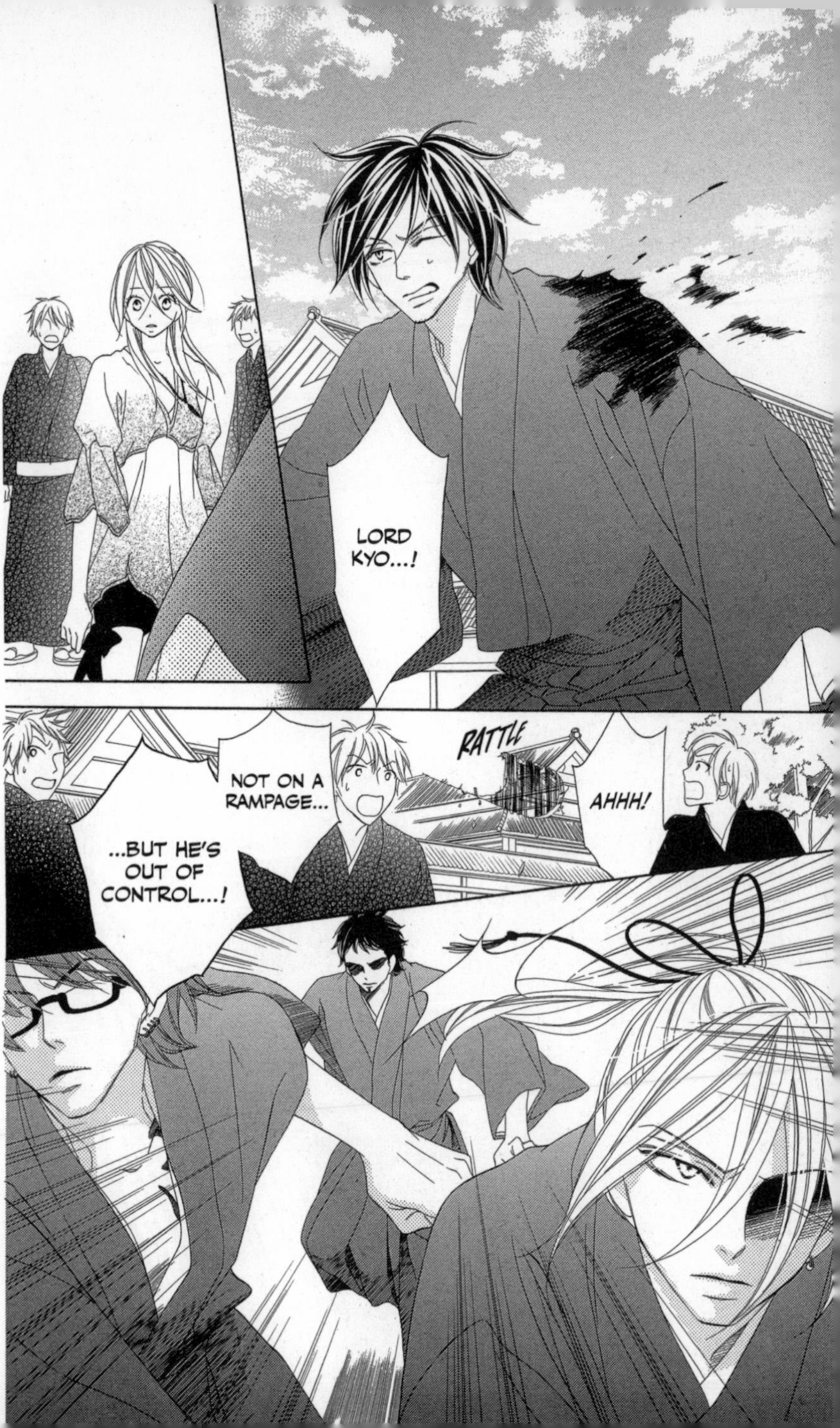
LORD KYO...!
AHHH!
RATTLE
NOT ON A RAMPAGE...
...BUT HE'S OUT OF CONTROL...!

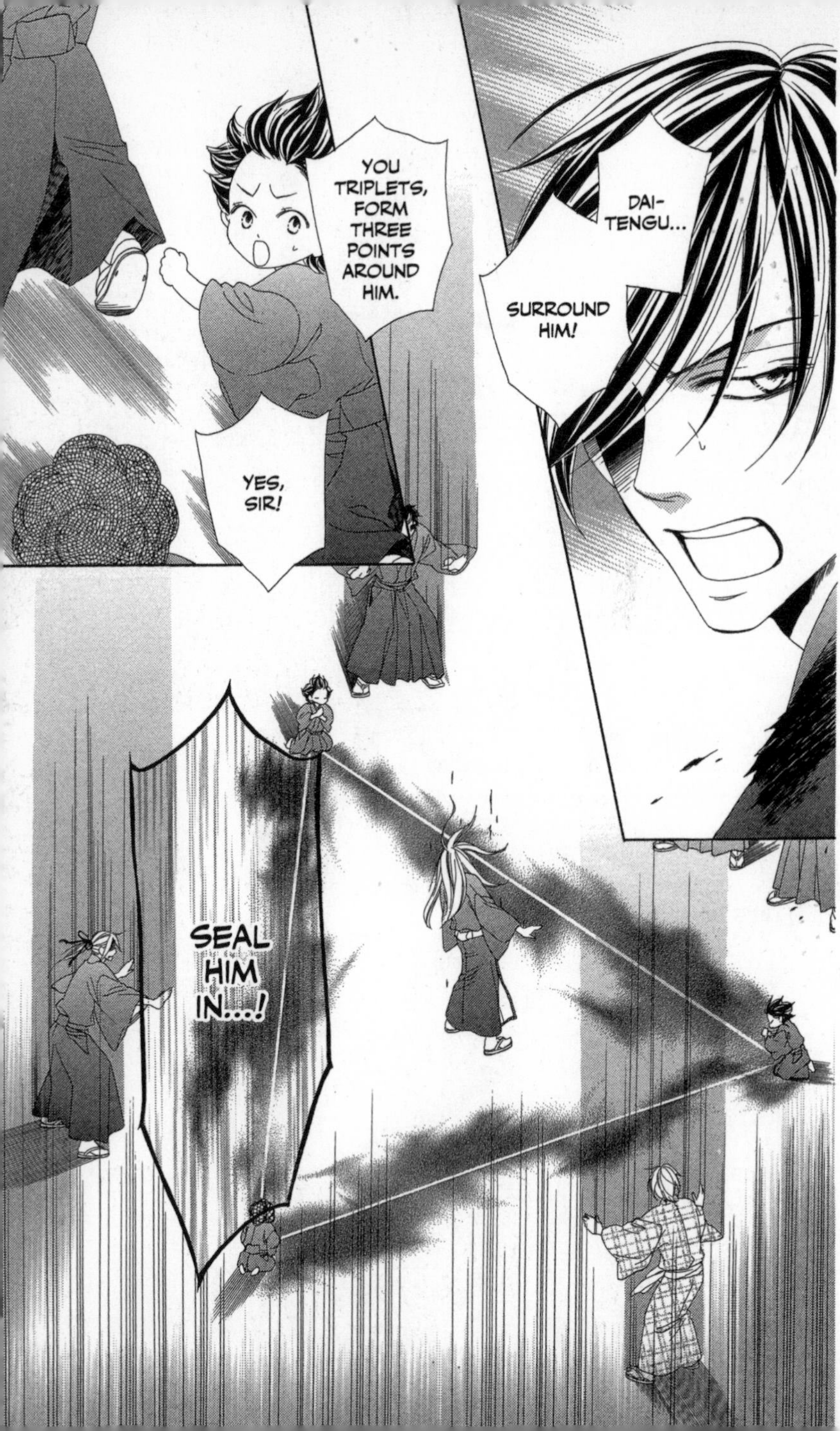
DAI-TENGU...
SURROUND HIM!
YOU TRIPLETS, FORM THREE POINTS AROUND HIM.
YES, SIR!
SEAL HIM IN...!

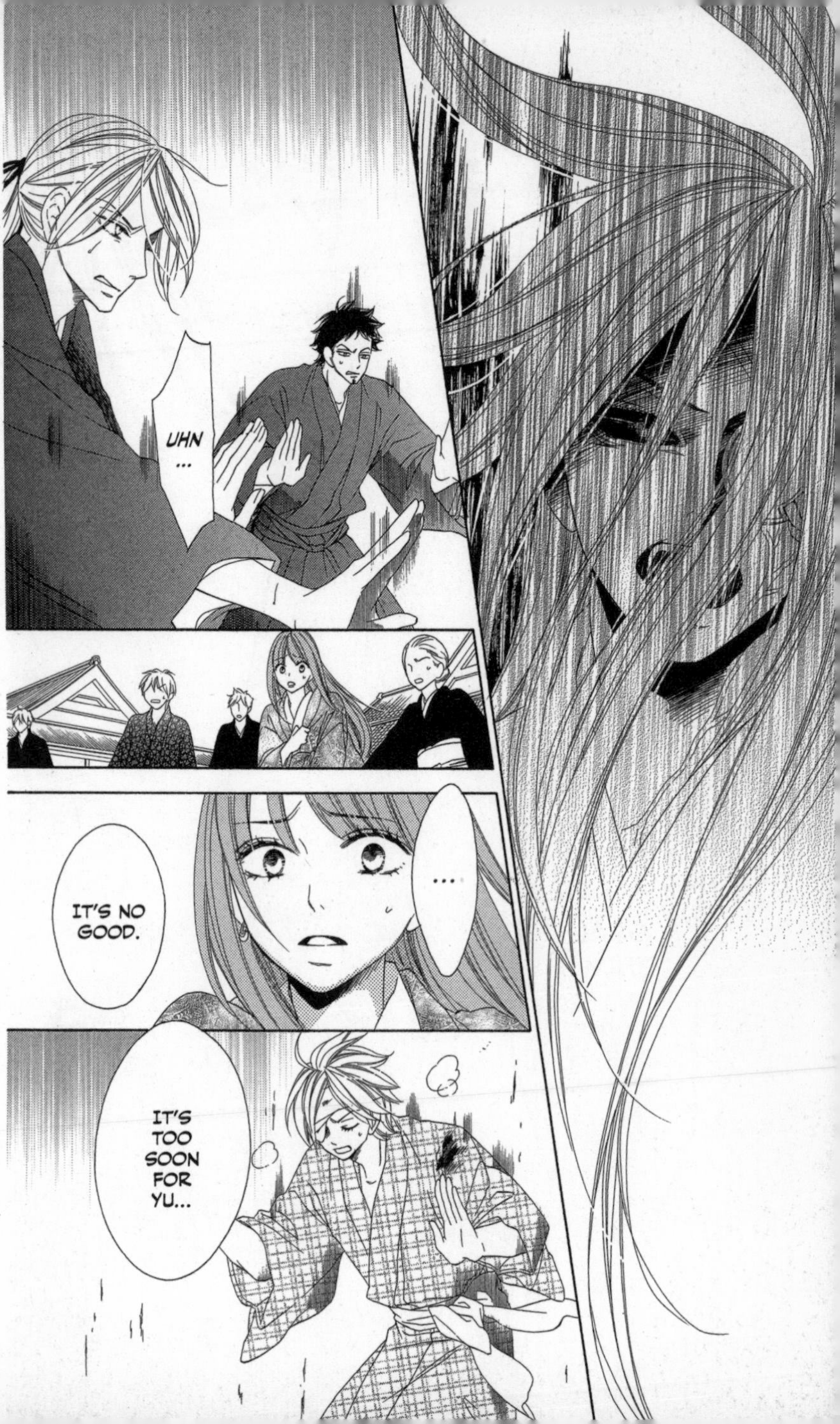
UHN ...
...
IT'S NO GOOD.
IT'S TOO SOON FOR YU...

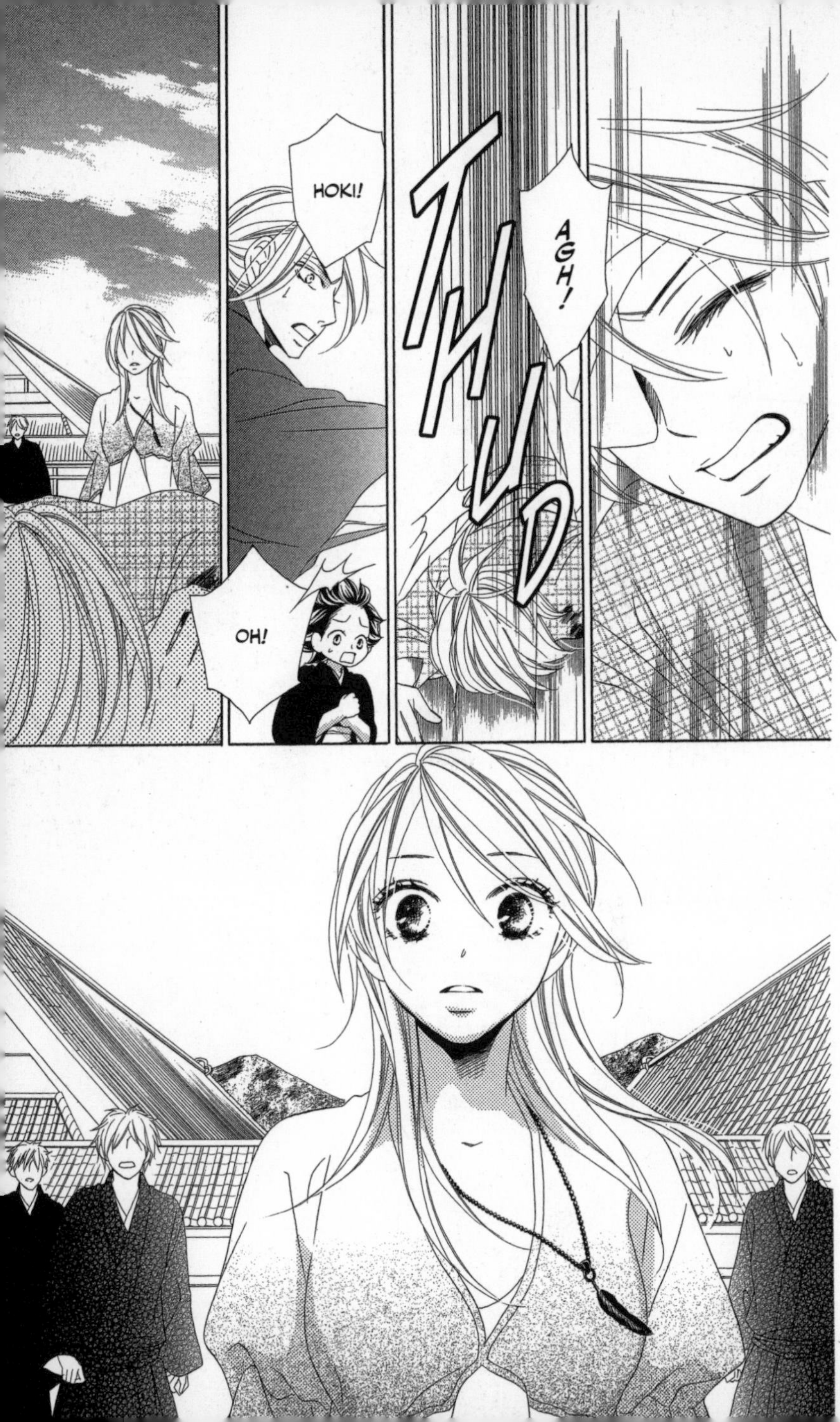
AGH!
THUD
HOKI!
OH!

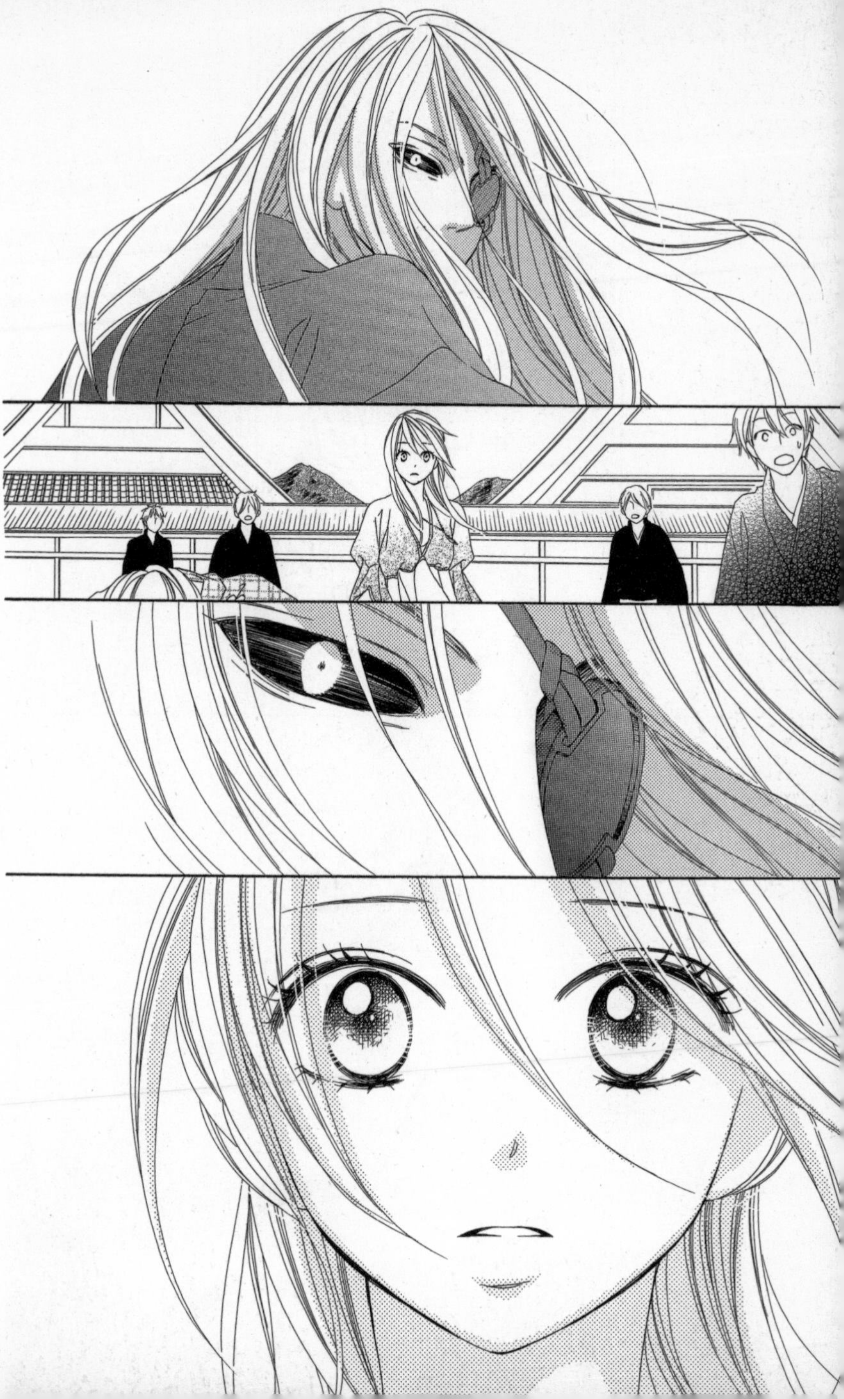

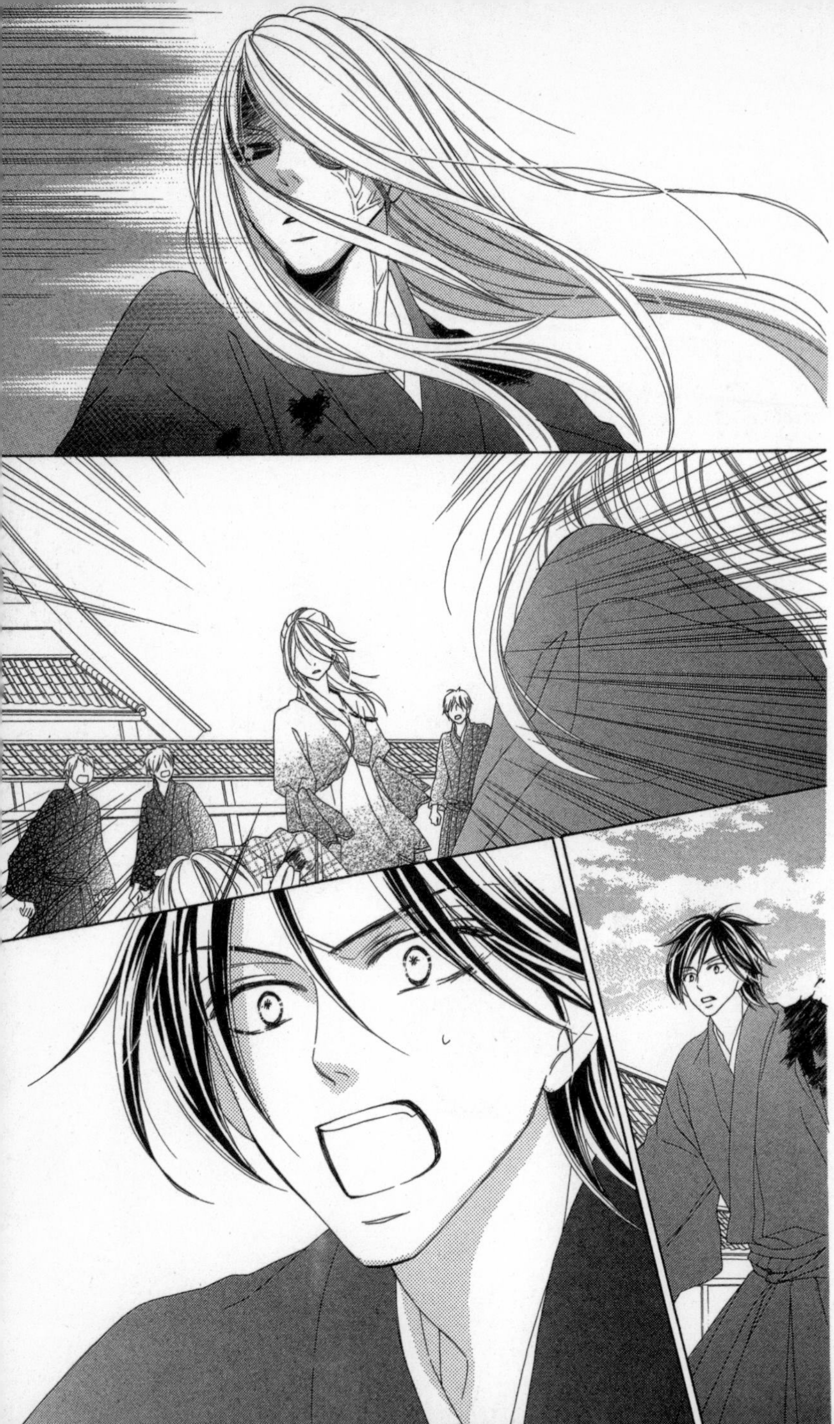

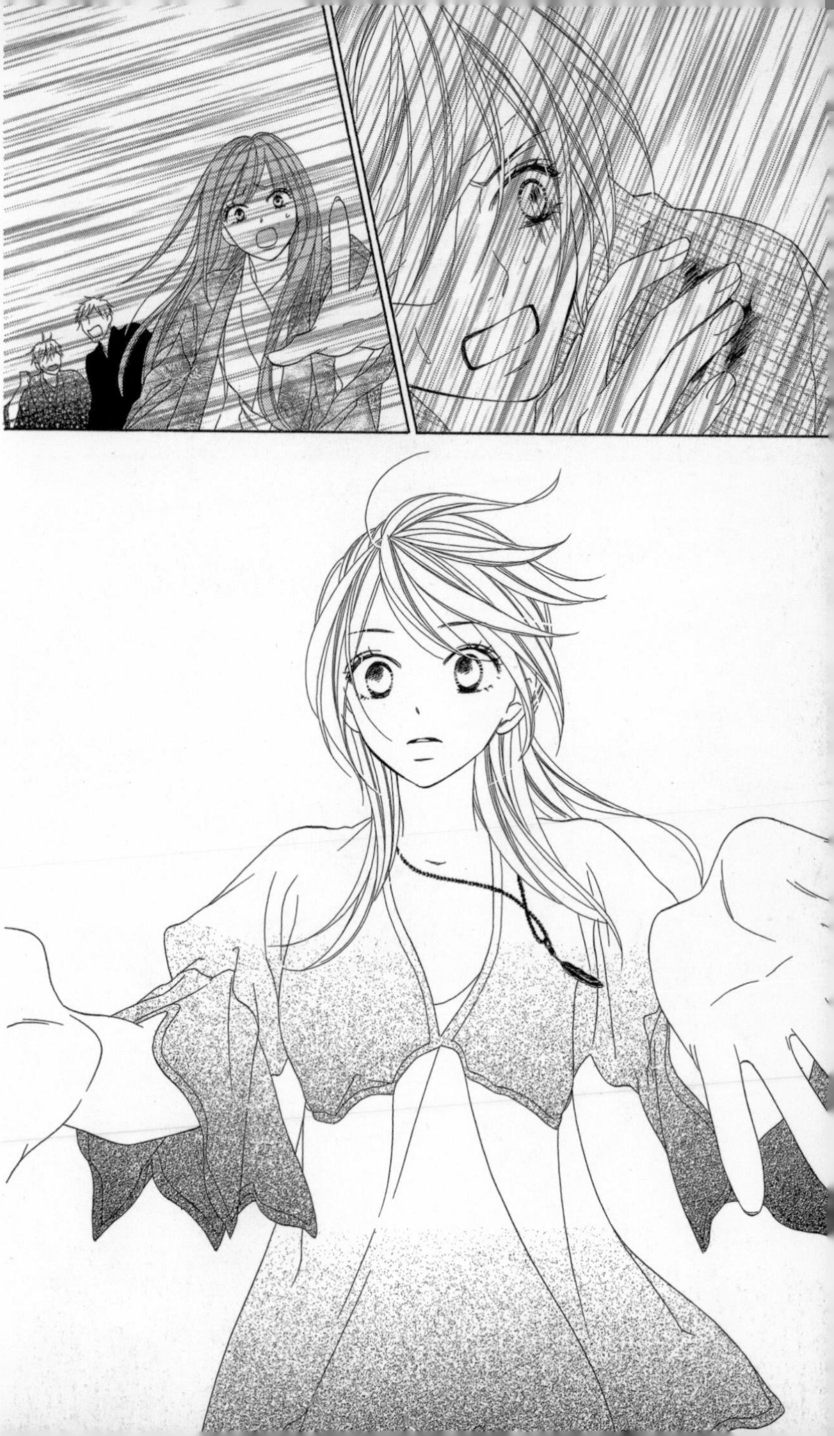

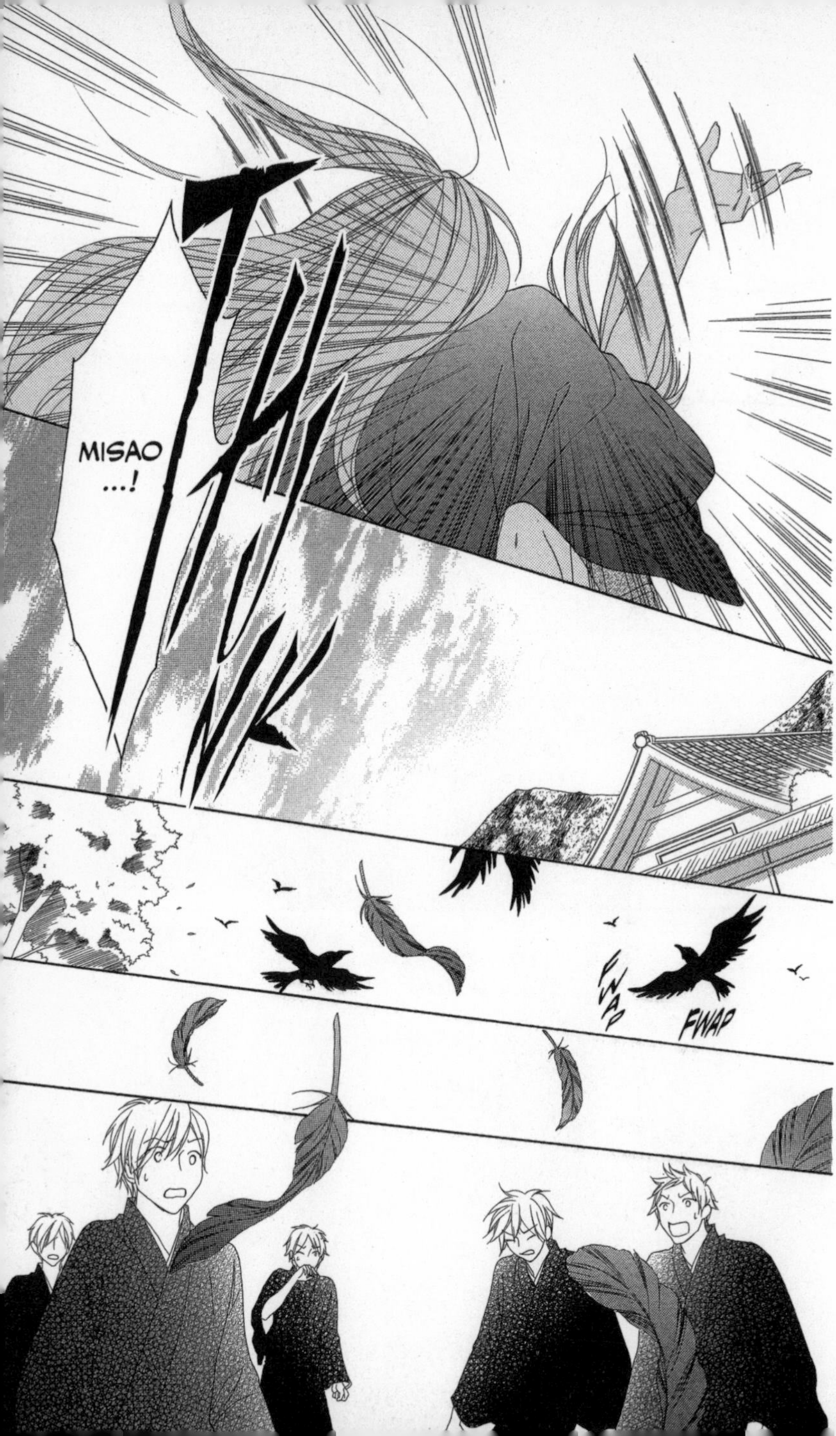
MISAO ...!
FWAP
FWAP

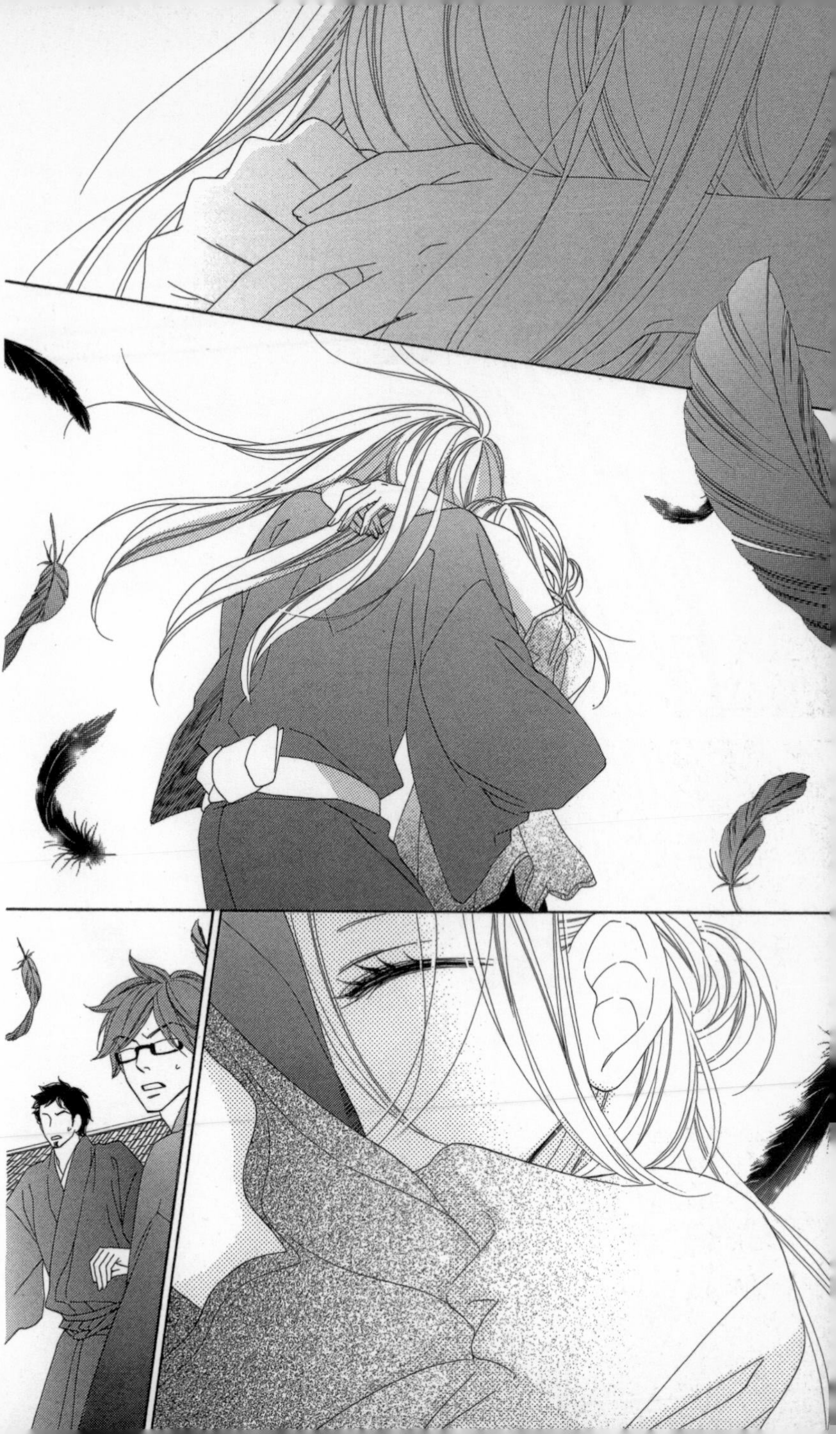

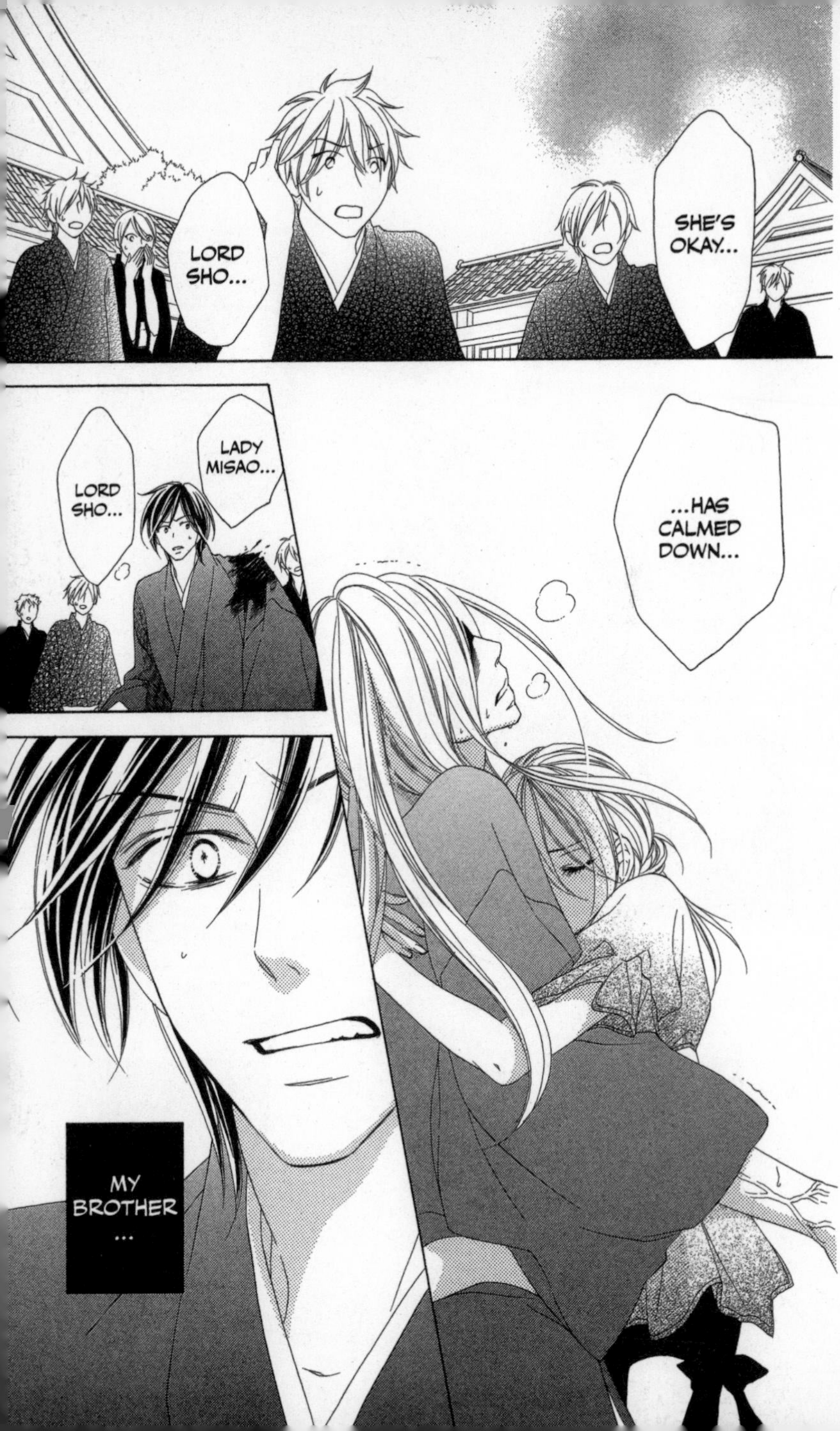
SHE'S OKAY...
LORD SHO...
...HAS CALMED DOWN...
LADY MISAO...
LORD SHO...
MY BROTHER ...

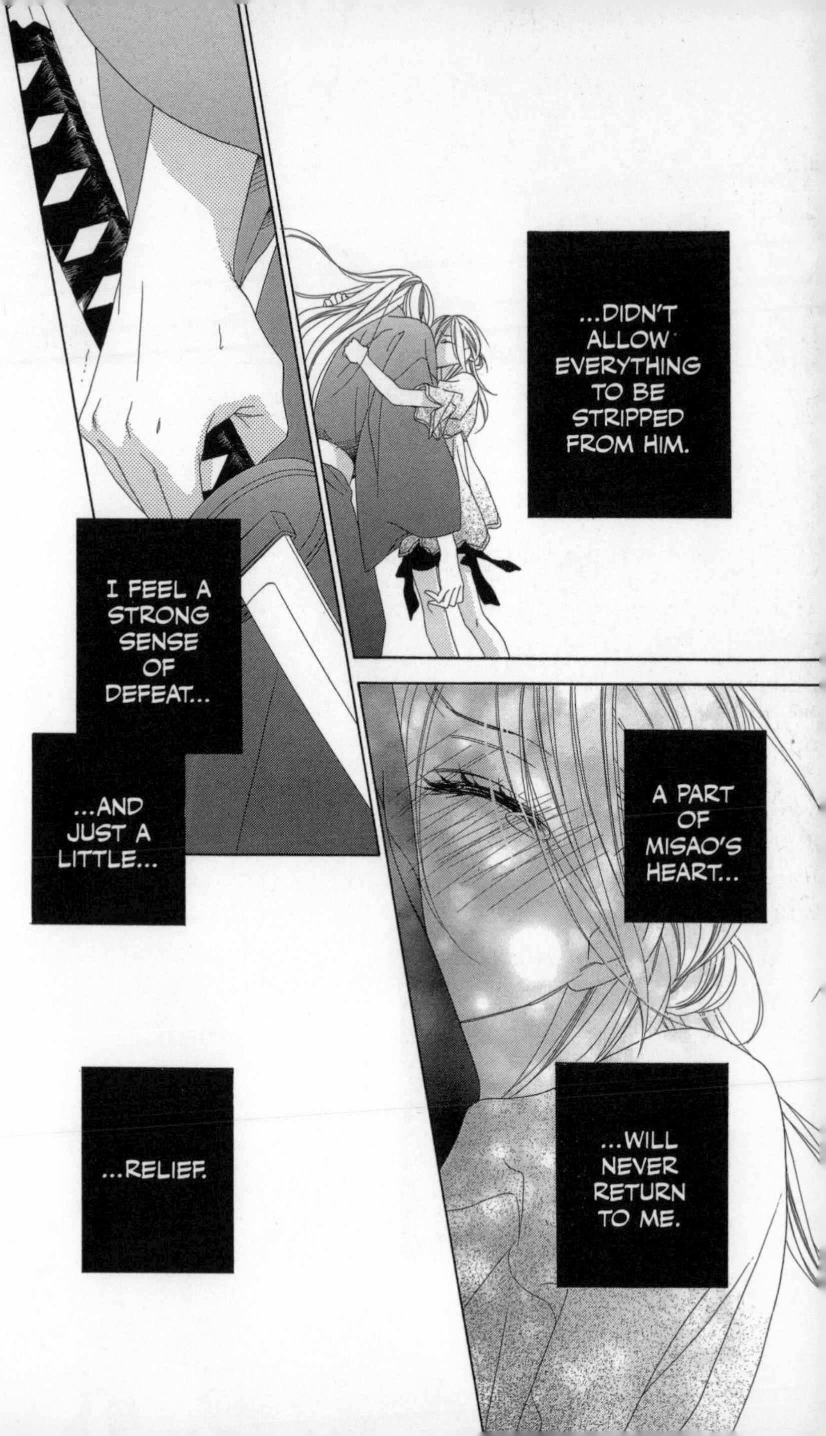
...DIDN'T ALLOW EVERYTHING TO BE STRIPPED FROM HIM.
A PART OF MISAO'S HEART...
...WILL NEVER RETURN TO ME.
I FEEL A STRONG SENSE OF DEFEAT...
...AND JUST A LITTLE...
...RELIEF.

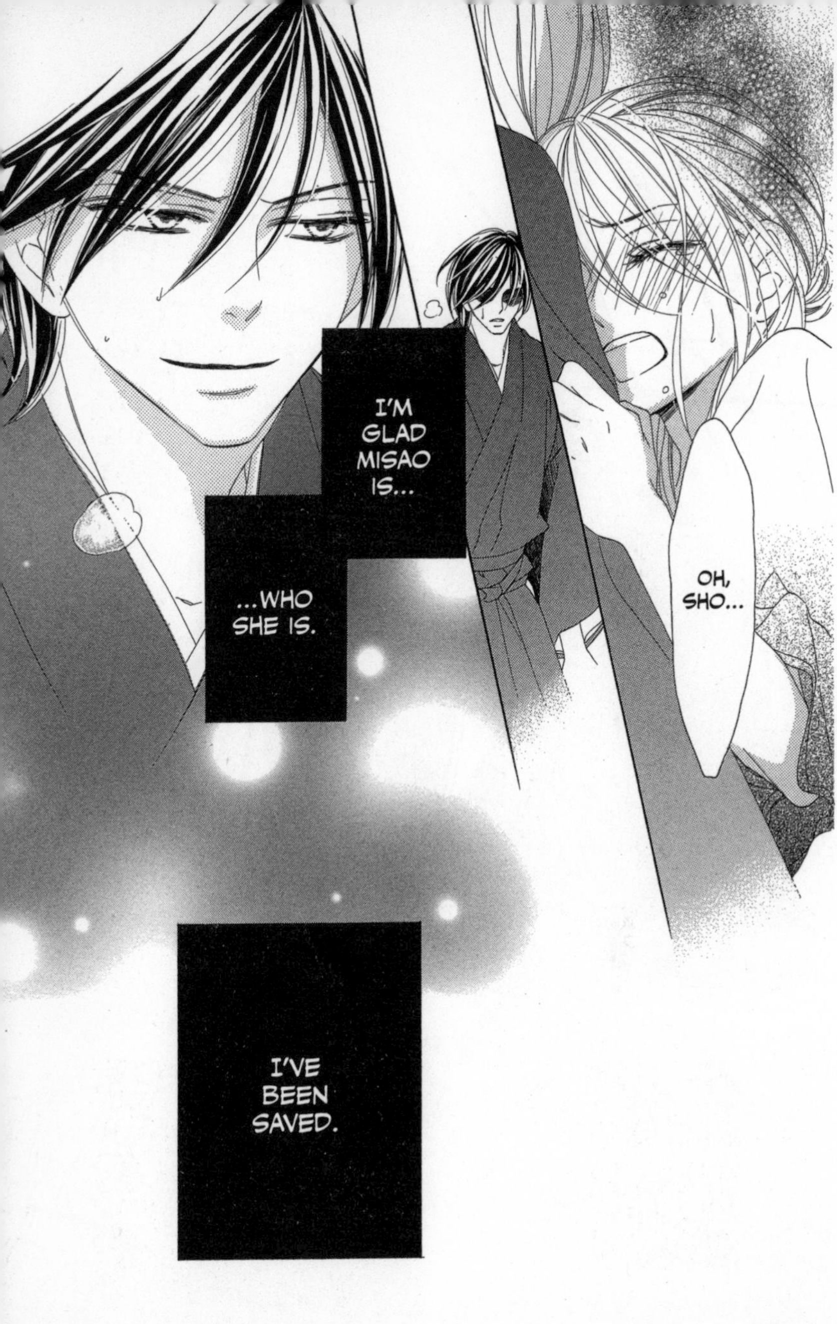
OH, SHO...
I'M GLAD MISAO IS...
...WHO SHE IS.
I'VE BEEN SAVED.

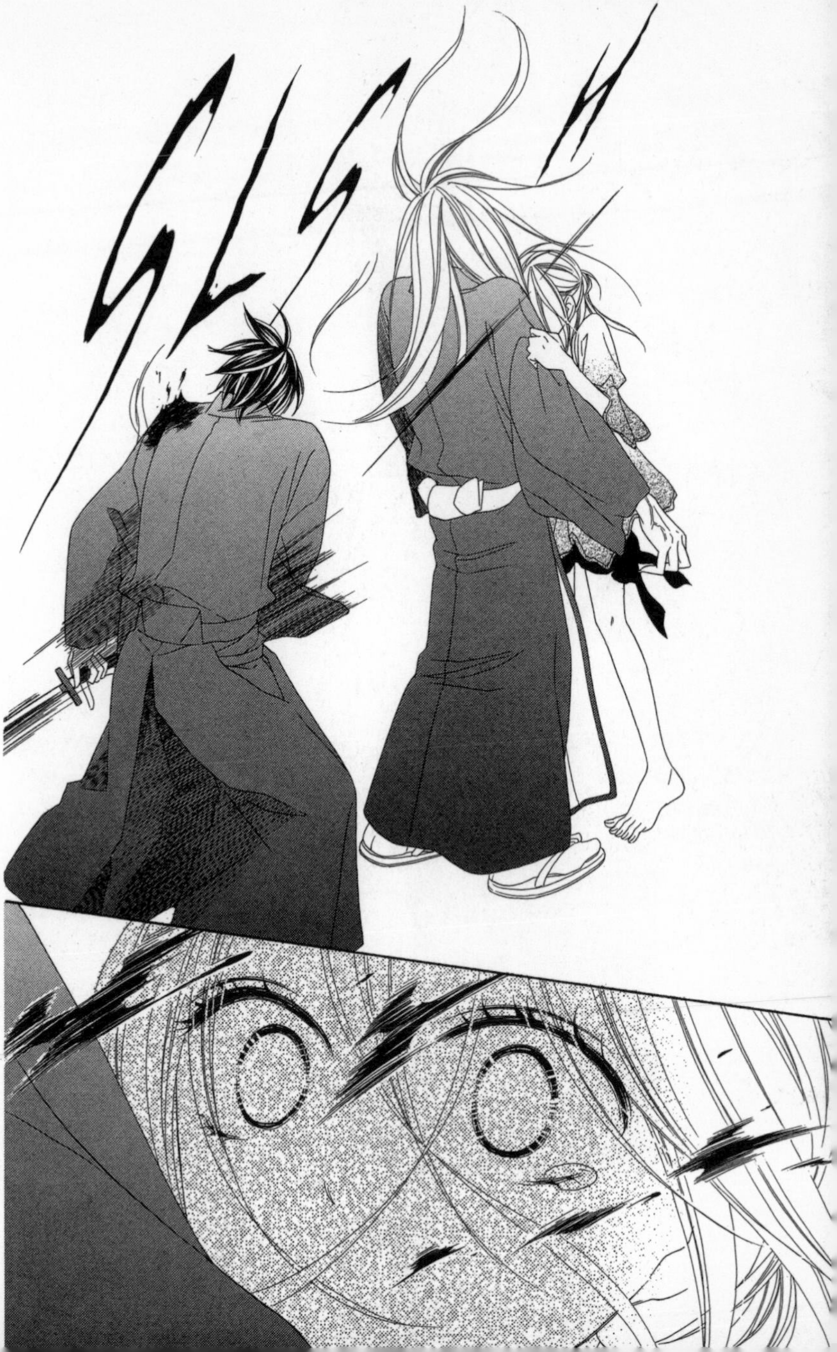
SLSH

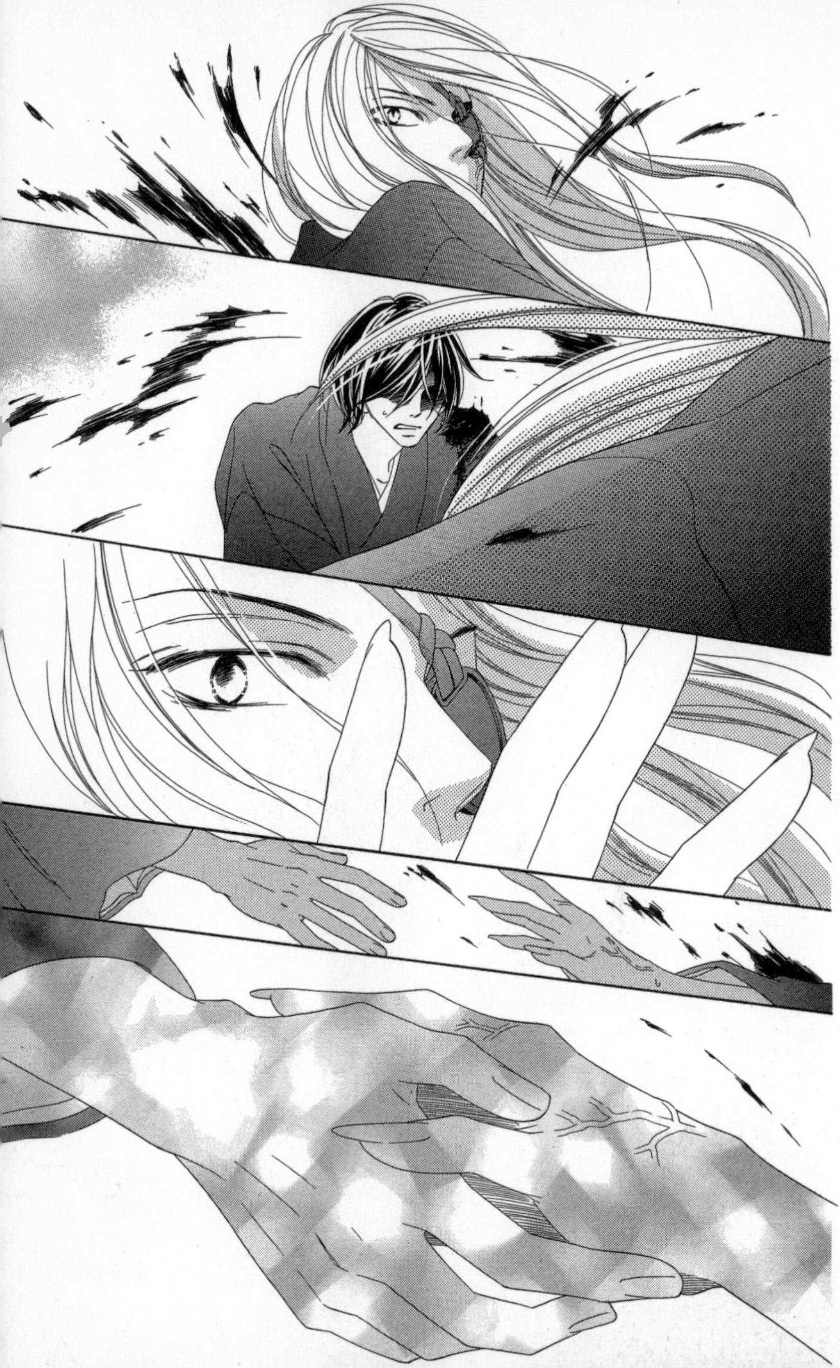

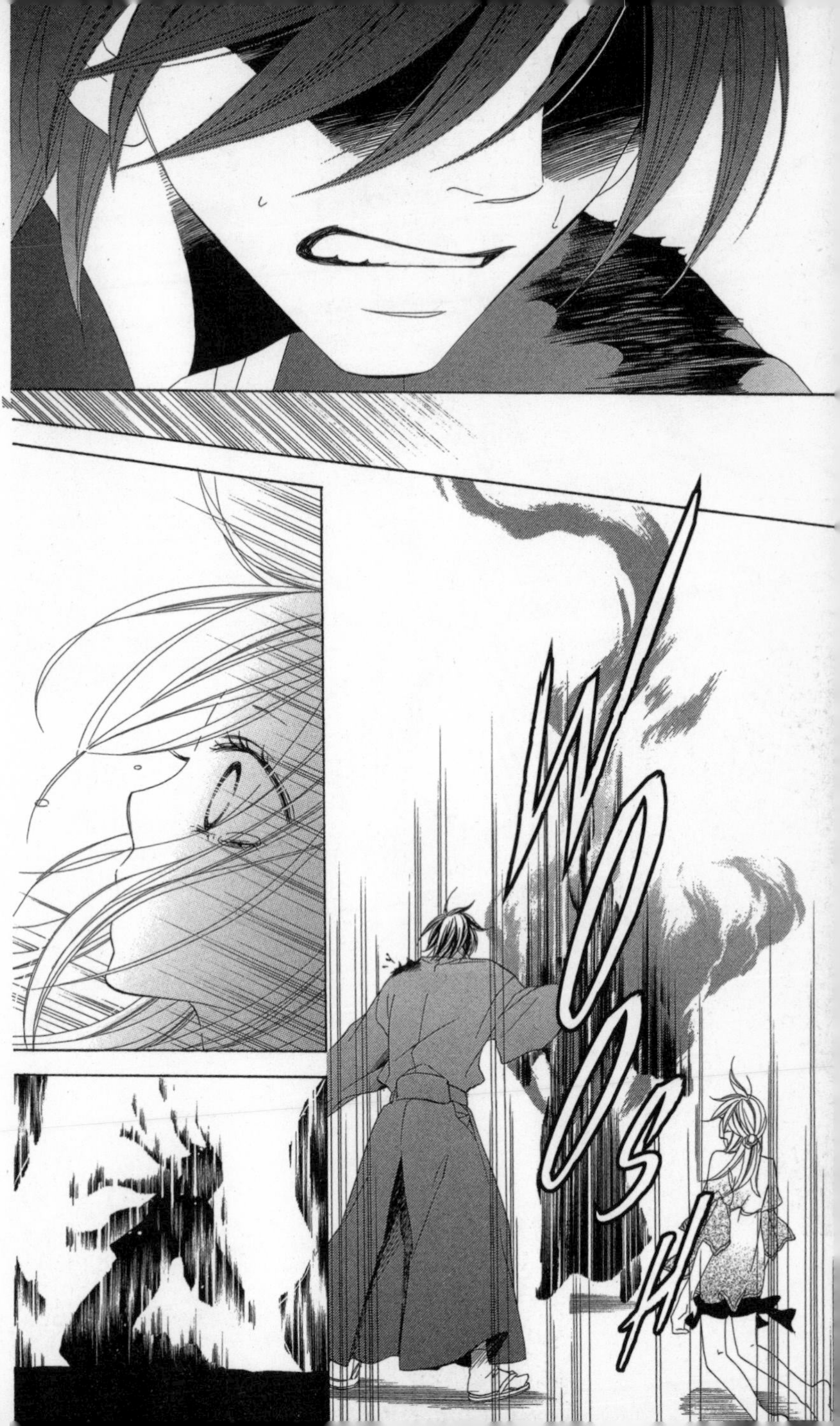
WHOOSH

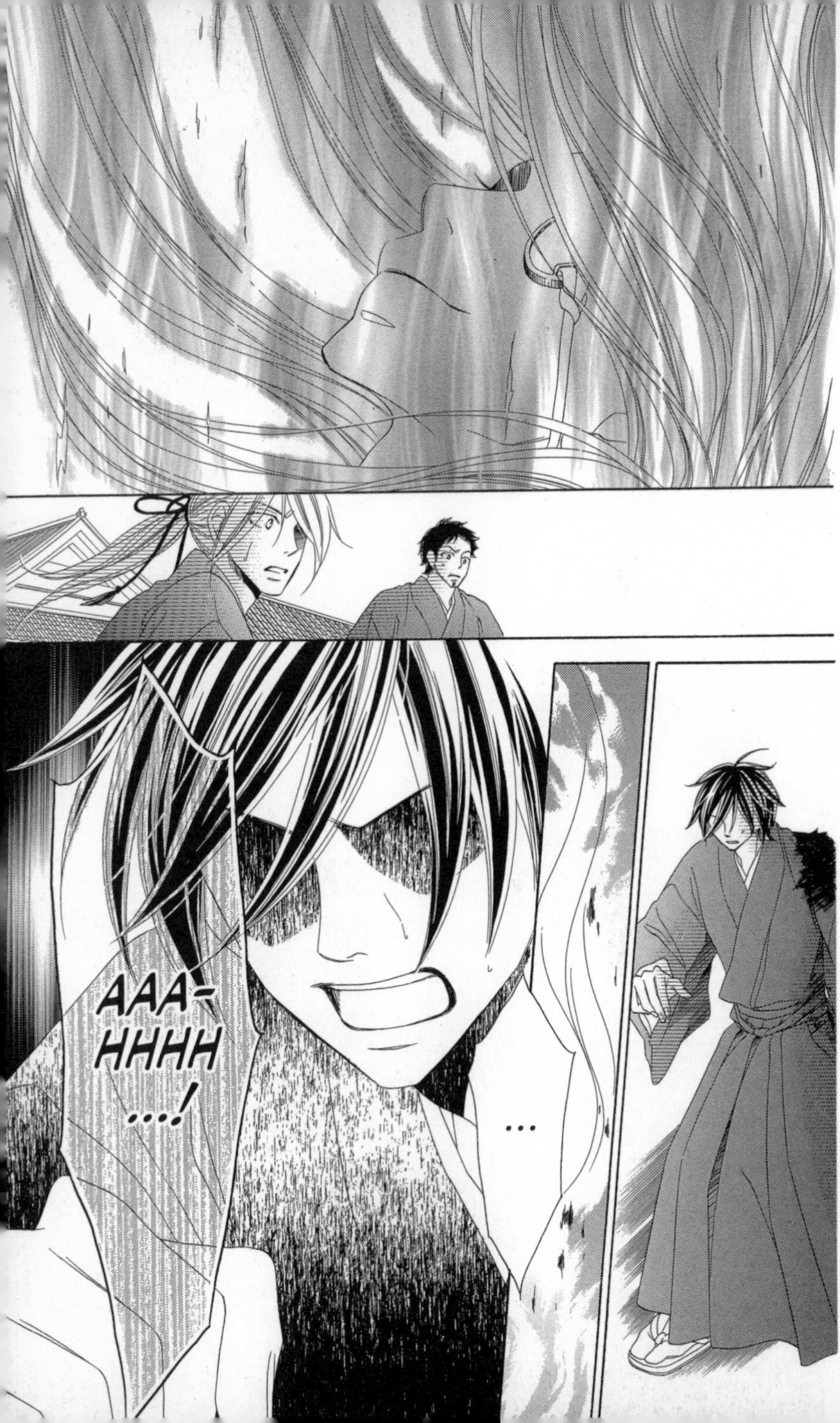
...
AAA-
HHHH
...!

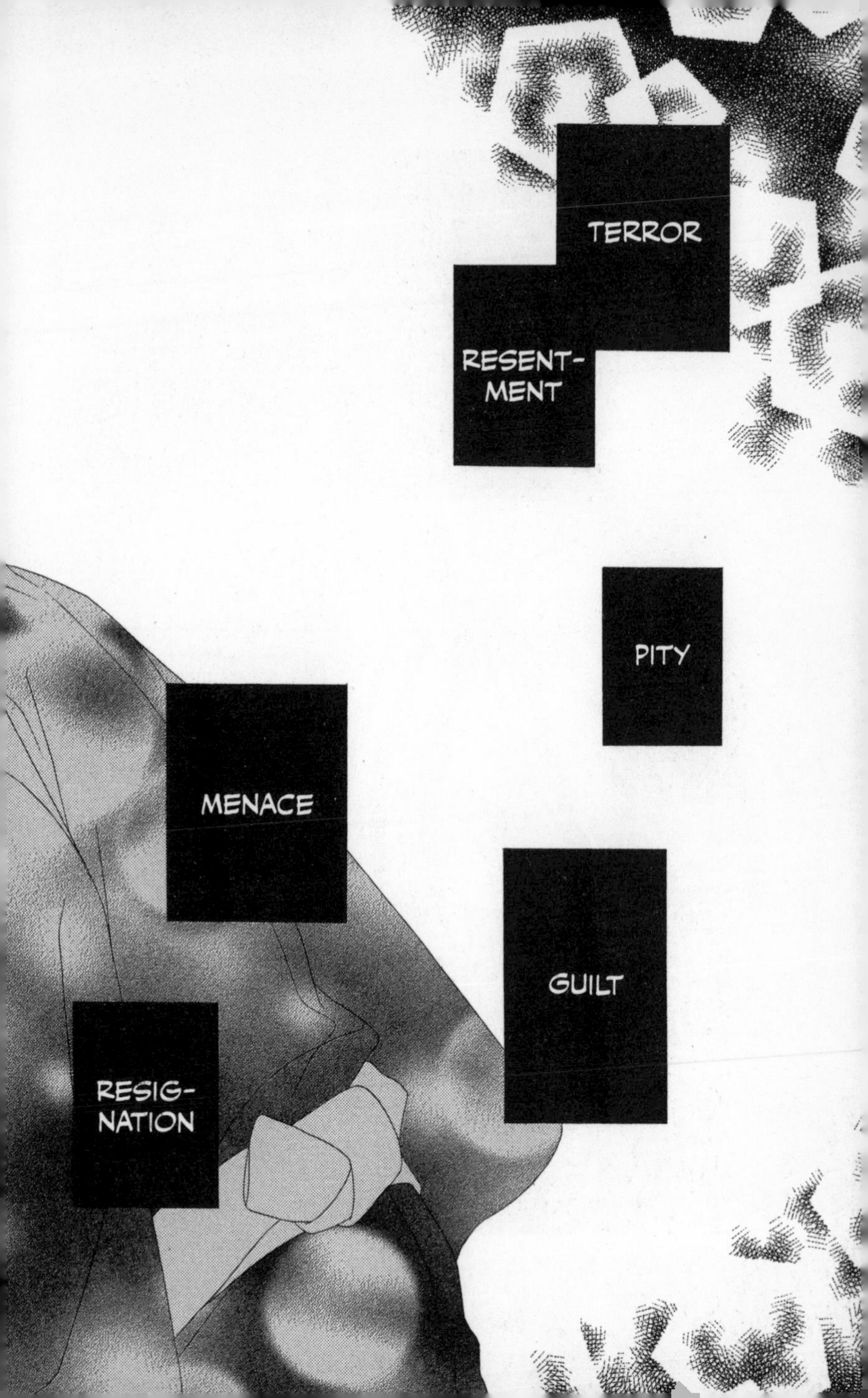
TERROR
RESENT-
MENT
PITY
MENACE
GUILT
RESIG-
NATION

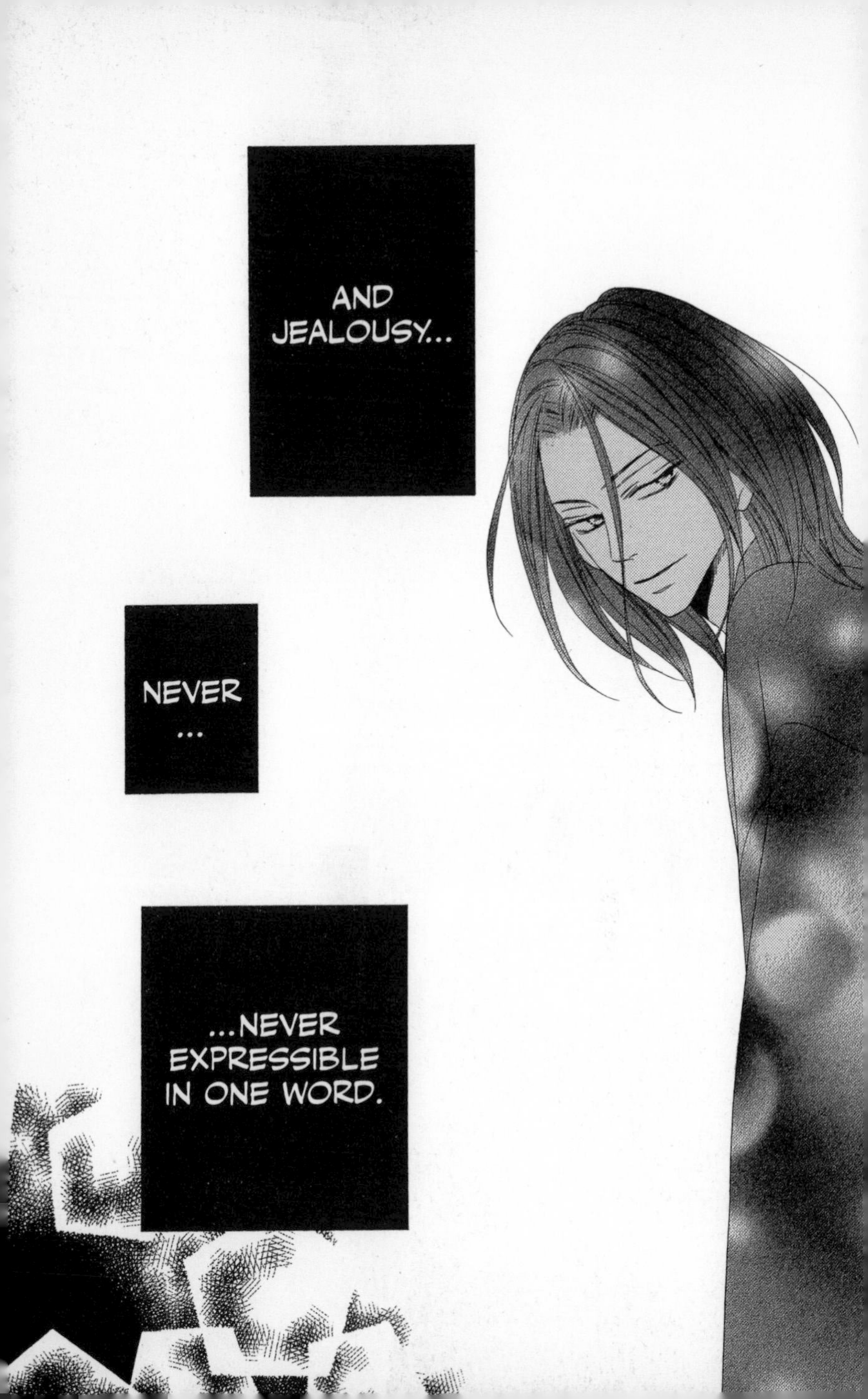
AND JEALOUSY...
NEVER ...
...NEVER EXPRESSIBLE IN ONE WORD.

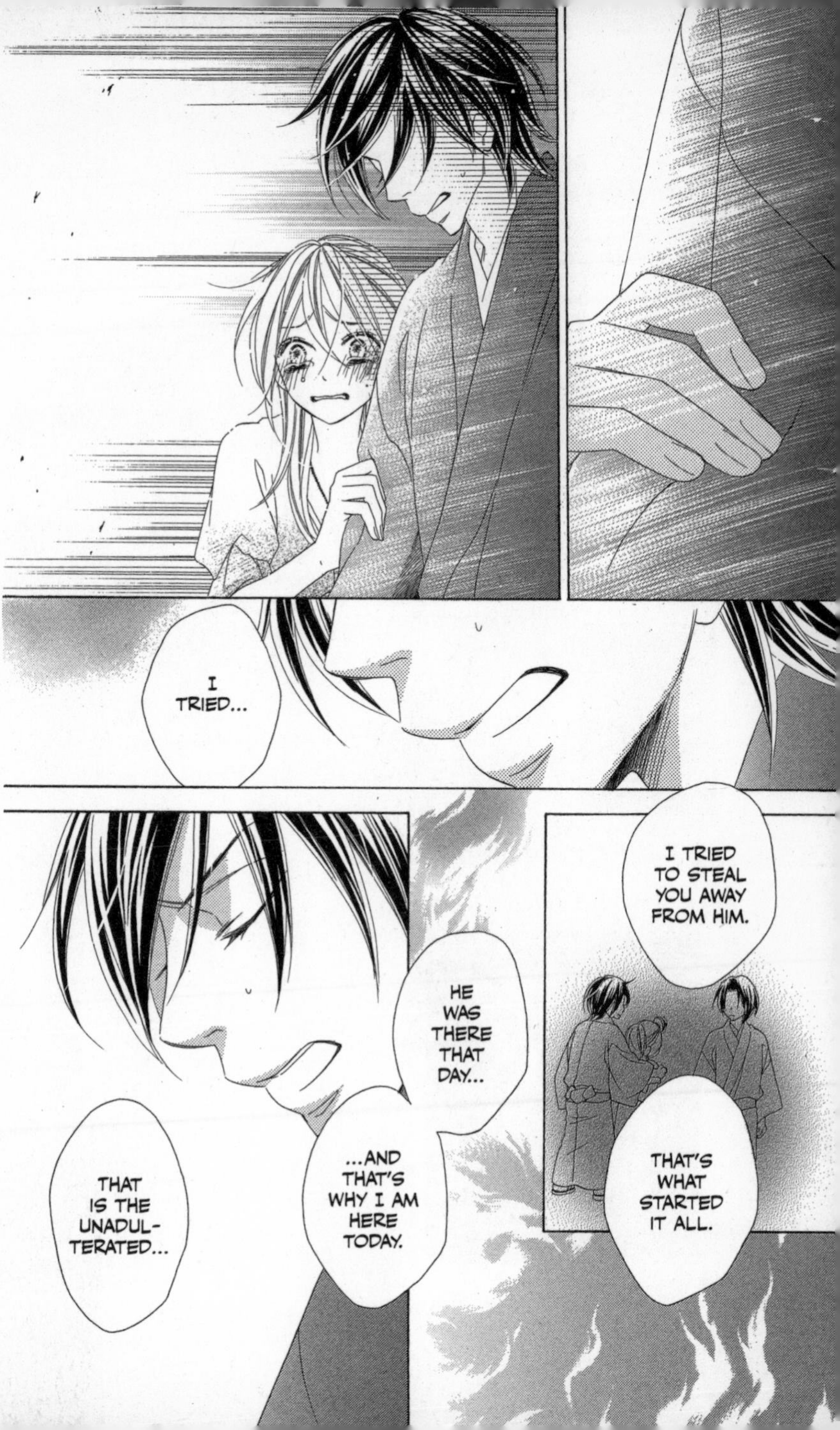
I TRIED...
I TRIED TO STEAL YOU AWAY FROM HIM.
THAT'S WHAT STARTED IT ALL.
HE WAS THERE THAT DAY...
...AND THAT'S WHY I AM HERE TODAY.
THAT IS THE UNADULTERATED...

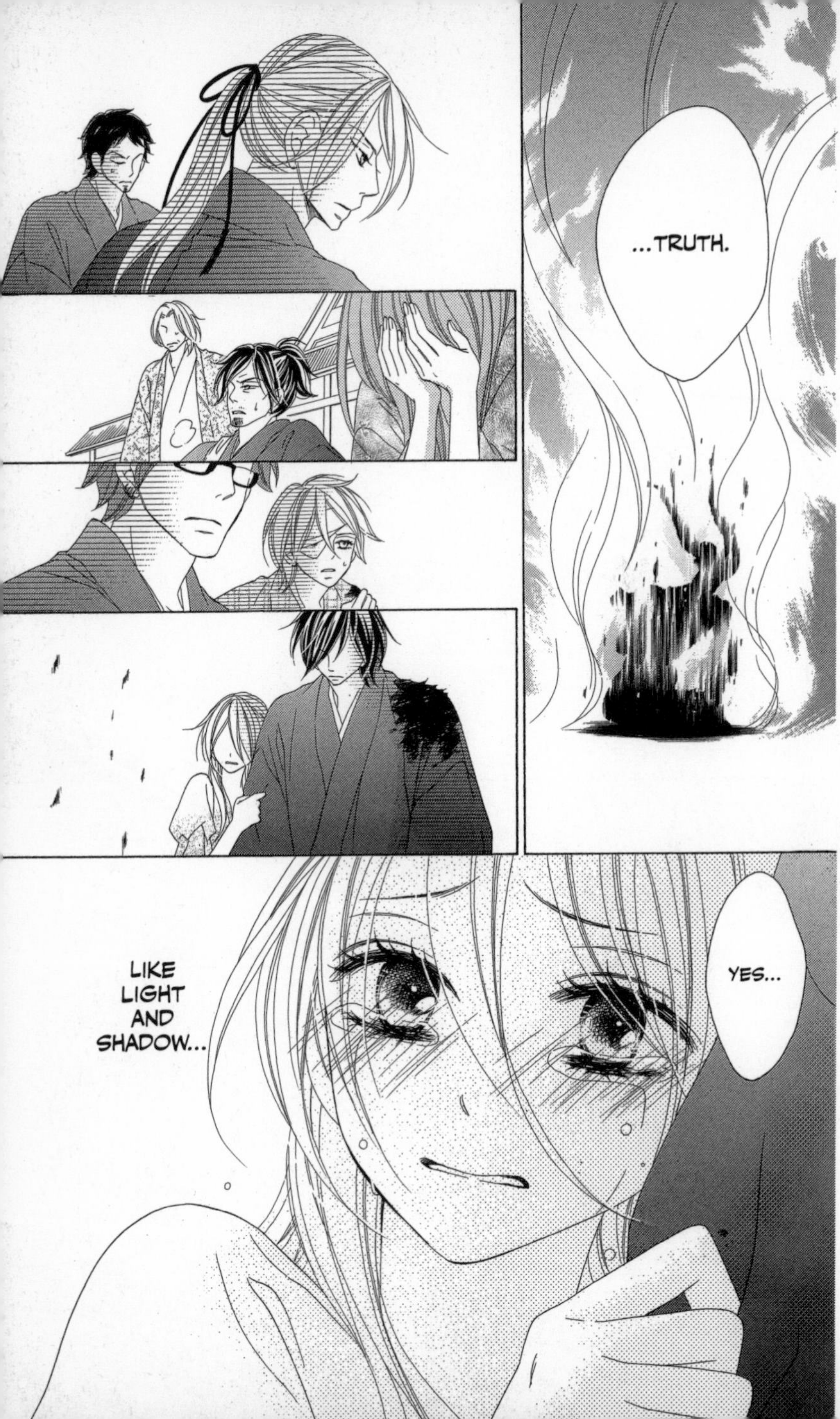
...TRUTH.
YES...
LIKE LIGHT AND SHADOW...

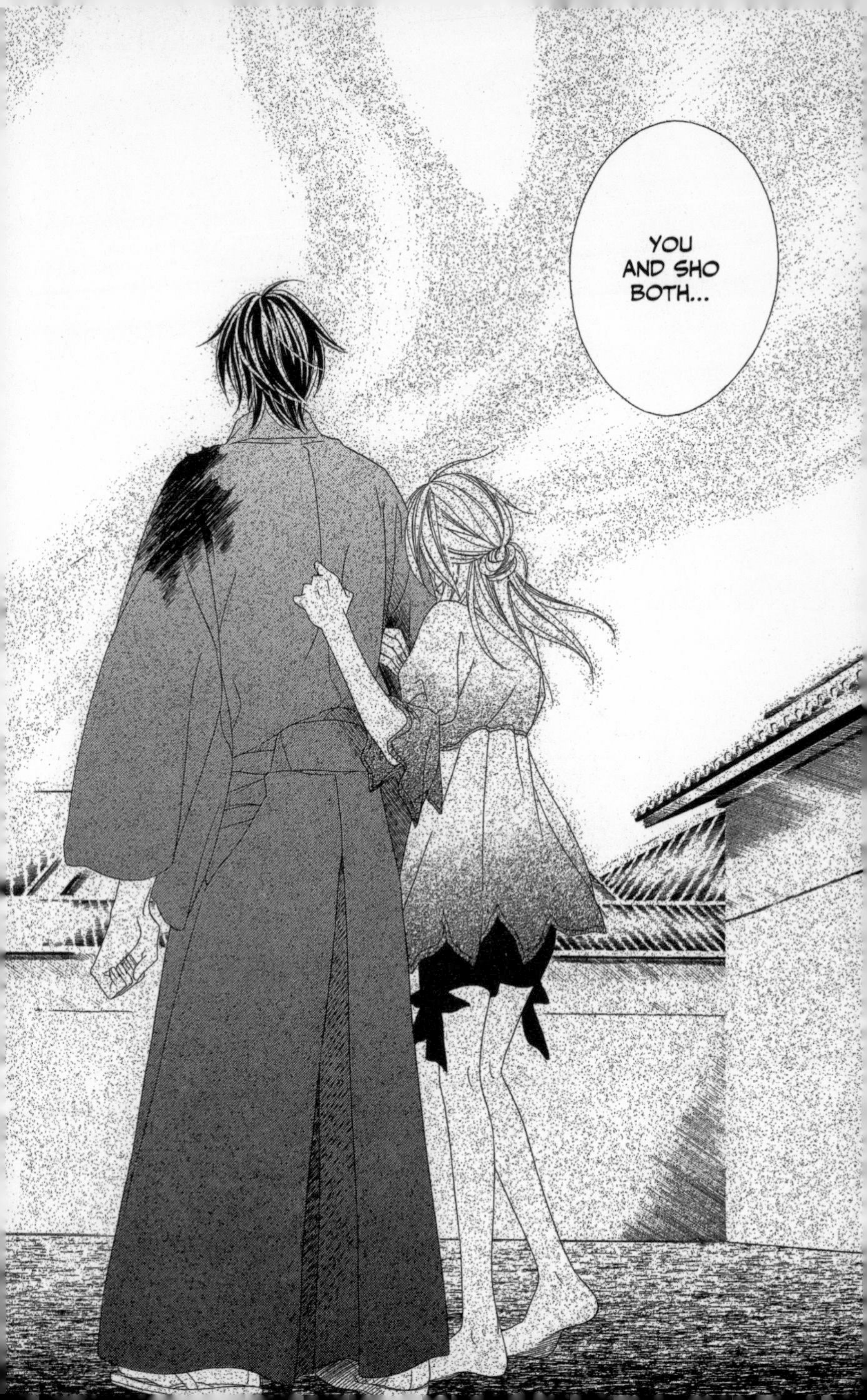
YOU AND SHO BOTH...

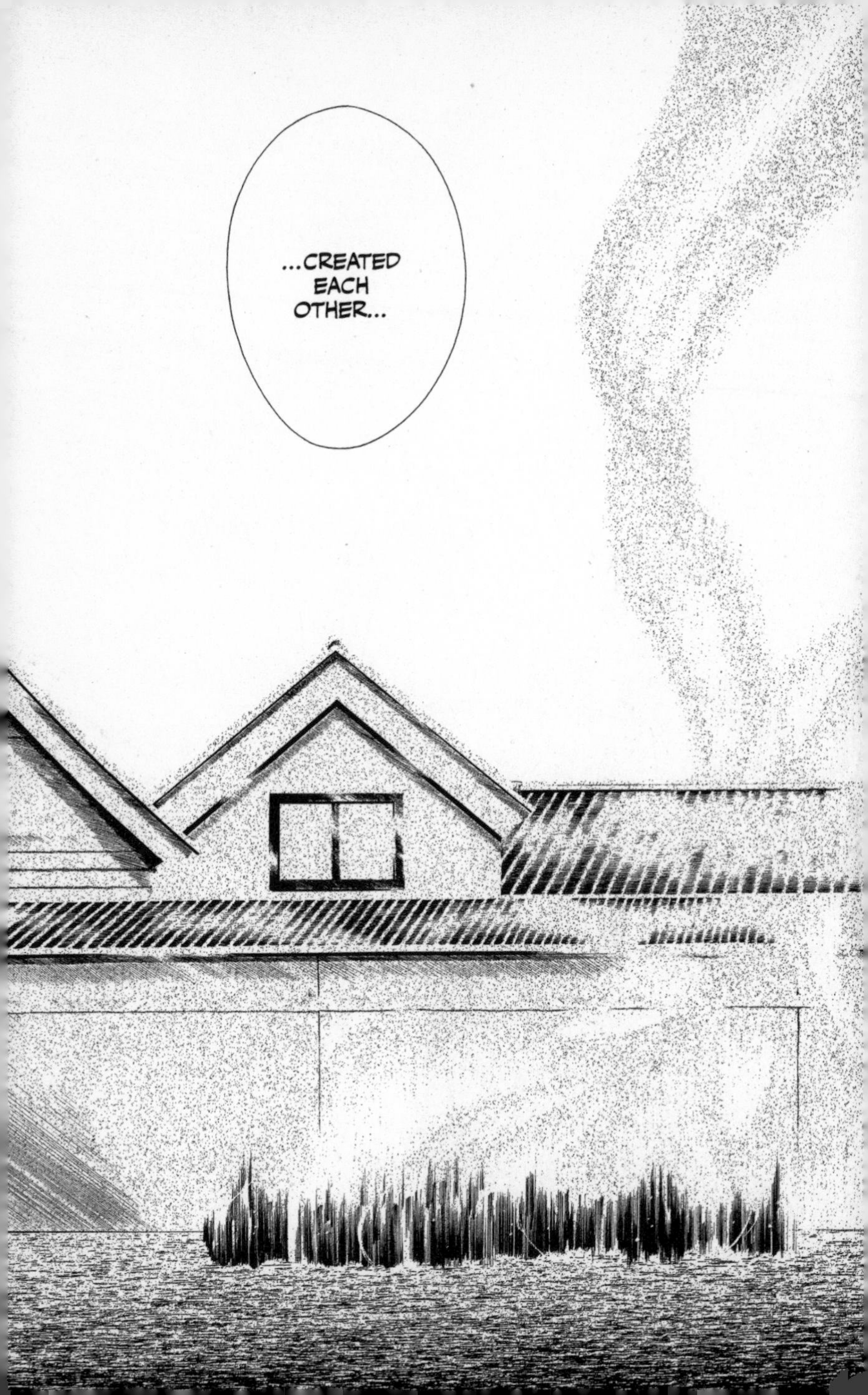
...CREATED EACH OTHER...

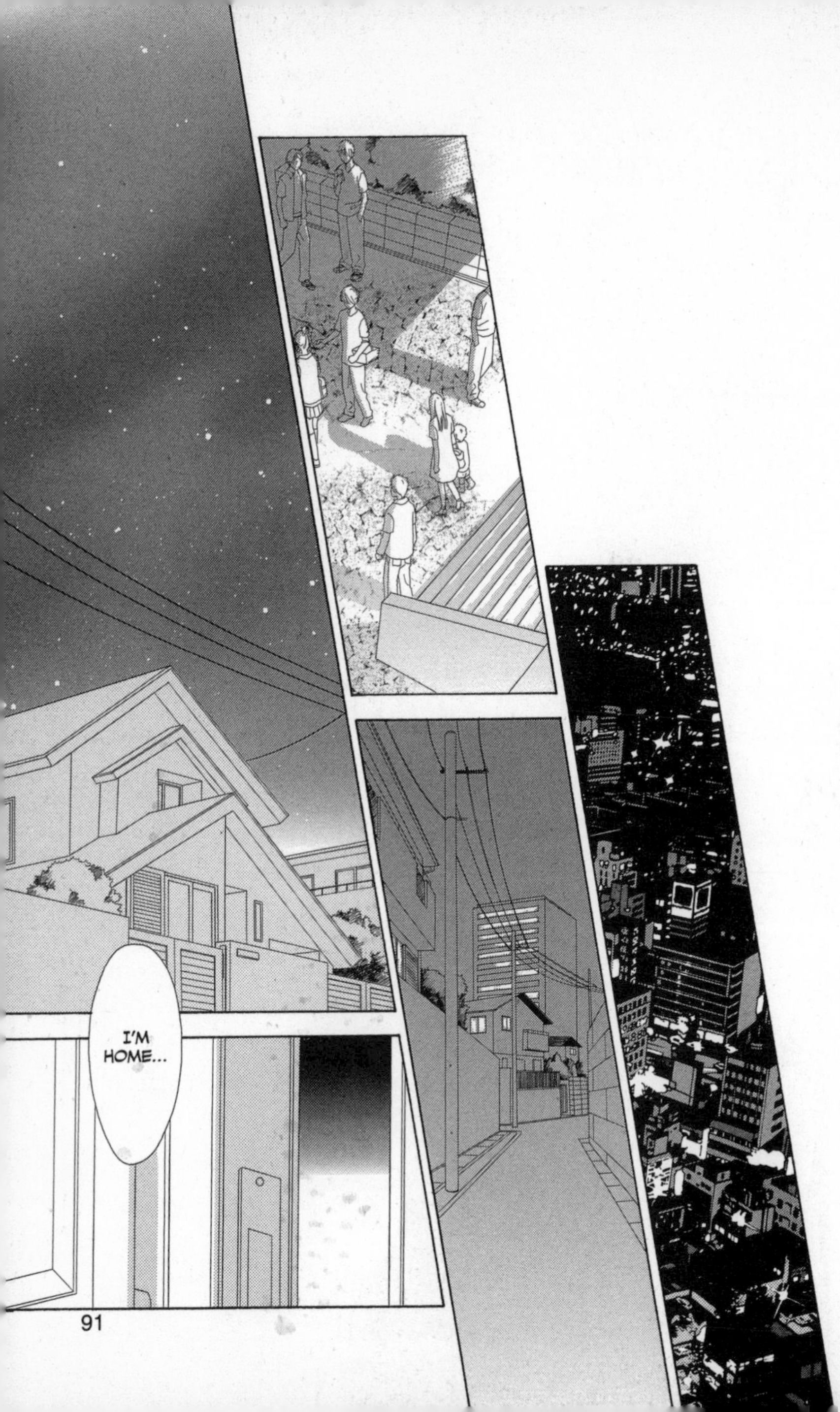
I'M HOME...

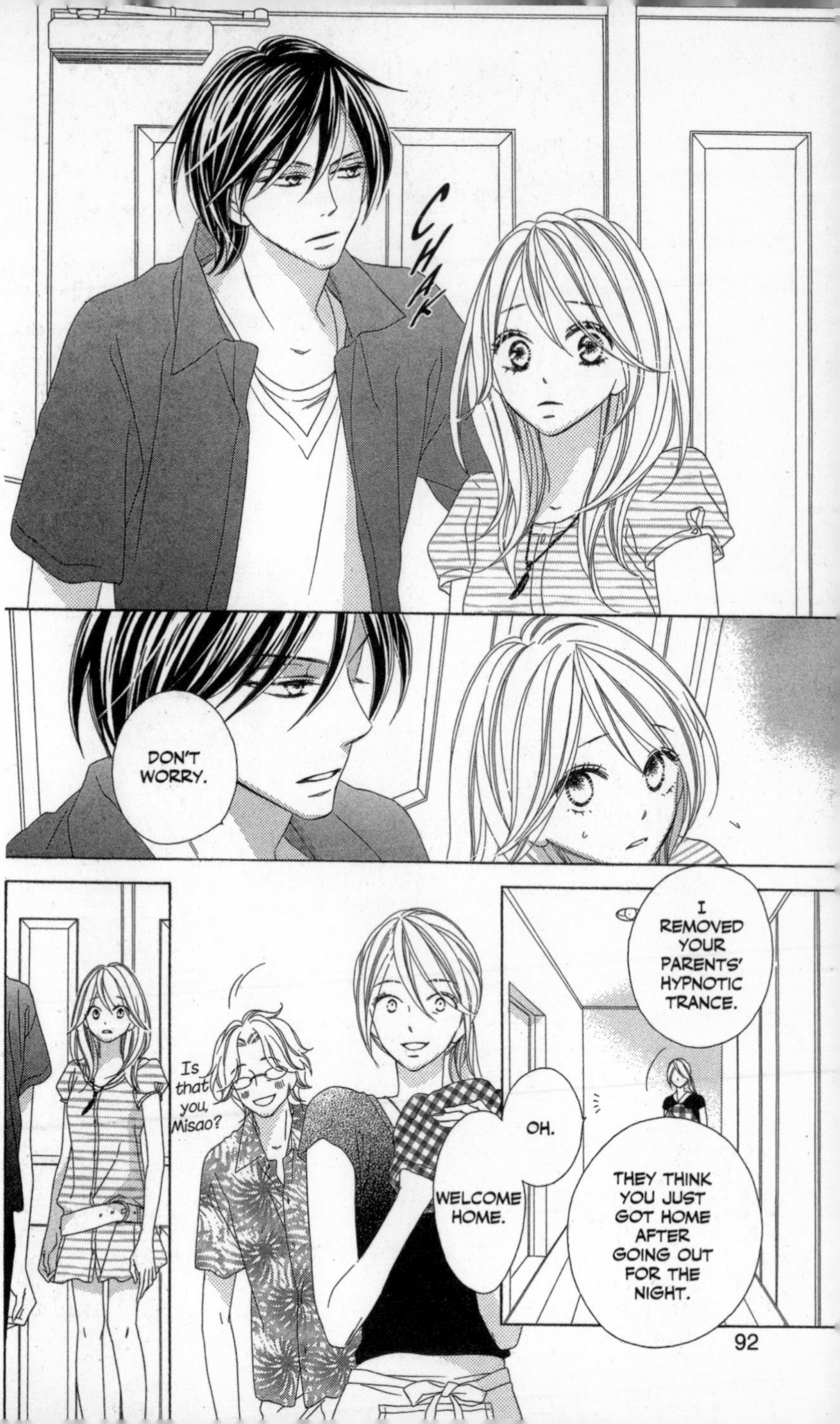
CHAK
DON'T WORRY.
I REMOVED YOUR PARENTS' HYPNOTIC TRANCE.
THEY THINK YOU JUST GOT HOME AFTER GOING OUT FOR THE NIGHT.
OH.
WELCOME HOME.
Is that you, Misao?

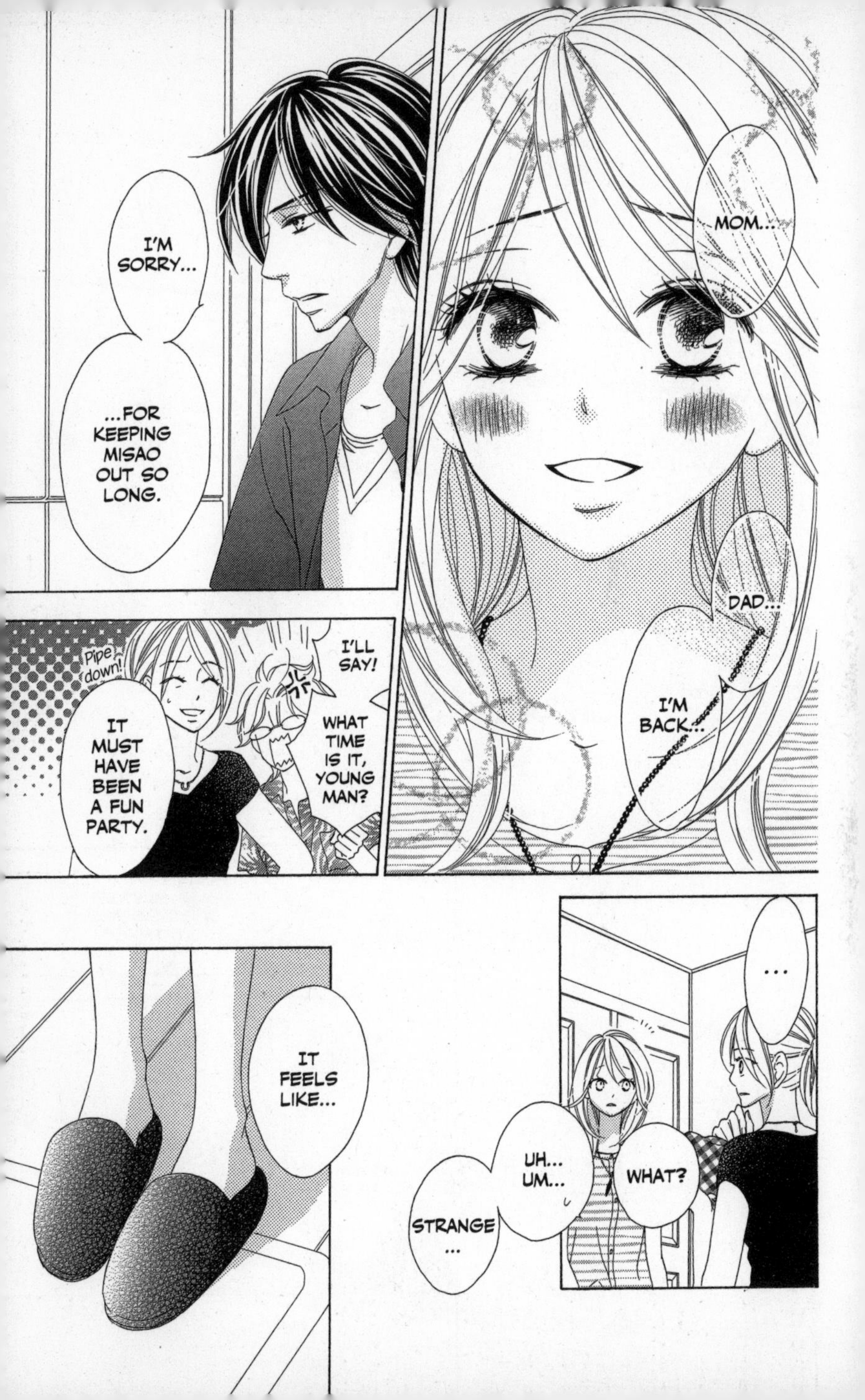

...MOM...
DAD...
I'M BACK...
I'M SORRY...
...FOR KEEPING MISAO OUT SO LONG.
I'LL SAY!
WHAT TIME IS IT, YOUNG MAN?
Pipe down!
IT MUST HAVE BEEN A FUN PARTY.
...
WHAT?
UH... UM...
IT FEELS LIKE...
STRANGE...

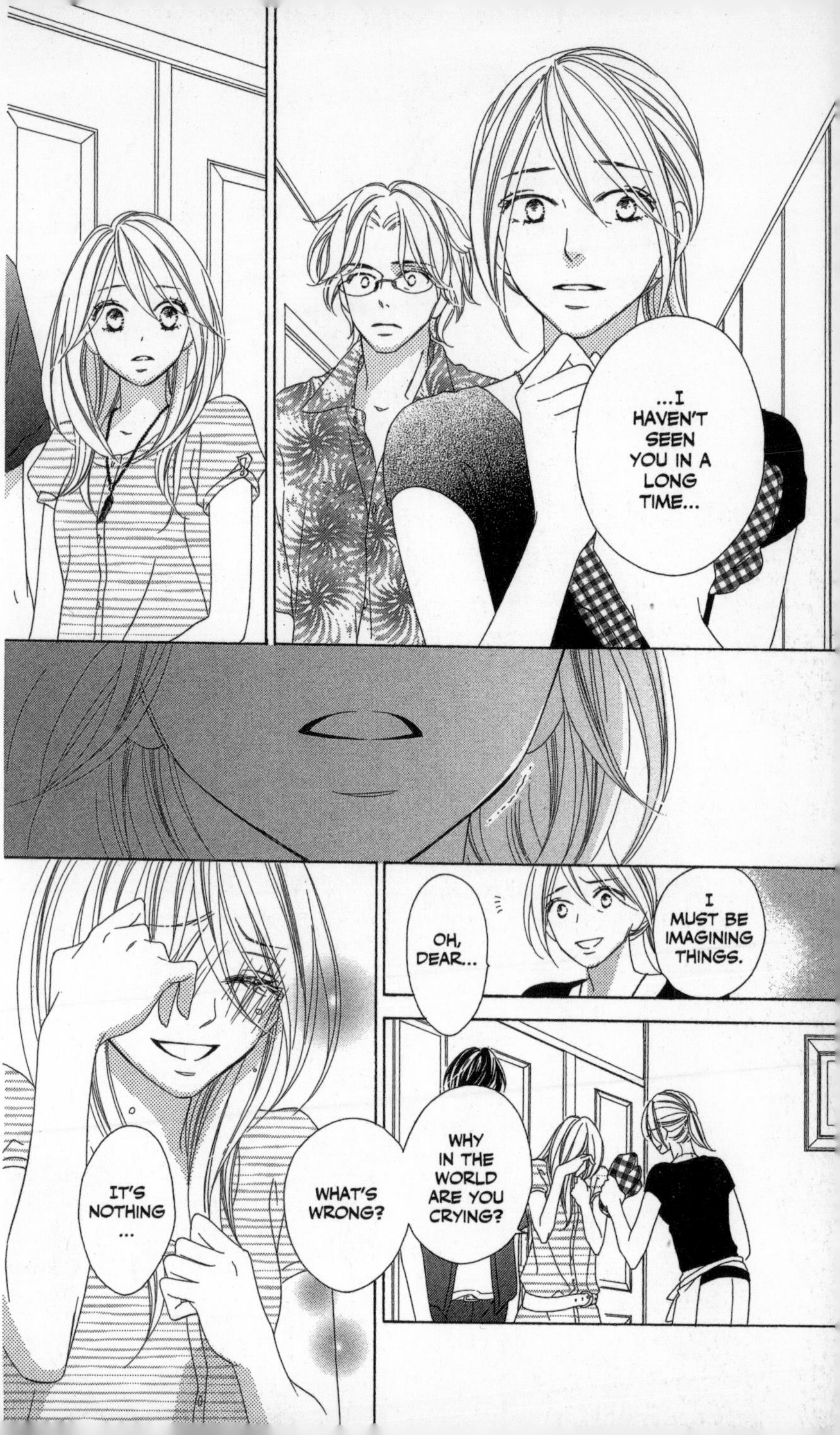
...I HAVEN'T SEEN YOU IN A LONG TIME...
I MUST BE IMAGINING THINGS.
OH, DEAR...
WHY IN THE WORLD ARE YOU CRYING?
WHAT'S WRONG?
IT'S NOTHING...

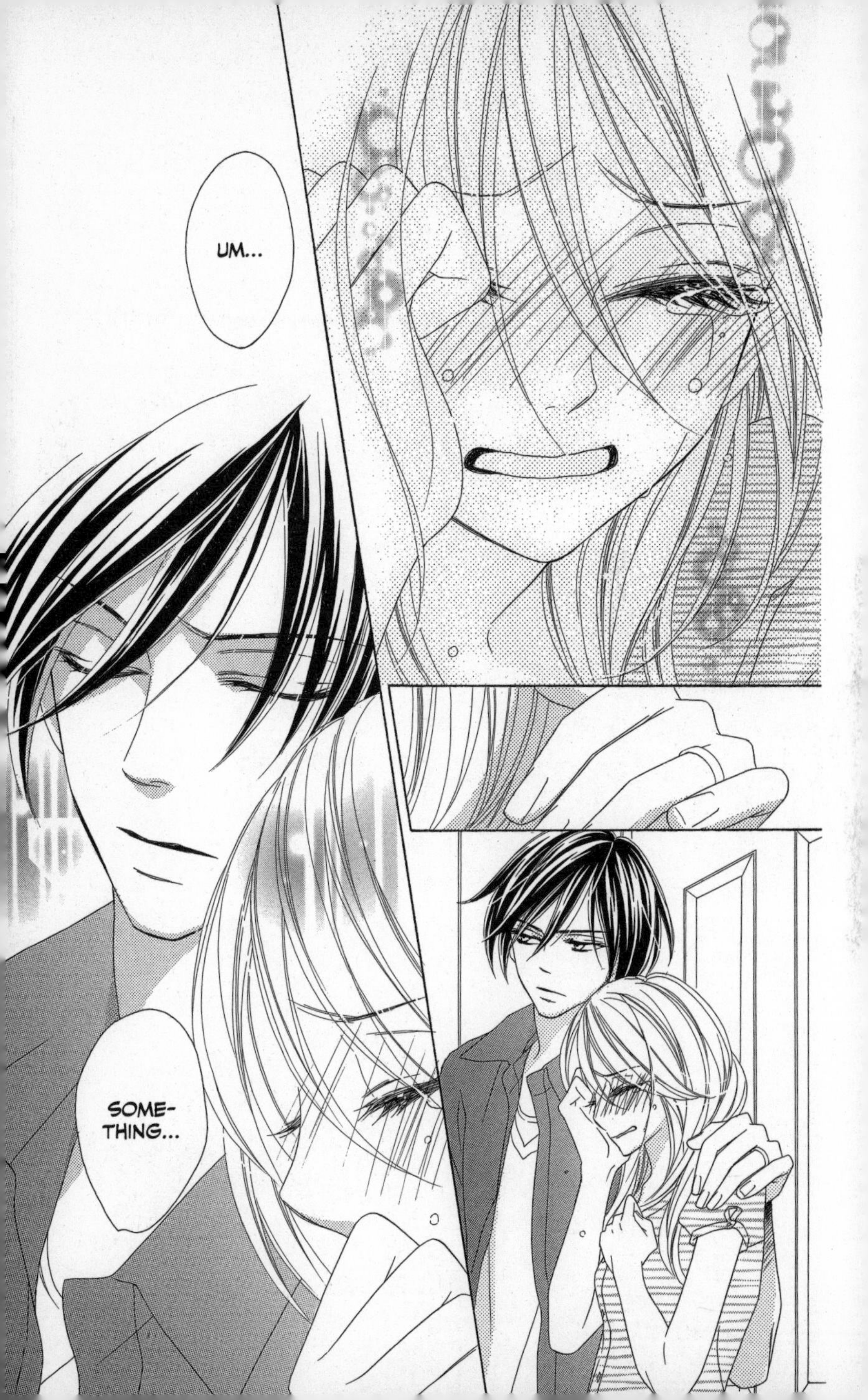
UM...
SOME-
THING...

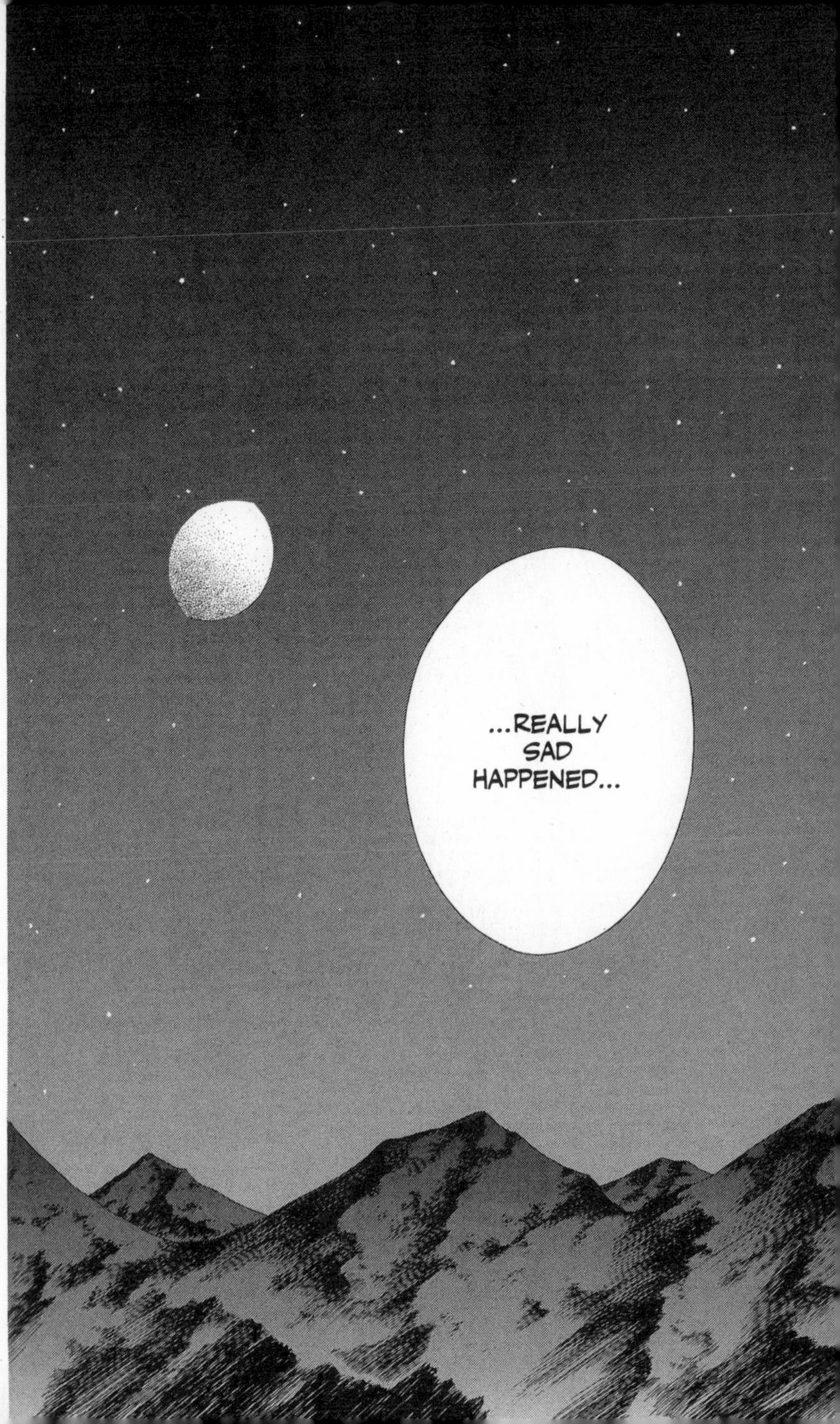
...REALLY SAD HAPPENED...

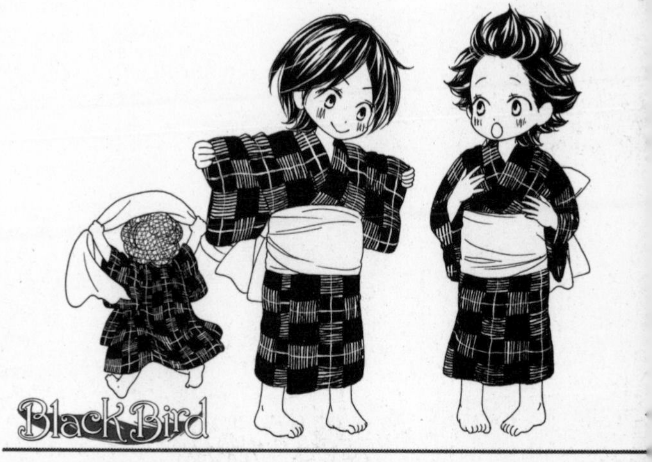
Black Bird

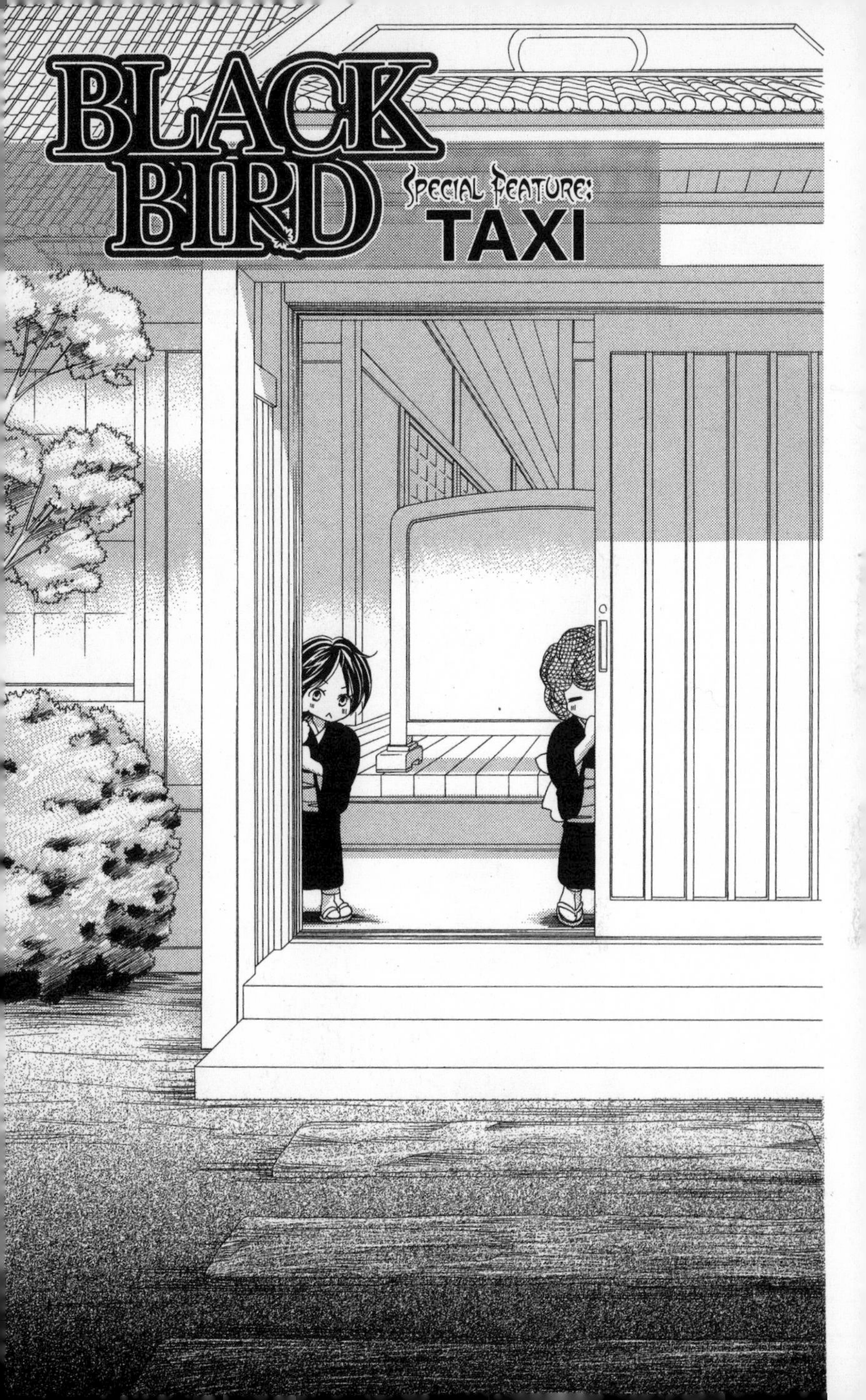
BLACK BIRD
Special Feature:
TAXI

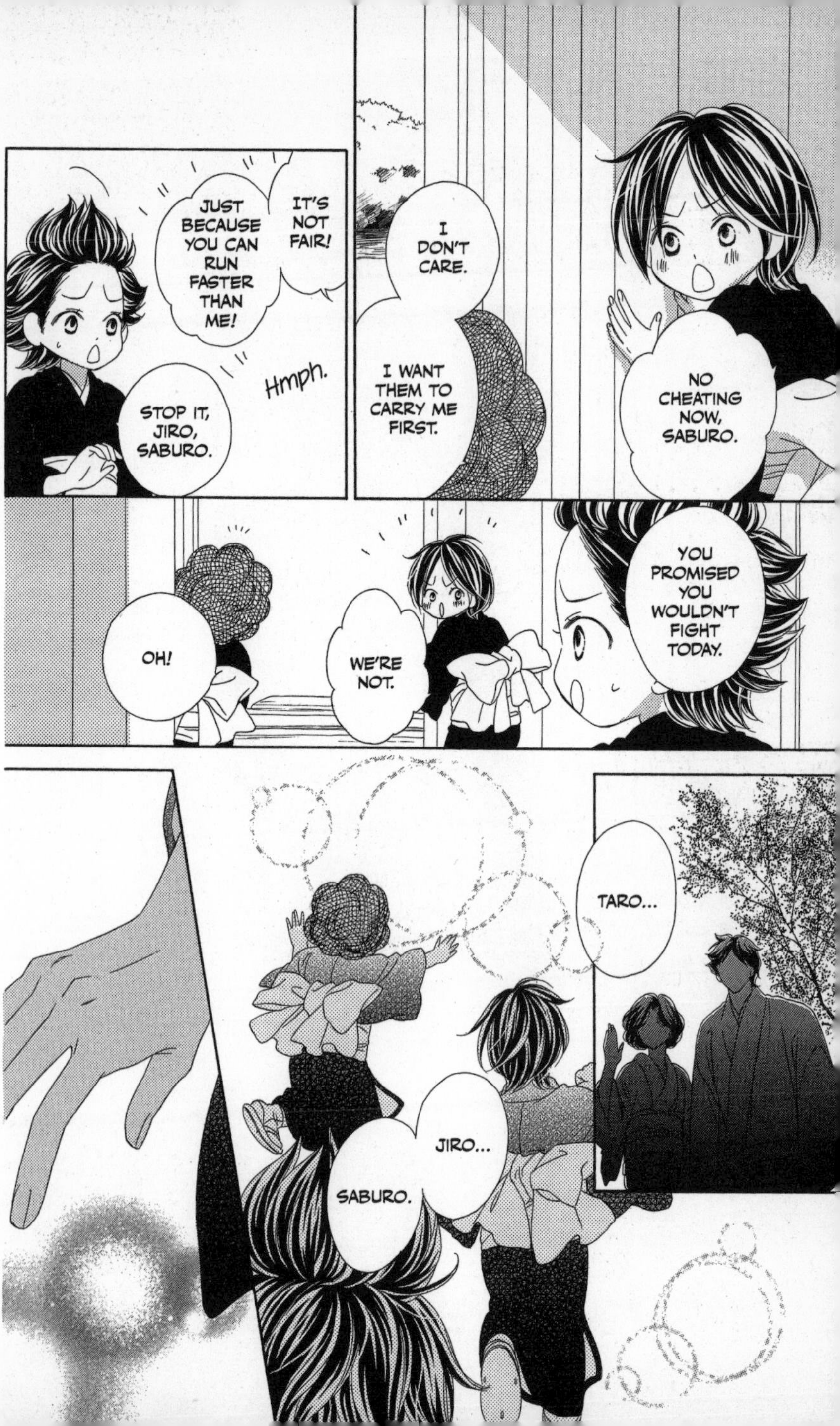
NO CHEATING NOW, SABURO.
I DON'T CARE.
I WANT THEM TO CARRY ME FIRST.
IT'S NOT FAIR!
JUST BECAUSE YOU CAN RUN FASTER THAN ME!
Hmph.
STOP IT, JIRO, SABURO.
YOU PROMISED YOU WOULDN'T FIGHT TODAY.
WE'RE NOT.
OH!
TARO...
JIRO...
SABURO.

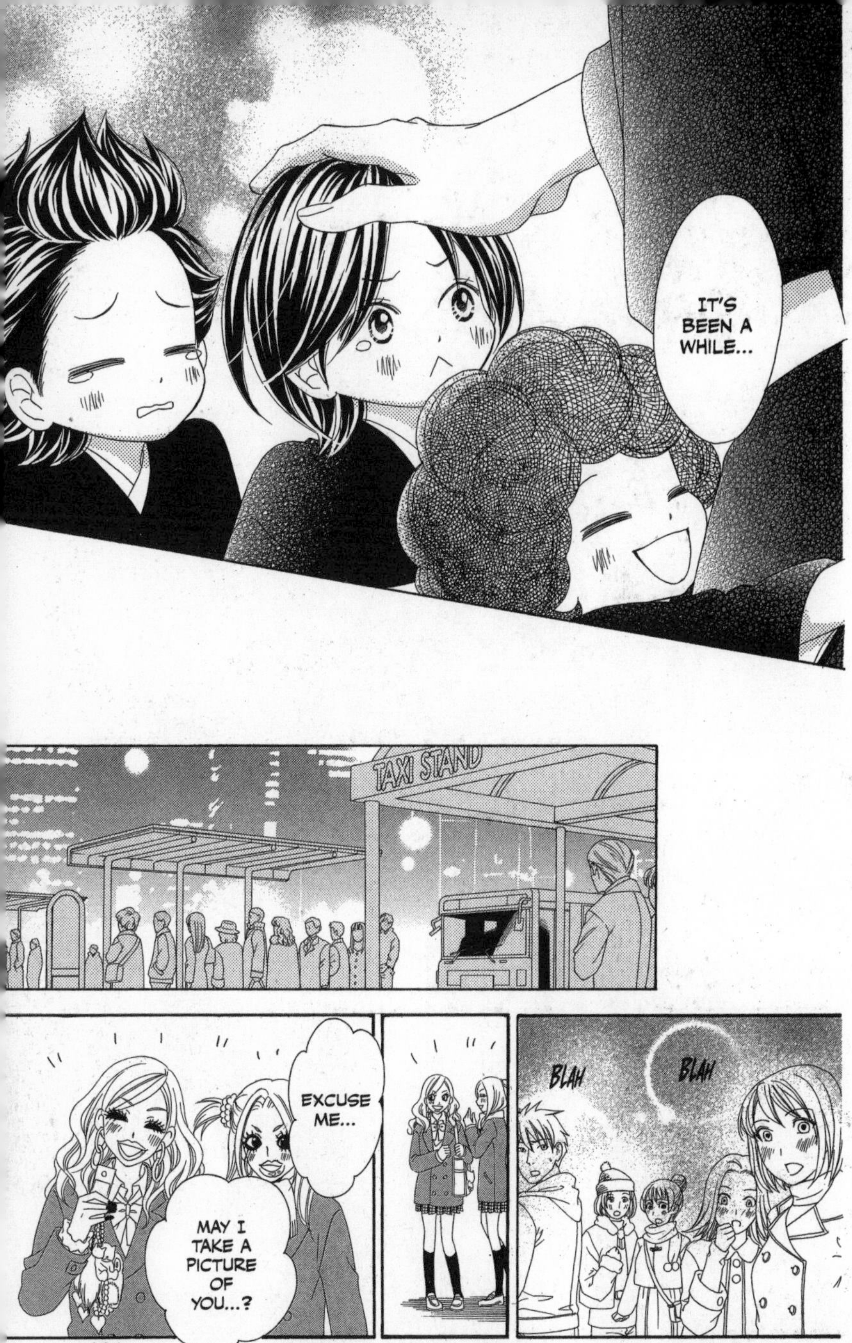
IT'S BEEN A WHILE...
TAXI STAND
BLAH
BLAH
EXCUSE ME...
MAY I TAKE A PICTURE OF YOU...?

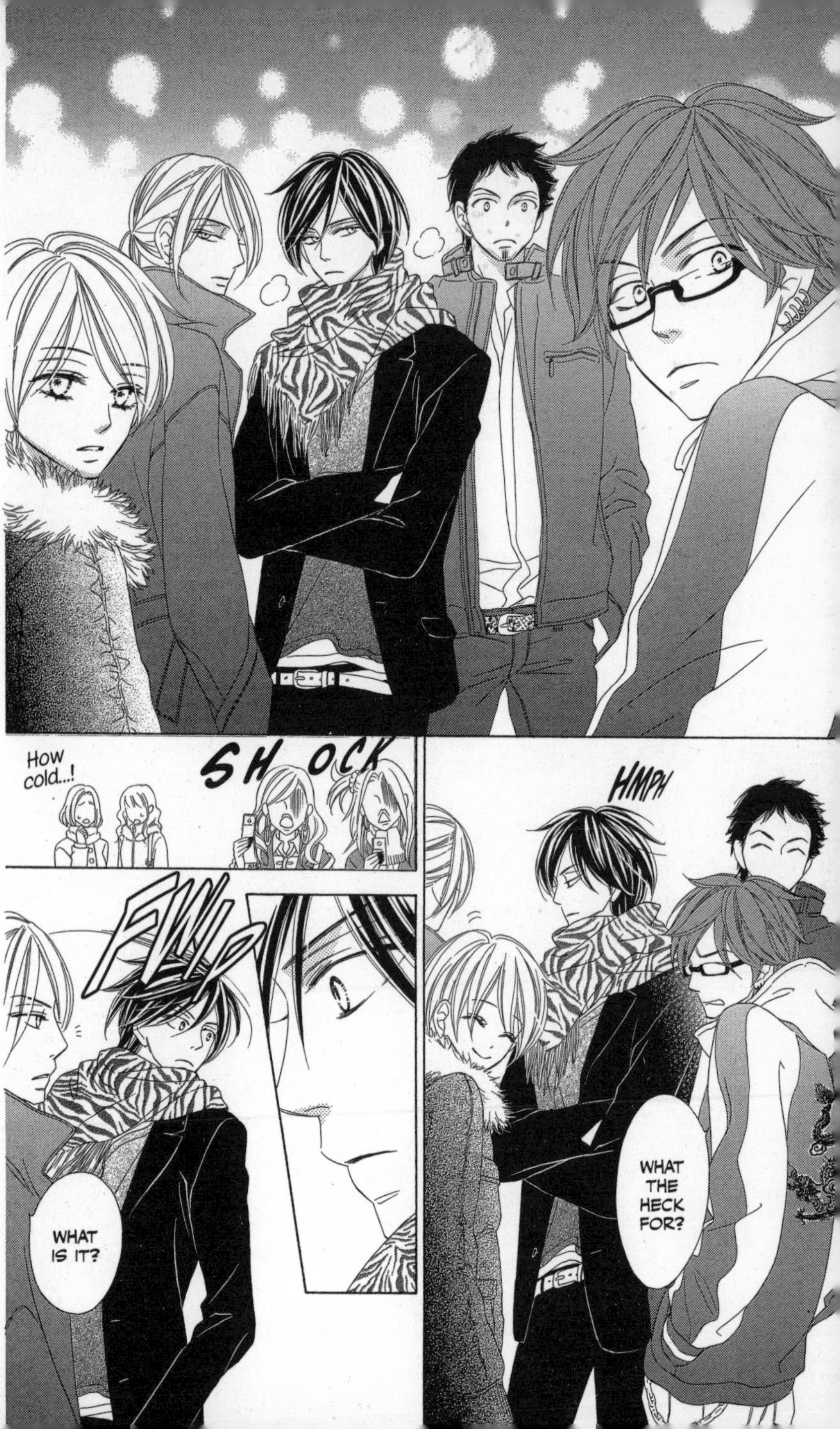
HMPH
WHAT THE HECK FOR?
How cold...!
SHOCK
FWIP
WHAT IS IT?

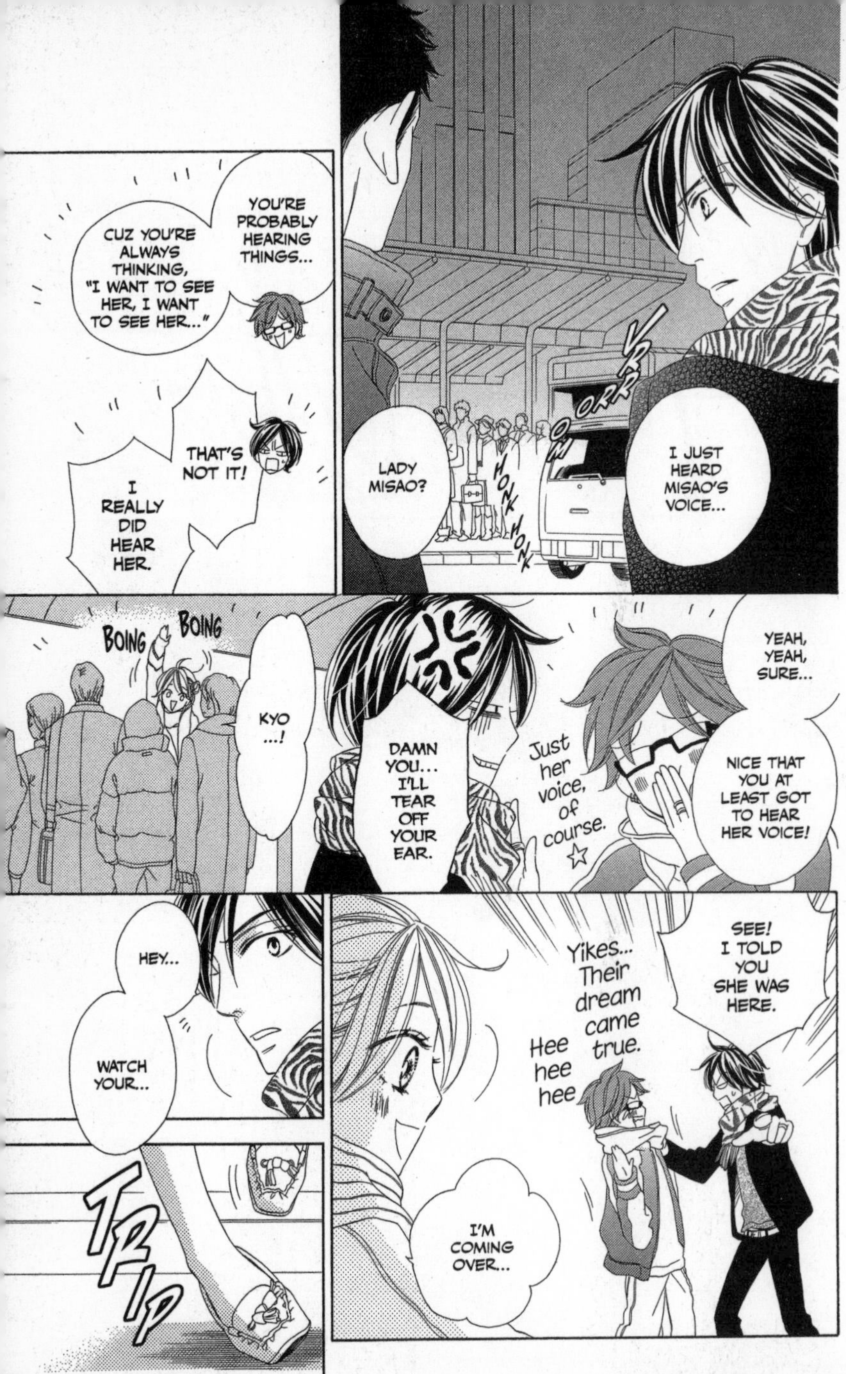
I JUST HEARD MISAO'S VOICE...
HONK HONK
LADY MISAO?
YOU'RE PROBABLY HEARING THINGS...
CUZ YOU'RE ALWAYS THINKING, "I WANT TO SEE HER, I WANT TO SEE HER..."
THAT'S NOT IT!
I REALLY DID HEAR HER.
YEAH, YEAH, SURE...
NICE THAT YOU AT LEAST GOT TO HEAR HER VOICE!
Just her voice, of course. ☆
DAMN YOU... I'LL TEAR OFF YOUR EAR.
KYO ...!
BOING BOING
SEE! I TOLD YOU SHE WAS HERE.
Yikes... Their dream came true.
Hee hee hee
I'M COMING OVER...
HEY...
WATCH YOUR...
TRIP

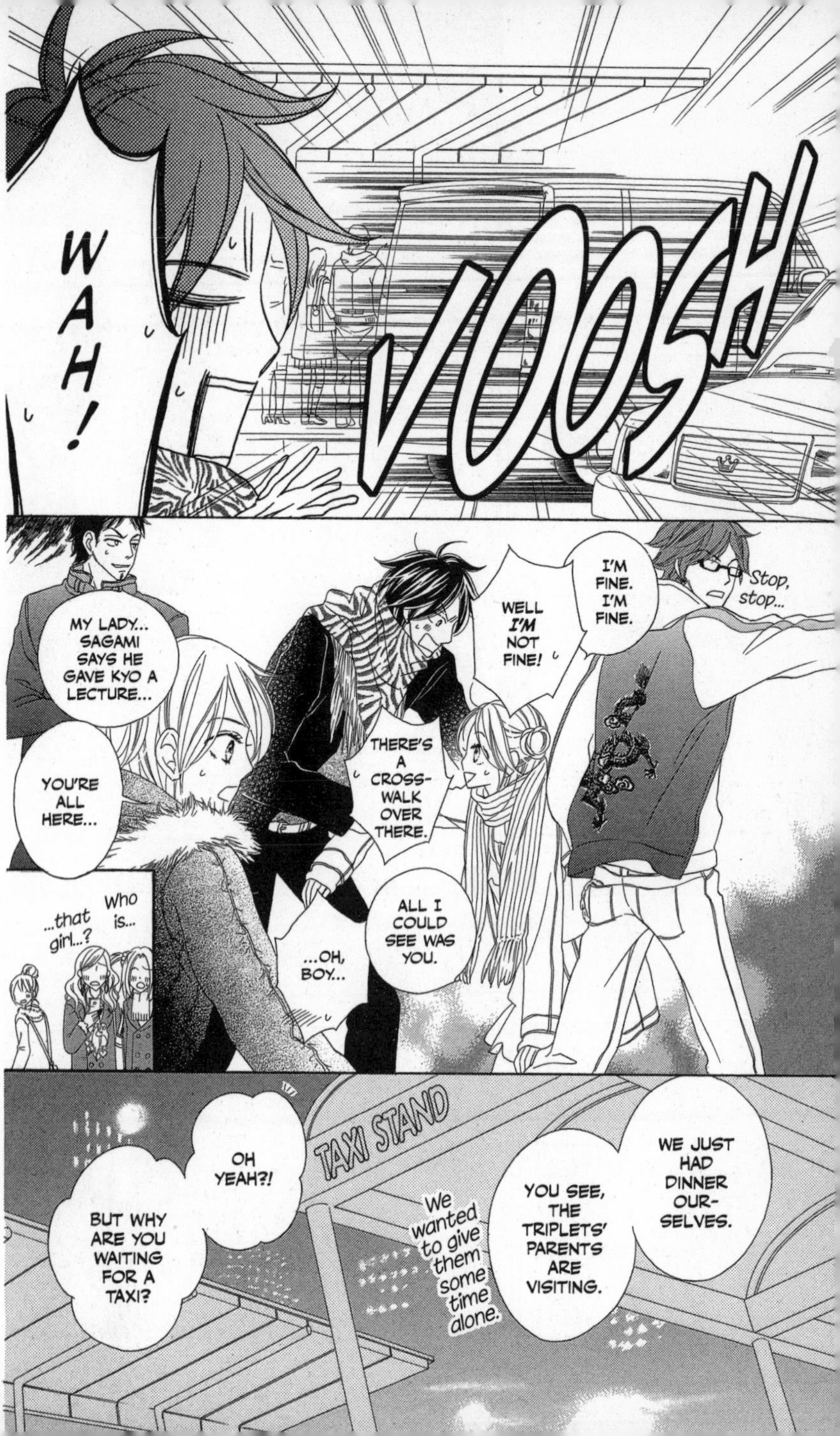
VOOSH
WAH!
Stop, stop...
I'M FINE. I'M FINE.
WELL *I'M* NOT FINE!
THERE'S A CROSS-WALK OVER THERE.
MY LADY... SAGAMI SAYS HE GAVE KYO A LECTURE...
YOU'RE ALL HERE...
ALL I COULD SEE WAS YOU.
...OH, BOY...
Who is... ...that girl...?
WE JUST HAD DINNER OUR-SELVES.
YOU SEE, THE TRIPLETS' PARENTS ARE VISITING.
We wanted to give them some time alone.
TAXI STAND
OH YEAH?!
BUT WHY ARE YOU WAITING FOR A TAXI?

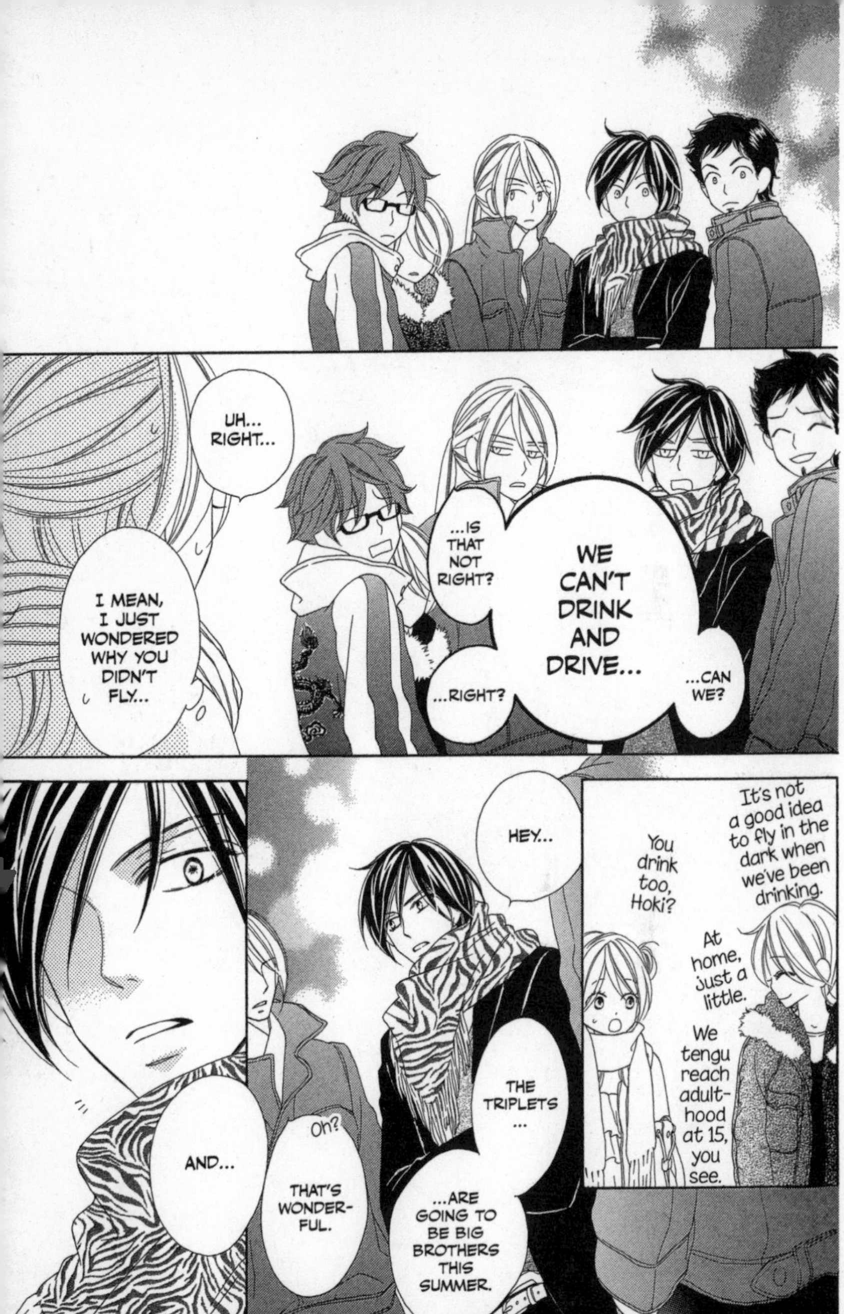
...CAN WE?
WE CAN'T DRINK AND DRIVE...
...RIGHT?
...IS THAT NOT RIGHT?
UH... RIGHT...
I MEAN, I JUST WONDERED WHY YOU DIDN'T FLY...
It's not a good idea to fly in the dark when we've been drinking.
You drink too, Hoki?
At home, just a little.
We tengu reach adulthood at 15, you see.
HEY...
THE TRIPLETS...
...ARE GOING TO BE BIG BROTHERS THIS SUMMER.
Oh?
THAT'S WONDERFUL.
AND...

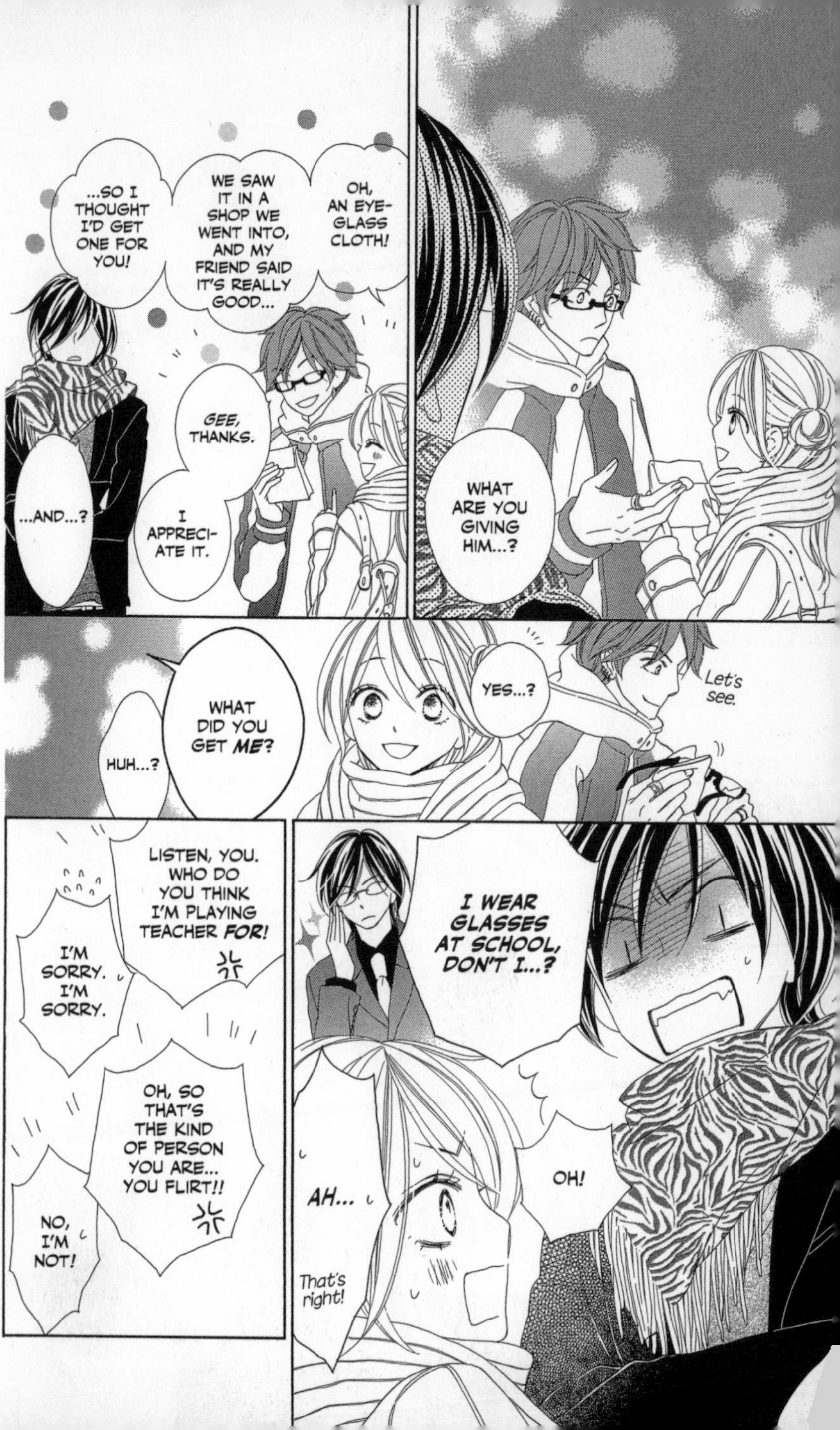
WHAT ARE YOU GIVING HIM...?
OH, AN EYE-GLASS CLOTH!
WE SAW IT IN A SHOP WE WENT INTO, AND MY FRIEND SAID IT'S REALLY GOOD...
...SO I THOUGHT I'D GET ONE FOR YOU!
GEE, THANKS.
I APPRECIATE IT.
...AND...?
Let's see.
YES...?
WHAT DID YOU GET ME?
HUH...?
I WEAR GLASSES AT SCHOOL, DON'T I...?
OH!
AH...
That's right!
LISTEN, YOU. WHO DO YOU THINK I'M PLAYING TEACHER FOR!
I'M SORRY. I'M SORRY.
OH, SO THAT'S THE KIND OF PERSON YOU ARE... YOU FLIRT!!
NO, I'M NOT!

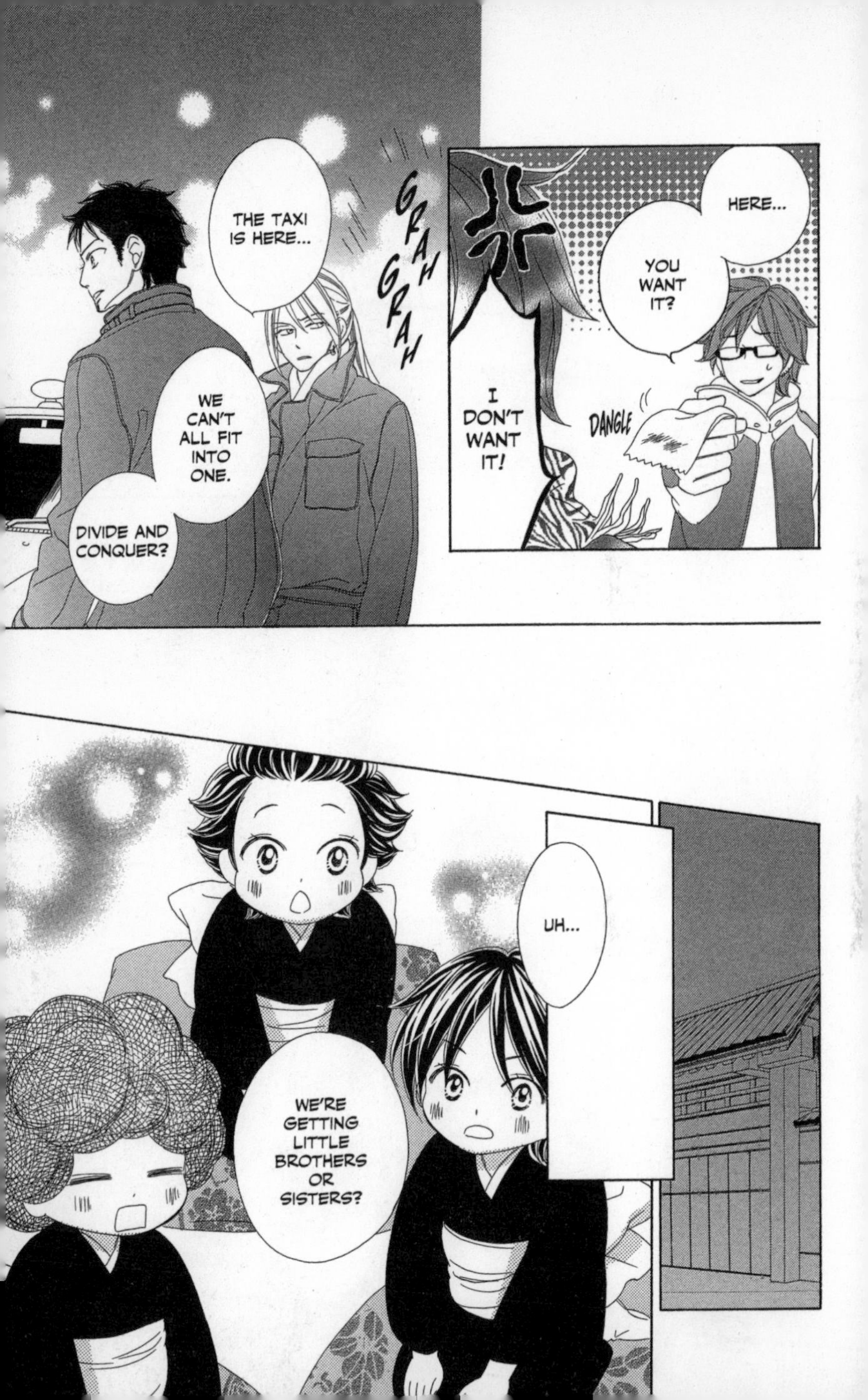
HERE...
YOU WANT IT?
DANGLE
I DON'T WANT IT!
THE TAXI IS HERE...
GRAH GRAH
WE CAN'T ALL FIT INTO ONE.
DIVIDE AND CONQUER?
UH...
WE'RE GETTING LITTLE BROTHERS OR SISTERS?

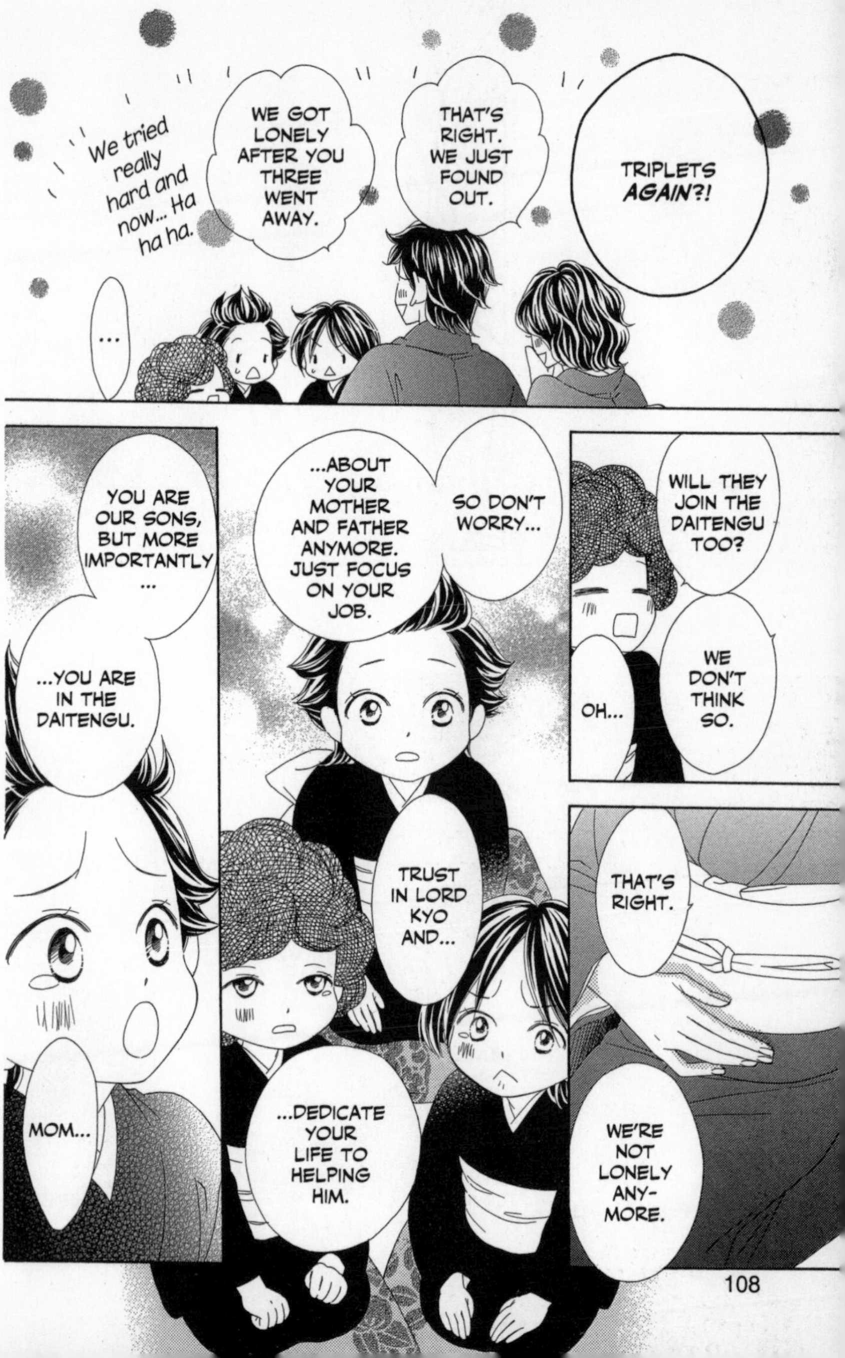
TRIPLETS AGAIN?!
THAT'S RIGHT. WE JUST FOUND OUT.
WE GOT LONELY AFTER YOU THREE WENT AWAY.
We tried really hard and now... Ha ha ha.
...
WILL THEY JOIN THE DAITENGU TOO?
WE DON'T THINK SO.
OH...
THAT'S RIGHT.
WE'RE NOT LONELY ANY-MORE.
SO DON'T WORRY...
...ABOUT YOUR MOTHER AND FATHER ANYMORE. JUST FOCUS ON YOUR JOB.
TRUST IN LORD KYO AND...
...DEDICATE YOUR LIFE TO HELPING HIM.
YOU ARE OUR SONS, BUT MORE IMPORTANTLY...
...YOU ARE IN THE DAITENGU.
MOM...

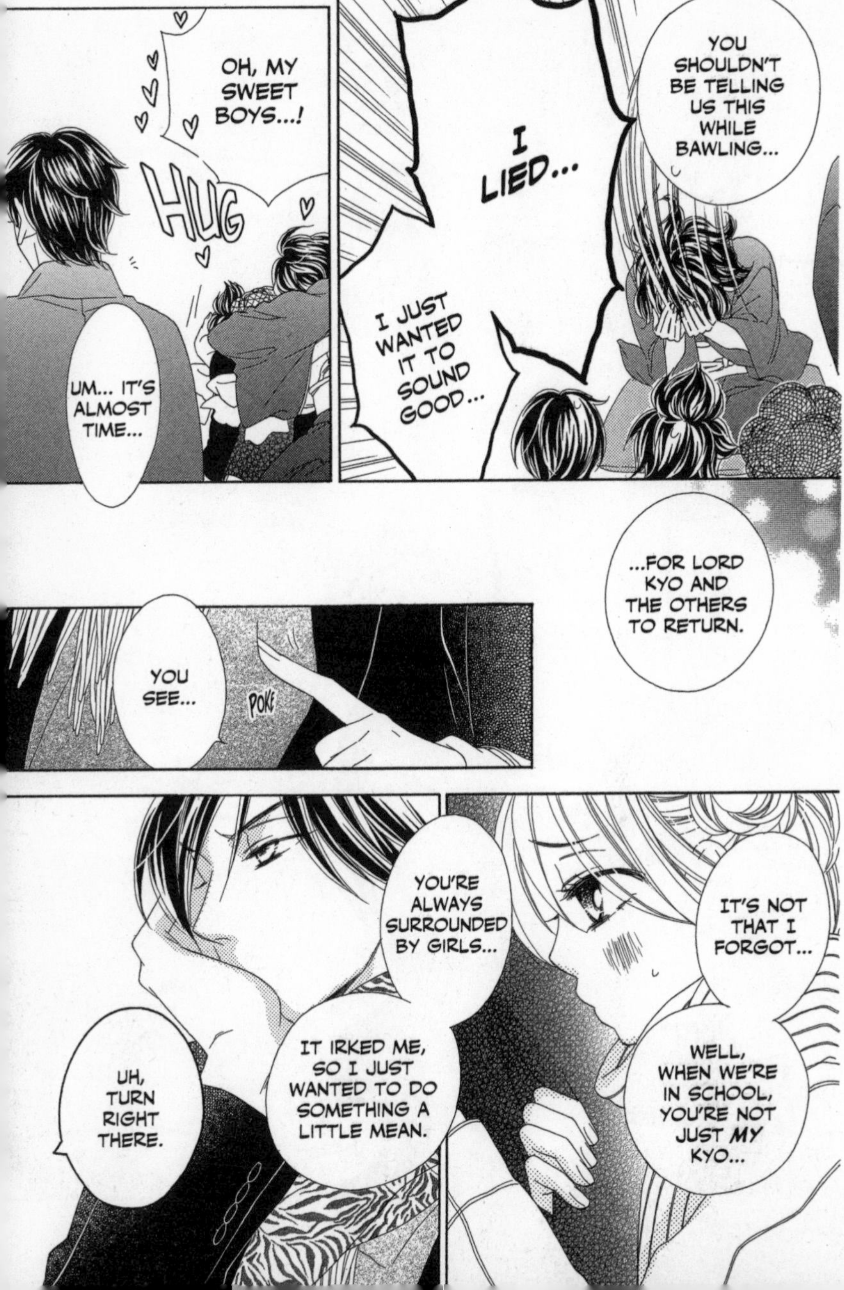
YOU SHOULDN'T BE TELLING US THIS WHILE BAWLING...
I LIED...
I JUST WANTED IT TO SOUND GOOD...
OH, MY SWEET BOYS...!
HUG
UM... IT'S ALMOST TIME...
...FOR LORD KYO AND THE OTHERS TO RETURN.
YOU SEE...
POKE
IT'S NOT THAT I FORGOT...
WELL, WHEN WE'RE IN SCHOOL, YOU'RE NOT JUST *MY* KYO...
YOU'RE ALWAYS SURROUNDED BY GIRLS...
IT IRKED ME, SO I JUST WANTED TO DO SOMETHING A LITTLE MEAN.
UH, TURN RIGHT THERE.

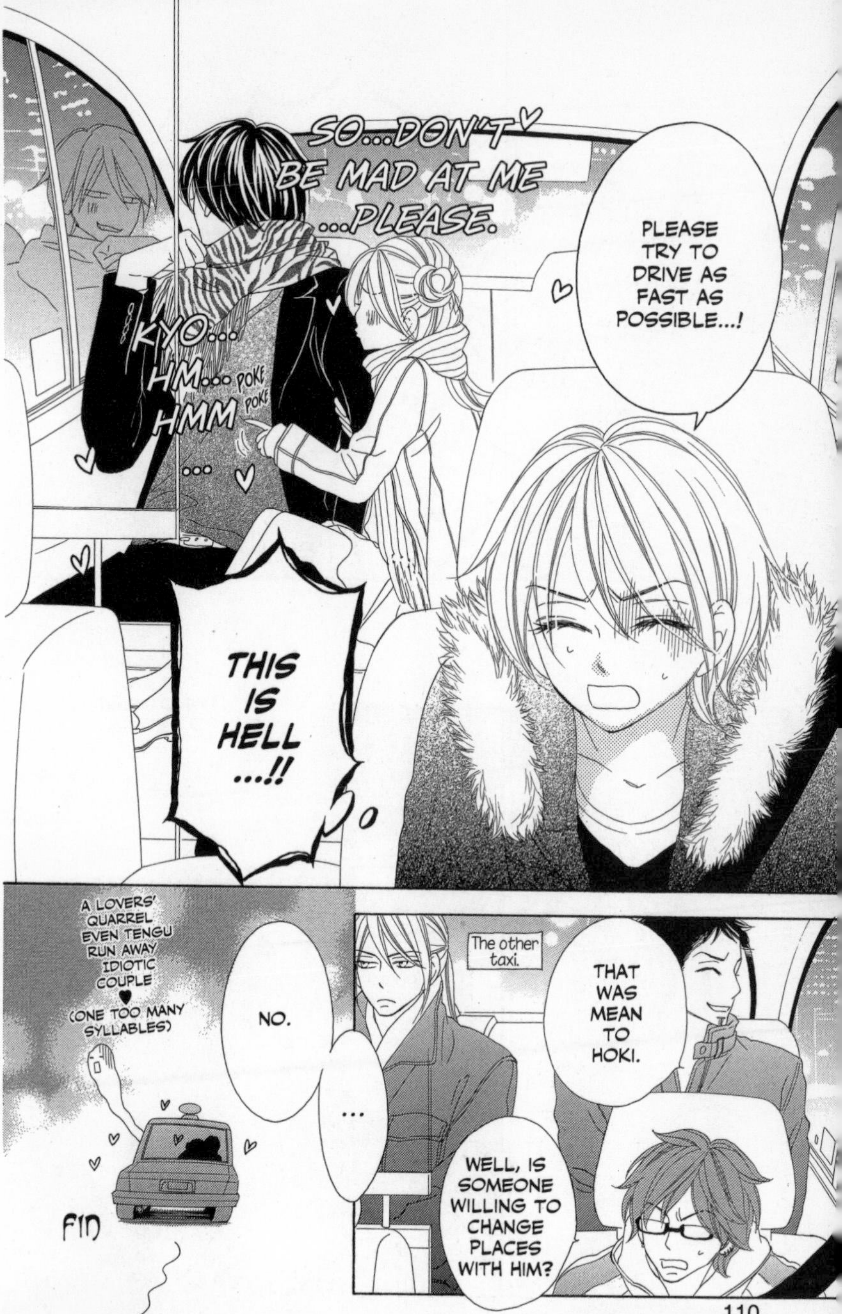
PLEASE TRY TO DRIVE AS FAST AS POSSIBLE...!
SO...DON'T BE MAD AT ME ...PLEASE.
KYO... HM... HMM ...
POKE POKE
THIS IS HELL ...!!
The other taxi.
THAT WAS MEAN TO HOKI.
NO.
...
WELL, IS SOMEONE WILLING TO CHANGE PLACES WITH HIM?
A LOVERS' QUARREL EVEN TENGU RUN AWAY IDIOTIC COUPLE ♥ (ONE TOO MANY SYLLABLES)
FIN

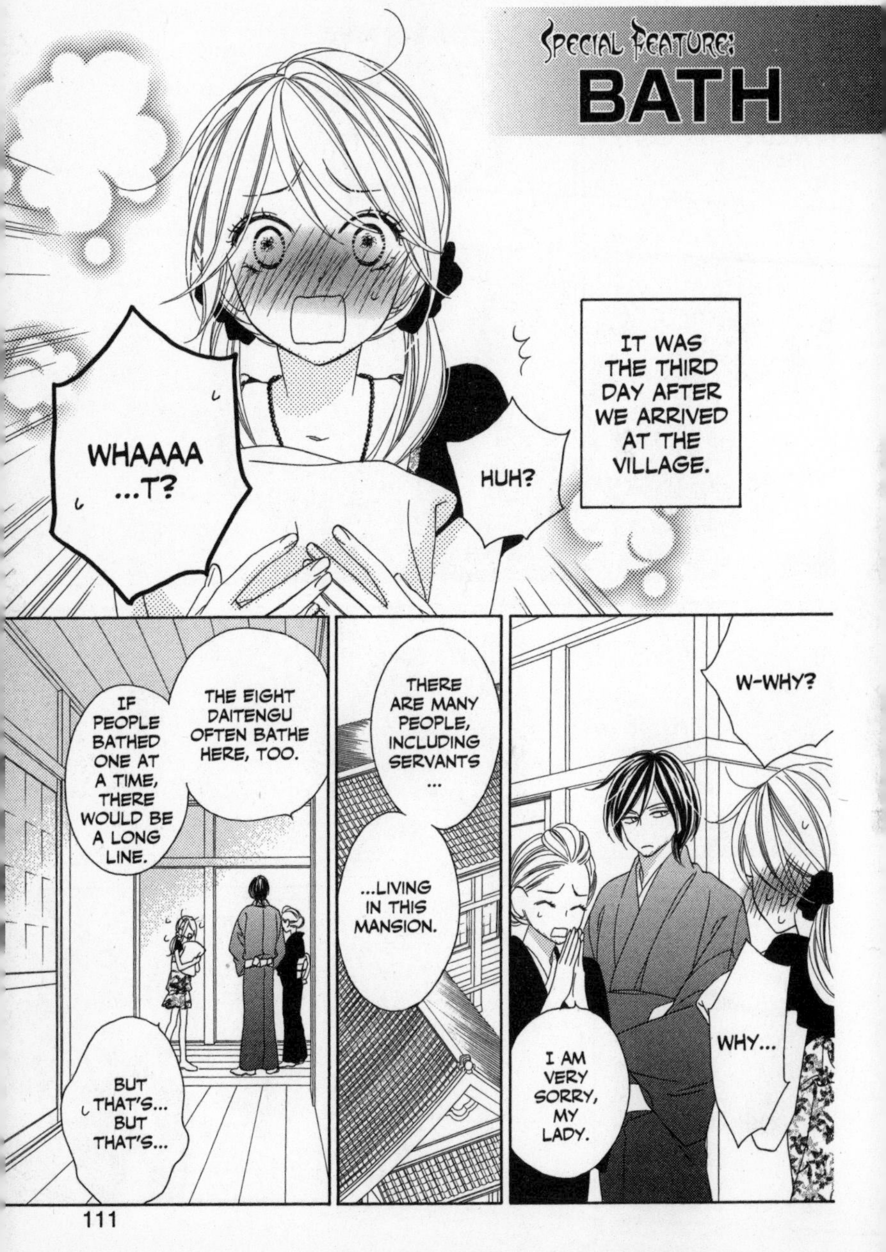
Special Feature:
BATH
IT WAS THE THIRD DAY AFTER WE ARRIVED AT THE VILLAGE.
HUH?
WHAAAA ...T?
W-WHY?
WHY...
I AM VERY SORRY, MY LADY.
THERE ARE MANY PEOPLE, INCLUDING SERVANTS ...
...LIVING IN THIS MANSION.
THE EIGHT DAITENGU OFTEN BATHE HERE, TOO.
IF PEOPLE BATHED ONE AT A TIME, THERE WOULD BE A LONG LINE.
BUT THAT'S... BUT THAT'S...

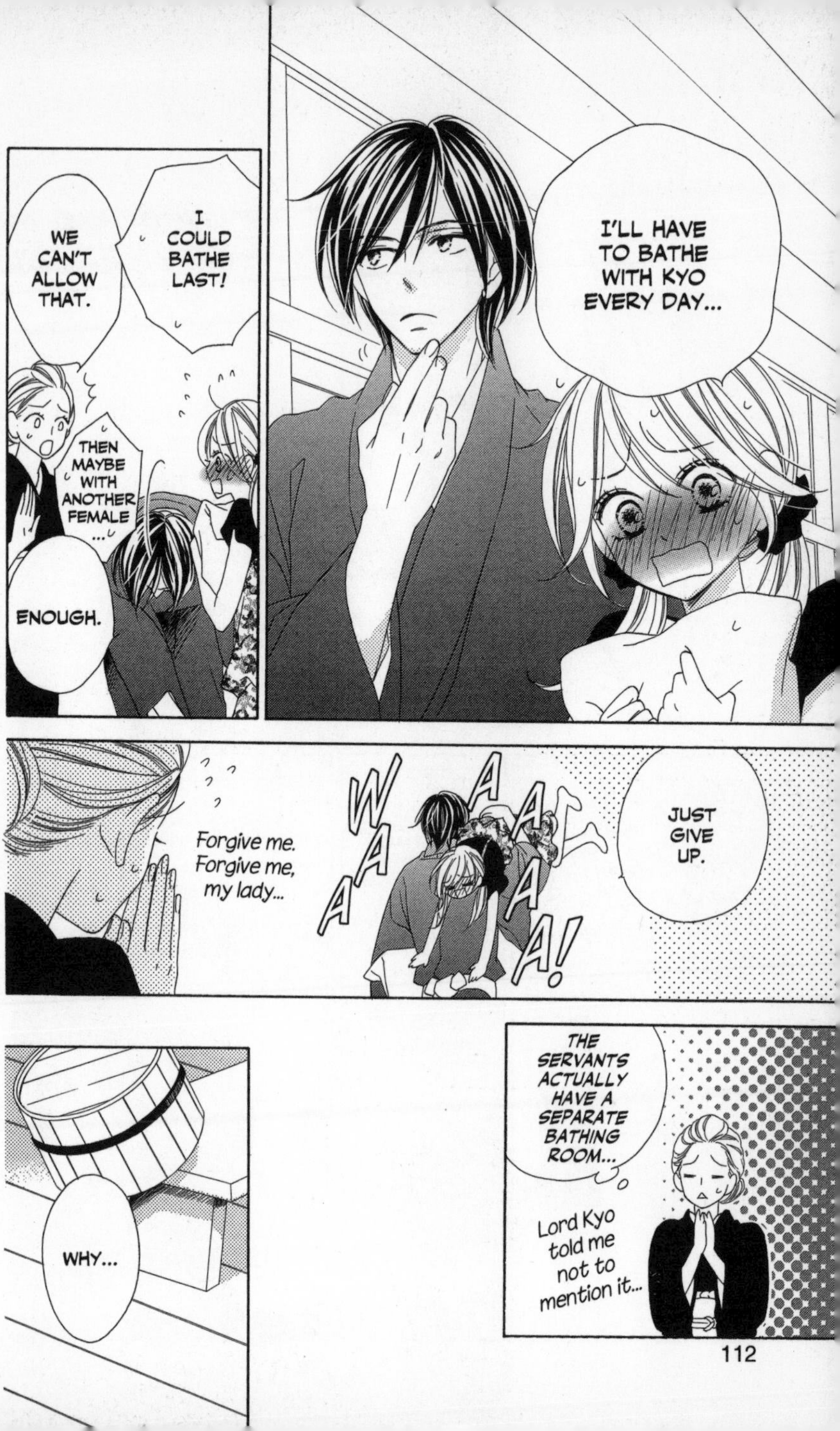
I'LL HAVE TO BATHE WITH KYO EVERY DAY...
I COULD BATHE LAST!
WE CAN'T ALLOW THAT.
THEN MAYBE WITH ANOTHER FEMALE ...
ENOUGH.
JUST GIVE UP.
WAAAAAAAA!
Forgive me. Forgive me, my lady...
THE SERVANTS ACTUALLY HAVE A SEPARATE BATHING ROOM...
Lord Kyo told me not to mention it...
WHY...

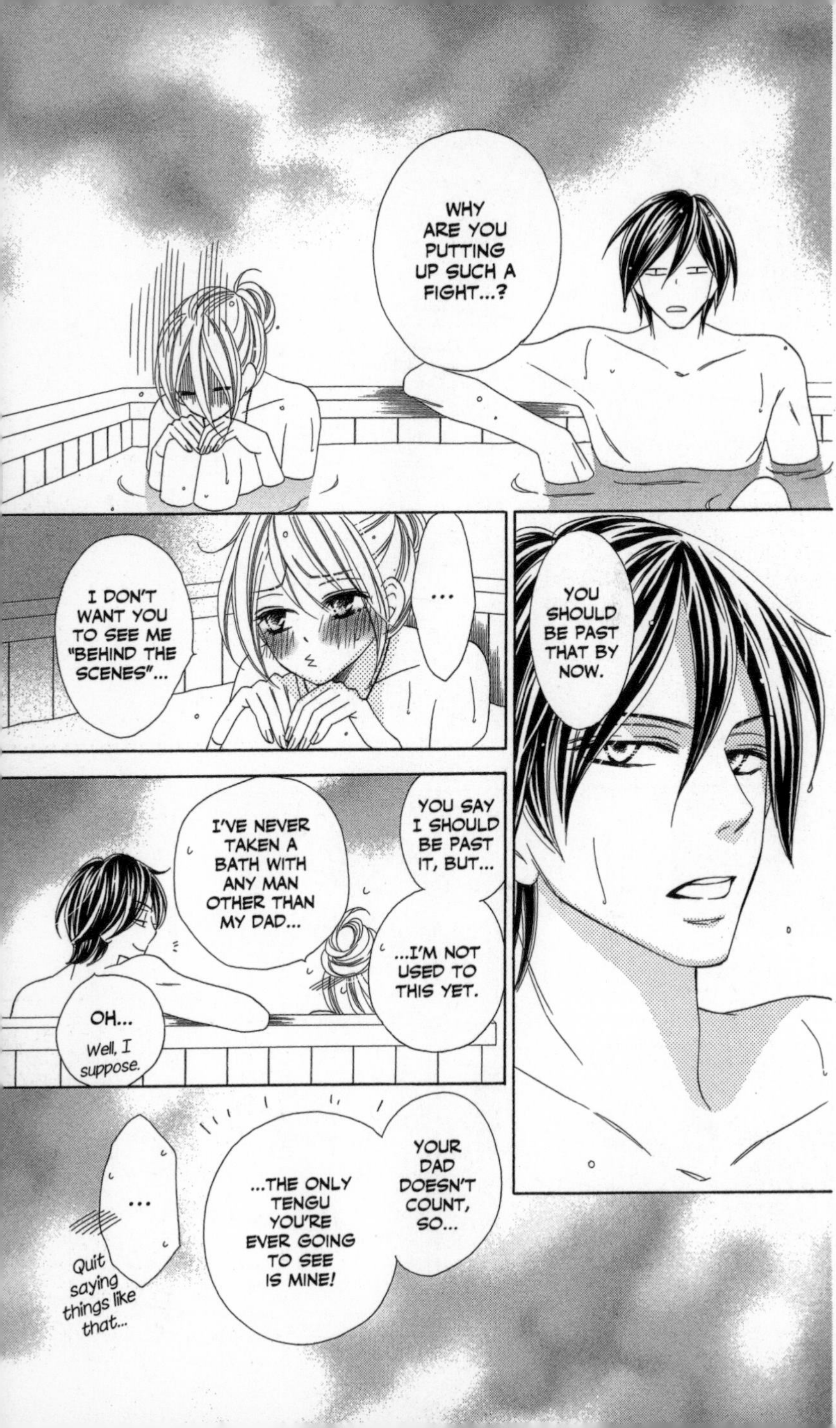
WHY ARE YOU PUTTING UP SUCH A FIGHT...?
YOU SHOULD BE PAST THAT BY NOW.
...
I DON'T WANT YOU TO SEE ME "BEHIND THE SCENES"...
YOU SAY I SHOULD BE PAST IT, BUT...
...I'M NOT USED TO THIS YET.
I'VE NEVER TAKEN A BATH WITH ANY MAN OTHER THAN MY DAD...
OH...
Well, I suppose.
YOUR DAD DOESN'T COUNT, SO...
...THE ONLY TENGU YOU'RE EVER GOING TO SEE IS MINE!
...
Quit saying things like that...

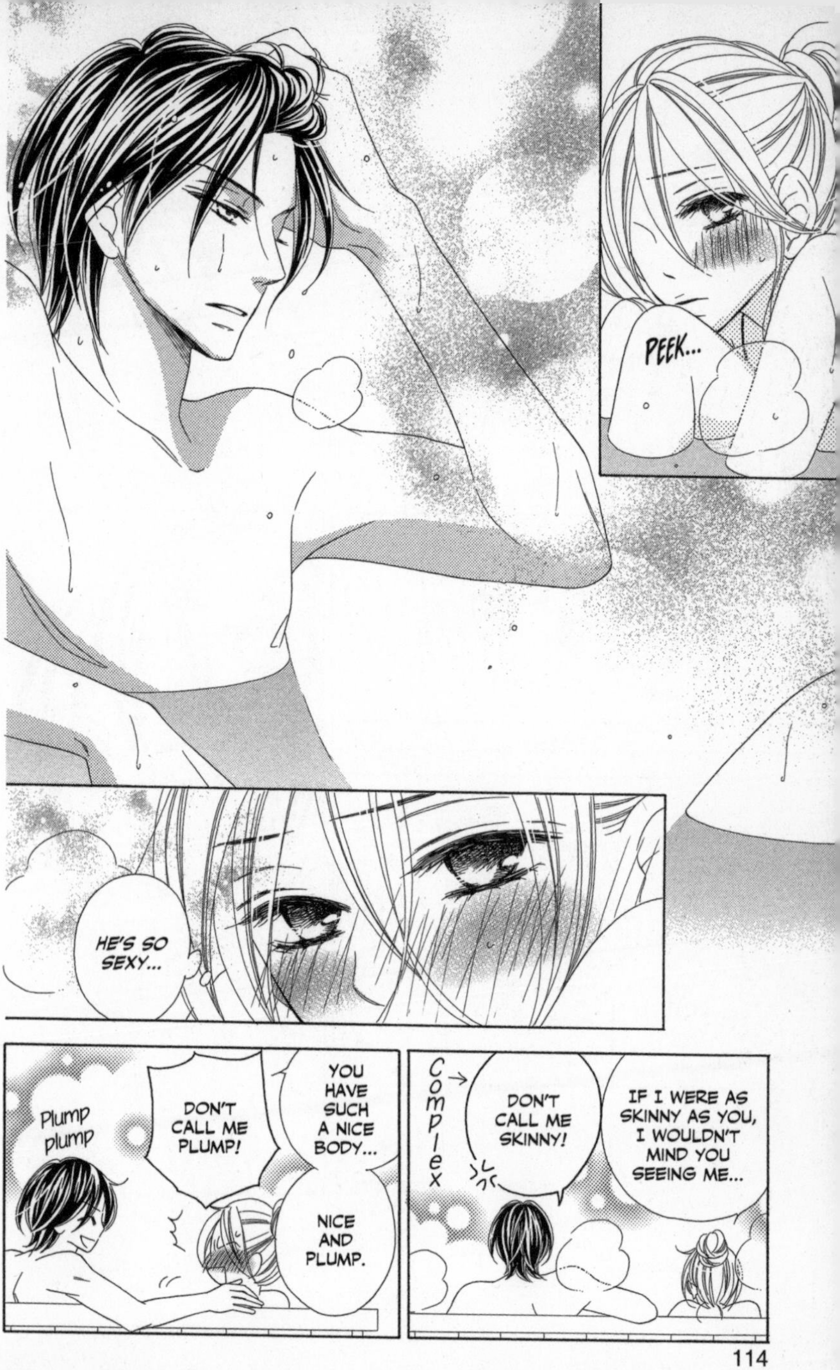
PEEK...
HE'S SO SEXY...
IF I WERE AS SKINNY AS YOU, I WOULDN'T MIND YOU SEEING ME...
DON'T CALL ME SKINNY!
Complex
YOU HAVE SUCH A NICE BODY...
NICE AND PLUMP.
DON'T CALL ME PLUMP!
Plump plump

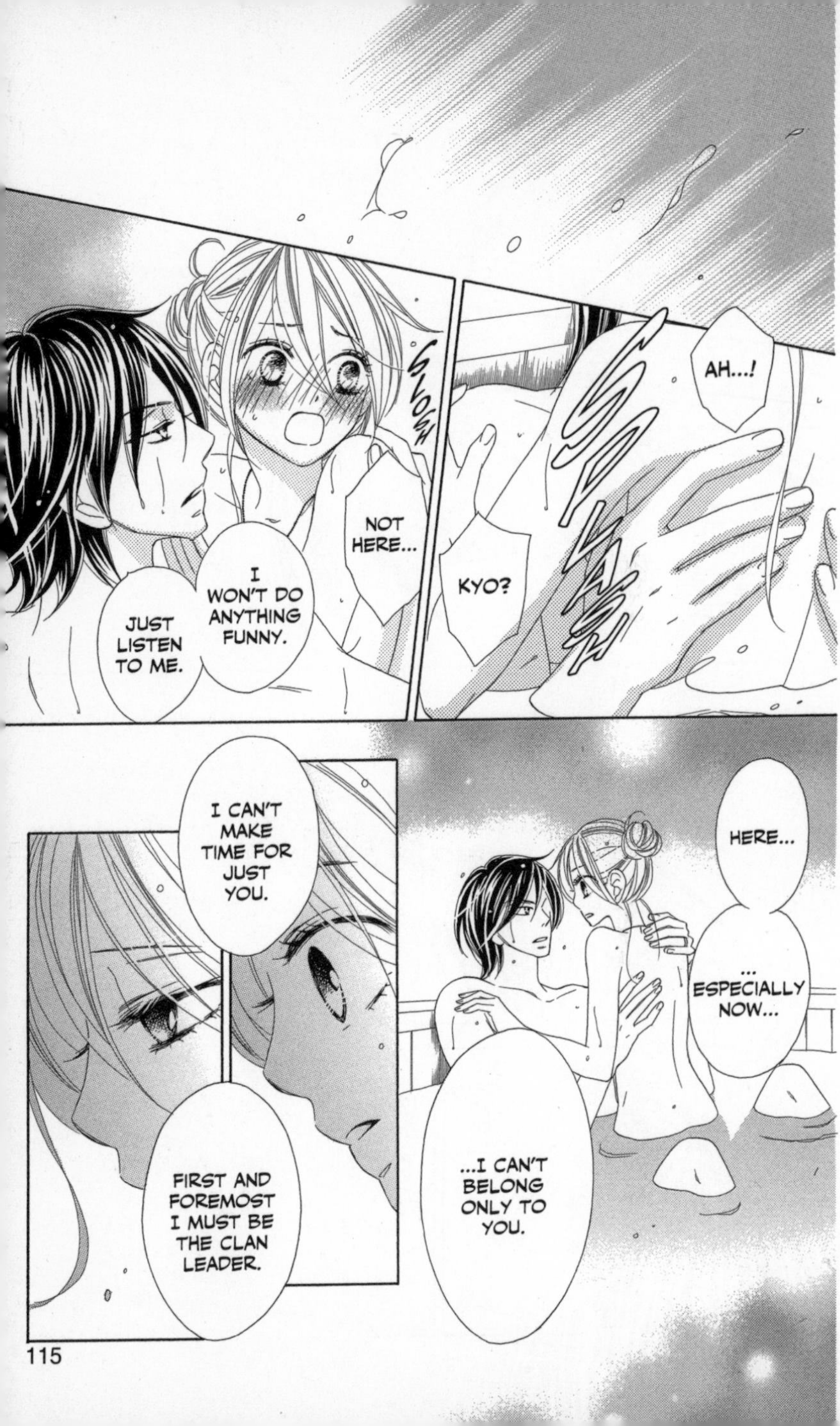
AH...!
KYO?
NOT HERE...
I WON'T DO ANYTHING FUNNY.
JUST LISTEN TO ME.
HERE...
...ESPECIALLY NOW...
...I CAN'T BELONG ONLY TO YOU.
I CAN'T MAKE TIME FOR JUST YOU.
FIRST AND FOREMOST I MUST BE THE CLAN LEADER.

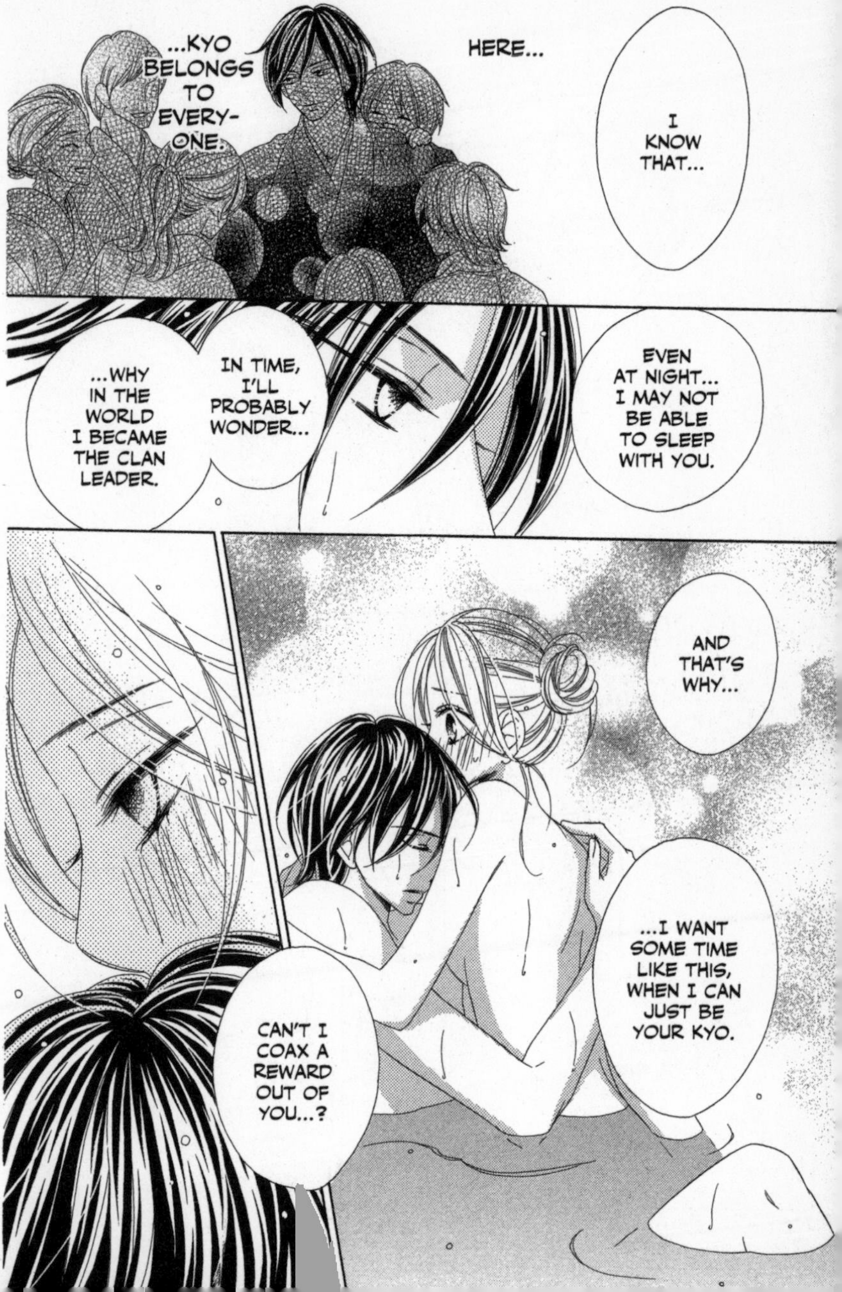
I KNOW THAT...
HERE...
...KYO BELONGS TO EVERY-ONE.
EVEN AT NIGHT... I MAY NOT BE ABLE TO SLEEP WITH YOU.
IN TIME, I'LL PROBABLY WONDER...
...WHY IN THE WORLD I BECAME THE CLAN LEADER.
AND THAT'S WHY...
...I WANT SOME TIME LIKE THIS, WHEN I CAN JUST BE YOUR KYO.
CAN'T I COAX A REWARD OUT OF YOU...?

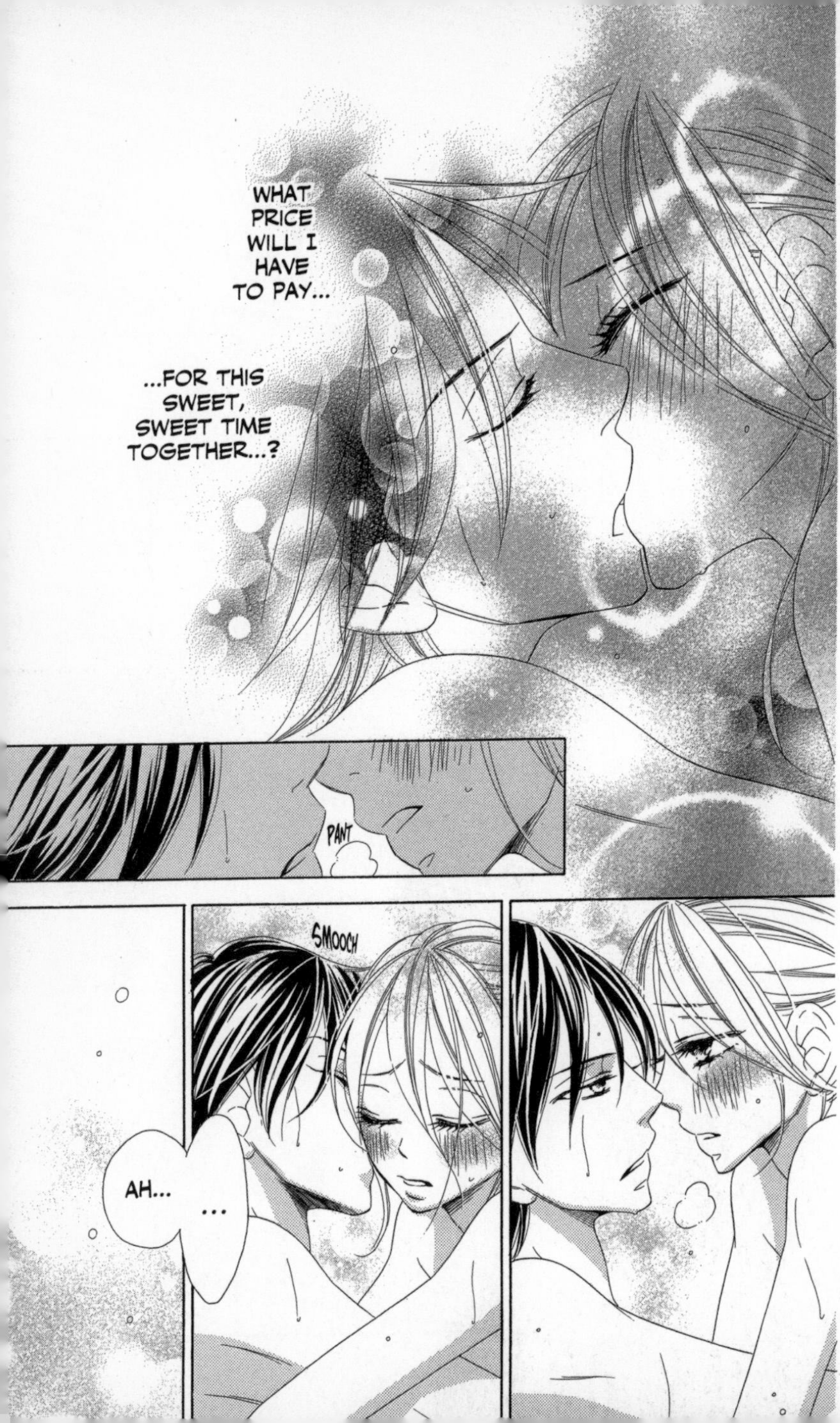
WHAT PRICE WILL I HAVE TO PAY...
...FOR THIS SWEET, SWEET TIME TOGETHER...?
PANT
SMOOCH
...
AH...

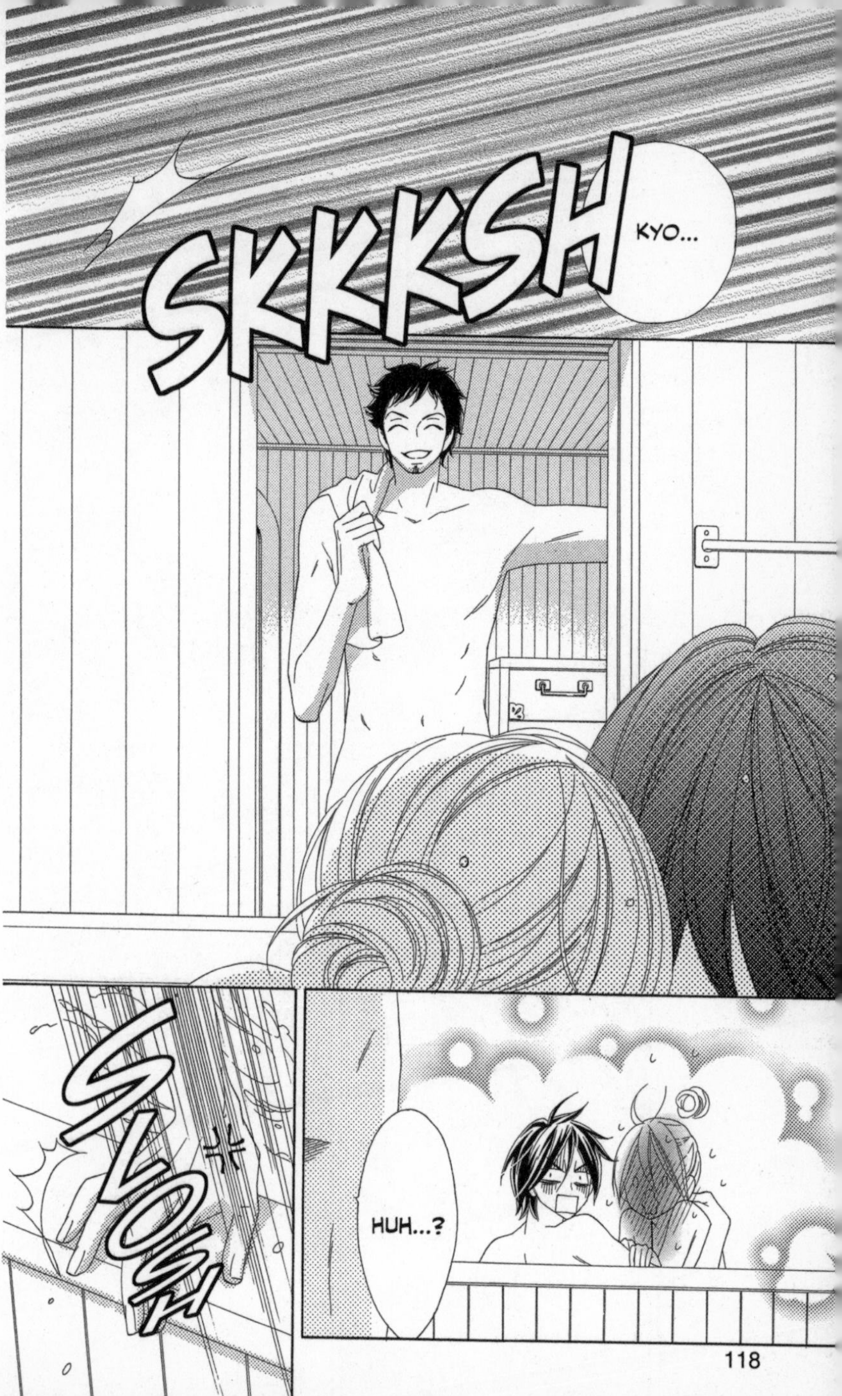
KYO...
SKKKSH
HUH...?
SLOSH

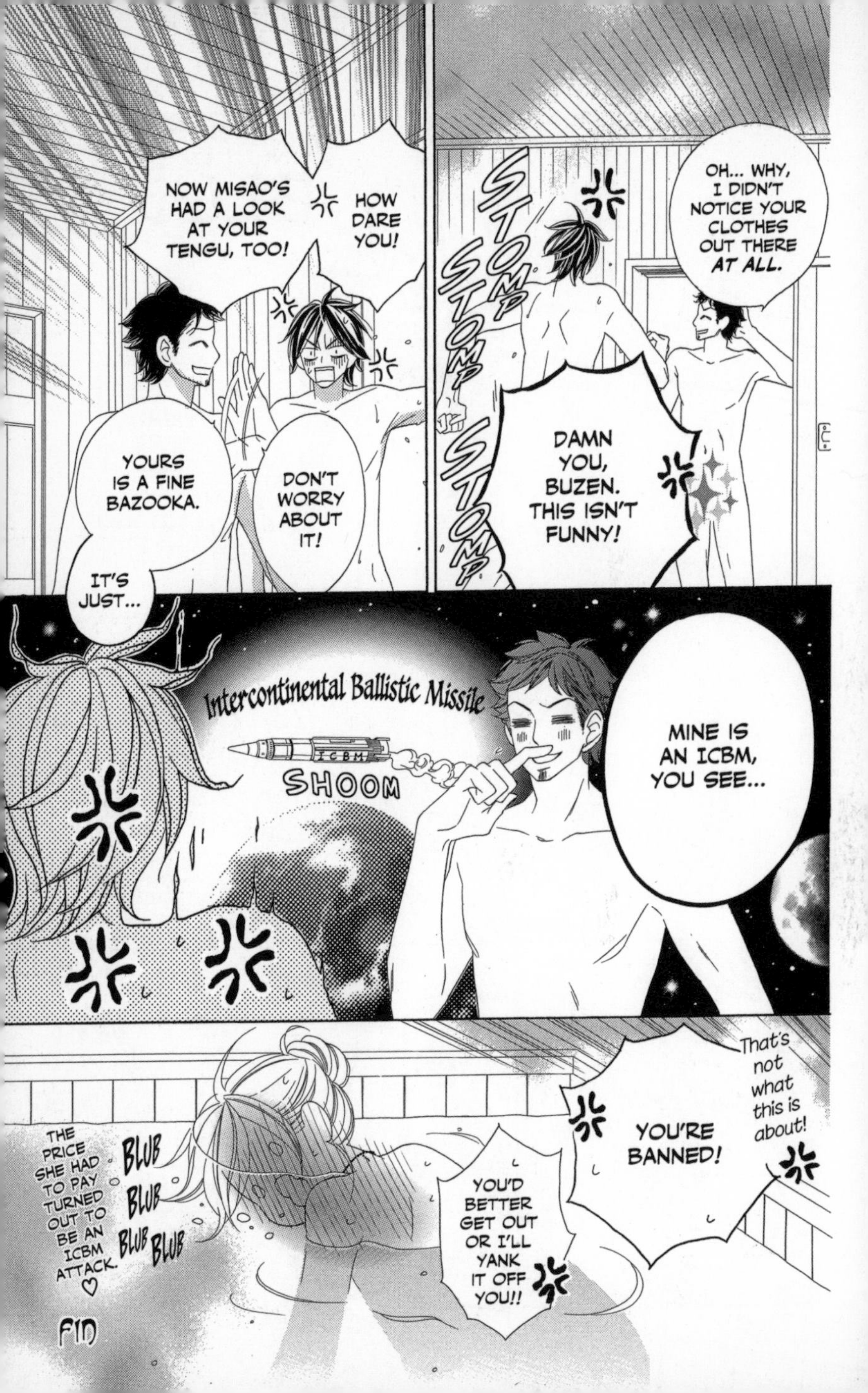
OH... WHY, I DIDN'T NOTICE YOUR CLOTHES OUT THERE AT ALL.
STOMP
STOMP
STOMP
DAMN YOU, BUZEN. THIS ISN'T FUNNY!
NOW MISAO'S HAD A LOOK AT YOUR TENGU, TOO!
HOW DARE YOU!
DON'T WORRY ABOUT IT!
YOURS IS A FINE BAZOOKA.
IT'S JUST...
MINE IS AN ICBM, YOU SEE...
Intercontinental Ballistic Missile
ICBM
SHOOM
That's not what this is about!
YOU'RE BANNED!
YOU'D BETTER GET OUT OR I'LL YANK IT OFF YOU!!
BLUB
BLUB
BLUB BLUB
THE PRICE SHE HAD TO PAY TURNED OUT TO BE AN ICBM ATTACK. ♡
FIN

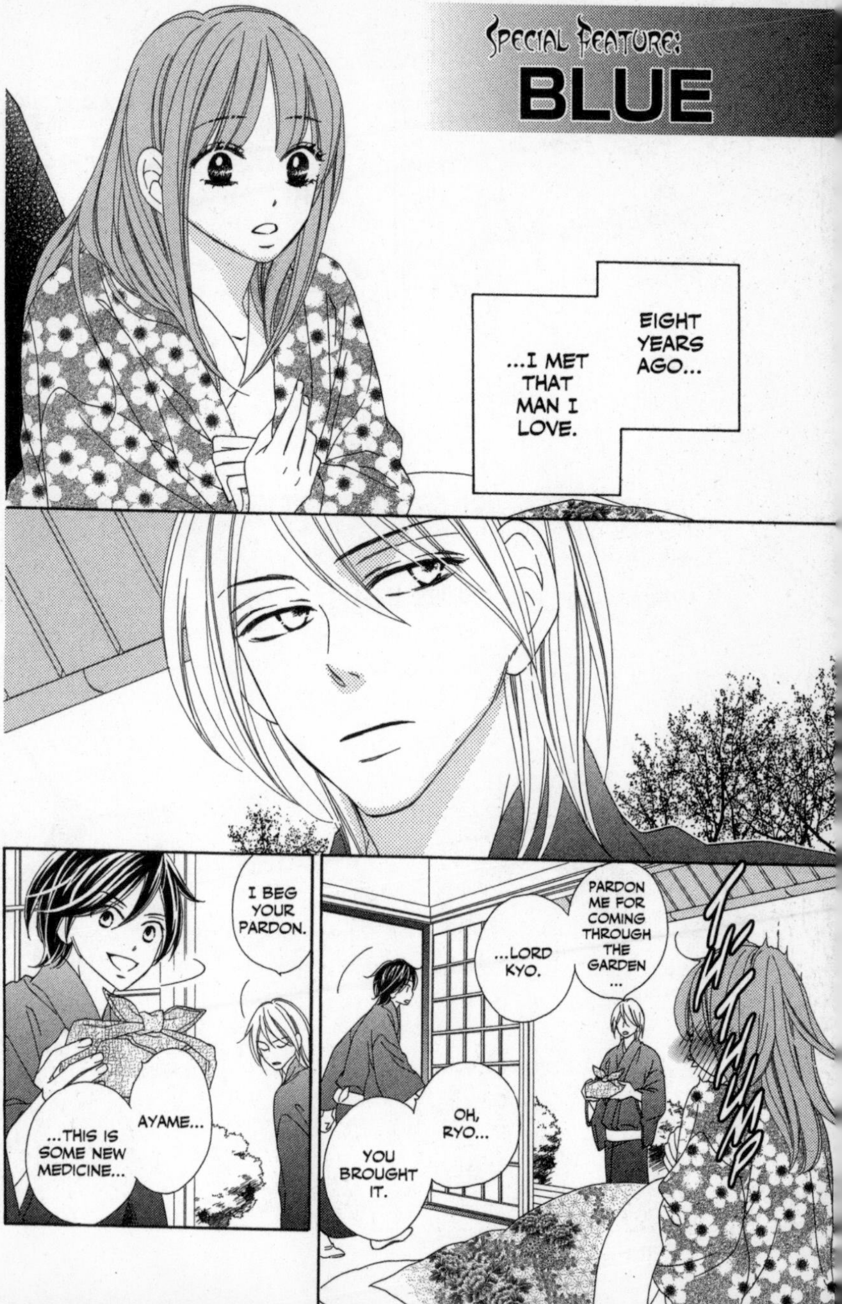
Special Feature:
BLUE
EIGHT YEARS AGO...
...I MET THAT MAN I LOVE.
PARDON ME FOR COMING THROUGH THE GARDEN ...
...LORD KYO.
OH, RYO...
YOU BROUGHT IT.
I BEG YOUR PARDON.
AYAME...
...THIS IS SOME NEW MEDICINE...

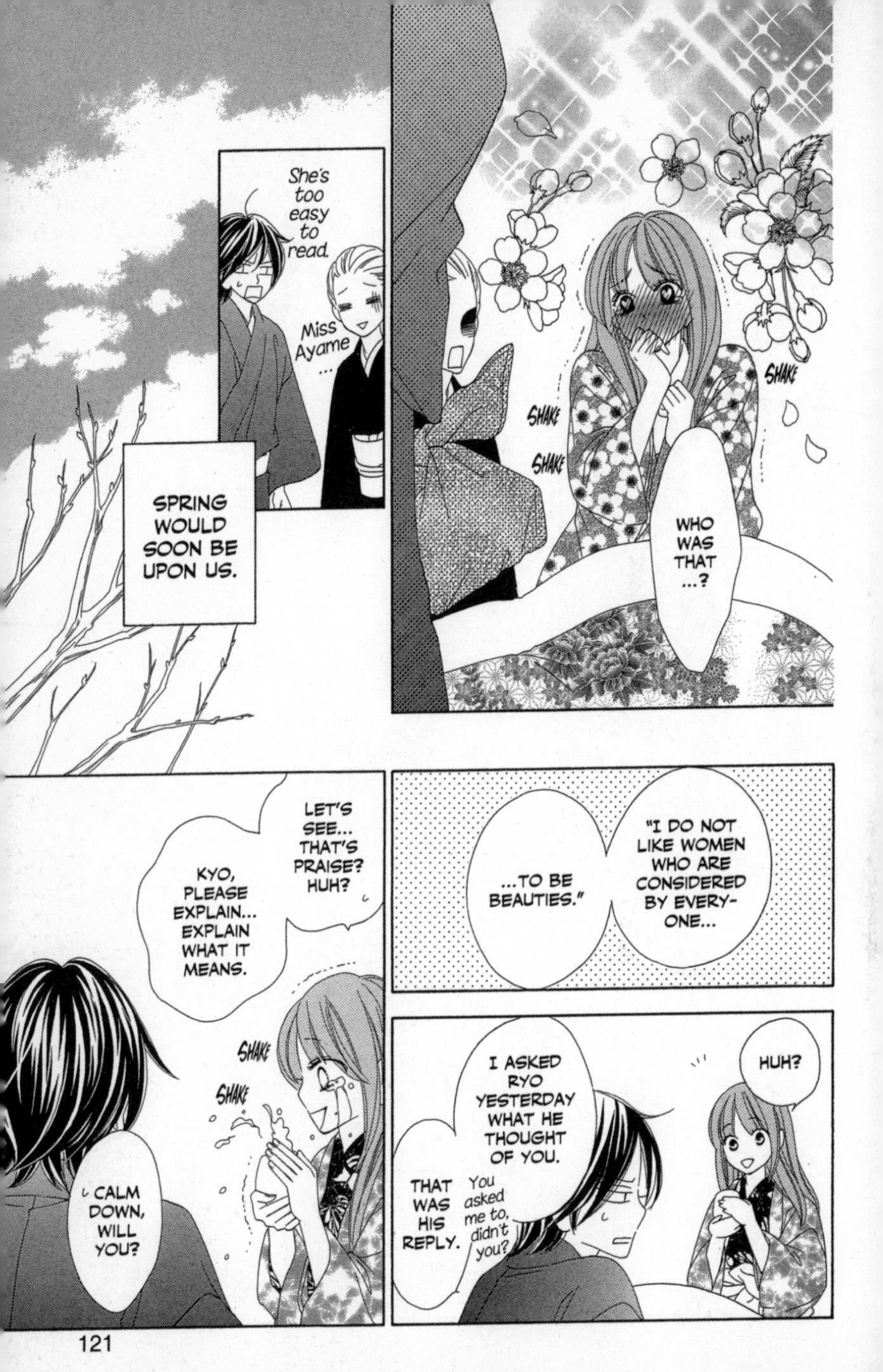
SHAKE
SHAKE
SHAKE
WHO WAS THAT ...?
She's too easy to read.
Miss Ayame ...
SPRING WOULD SOON BE UPON US.
"I DO NOT LIKE WOMEN WHO ARE CONSIDERED BY EVERY-ONE...
...TO BE BEAUTIES."
HUH?
I ASKED RYO YESTERDAY WHAT HE THOUGHT OF YOU.
THAT WAS HIS REPLY.
You asked me to, didn't you?
LET'S SEE... THAT'S PRAISE? HUH?
KYO, PLEASE EXPLAIN... EXPLAIN WHAT IT MEANS.
SHAKE
SHAKE
CALM DOWN, WILL YOU?

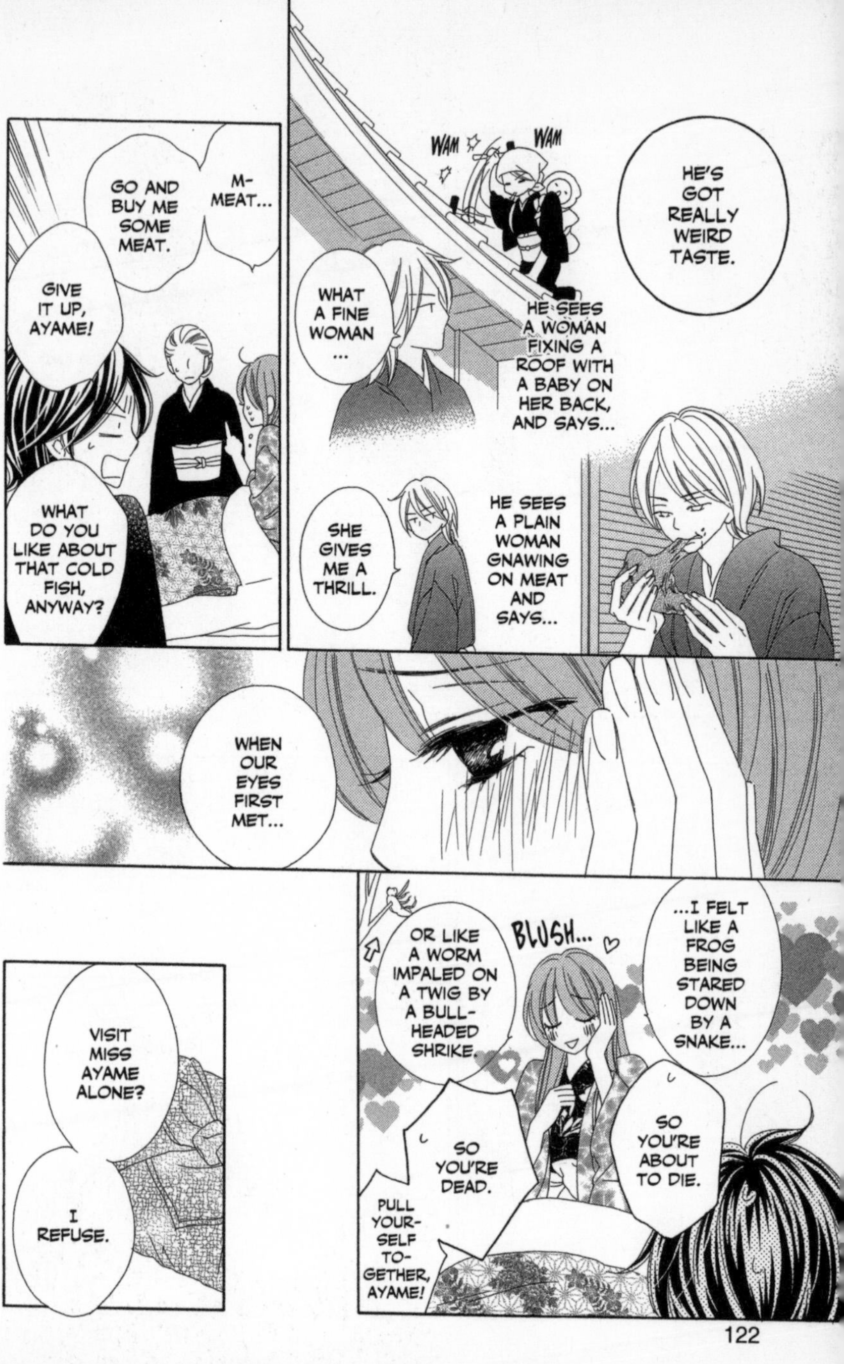
HE'S GOT REALLY WEIRD TASTE.
WAM
WAM
HE SEES A WOMAN FIXING A ROOF WITH A BABY ON HER BACK, AND SAYS...
WHAT A FINE WOMAN ...
HE SEES A PLAIN WOMAN GNAWING ON MEAT AND SAYS...
SHE GIVES ME A THRILL.
M-MEAT...
GO AND BUY ME SOME MEAT.
GIVE IT UP, AYAME!
WHAT DO YOU LIKE ABOUT THAT COLD FISH, ANYWAY?
WHEN OUR EYES FIRST MET...
...I FELT LIKE A FROG BEING STARED DOWN BY A SNAKE...
BLUSH...
OR LIKE A WORM IMPALED ON A TWIG BY A BULL-HEADED SHRIKE.
SO YOU'RE ABOUT TO DIE.
SO YOU'RE DEAD.
PULL YOURSELF TOGETHER, AYAME!
VISIT MISS AYAME ALONE?
I REFUSE.

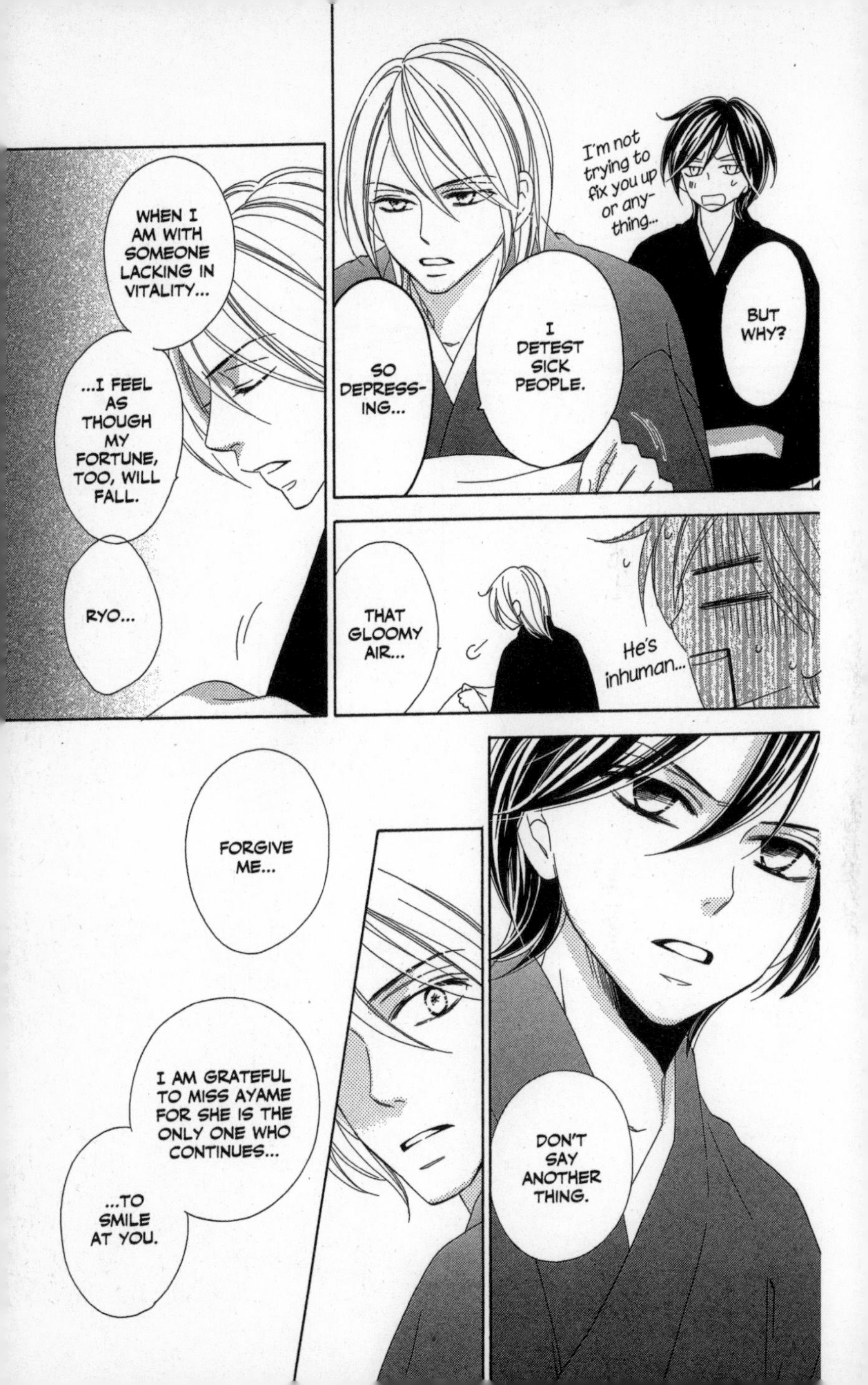
I'm not trying to fix you up or anything...
BUT WHY?
I DETEST SICK PEOPLE.
SO DEPRESSING...
He's inhuman...
THAT GLOOMY AIR...
WHEN I AM WITH SOMEONE LACKING IN VITALITY...
...I FEEL AS THOUGH MY FORTUNE, TOO, WILL FALL.
RYO...
FORGIVE ME...
I AM GRATEFUL TO MISS AYAME FOR SHE IS THE ONLY ONE WHO CONTINUES...
...TO SMILE AT YOU.
DON'T SAY ANOTHER THING.

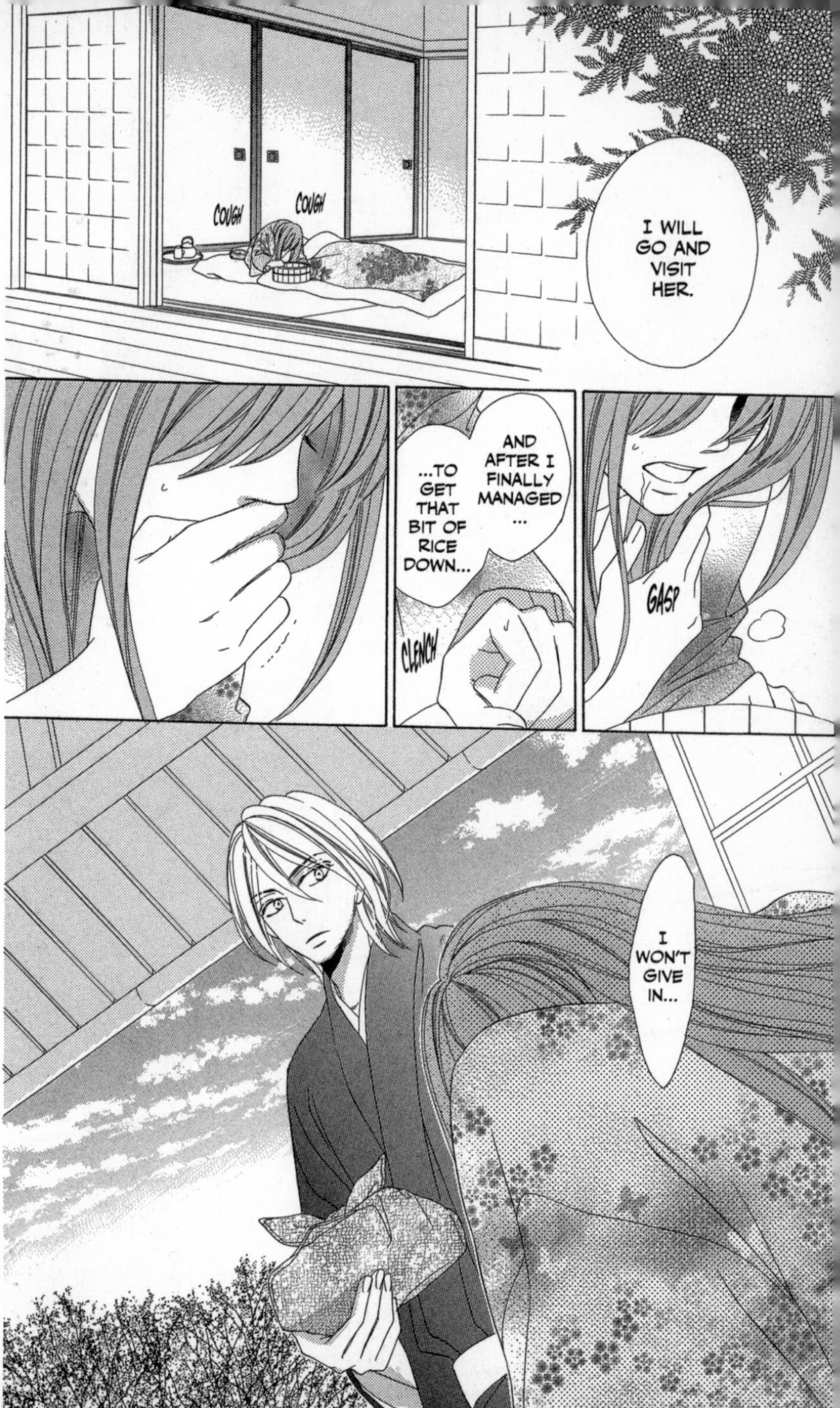
I WILL GO AND VISIT HER.
COUGH
COUGH
GASP
AND AFTER I FINALLY MANAGED ...
...TO GET THAT BIT OF RICE DOWN...
CLENCH
I WON'T GIVE IN...

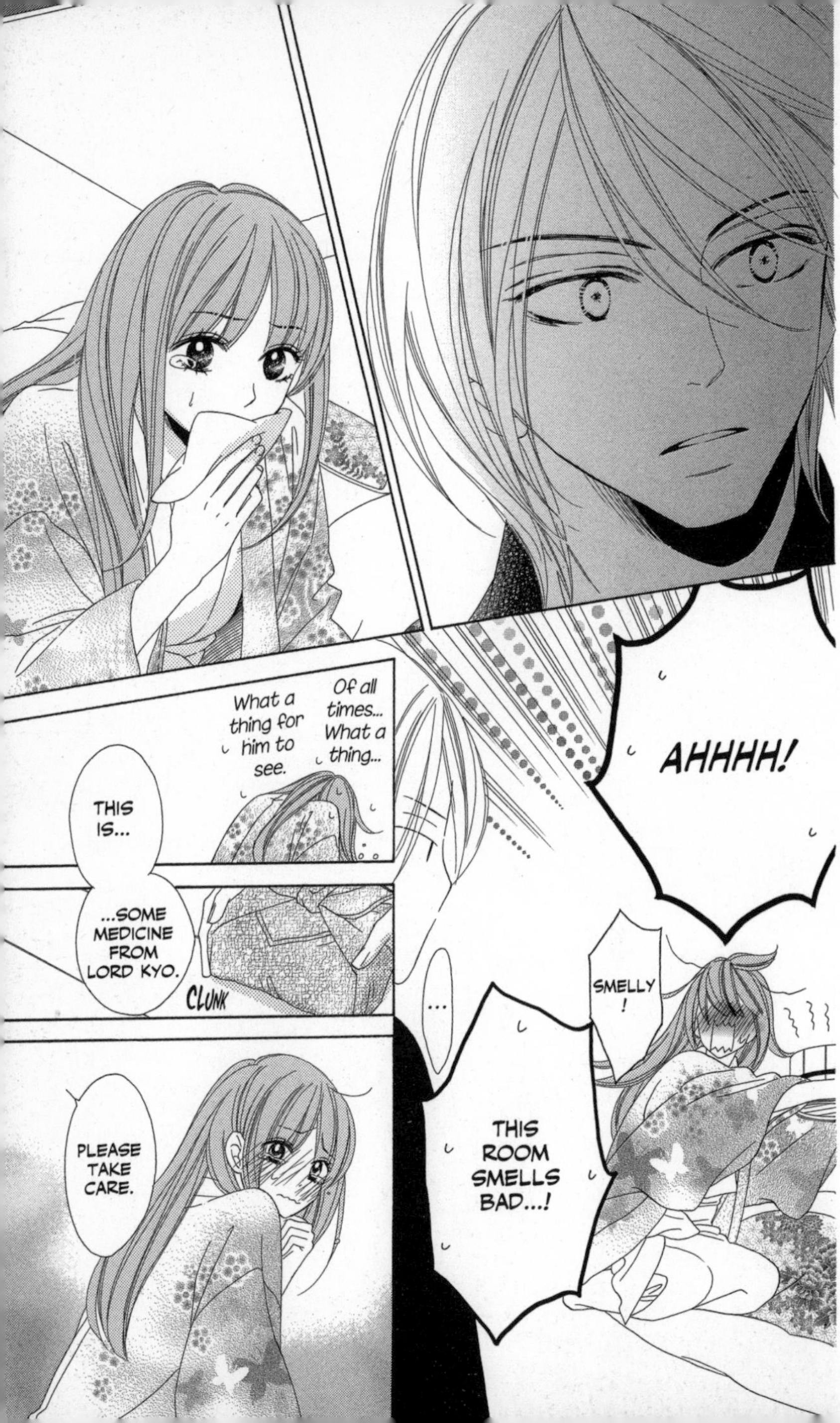
AHHHH!
SMELLY!
...
THIS ROOM SMELLS BAD...!
Of all times... What a thing...
What a thing for him to see.
THIS IS...
...SOME MEDICINE FROM LORD KYO.
CLUNK
PLEASE TAKE CARE.

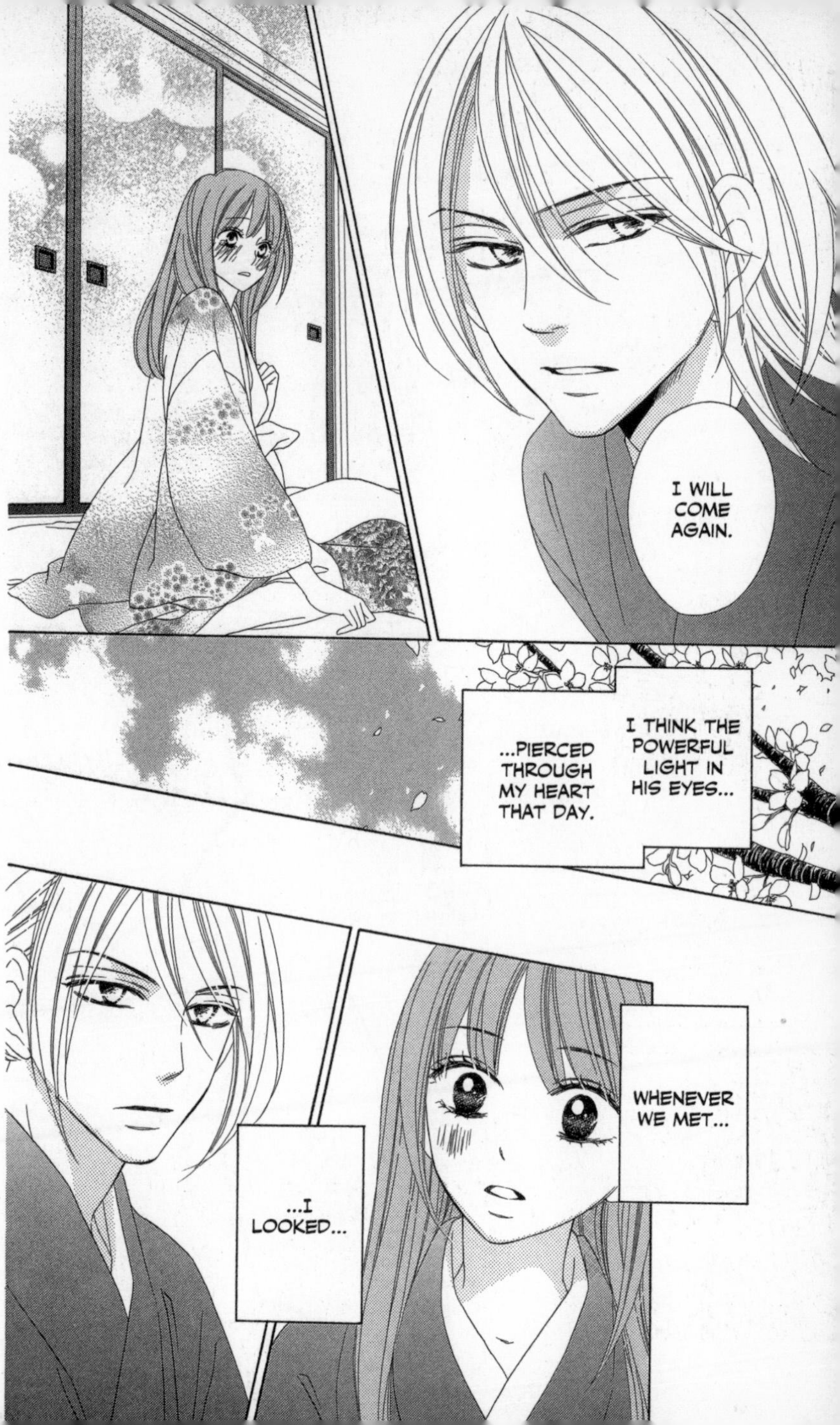
I WILL COME AGAIN.
I THINK THE POWERFUL LIGHT IN HIS EYES...
...PIERCED THROUGH MY HEART THAT DAY.
WHENEVER WE MET...
...I LOOKED...

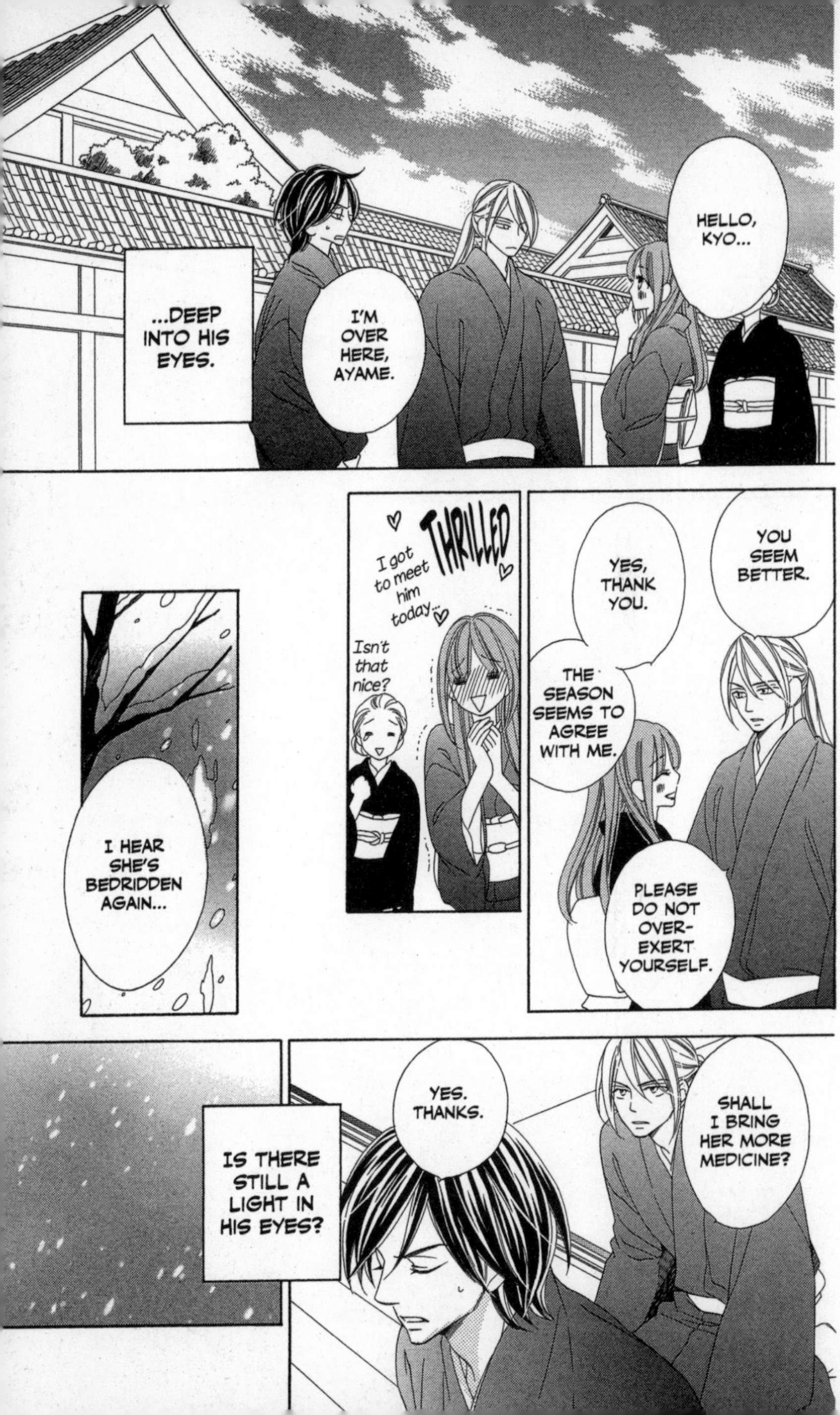
HELLO, KYO...
I'M OVER HERE, AYAME.
...DEEP INTO HIS EYES.
YOU SEEM BETTER.
YES, THANK YOU.
THE SEASON SEEMS TO AGREE WITH ME.
PLEASE DO NOT OVER-EXERT YOURSELF.
THRILLED
I got to meet him today...
Isn't that nice?
I HEAR SHE'S BEDRIDDEN AGAIN...
SHALL I BRING HER MORE MEDICINE?
YES. THANKS.
IS THERE STILL A LIGHT IN HIS EYES?

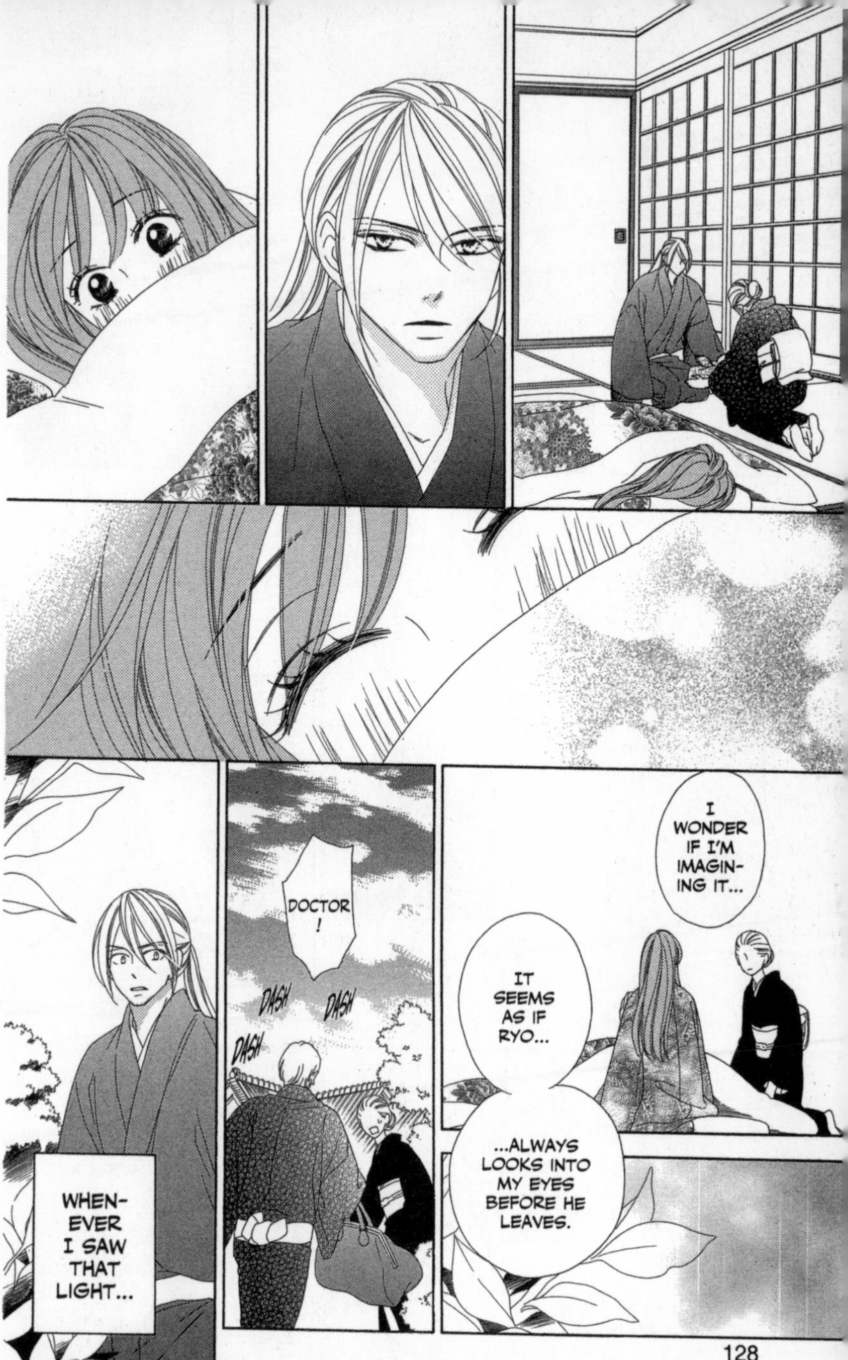
I WONDER IF I'M IMAGINING IT...
IT SEEMS AS IF RYO...
...ALWAYS LOOKS INTO MY EYES BEFORE HE LEAVES.
DOCTOR!
DASH
DASH
DASH
WHENEVER I SAW THAT LIGHT...

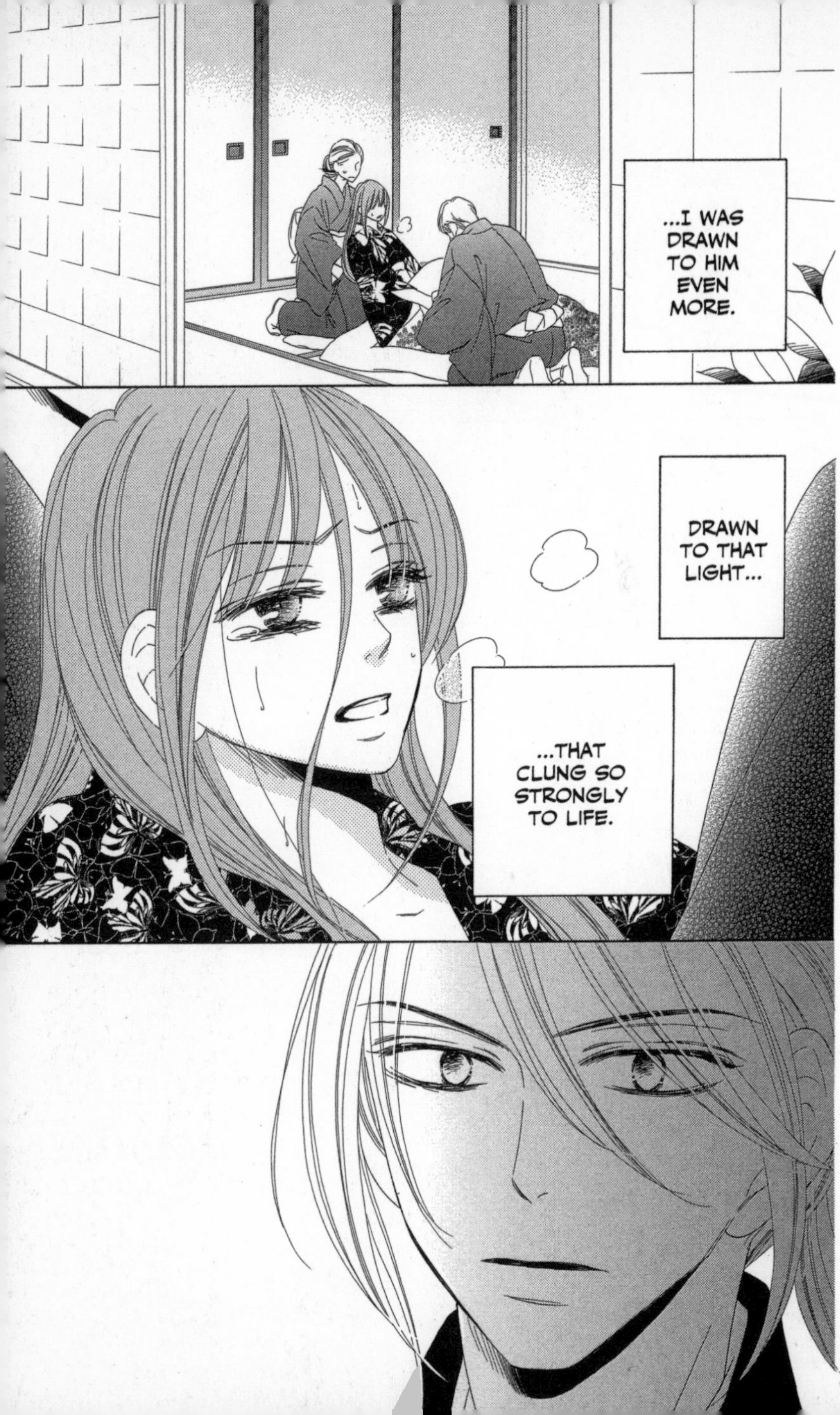
...I WAS DRAWN TO HIM EVEN MORE.
DRAWN TO THAT LIGHT...
...THAT CLUNG SO STRONGLY TO LIFE.

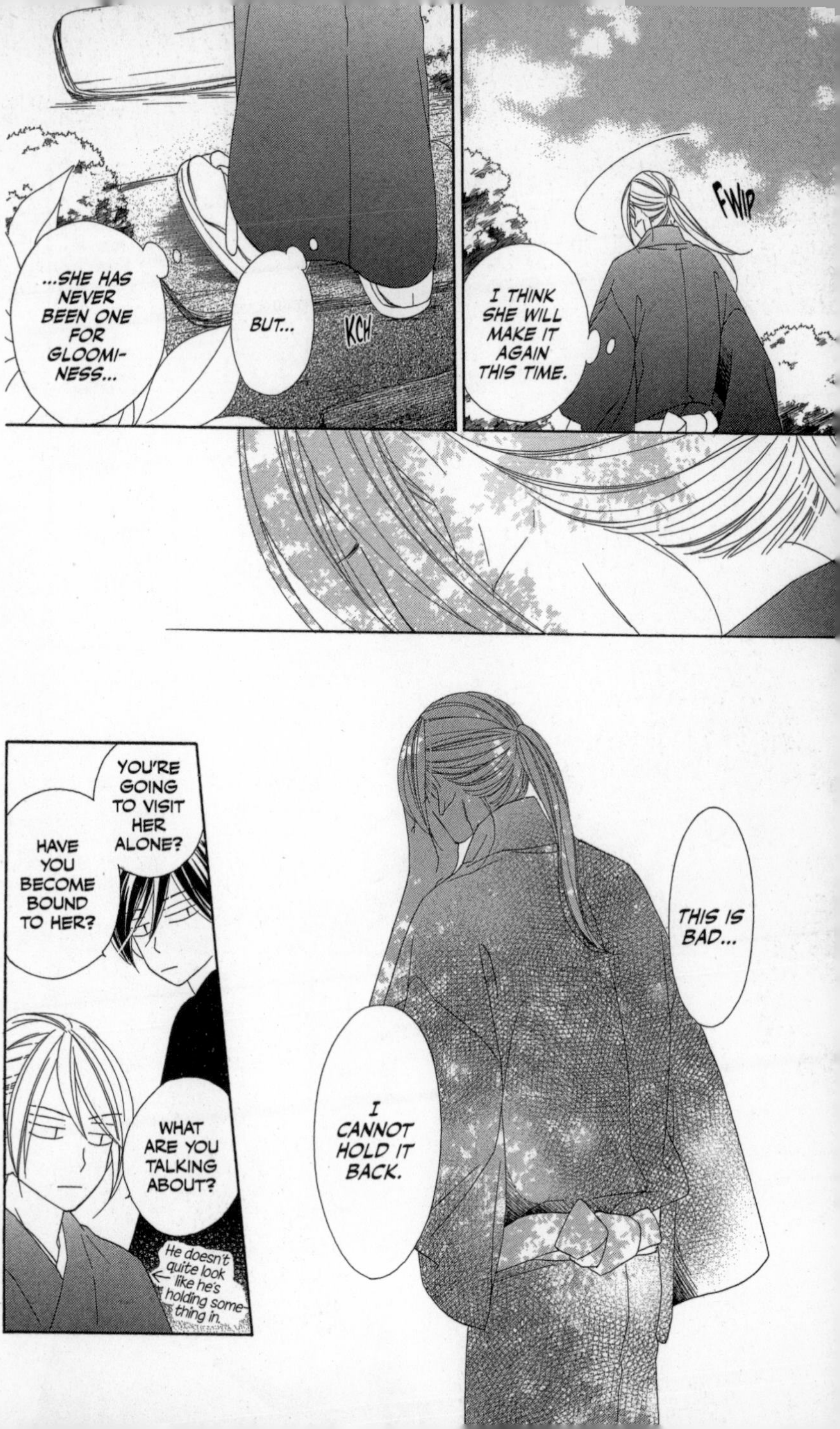
FWIP
I THINK SHE WILL MAKE IT AGAIN THIS TIME.
BUT...
KCH
...SHE HAS NEVER BEEN ONE FOR GLOOMINESS...
THIS IS BAD...
I CANNOT HOLD IT BACK.
YOU'RE GOING TO VISIT HER ALONE?
HAVE YOU BECOME BOUND TO HER?
WHAT ARE YOU TALKING ABOUT?
He doesn't quite look like he's holding something in.

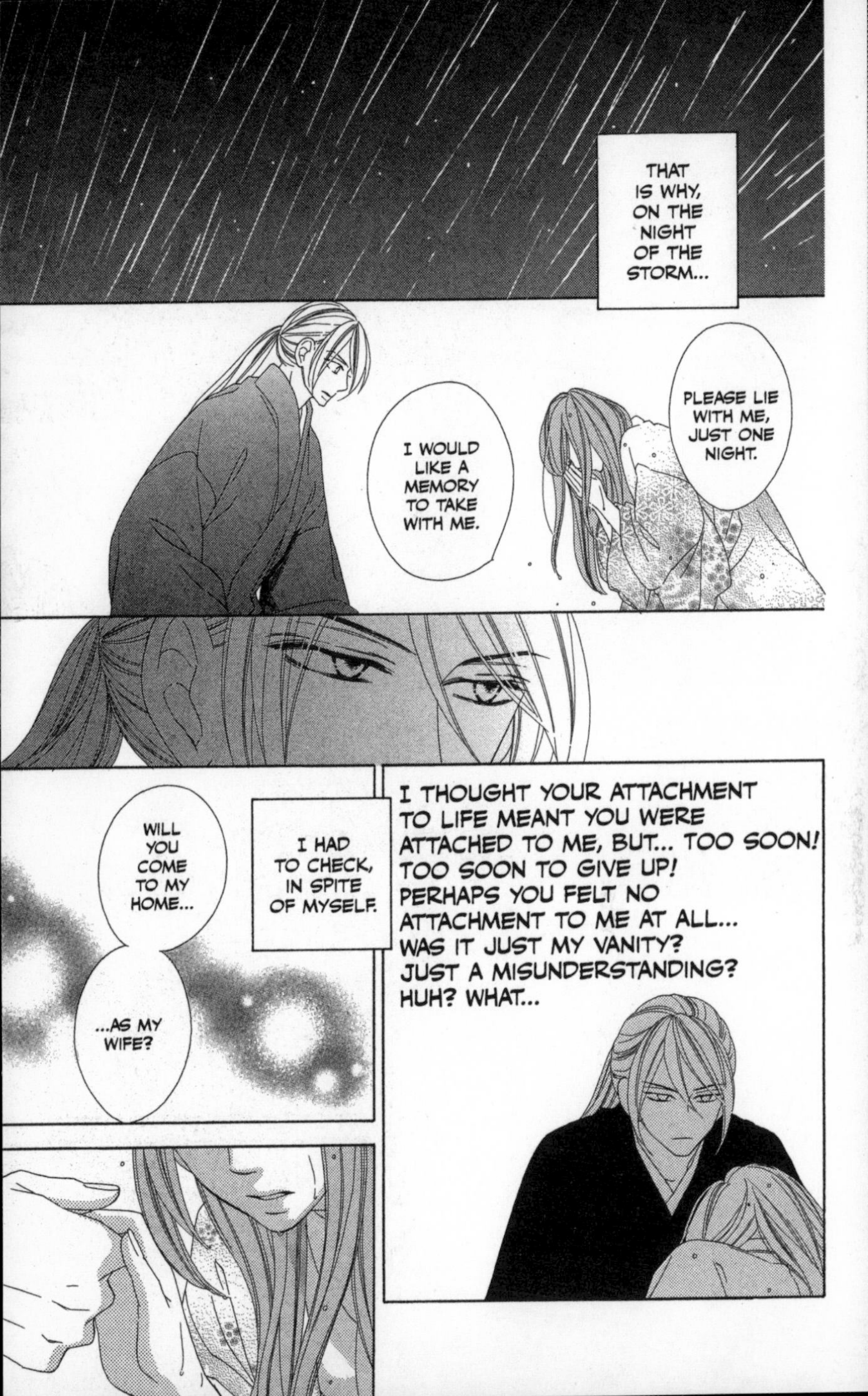
THAT IS WHY, ON THE NIGHT OF THE STORM...
PLEASE LIE WITH ME, JUST ONE NIGHT.
I WOULD LIKE A MEMORY TO TAKE WITH ME.
I THOUGHT YOUR ATTACHMENT TO LIFE MEANT YOU WERE ATTACHED TO ME, BUT... TOO SOON! TOO SOON TO GIVE UP! PERHAPS YOU FELT NO ATTACHMENT TO ME AT ALL... WAS IT JUST MY VANITY? JUST A MISUNDERSTANDING? HUH? WHAT...
I HAD TO CHECK, IN SPITE OF MYSELF.
WILL YOU COME TO MY HOME...
...AS MY WIFE?

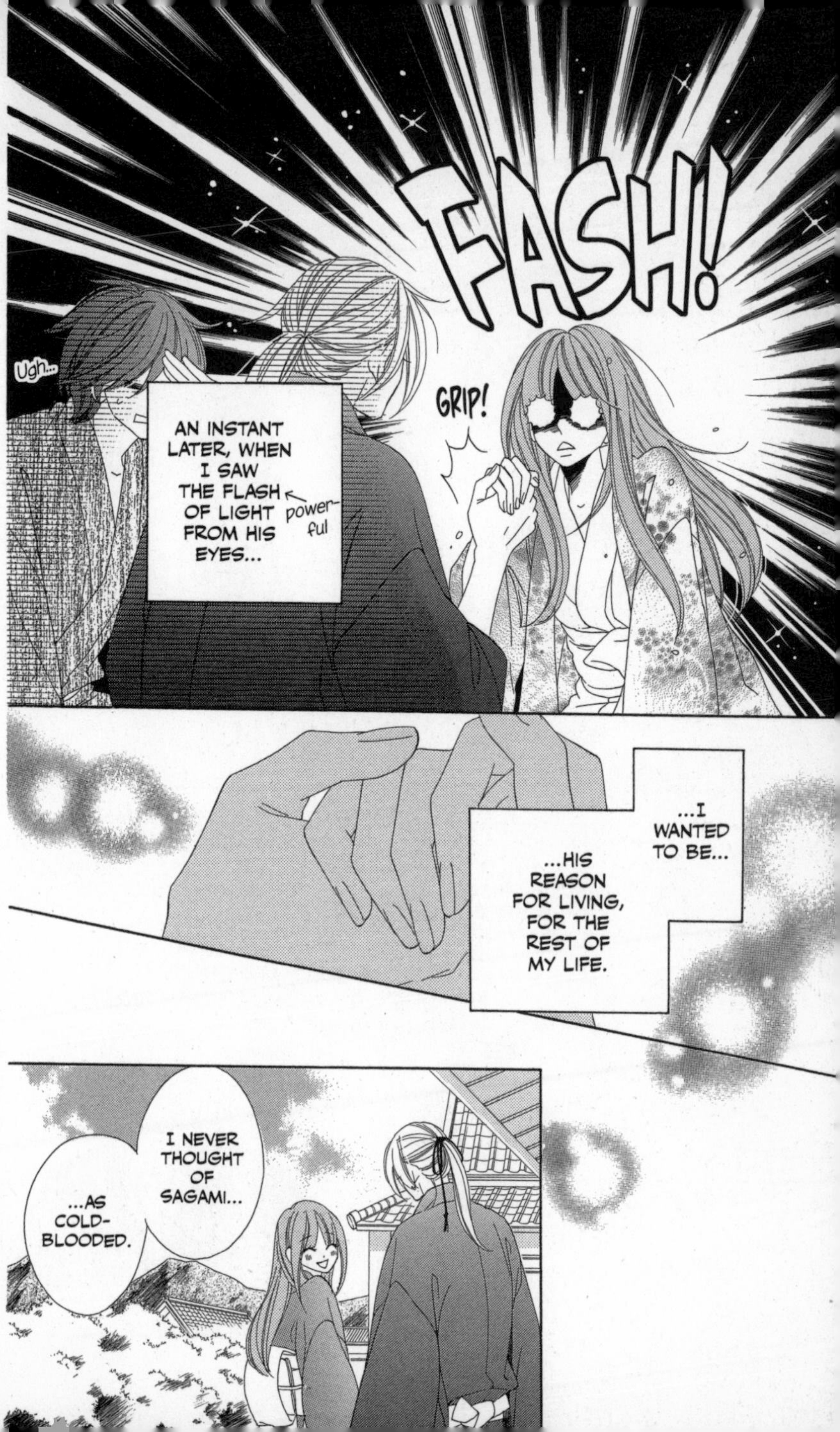
FASH!
GRIP!
AN INSTANT LATER, WHEN I SAW THE FLASH OF LIGHT FROM HIS EYES...
powerful
Ugh...
...I WANTED TO BE...
...HIS REASON FOR LIVING, FOR THE REST OF MY LIFE.
I NEVER THOUGHT OF SAGAMI...
...AS COLD-BLOODED.

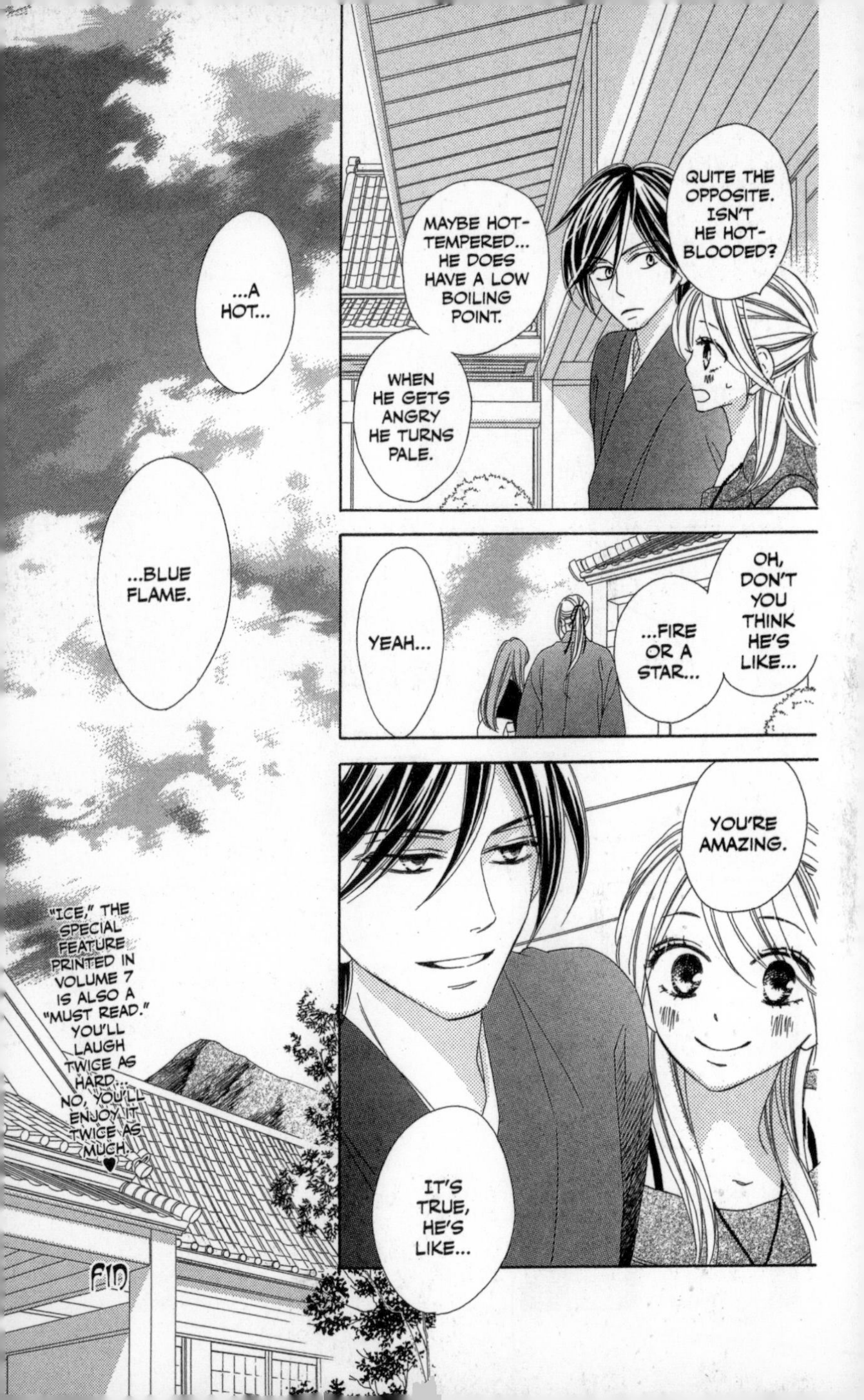
QUITE THE OPPOSITE. ISN'T HE HOT-BLOODED?
MAYBE HOT-TEMPERED... HE DOES HAVE A LOW BOILING POINT.
WHEN HE GETS ANGRY HE TURNS PALE.
OH, DON'T YOU THINK HE'S LIKE...
...FIRE OR A STAR...
YEAH...
YOU'RE AMAZING.
IT'S TRUE, HE'S LIKE...
...A HOT...
...BLUE FLAME.
"ICE," THE SPECIAL FEATURE PRINTED IN VOLUME 7 IS ALSO A "MUST READ." YOU'LL LAUGH TWICE AS HARD... NO, YOU'LL ENJOY IT TWICE AS MUCH.♥
FIN

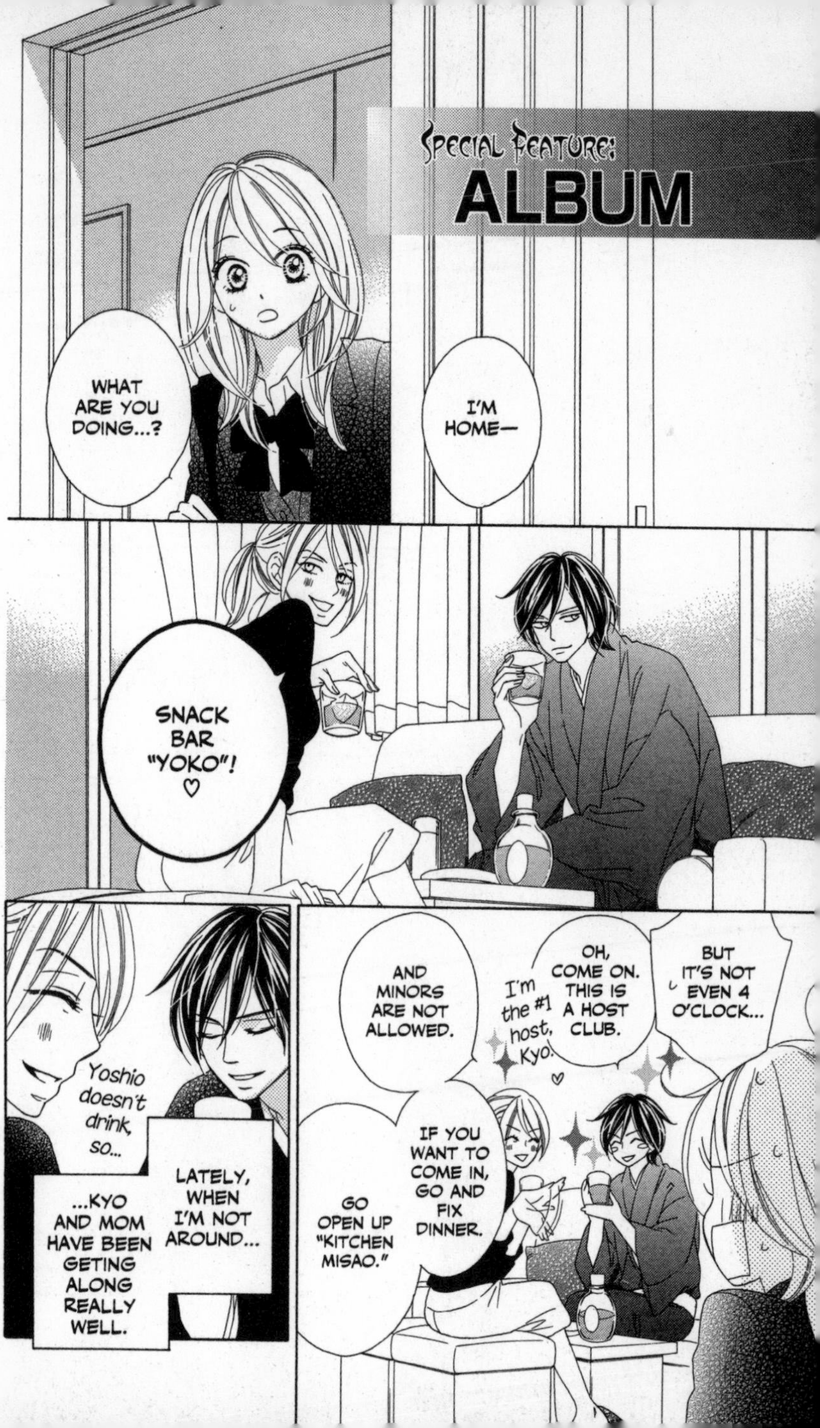
Special Feature:
ALBUM
I'M HOME—
WHAT ARE YOU DOING...?
SNACK BAR "YOKO"! ♡
BUT IT'S NOT EVEN 4 O'CLOCK...
OH, COME ON. THIS IS A HOST CLUB.
I'm the #1 host, Kyo. ♡
AND MINORS ARE NOT ALLOWED.
IF YOU WANT TO COME IN, GO AND FIX DINNER.
GO OPEN UP "KITCHEN MISAO."
LATELY, WHEN I'M NOT AROUND...
...KYO AND MOM HAVE BEEN GETING ALONG REALLY WELL.
Yoshio doesn't drink, so...

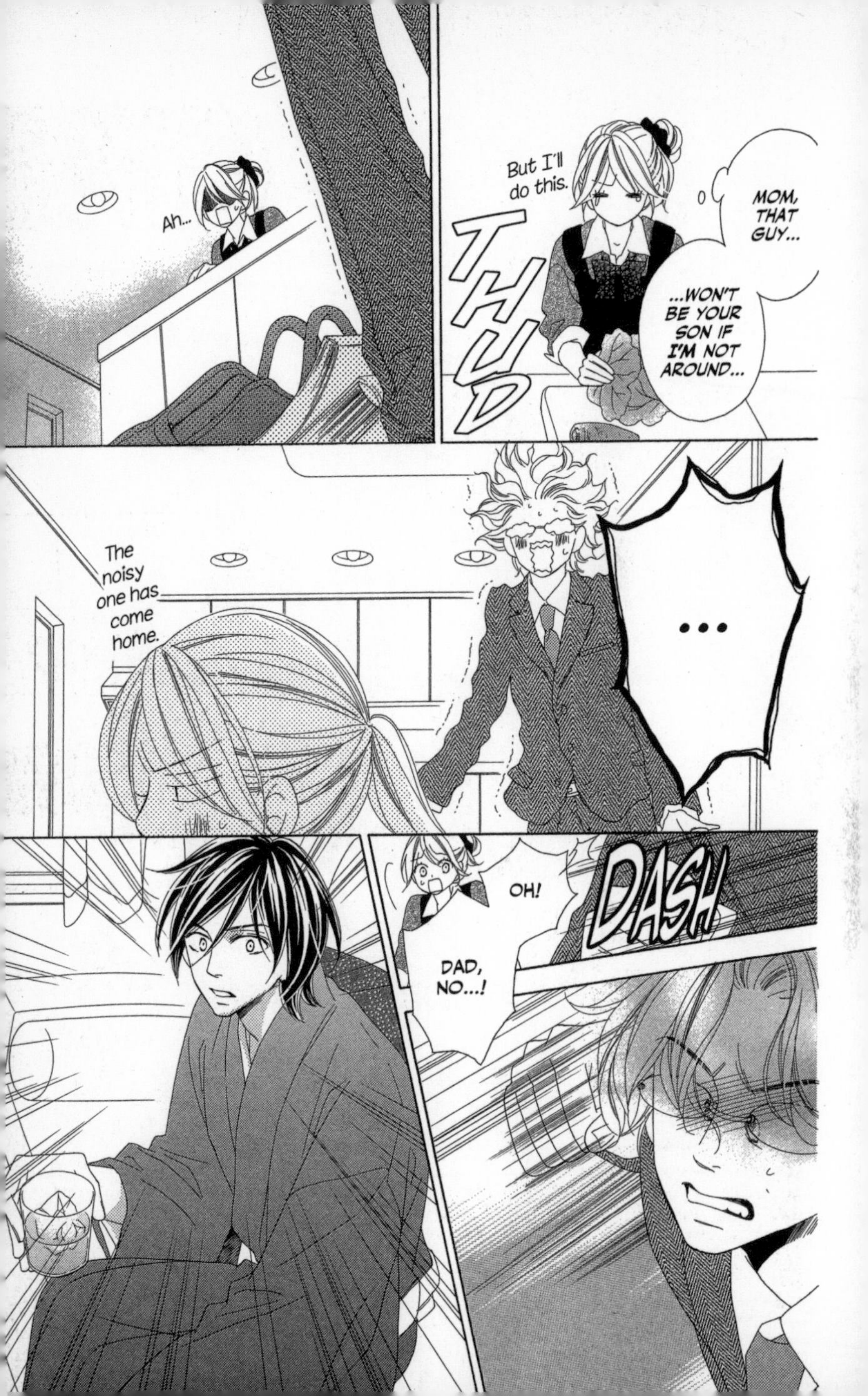
MOM, THAT GUY...
...WON'T BE YOUR SON IF I'M NOT AROUND...
But I'll do this.
THUD
Ah...
...
The noisy one has come home.
DASH
OH!
DAD, NO...!

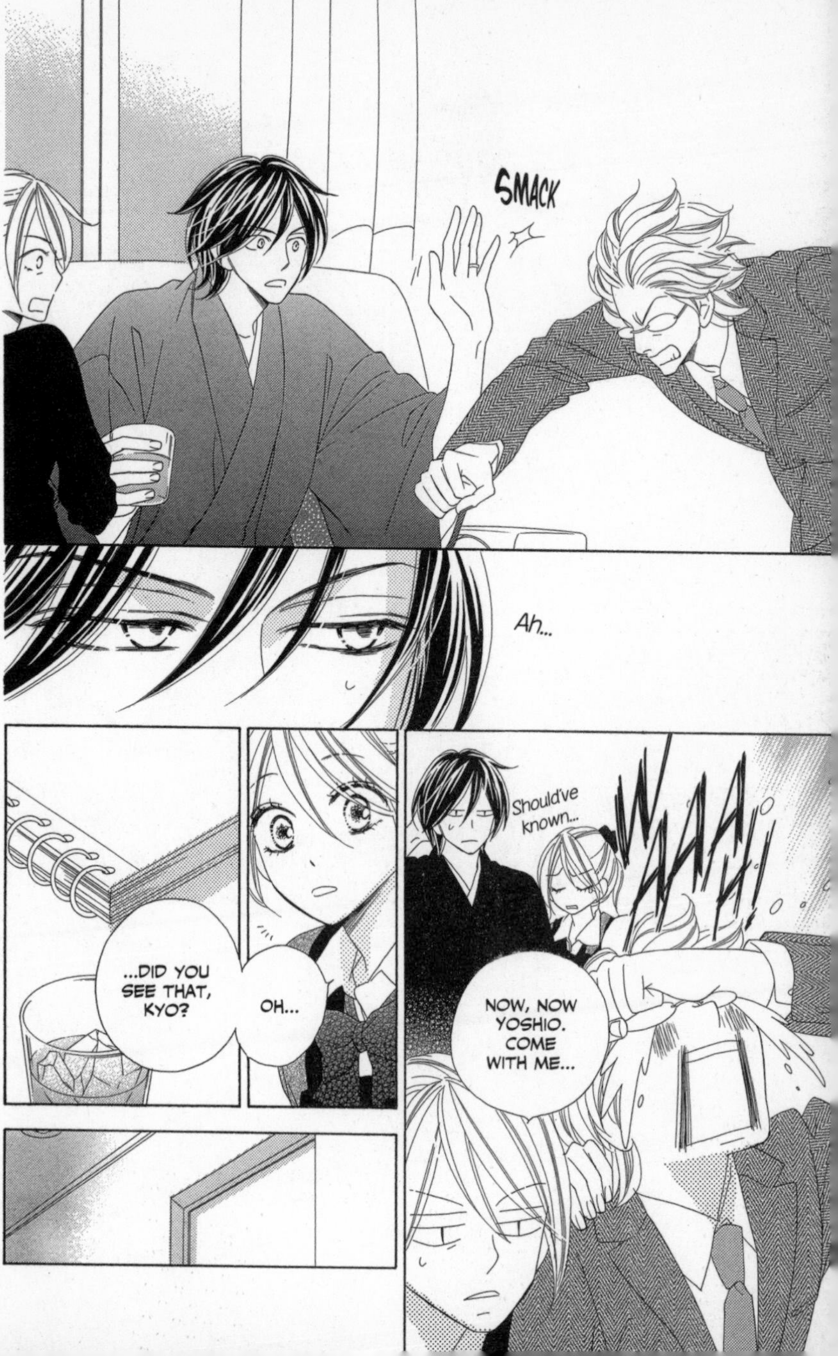
SMACK
Ah...
WAAAH!
Should've known...
NOW, NOW YOSHIO. COME WITH ME...
OH...
...DID YOU SEE THAT, KYO?

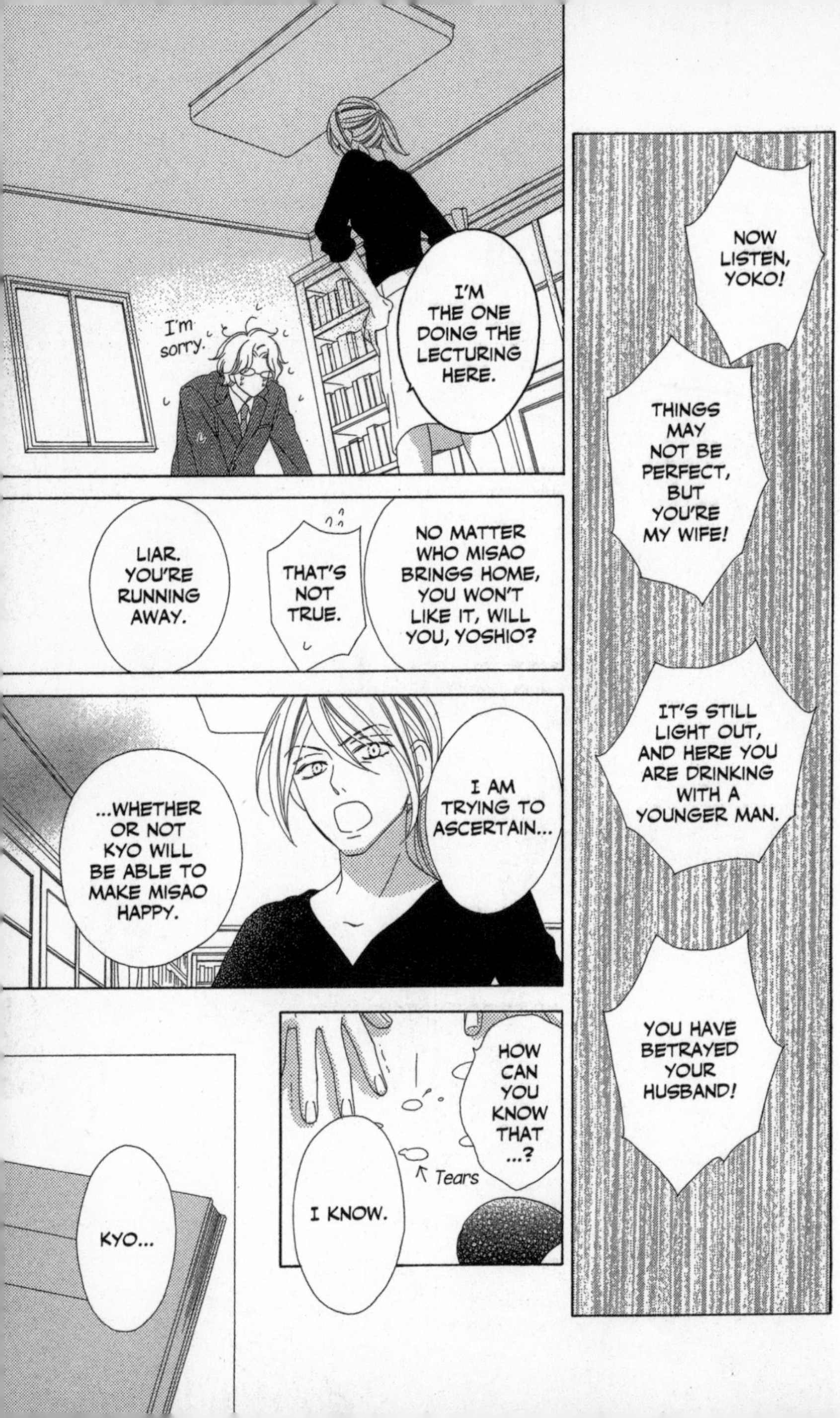
NOW LISTEN, YOKO!
THINGS MAY NOT BE PERFECT, BUT YOU'RE MY WIFE!
IT'S STILL LIGHT OUT, AND HERE YOU ARE DRINKING WITH A YOUNGER MAN.
YOU HAVE BETRAYED YOUR HUSBAND!
I'M THE ONE DOING THE LECTURING HERE.
I'm sorry.
NO MATTER WHO MISAO BRINGS HOME, YOU WON'T LIKE IT, WILL YOU, YOSHIO?
THAT'S NOT TRUE.
LIAR. YOU'RE RUNNING AWAY.
I AM TRYING TO ASCERTAIN...
...WHETHER OR NOT KYO WILL BE ABLE TO MAKE MISAO HAPPY.
HOW CAN YOU KNOW THAT ...?
Tears
I KNOW.
KYO...

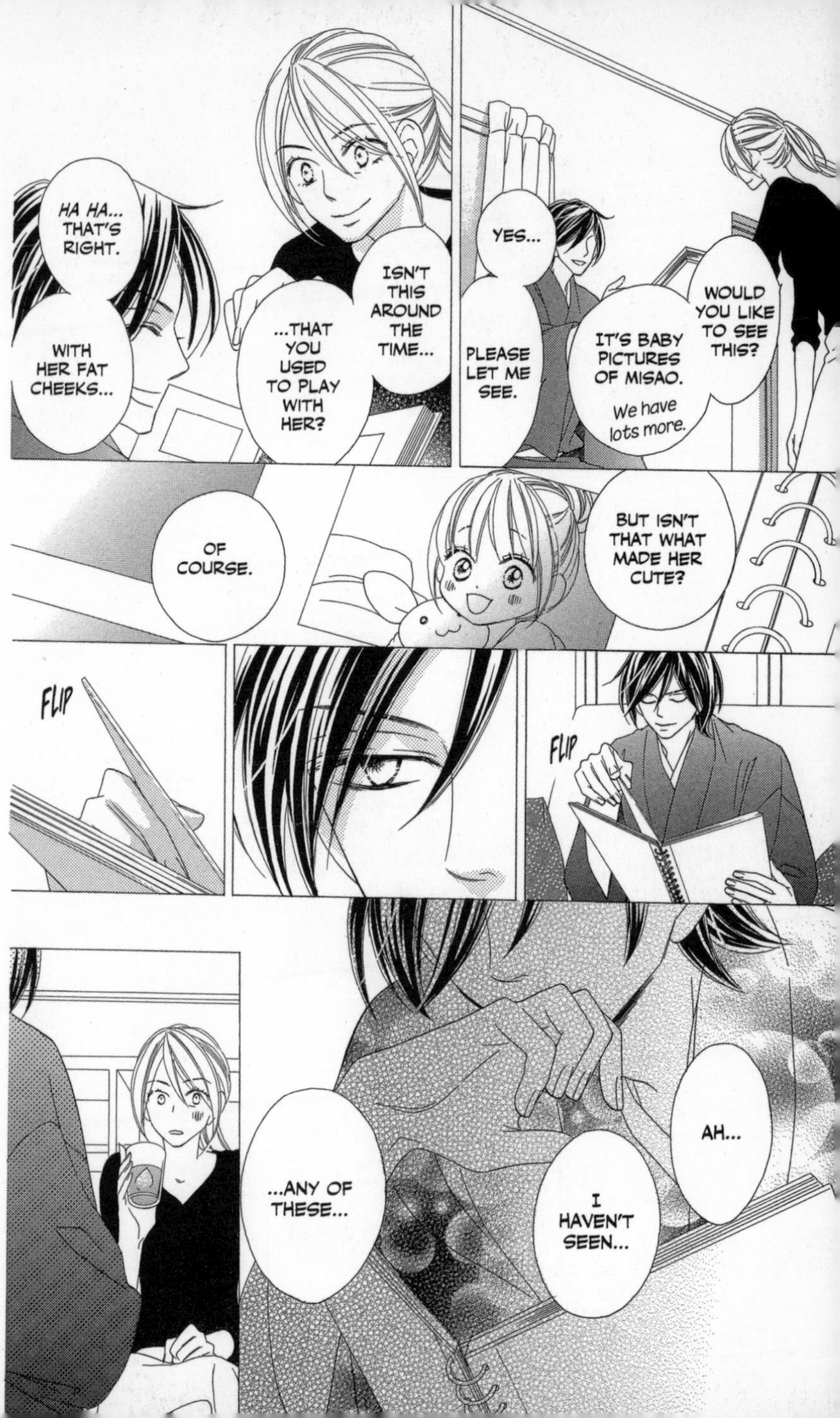
WOULD YOU LIKE TO SEE THIS?
IT'S BABY PICTURES OF MISAO.
We have lots more.
YES...
PLEASE LET ME SEE.
ISN'T THIS AROUND THE TIME...
...THAT YOU USED TO PLAY WITH HER?
HA HA... THAT'S RIGHT.
WITH HER FAT CHEEKS...
BUT ISN'T THAT WHAT MADE HER CUTE?
OF COURSE.
FLIP
FLIP
AH...
I HAVEN'T SEEN...
...ANY OF THESE...

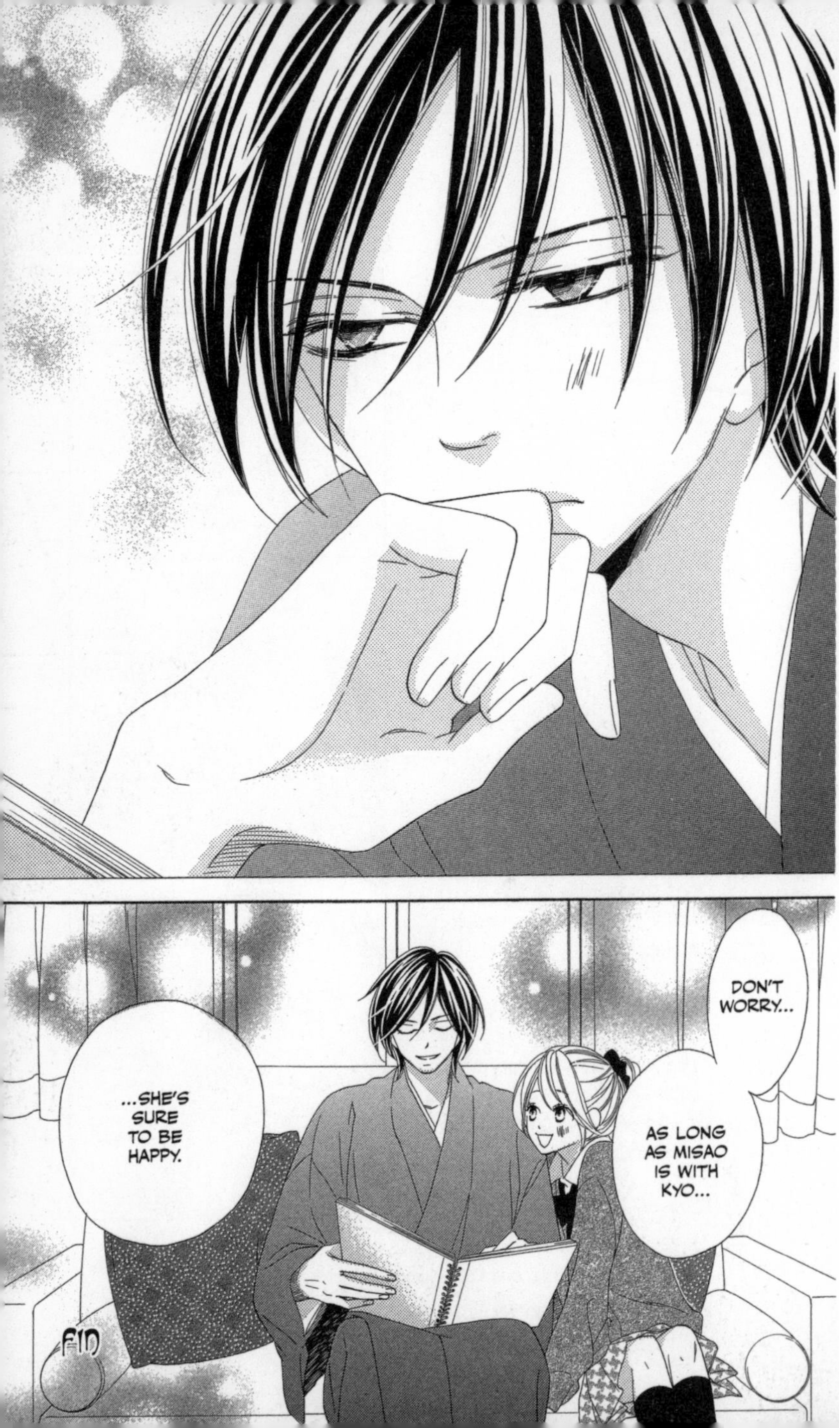
DON'T WORRY...
AS LONG AS MISAO IS WITH KYO...
...SHE'S SURE TO BE HAPPY.
FIN

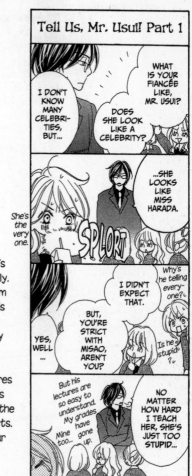

Tell Us, Mr. Usui! Part 1

WHAT IS YOUR FIANCÉE LIKE, MR. USUI?
DOES SHE LOOK LIKE A CELEBRITY?
I DON'T KNOW MANY CELEBRI-TIES, BUT...
...SHE LOOKS LIKE MISS HARADA.
SPLORT
She's the very one.
Why's he telling every-one?
I DIDN'T EXPECT THAT.
BUT, YOU'RE STRICT WITH MISAO, AREN'T YOU?
Is he stupid?
YES, WELL ...
NO MATTER HOW HARD I TEACH HER, SHE'S JUST TOO STUPID...
But his lectures are so easy to understand.
My grades have gone up.
Mine too...

The students' grades in Kyo's classes have improved rapidly. That's because Kyo has them lightly tranced. Misao, who is not susceptible to the trance※, is still doing poorly on her tests.

I enjoy doing special features because I can draw subjects that would never appear in the main story, or minor subjects. I was even able to draw four of them! ♡

※ At school. Renko and Raikoh won't fall under a trance, either.

← You'll find another "Tell us, Mr. Usui!" at the end of this volume!

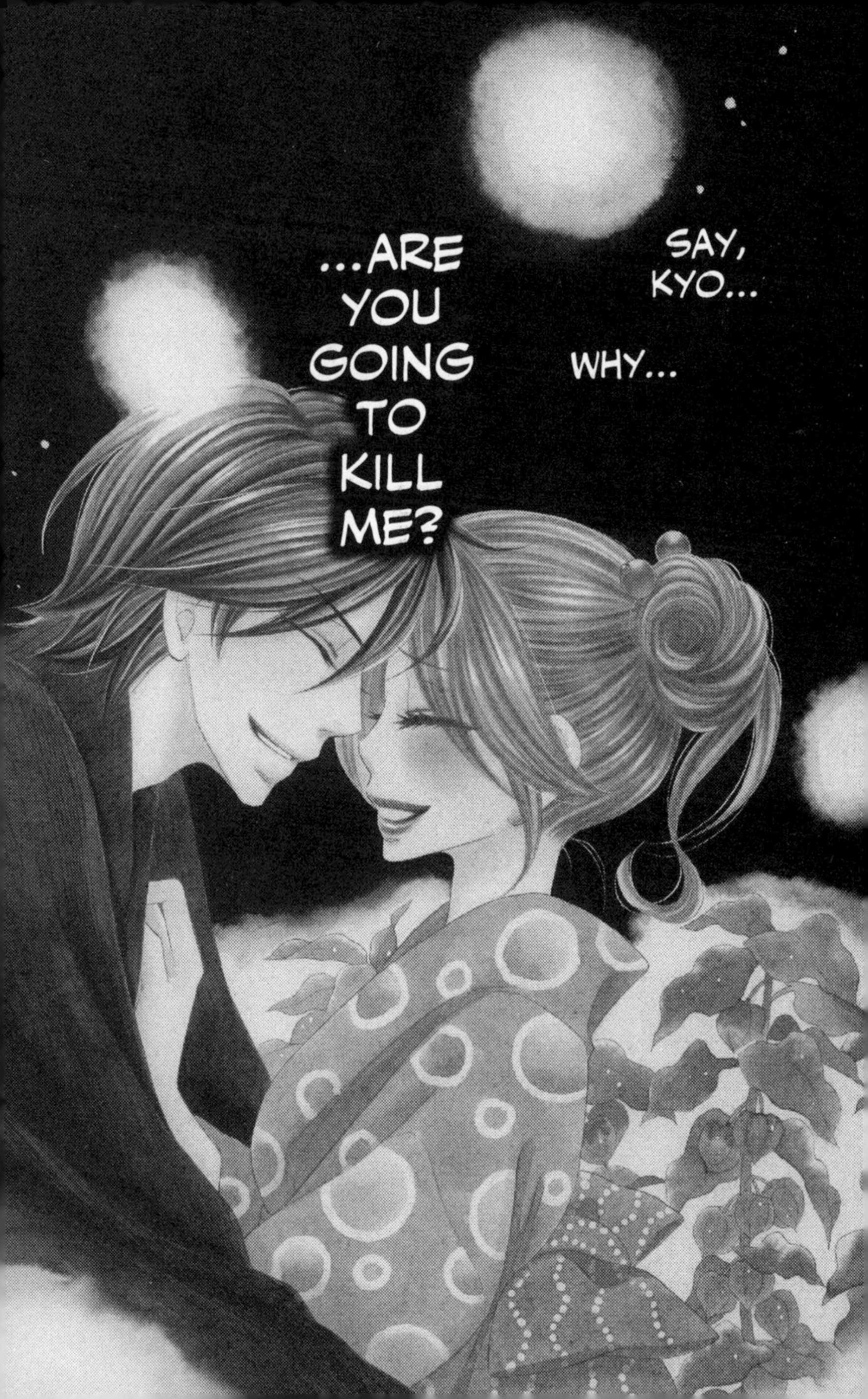
SAY, KYO...
WHY...
...ARE YOU GOING TO KILL ME?

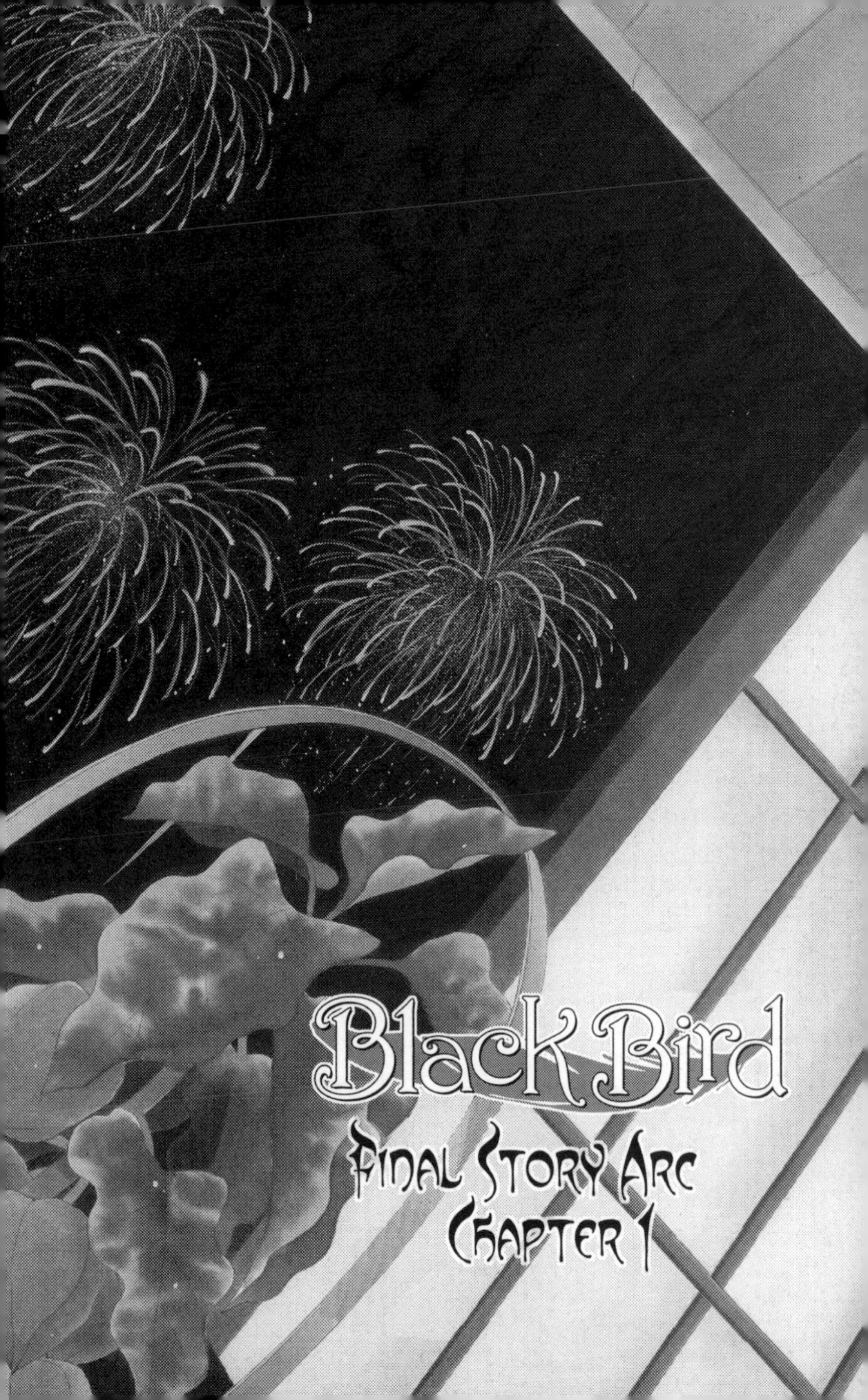
Black Bird
Final Story Arc
Chapter 1

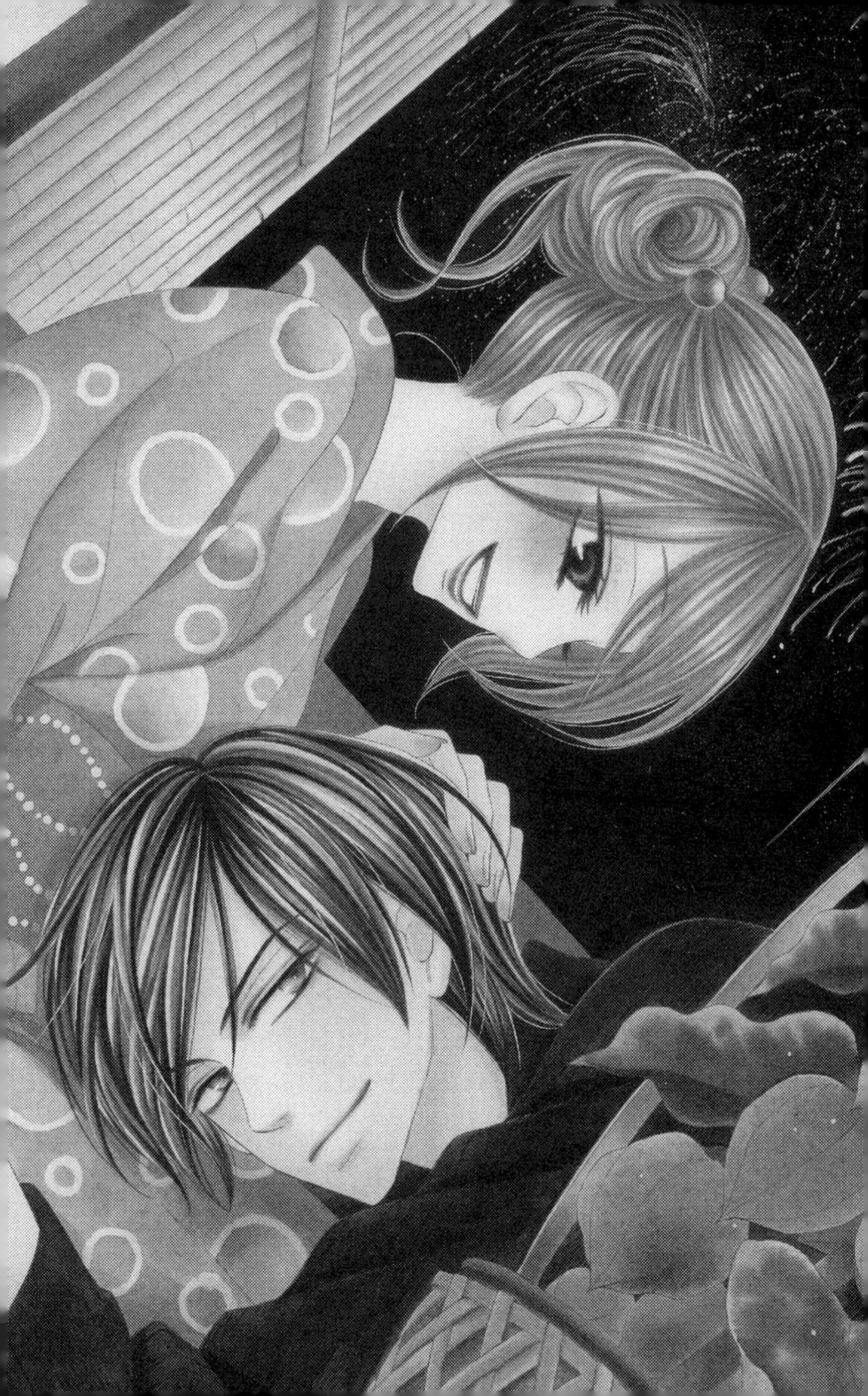

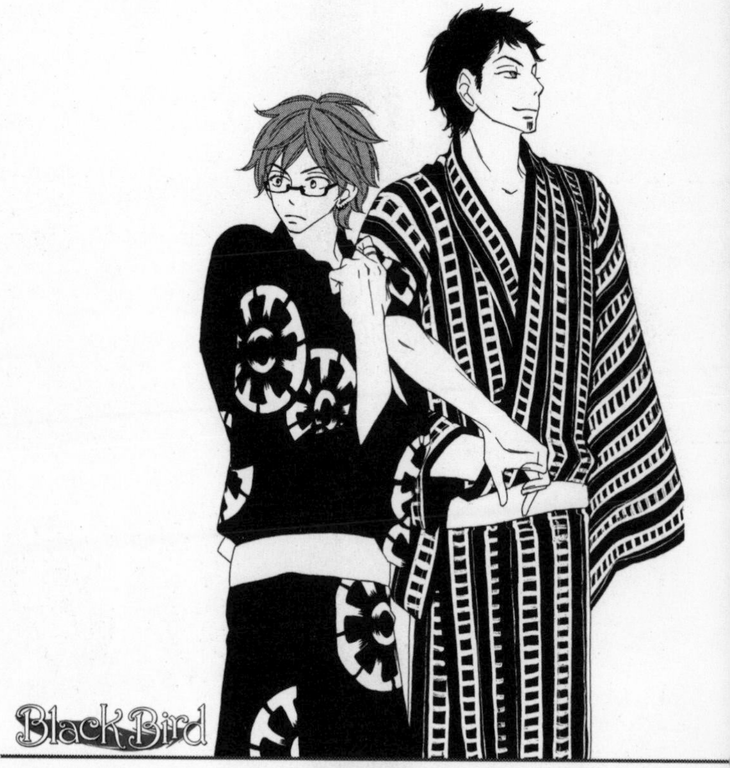
Black Bird

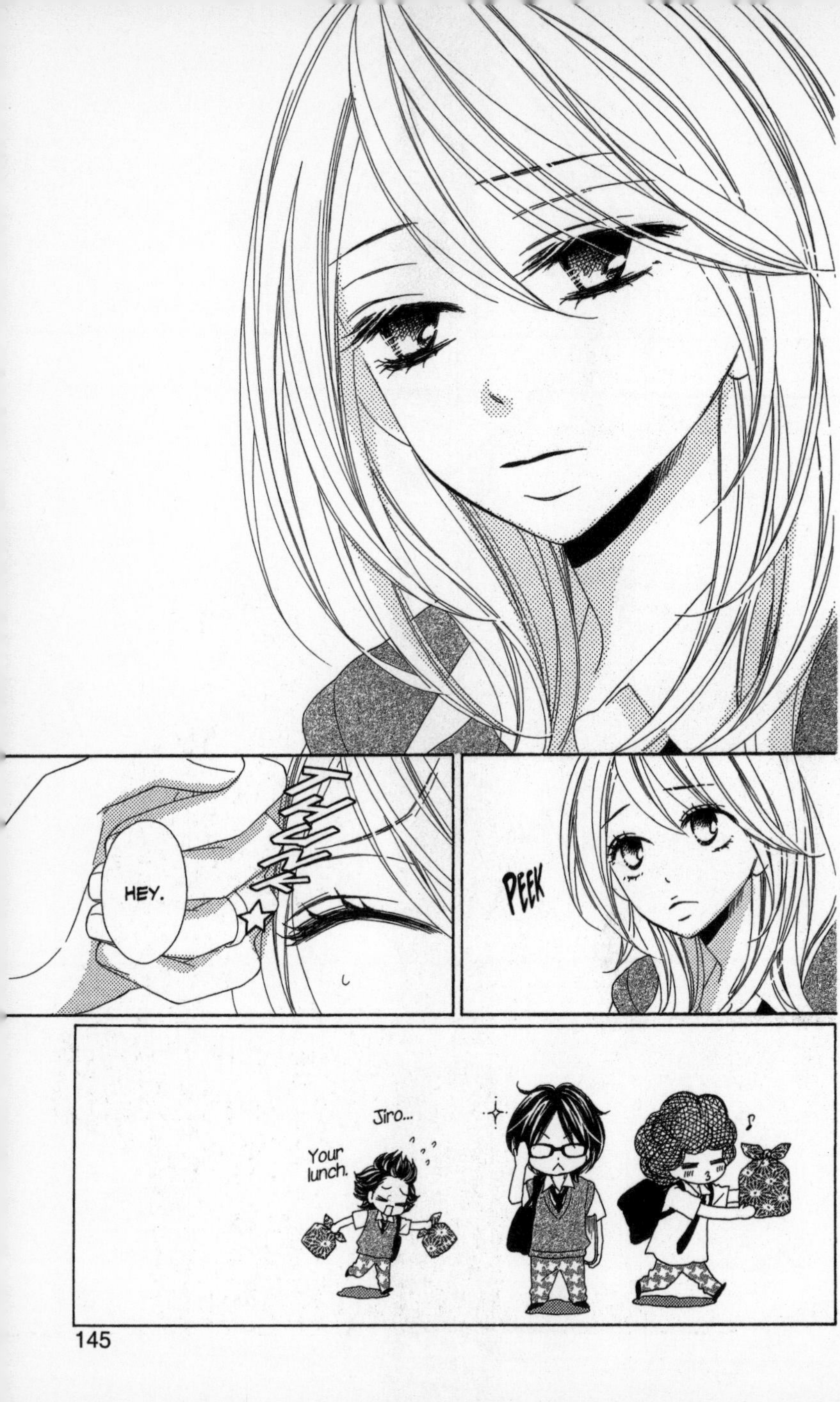
PEEK
THUNK
HEY.
Jiro...
Your lunch.

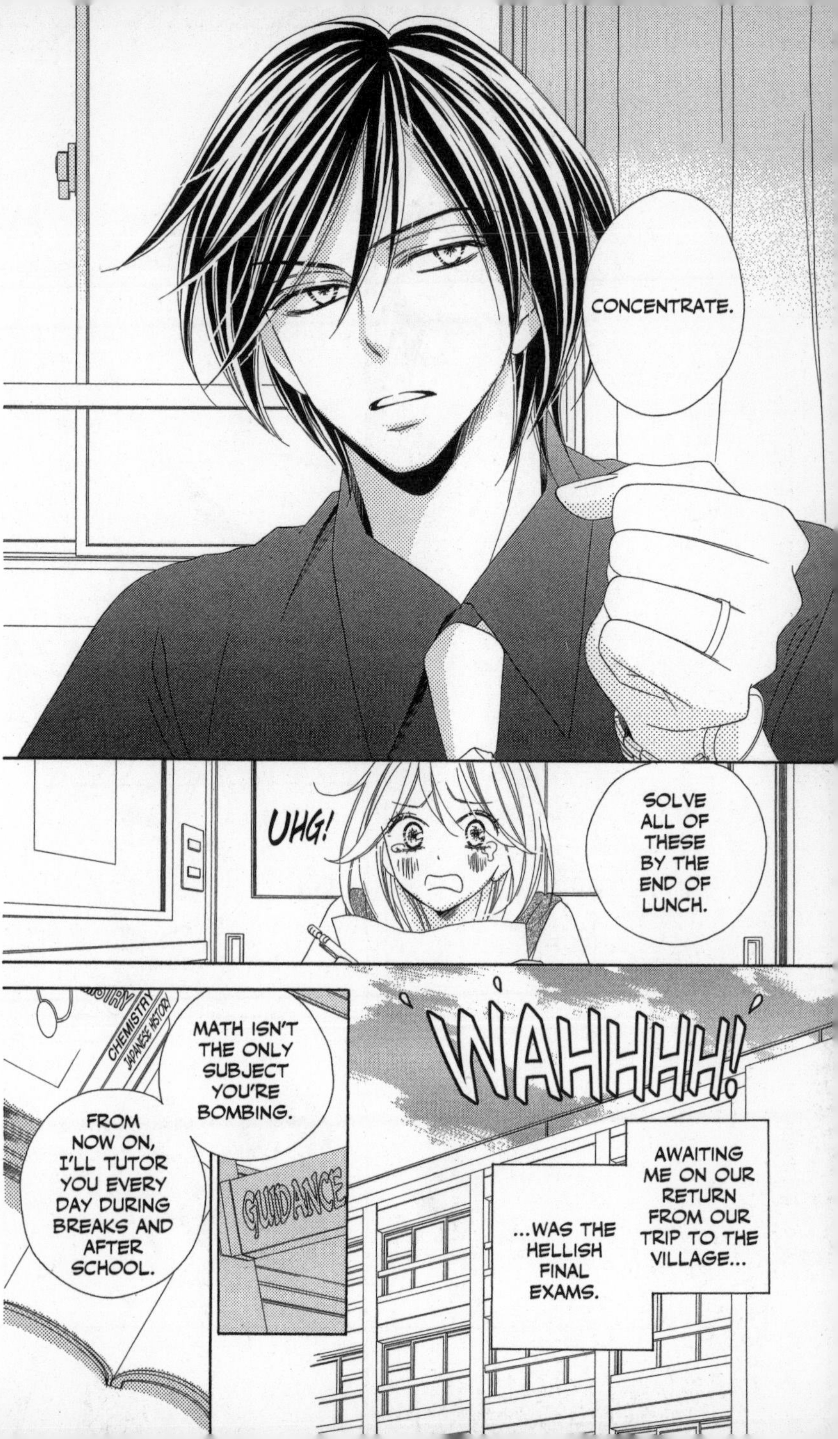
CONCENTRATE.
SOLVE ALL OF THESE BY THE END OF LUNCH.
UHG!
WAHHHH!
AWAITING ME ON OUR RETURN FROM OUR TRIP TO THE VILLAGE...
...WAS THE HELLISH FINAL EXAMS.
MATH ISN'T THE ONLY SUBJECT YOU'RE BOMBING.
FROM NOW ON, I'LL TUTOR YOU EVERY DAY DURING BREAKS AND AFTER SCHOOL.
CHEMISTRY
JAPANESE HISTORY
GUIDANCE

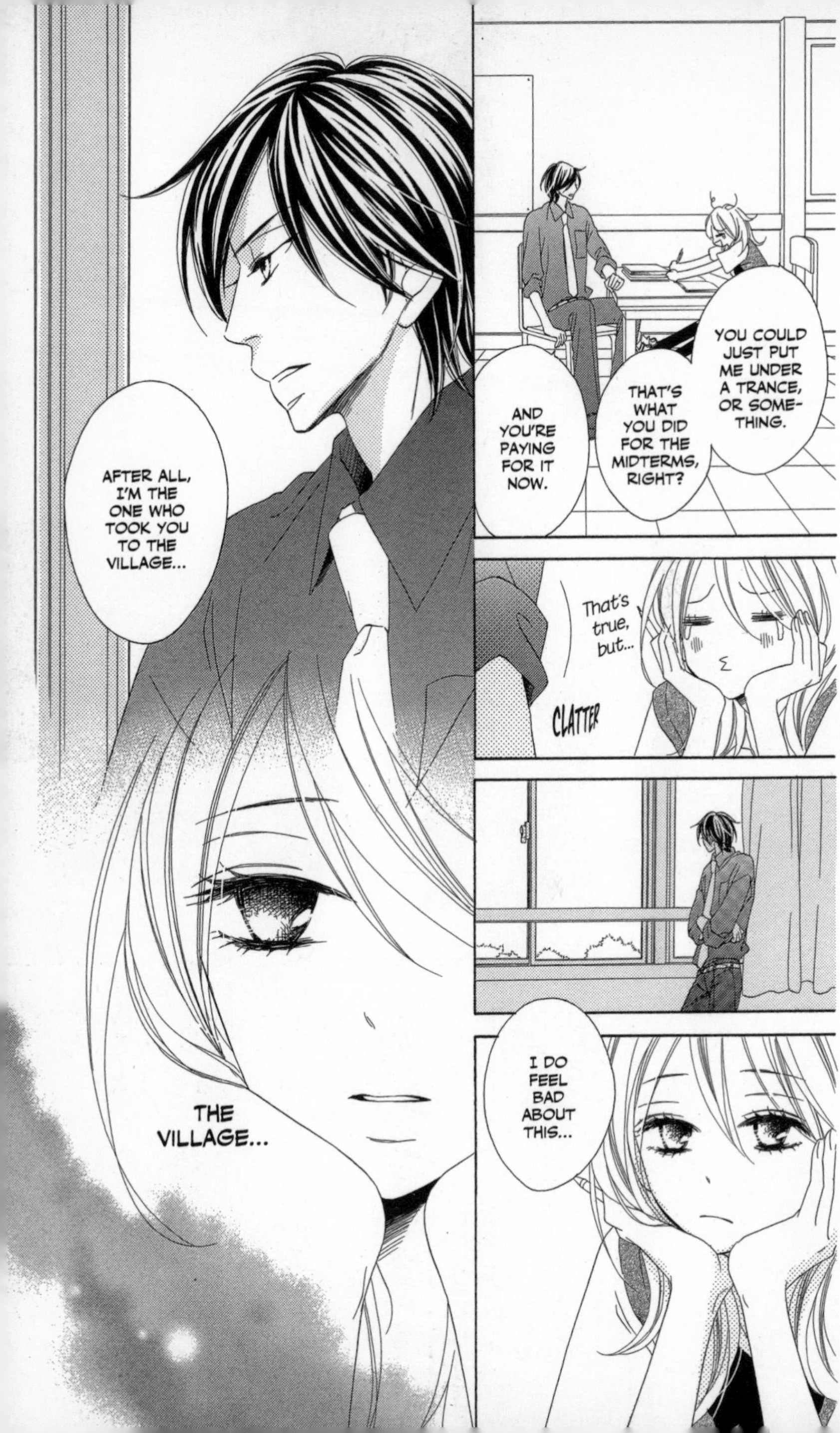
YOU COULD JUST PUT ME UNDER A TRANCE, OR SOME-THING.
THAT'S WHAT YOU DID FOR THE MIDTERMS, RIGHT?
AND YOU'RE PAYING FOR IT NOW.
That's true, but...
CLATTER
I DO FEEL BAD ABOUT THIS...
AFTER ALL, I'M THE ONE WHO TOOK YOU TO THE VILLAGE...
THE VILLAGE...

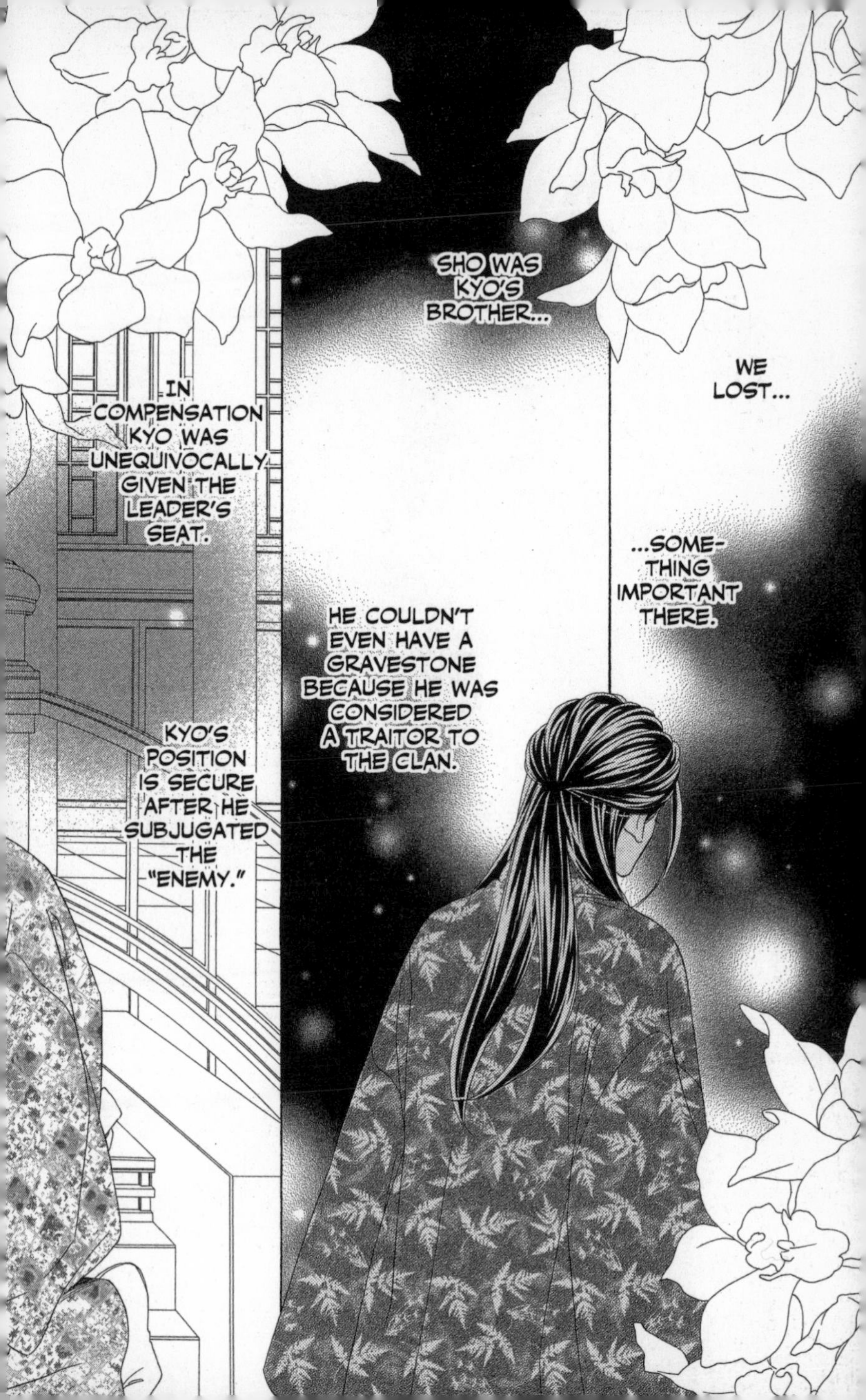
WE LOST...
...SOMETHING IMPORTANT THERE.
SHO WAS KYO'S BROTHER...
HE COULDN'T EVEN HAVE A GRAVESTONE BECAUSE HE WAS CONSIDERED A TRAITOR TO THE CLAN.
IN COMPENSATION KYO WAS UNEQUIVOCALLY GIVEN THE LEADER'S SEAT.
KYO'S POSITION IS SECURE AFTER HE SUBJUGATED THE "ENEMY."

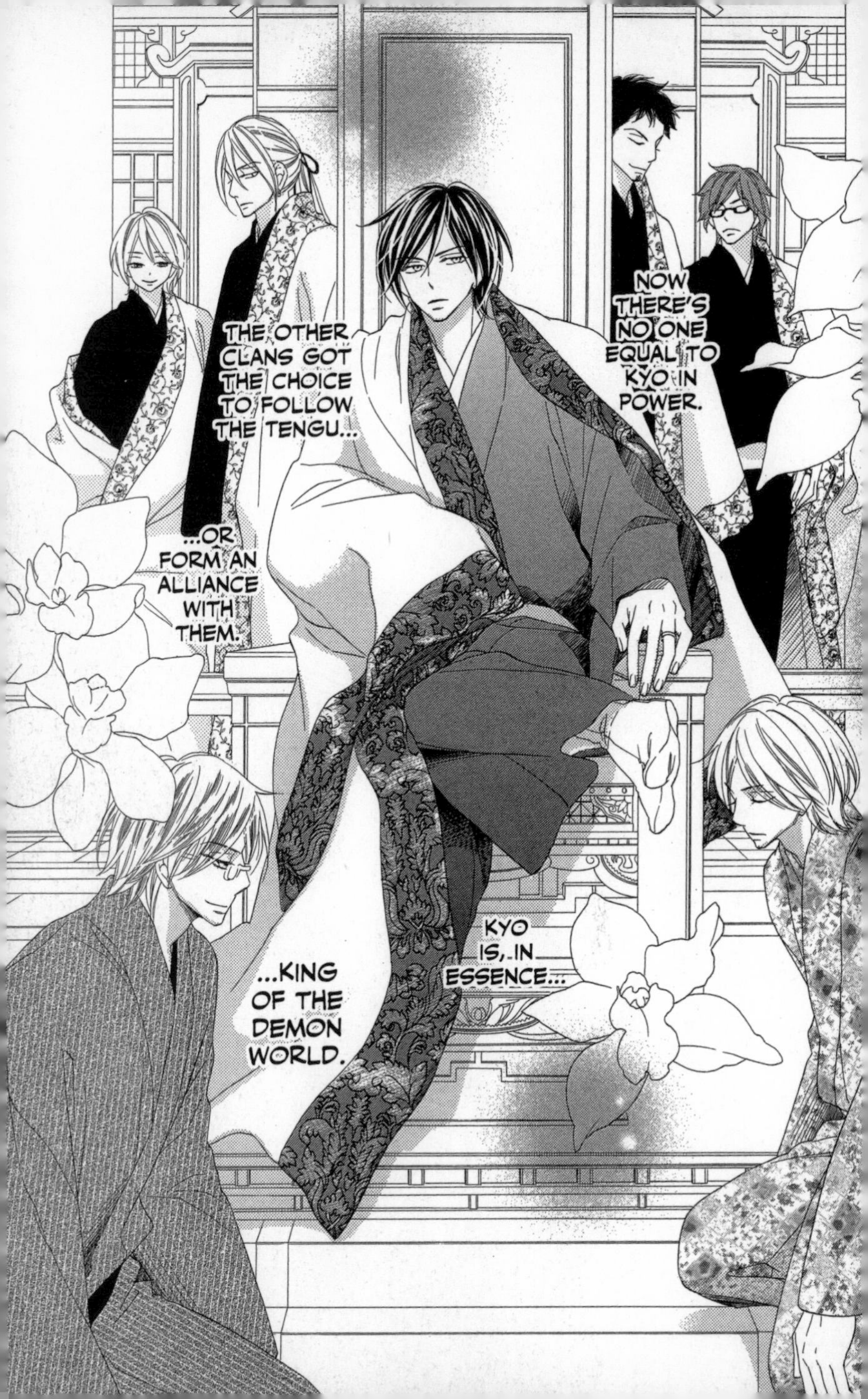
NOW THERE'S NO ONE EQUAL TO KYO IN POWER.
THE OTHER CLANS GOT THE CHOICE TO FOLLOW THE TENGU...
...OR FORM AN ALLIANCE WITH THEM.
KYO IS, IN ESSENCE...
...KING OF THE DEMON WORLD.

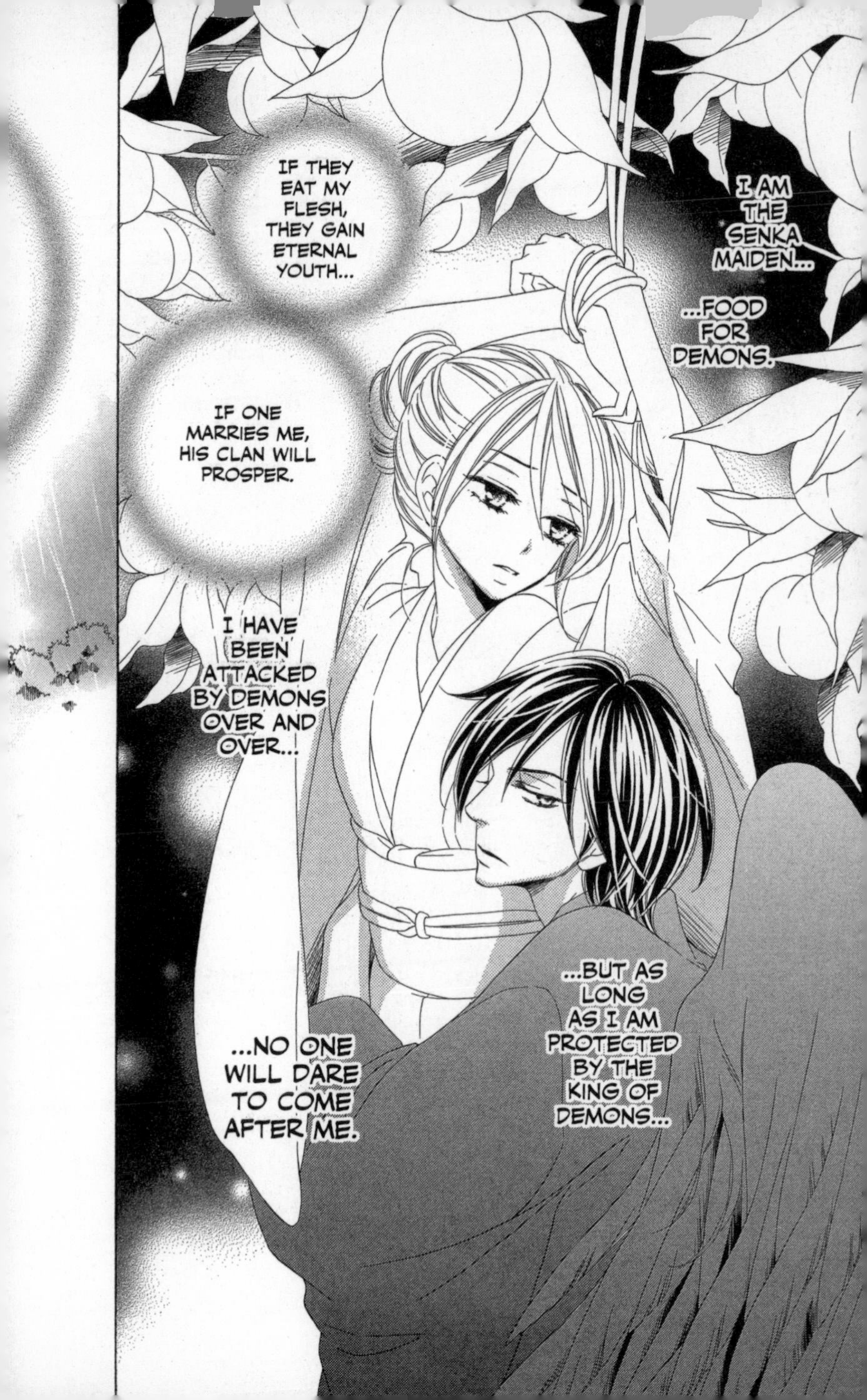
I AM THE SENKA MAIDEN...
...FOOD FOR DEMONS.
IF THEY EAT MY FLESH, THEY GAIN ETERNAL YOUTH...
IF ONE MARRIES ME, HIS CLAN WILL PROSPER.
I HAVE BEEN ATTACKED BY DEMONS OVER AND OVER...
...BUT AS LONG AS I AM PROTECTED BY THE KING OF DEMONS...
...NO ONE WILL DARE TO COME AFTER ME.

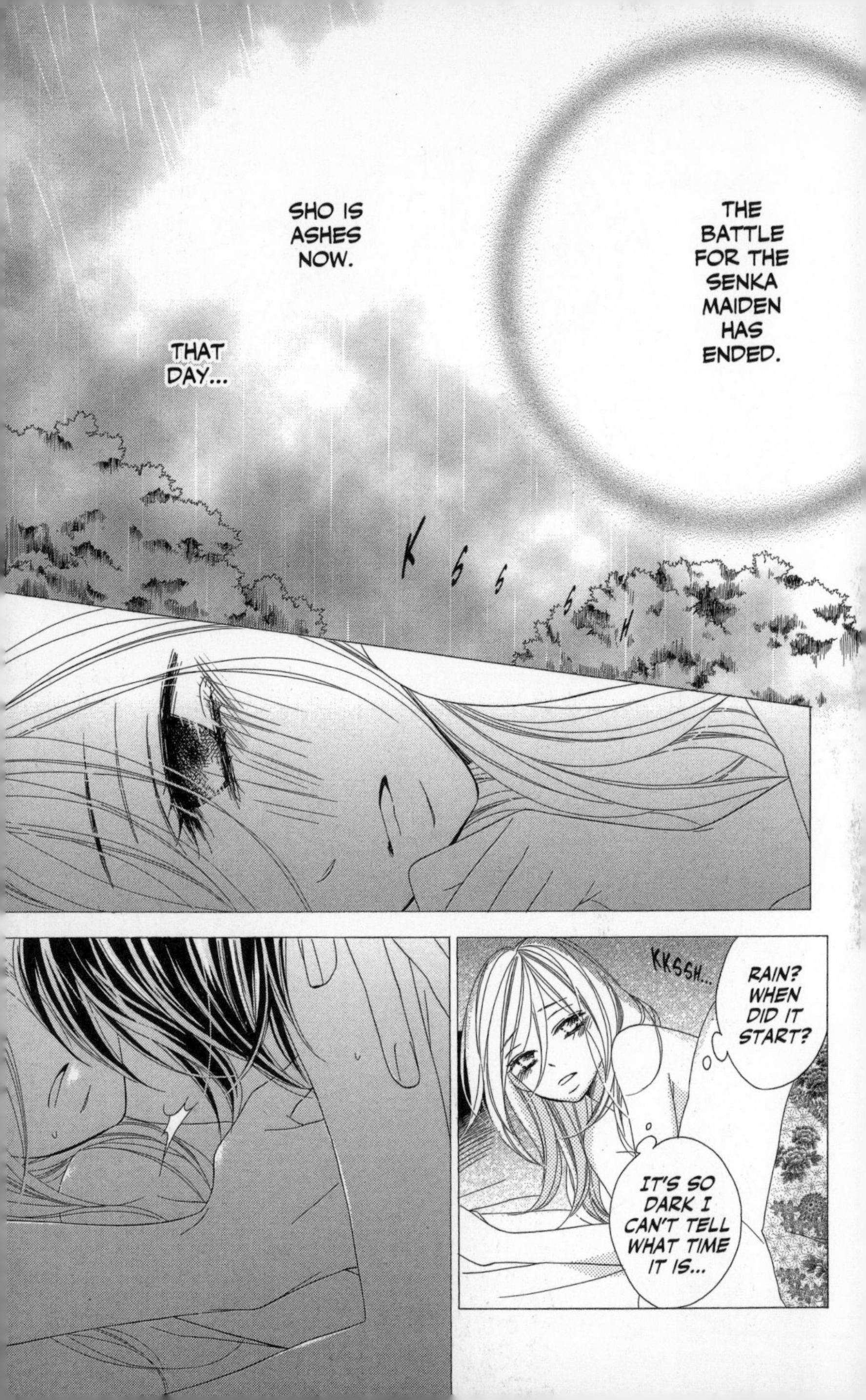
THE BATTLE FOR THE SENKA MAIDEN HAS ENDED.
SHO IS ASHES NOW.
THAT DAY...
KSSSSH
KKSSH...
RAIN? WHEN DID IT START?
IT'S SO DARK I CAN'T TELL WHAT TIME IT IS...

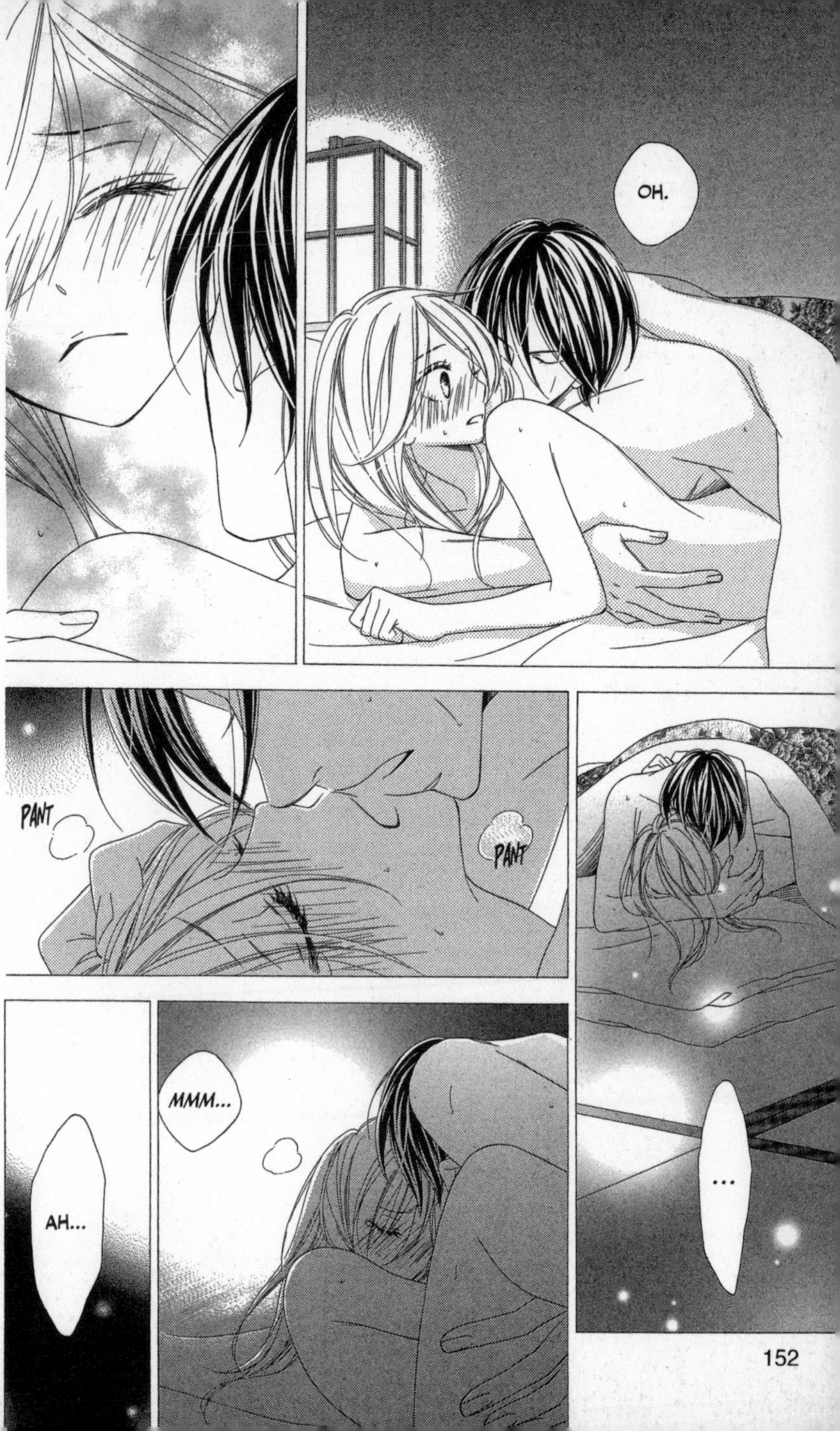
OH.
...
PANT
PANT
MMM...
AH...

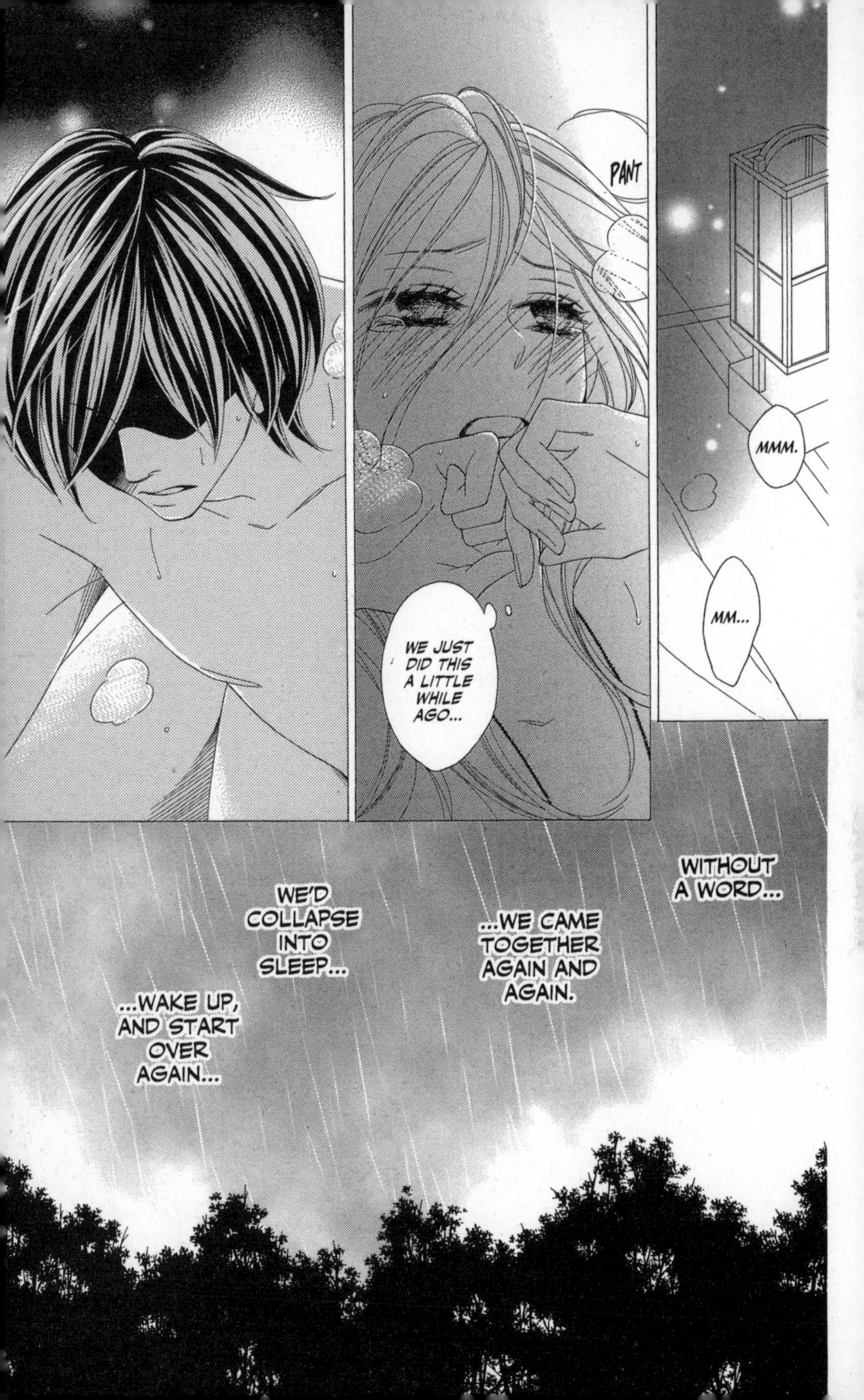
MMM.
MM...
PANT
WE JUST DID THIS A LITTLE WHILE AGO...
WITHOUT A WORD...
...WE CAME TOGETHER AGAIN AND AGAIN.
WE'D COLLAPSE INTO SLEEP...
...WAKE UP, AND START OVER AGAIN...

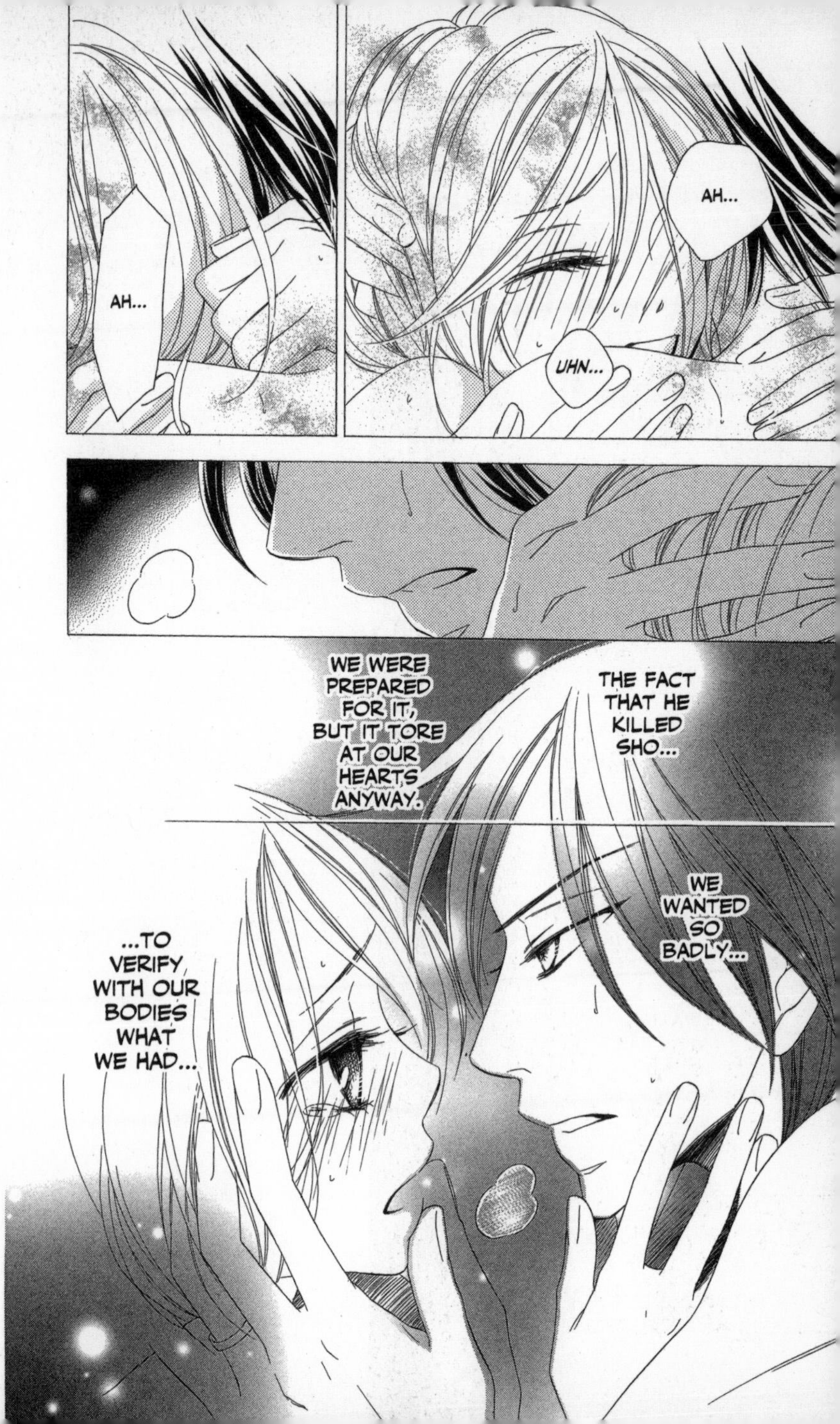
AH...
UHN...
AH...
THE FACT THAT HE KILLED SHO...
WE WERE PREPARED FOR IT, BUT IT TORE AT OUR HEARTS ANYWAY.
WE WANTED SO BADLY...
...TO VERIFY WITH OUR BODIES WHAT WE HAD...

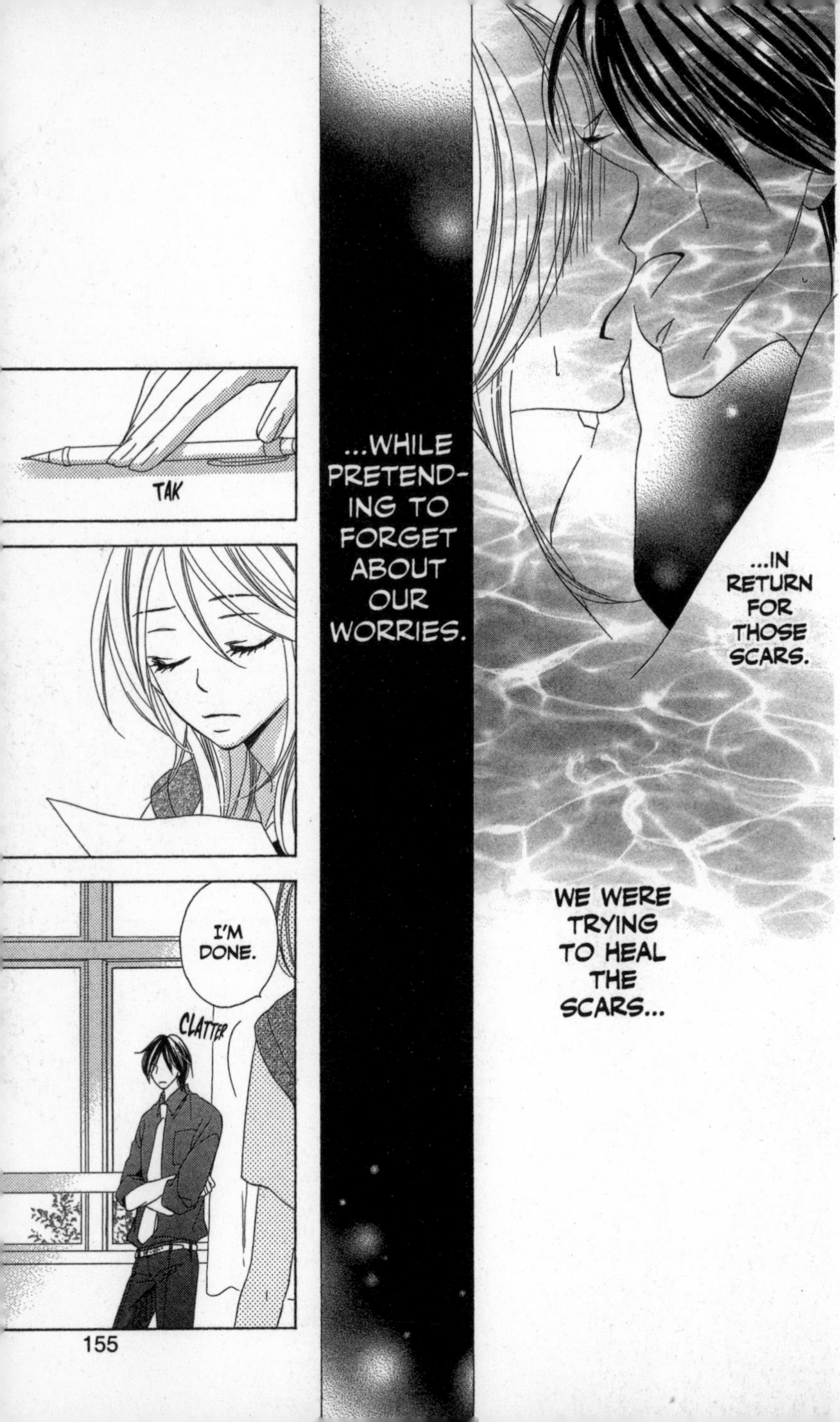
...IN RETURN FOR THOSE SCARS.
WE WERE TRYING TO HEAL THE SCARS...
...WHILE PRETEND-ING TO FORGET ABOUT OUR WORRIES.
TAK
I'M DONE.
CLATTER

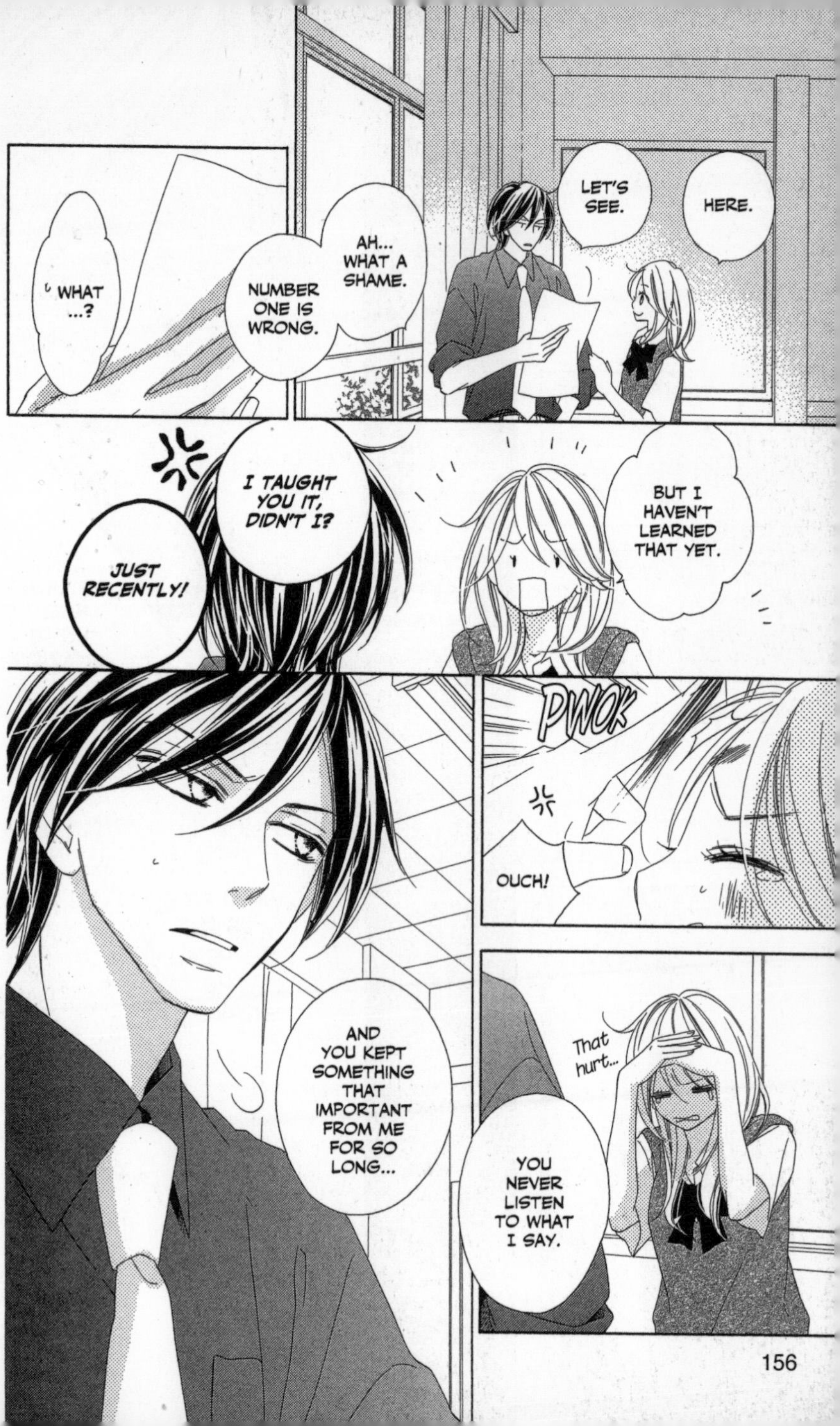
HERE.
LET'S SEE.
AH... WHAT A SHAME.
NUMBER ONE IS WRONG.
WHAT ...?
BUT I HAVEN'T LEARNED THAT YET.
I TAUGHT YOU IT, DIDN'T I?
JUST RECENTLY!
PWOK
OUCH!
That hurt...
YOU NEVER LISTEN TO WHAT I SAY.
AND YOU KEPT SOMETHING THAT IMPORTANT FROM ME FOR SO LONG...

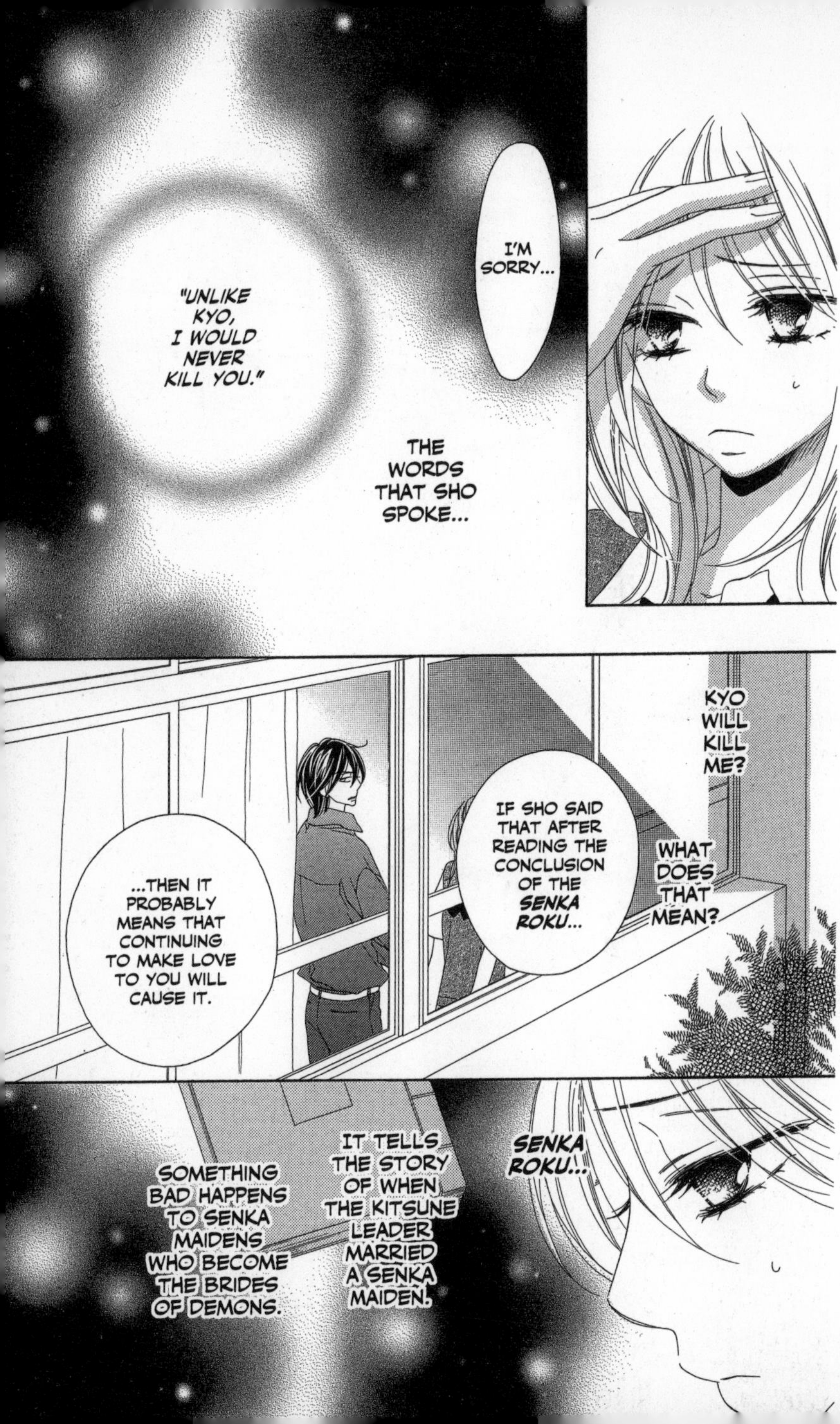
I'M SORRY...
"UNLIKE KYO, I WOULD NEVER KILL YOU."
THE WORDS THAT SHO SPOKE...
KYO WILL KILL ME?
WHAT DOES THAT MEAN?
IF SHO SAID THAT AFTER READING THE CONCLUSION OF THE *SENKA ROKU*...
...THEN IT PROBABLY MEANS THAT CONTINUING TO MAKE LOVE TO YOU WILL CAUSE IT.
SENKA ROKU...
IT TELLS THE STORY OF WHEN THE KITSUNE LEADER MARRIED A SENKA MAIDEN.
SOMETHING BAD HAPPENS TO SENKA MAIDENS WHO BECOME THE BRIDES OF DEMONS.

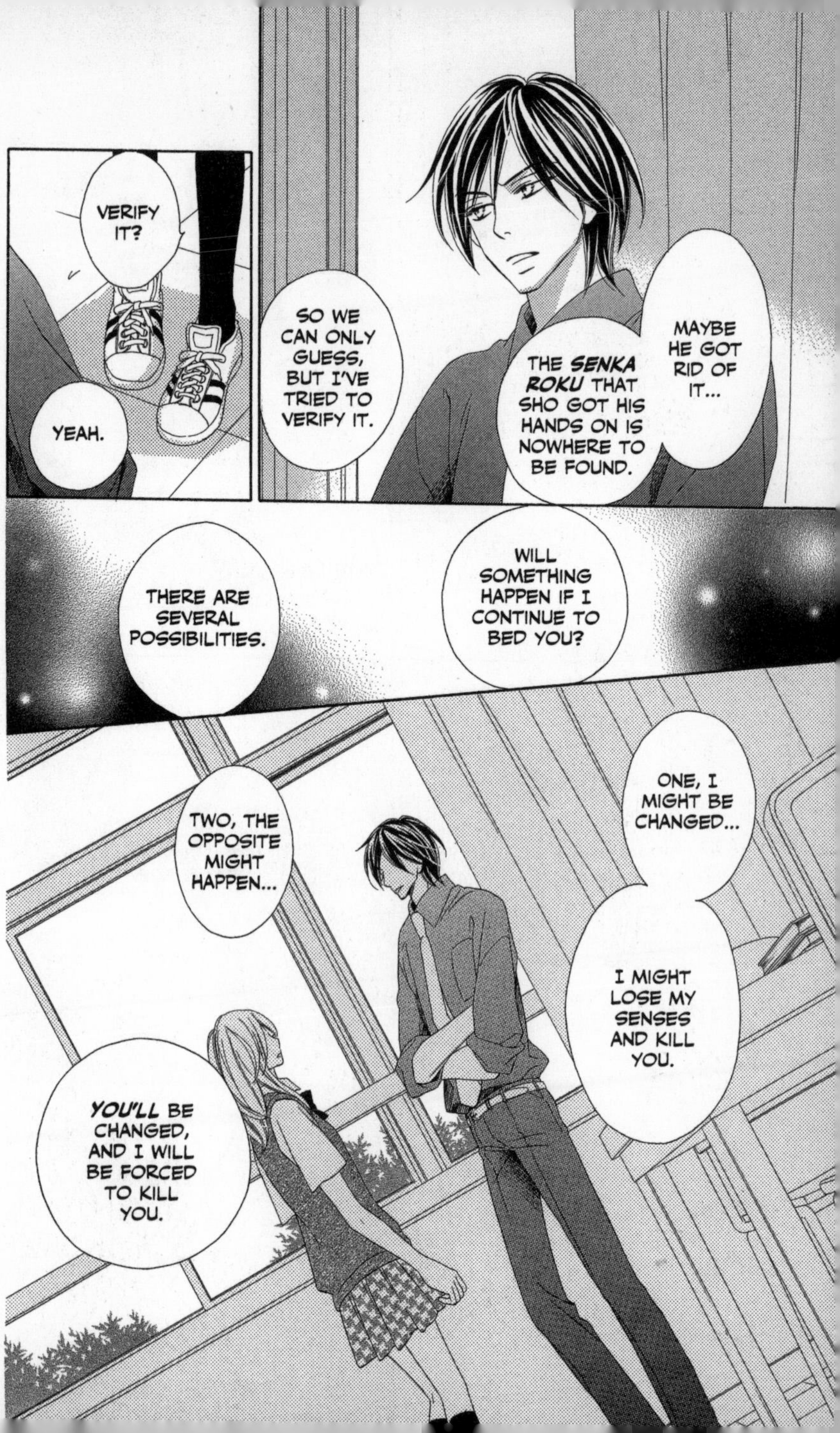
MAYBE HE GOT RID OF IT...
THE *SENKA ROKU* THAT SHO GOT HIS HANDS ON IS NOWHERE TO BE FOUND.
SO WE CAN ONLY GUESS, BUT I'VE TRIED TO VERIFY IT.
VERIFY IT?
YEAH.
WILL SOMETHING HAPPEN IF I CONTINUE TO BED YOU?
THERE ARE SEVERAL POSSIBILITIES.
ONE, I MIGHT BE CHANGED...
I MIGHT LOSE MY SENSES AND KILL YOU.
TWO, THE OPPOSITE MIGHT HAPPEN...
YOU'LL BE CHANGED, AND I WILL BE FORCED TO KILL YOU.

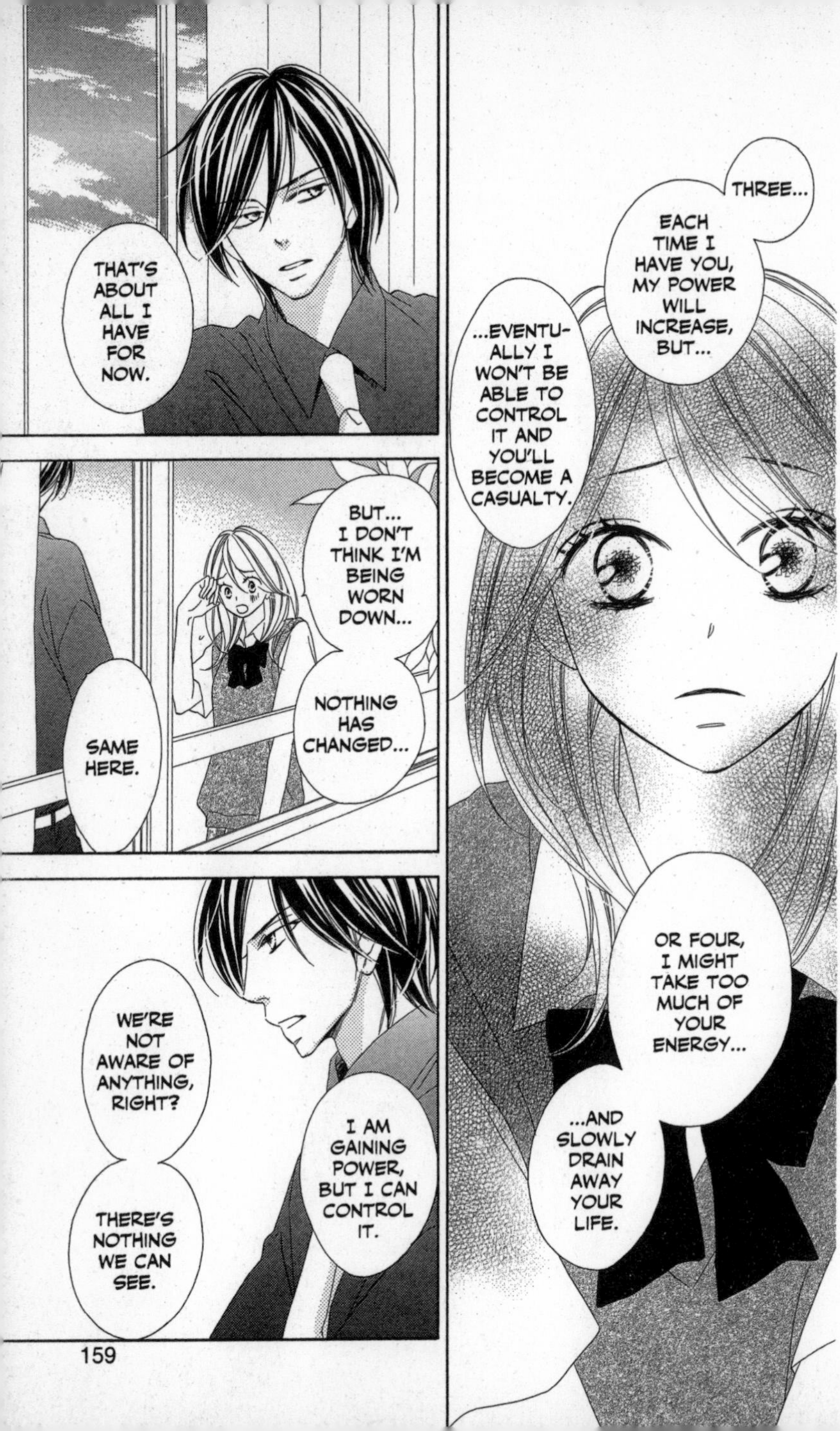
THREE...
EACH TIME I HAVE YOU, MY POWER WILL INCREASE, BUT...
...EVENTUALLY I WON'T BE ABLE TO CONTROL IT AND YOU'LL BECOME A CASUALTY.
OR FOUR, I MIGHT TAKE TOO MUCH OF YOUR ENERGY...
...AND SLOWLY DRAIN AWAY YOUR LIFE.
THAT'S ABOUT ALL I HAVE FOR NOW.
BUT... I DON'T THINK I'M BEING WORN DOWN...
NOTHING HAS CHANGED...
SAME HERE.
I AM GAINING POWER, BUT I CAN CONTROL IT.
WE'RE NOT AWARE OF ANYTHING, RIGHT?
THERE'S NOTHING WE CAN SEE.

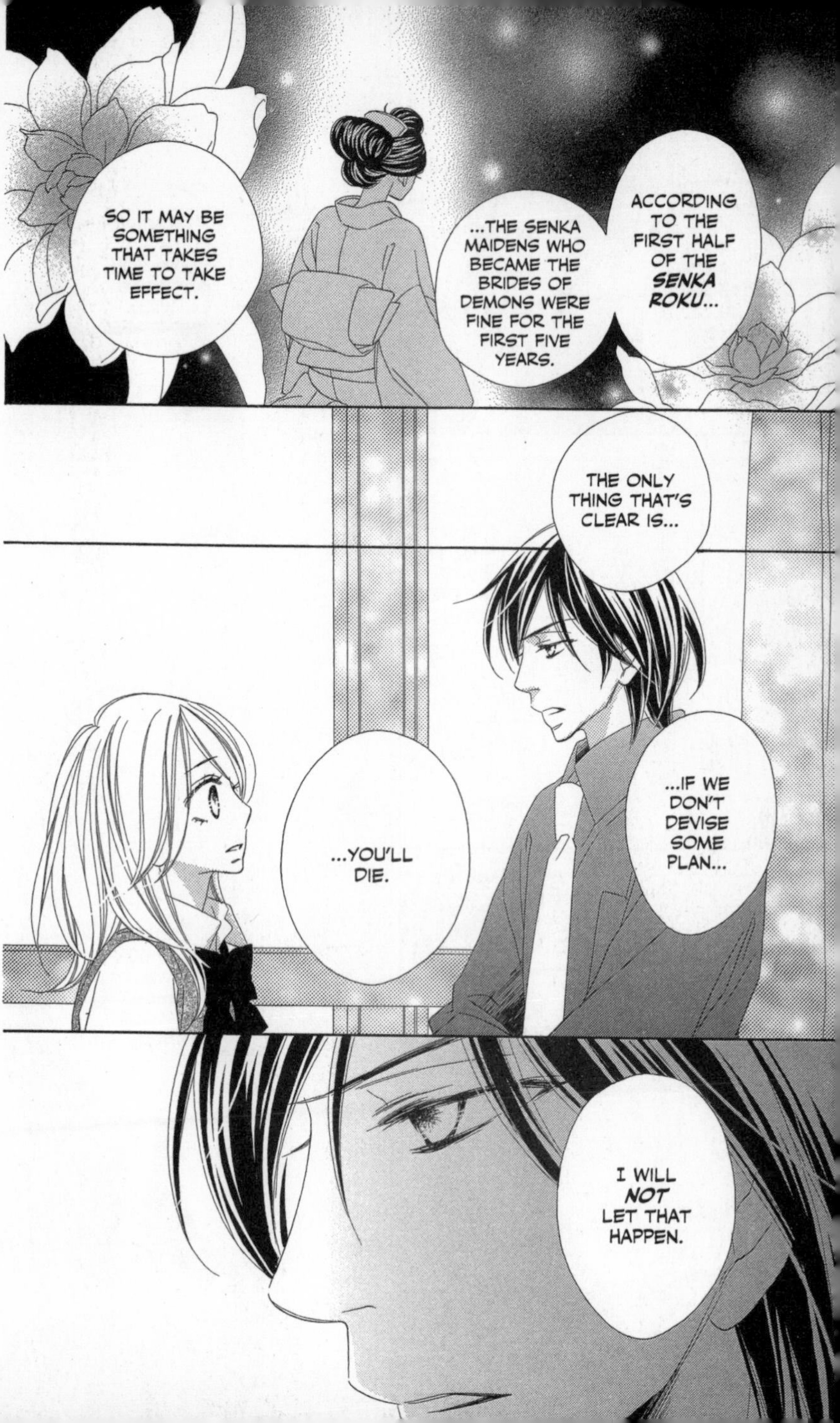
ACCORDING TO THE FIRST HALF OF THE *SENKA ROKU*...
...THE SENKA MAIDENS WHO BECAME THE BRIDES OF DEMONS WERE FINE FOR THE FIRST FIVE YEARS.
SO IT MAY BE SOMETHING THAT TAKES TIME TO TAKE EFFECT.
THE ONLY THING THAT'S CLEAR IS...
...IF WE DON'T DEVISE SOME PLAN...
...YOU'LL DIE.
I WILL ***NOT*** LET THAT HAPPEN.

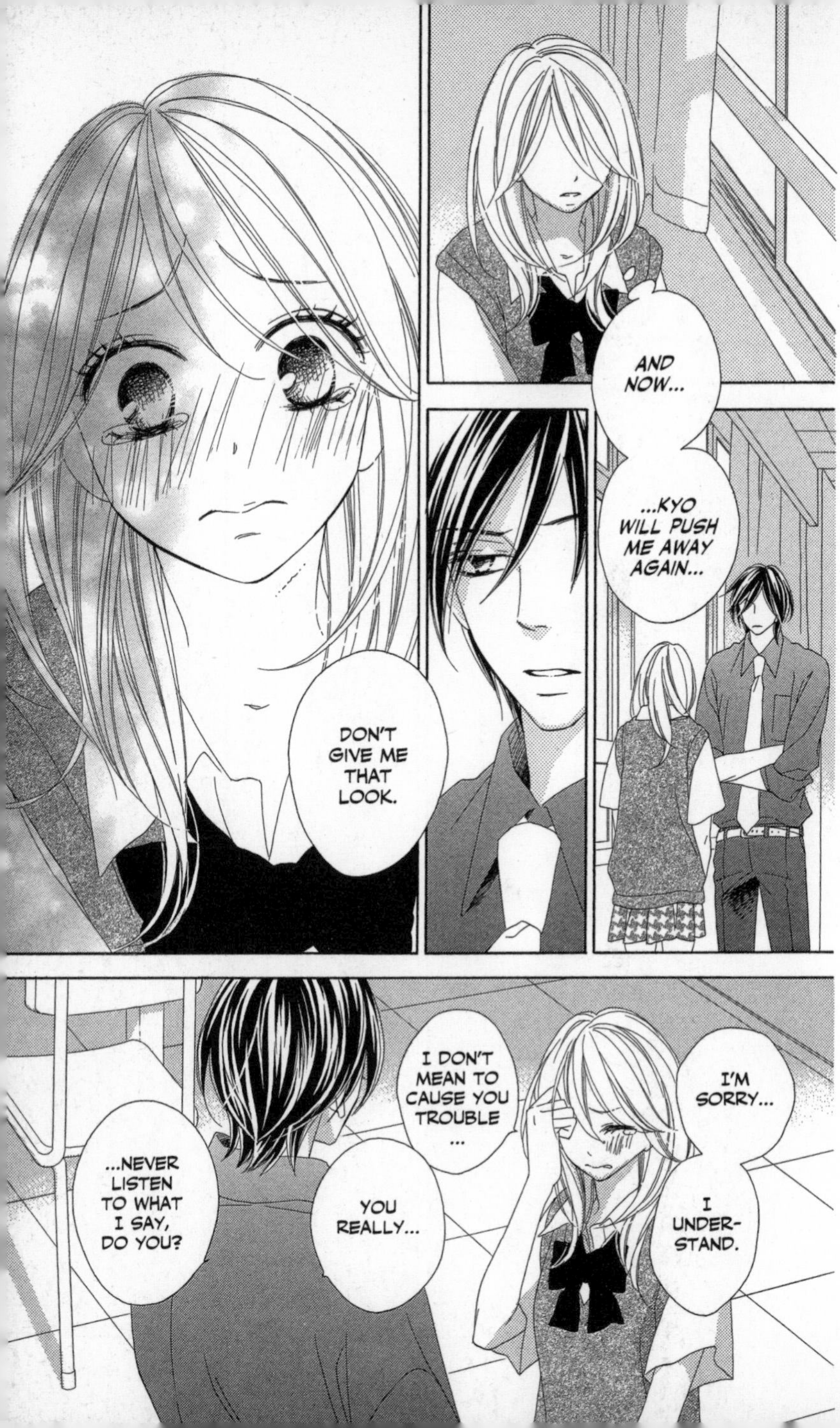
AND NOW...
...KYO WILL PUSH ME AWAY AGAIN...
DON'T GIVE ME THAT LOOK.
I'M SORRY...
I UNDERSTAND.
I DON'T MEAN TO CAUSE YOU TROUBLE ...
YOU REALLY...
...NEVER LISTEN TO WHAT I SAY, DO YOU?

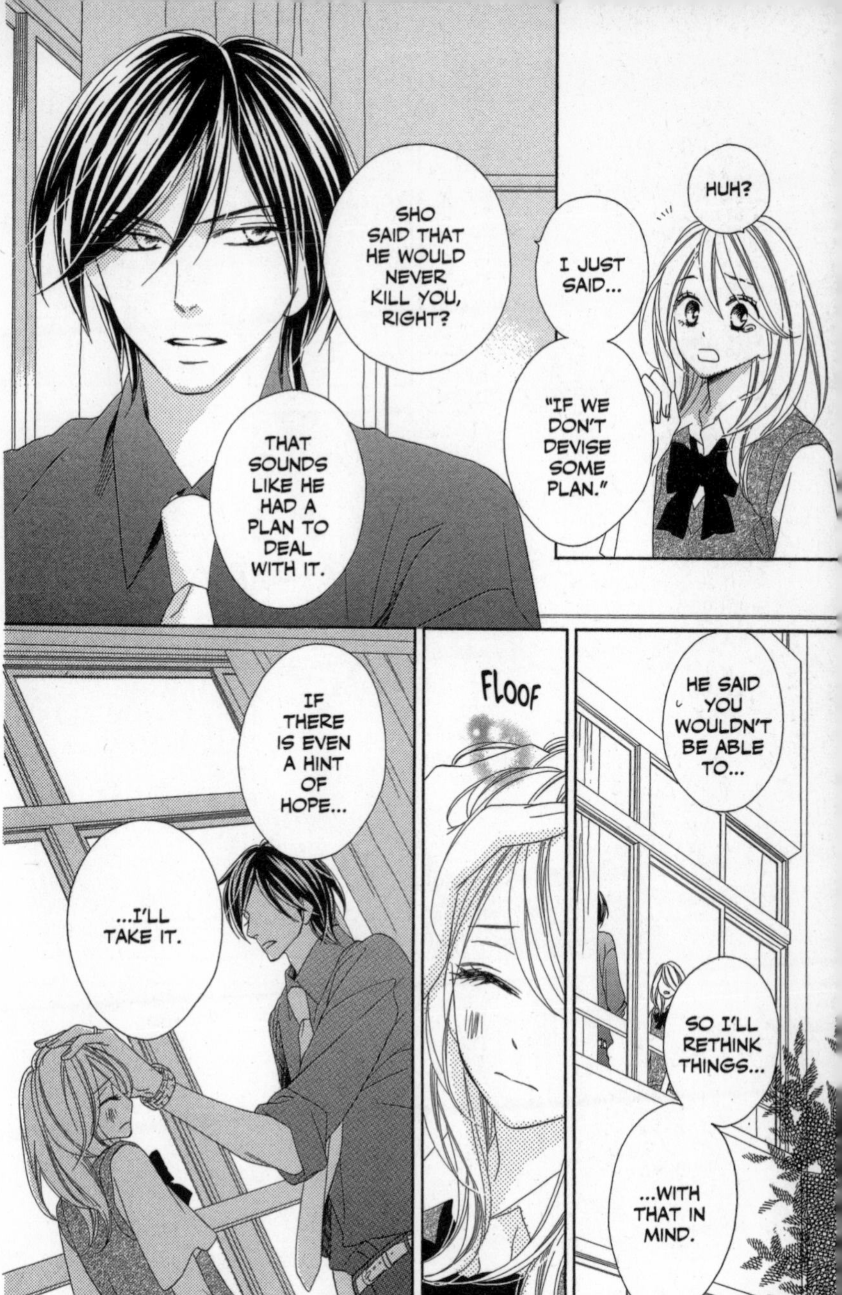
HUH?
I JUST SAID...
"IF WE DON'T DEVISE SOME PLAN."
SHO SAID THAT HE WOULD NEVER KILL YOU, RIGHT?
THAT SOUNDS LIKE HE HAD A PLAN TO DEAL WITH IT.
HE SAID YOU WOULDN'T BE ABLE TO...
SO I'LL RETHINK THINGS...
...WITH THAT IN MIND.
FLOOF
IF THERE IS EVEN A HINT OF HOPE...
...I'LL TAKE IT.

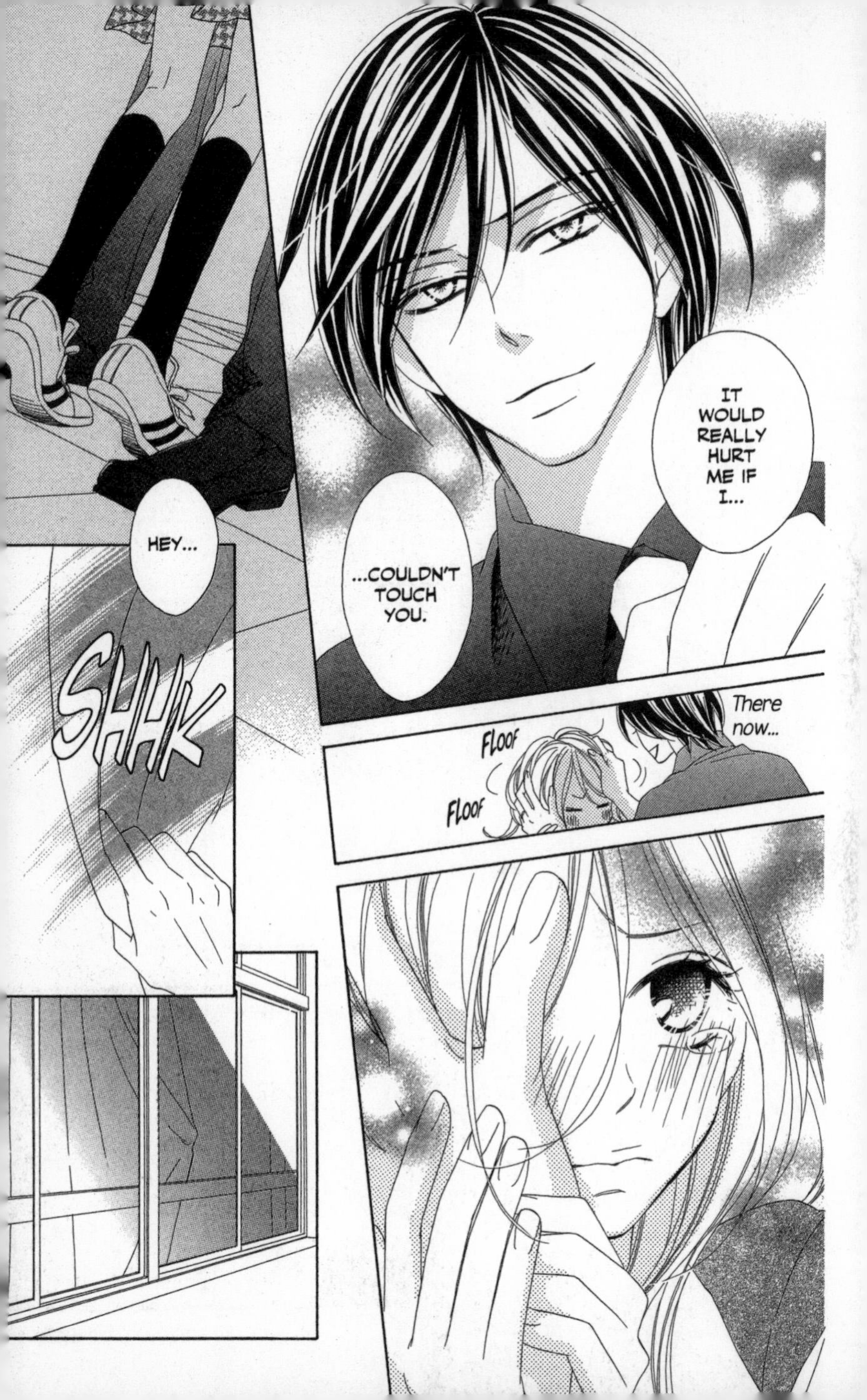
IT WOULD REALLY HURT ME IF I...
...COULDN'T TOUCH YOU.
There now...
FLOOF
FLOOF
HEY...
SHHK

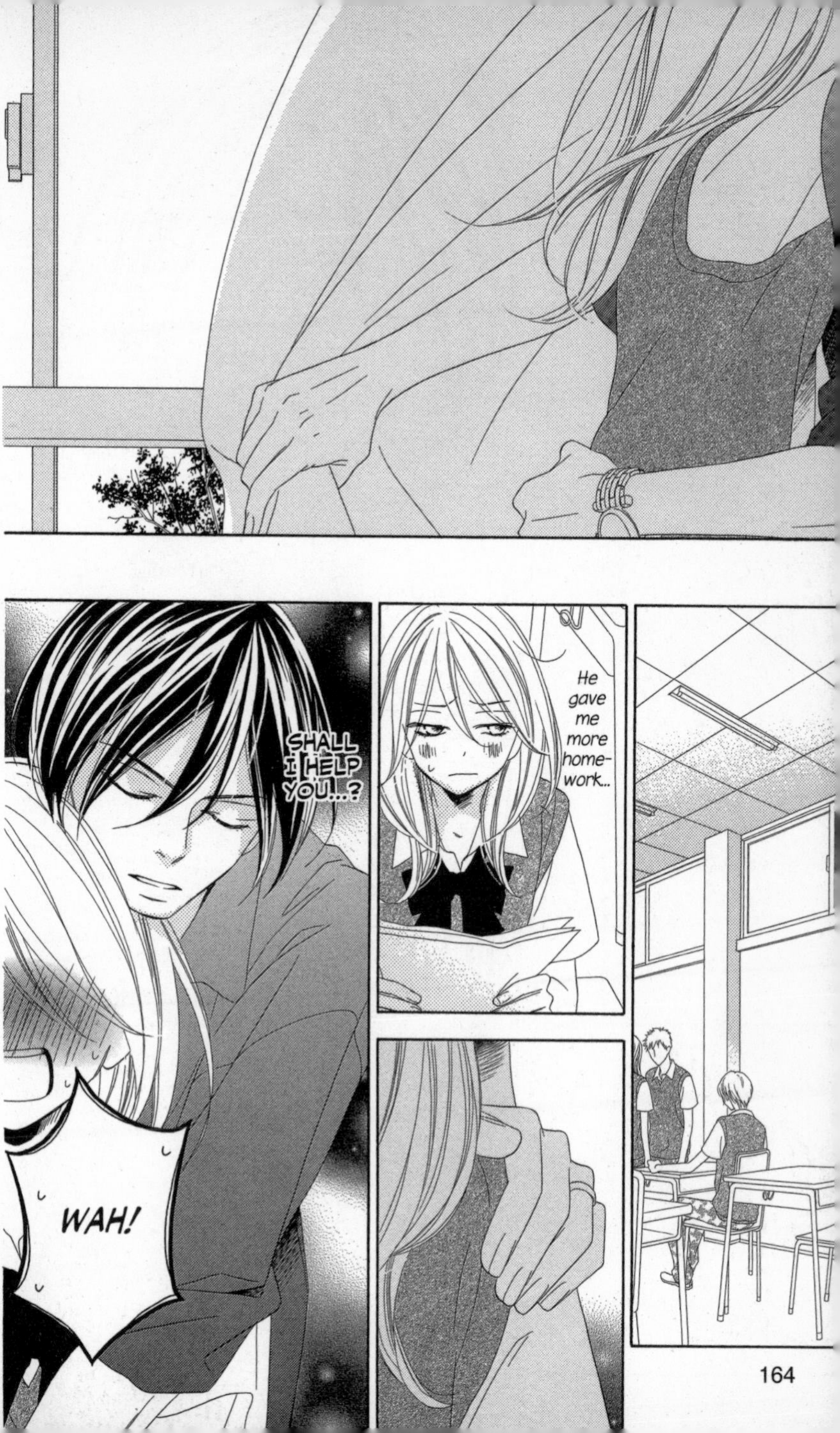
He gave me more home-work...
SHALL I HELP YOU...?
WAH!

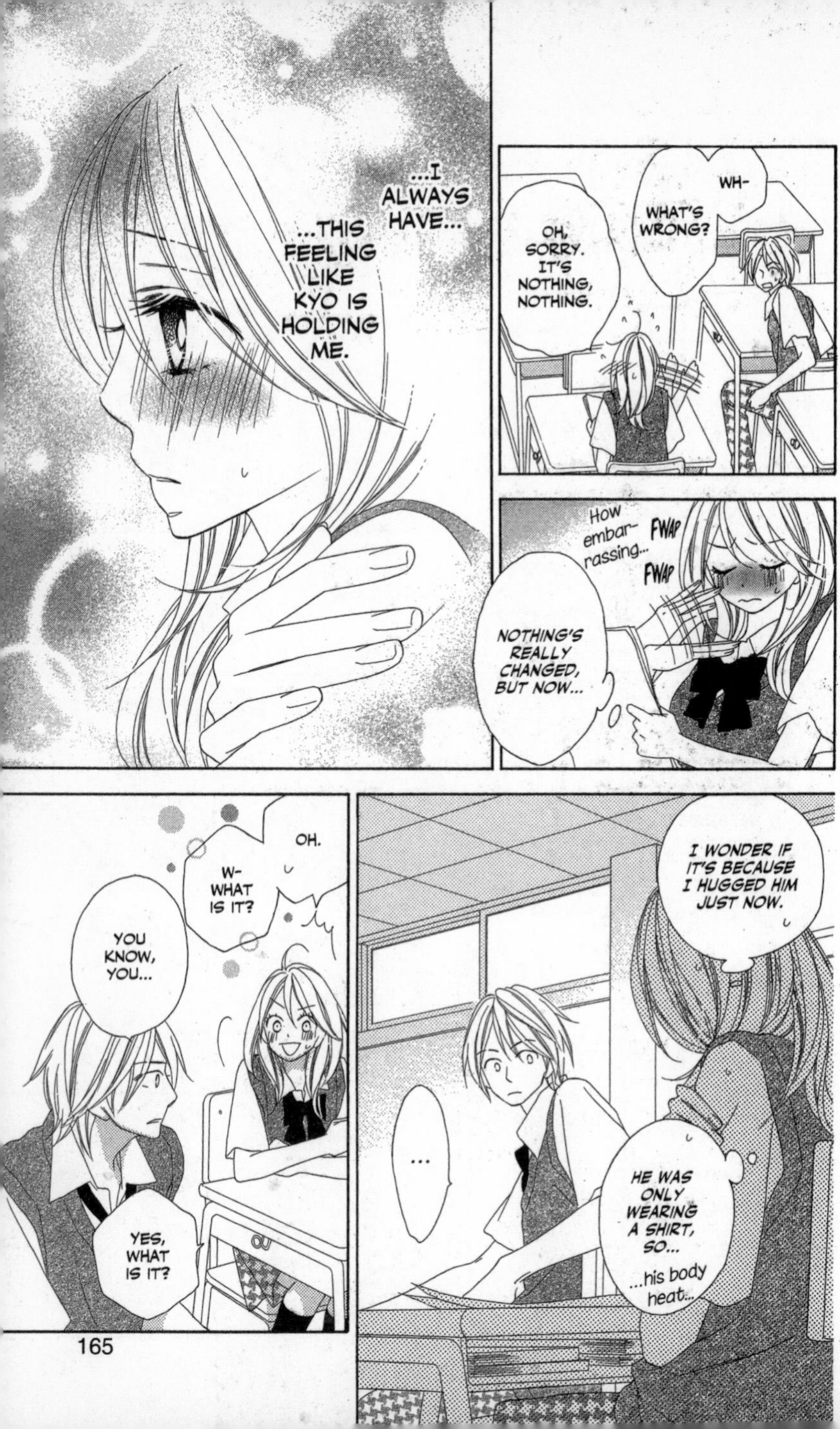
WH-
WHAT'S WRONG?
OH, SORRY. IT'S NOTHING, NOTHING.
How embar-rassing...
FWAP
FWAP
NOTHING'S REALLY CHANGED, BUT NOW...
...I ALWAYS HAVE...
...THIS FEELING LIKE KYO IS HOLDING ME.
I WONDER IF IT'S BECAUSE I HUGGED HIM JUST NOW.
...
HE WAS ONLY WEARING A SHIRT, SO...
...his body heat...
OH.
W-WHAT IS IT?
YOU KNOW, YOU...
YES, WHAT IS IT?

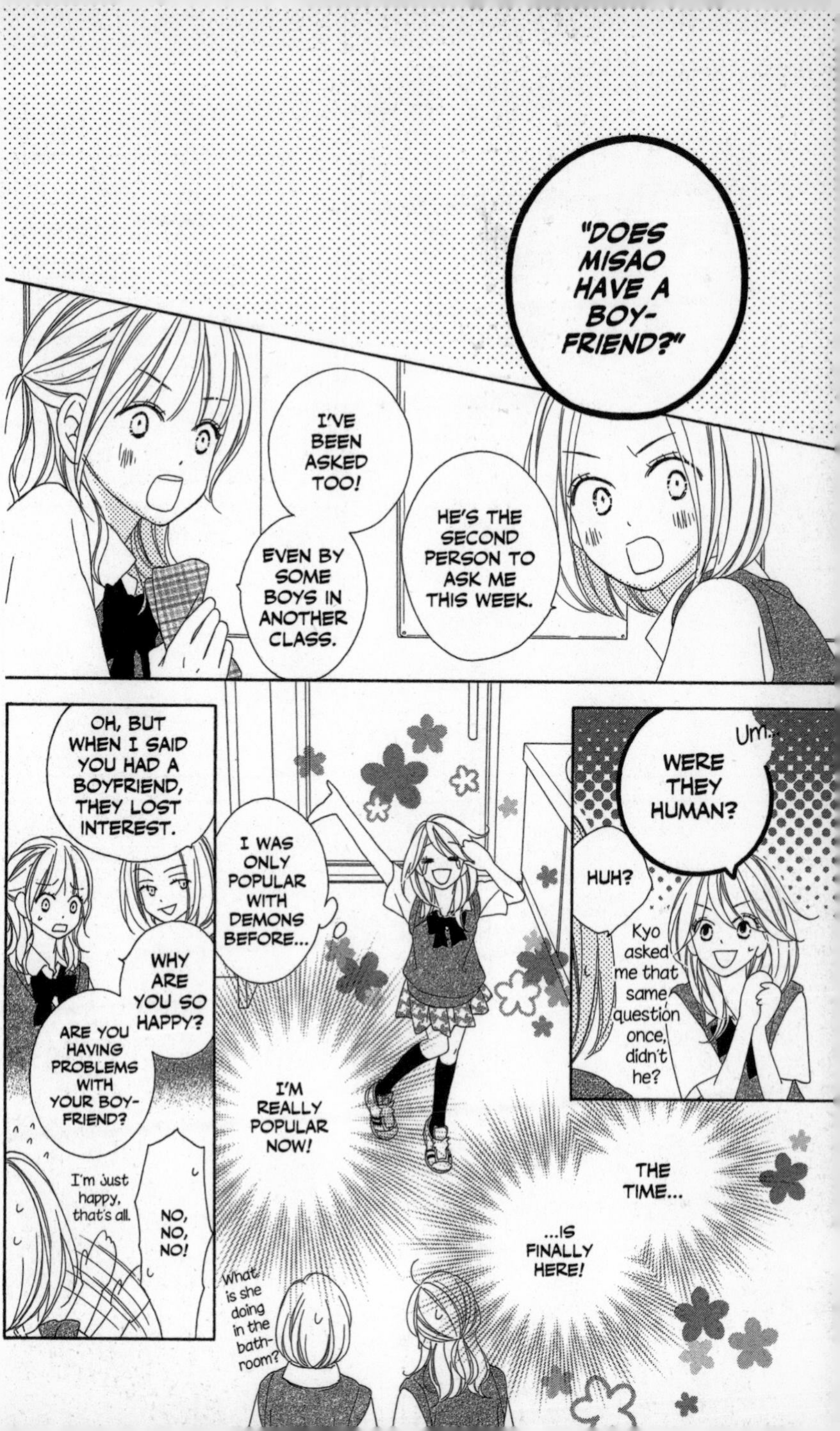
"DOES MISAO HAVE A BOY-FRIEND?"
HE'S THE SECOND PERSON TO ASK ME THIS WEEK.
I'VE BEEN ASKED TOO!
EVEN BY SOME BOYS IN ANOTHER CLASS.
Um...
WERE THEY HUMAN?
HUH?
Kyo asked me that same question once, didn't he?
I WAS ONLY POPULAR WITH DEMONS BEFORE...
I'M REALLY POPULAR NOW!
THE TIME...
...IS FINALLY HERE!
What is she doing in the bath-room?
OH, BUT WHEN I SAID YOU HAD A BOYFRIEND, THEY LOST INTEREST.
WHY ARE YOU SO HAPPY?
ARE YOU HAVING PROBLEMS WITH YOUR BOY-FRIEND?
NO, NO, NO!
I'm just happy, that's all.

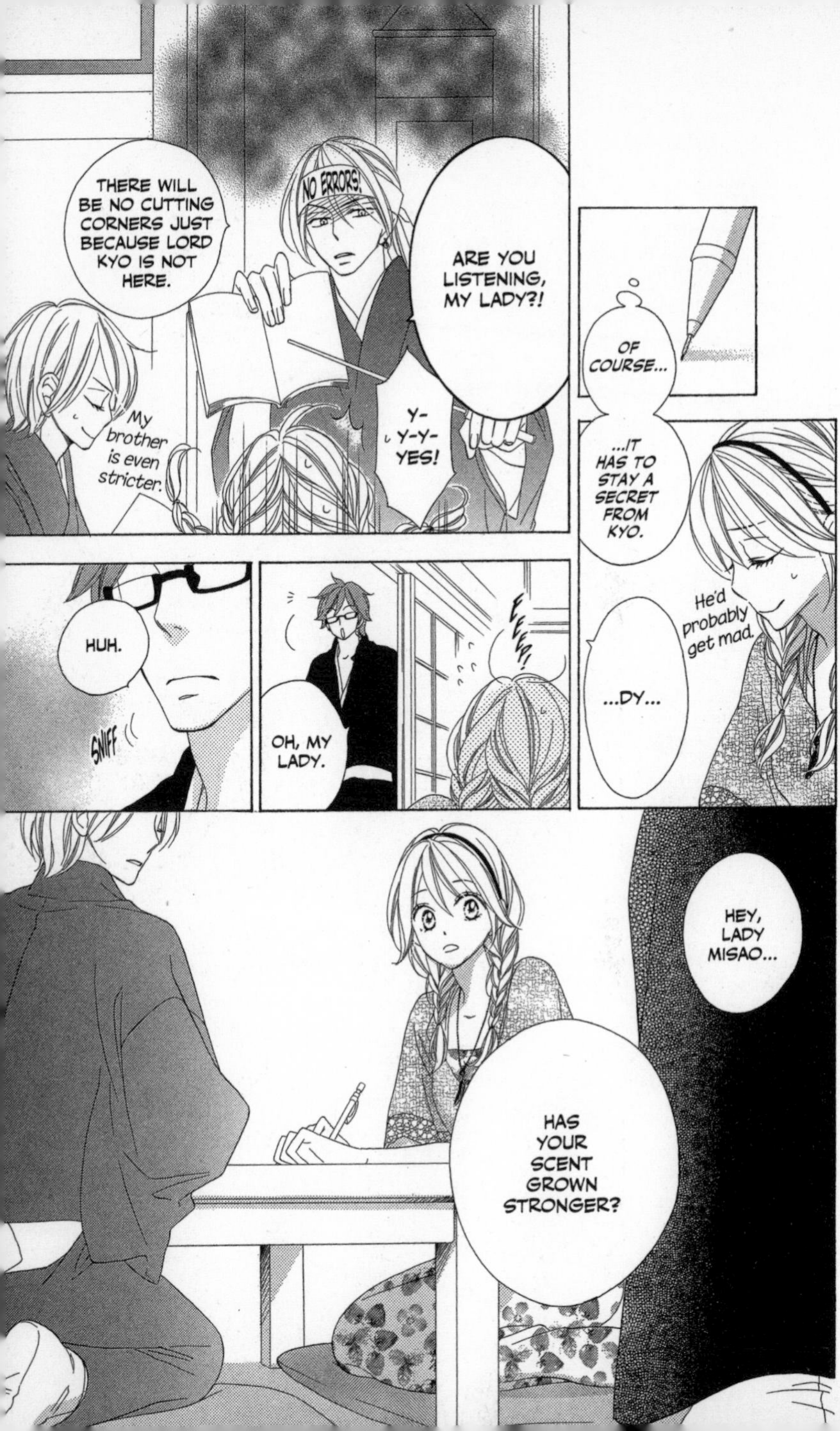
NO ERRORS!
THERE WILL BE NO CUTTING CORNERS JUST BECAUSE LORD KYO IS NOT HERE.
ARE YOU LISTENING, MY LADY?!
Y-Y-Y-YES!
My brother is even stricter.
OF COURSE...
...IT HAS TO STAY A SECRET FROM KYO.
He'd probably get mad.
...DY...
EEEP!
OH, MY LADY.
HUH.
SNIFF
HEY, LADY MISAO...
HAS YOUR SCENT GROWN STRONGER?

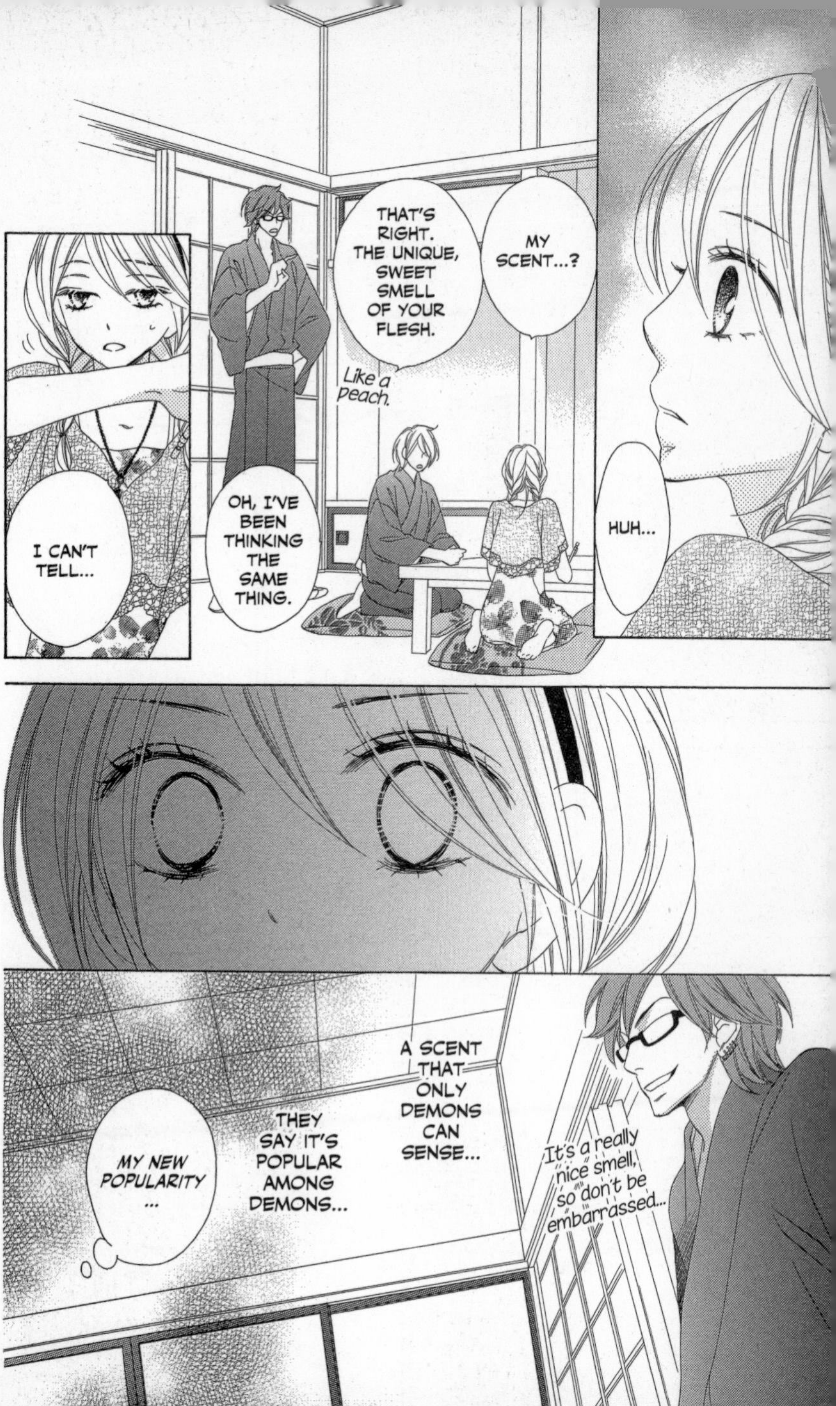
HUH...
MY SCENT...?
THAT'S RIGHT. THE UNIQUE, SWEET SMELL OF YOUR FLESH.
Like a peach.
OH, I'VE BEEN THINKING THE SAME THING.
I CAN'T TELL...
It's a really nice smell, so don't be embarrassed...
A SCENT THAT ONLY DEMONS CAN SENSE...
THEY SAY IT'S POPULAR AMONG DEMONS...
MY NEW POPULARITY ...

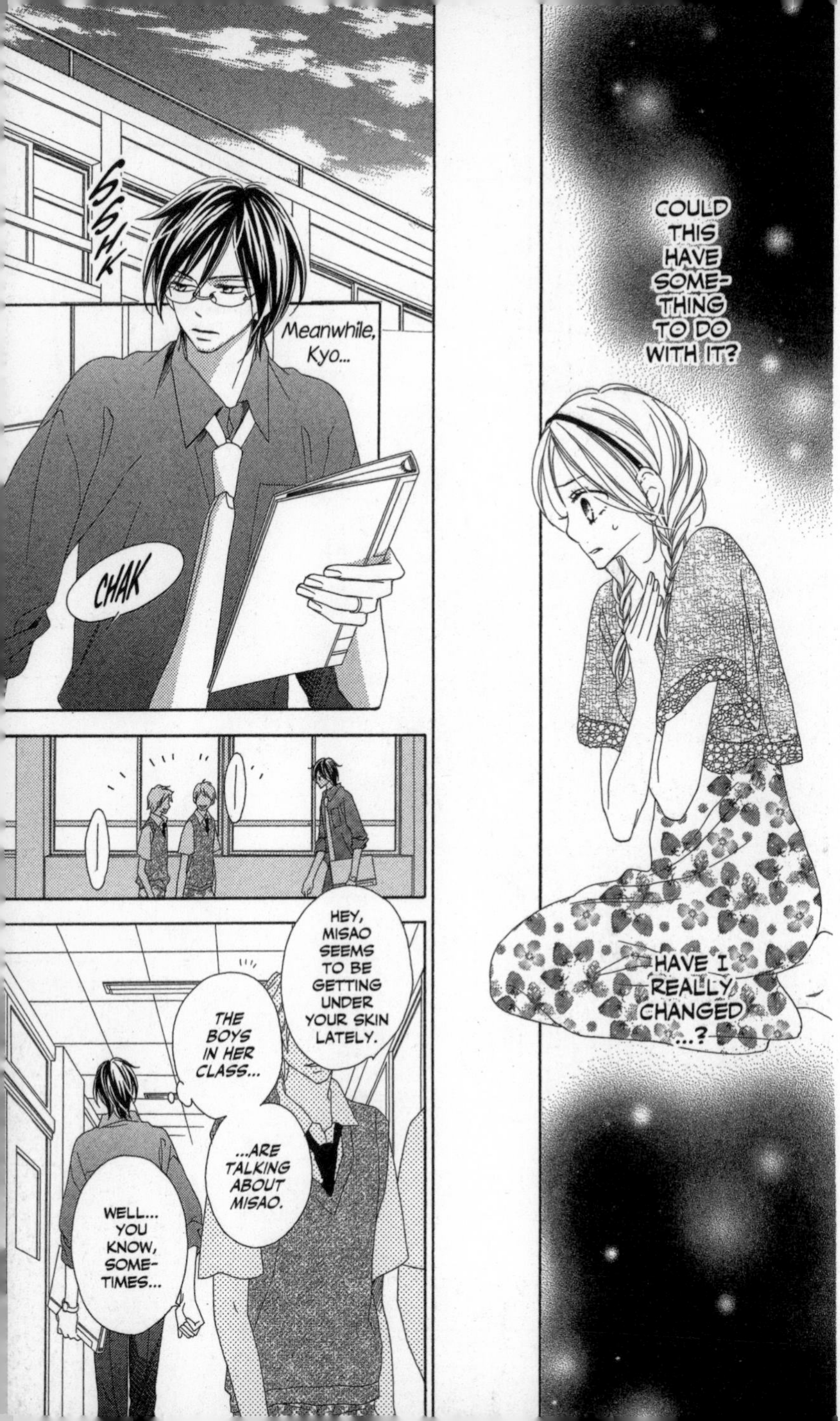
COULD THIS HAVE SOME-THING TO DO WITH IT?
HAVE I REALLY CHANGED ...?
SSHK
Meanwhile, Kyo...
CHAK
HEY, MISAO SEEMS TO BE GETTING UNDER YOUR SKIN LATELY.
THE BOYS IN HER CLASS...
...ARE TALKING ABOUT MISAO.
WELL... YOU KNOW, SOME-TIMES...

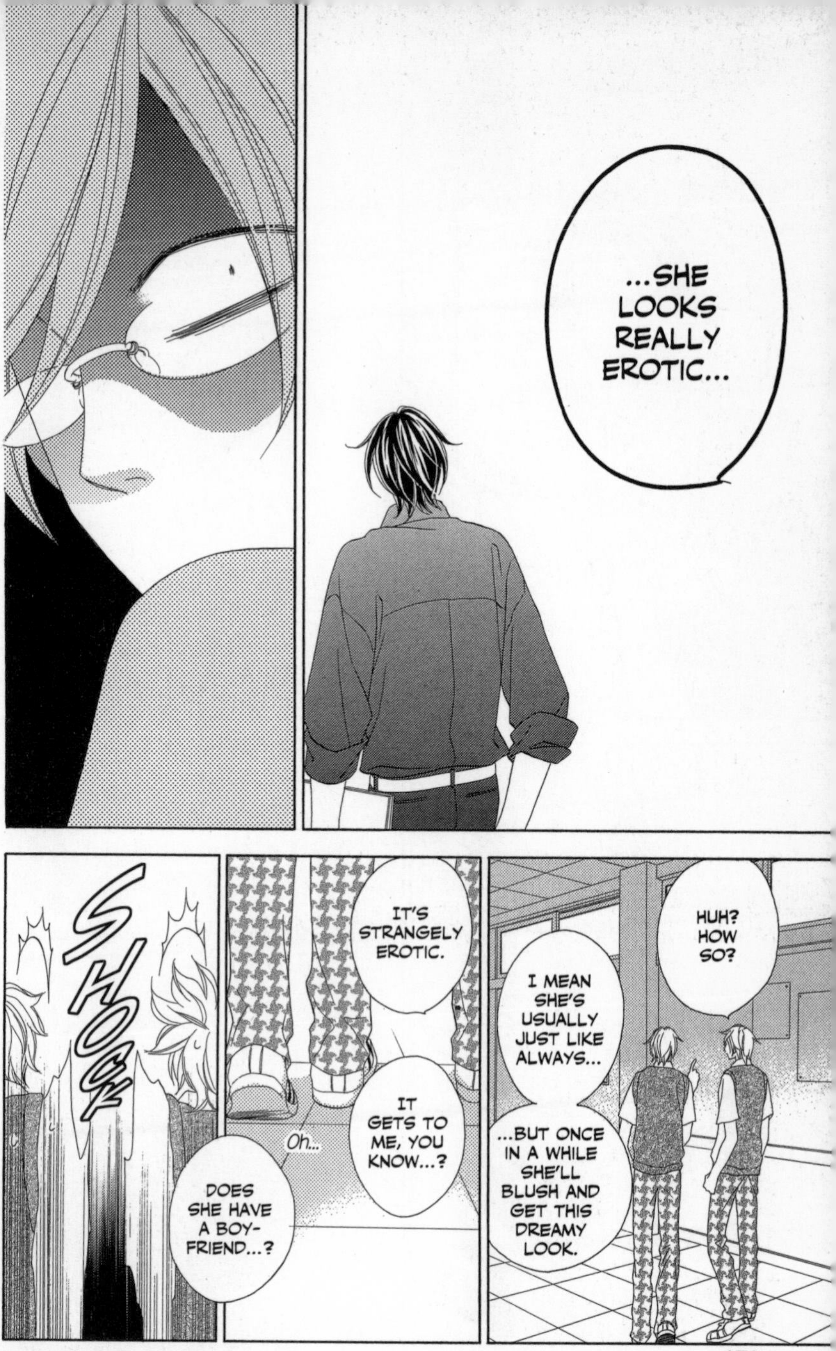
...SHE LOOKS REALLY EROTIC...
HUH? HOW SO?
I MEAN SHE'S USUALLY JUST LIKE ALWAYS...
...BUT ONCE IN A WHILE SHE'LL BLUSH AND GET THIS DREAMY LOOK.
IT'S STRANGELY EROTIC.
IT GETS TO ME, YOU KNOW...?
Oh...
DOES SHE HAVE A BOY-FRIEND...?
SHOCK

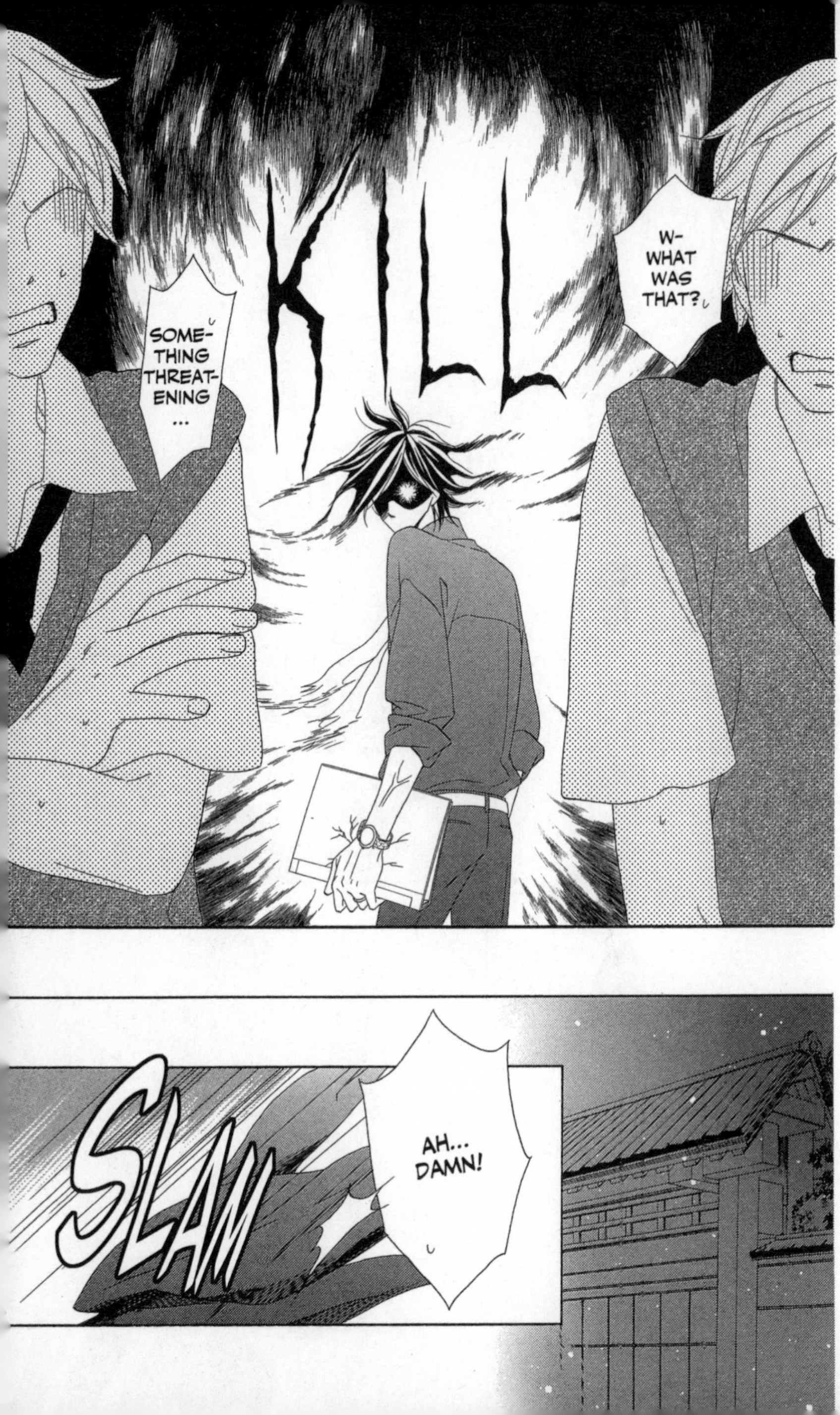
KILL
W-WHAT WAS THAT?
SOME-THING THREAT-ENING ...
AH... DAMN!
SLAM

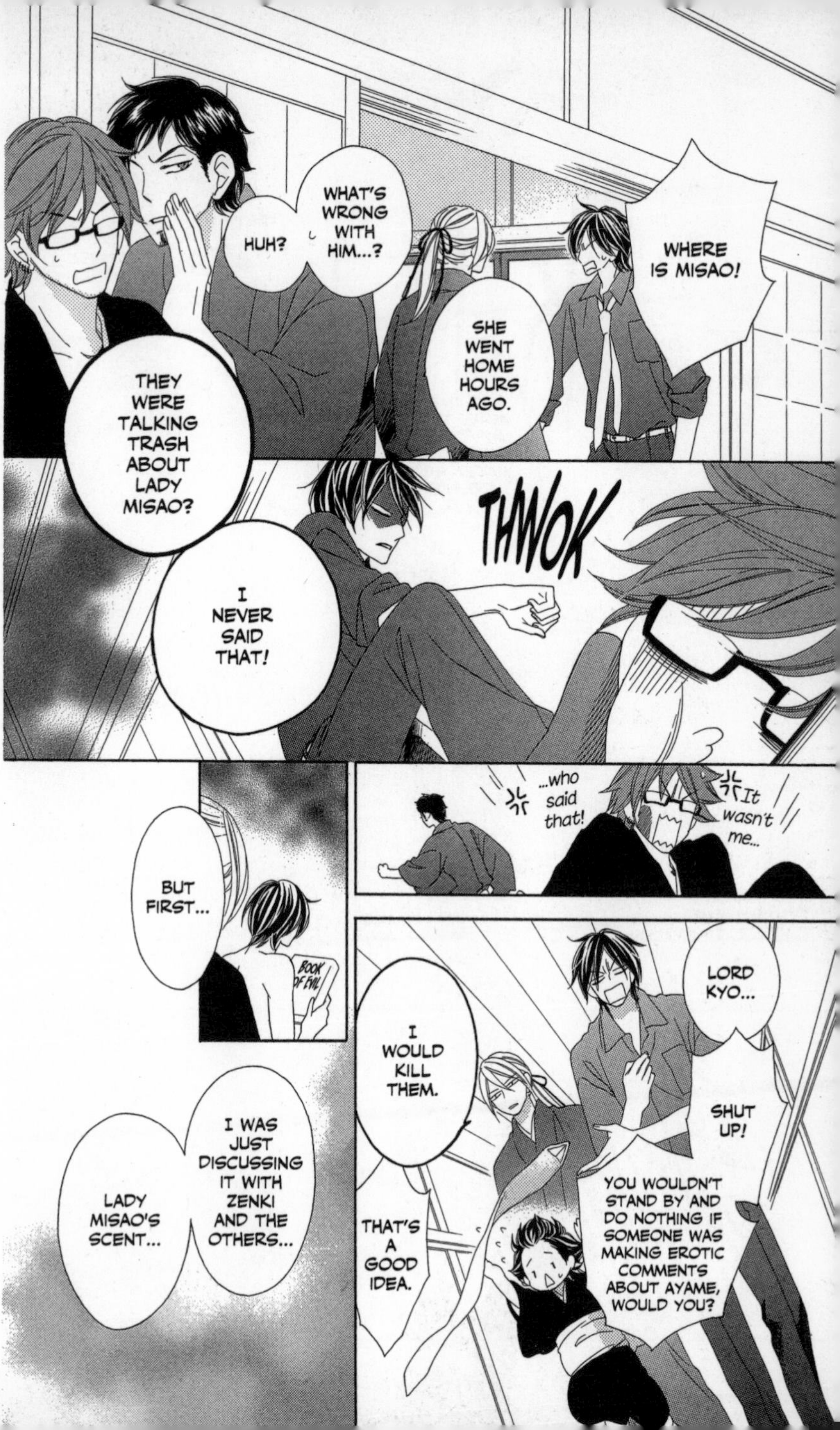
WHERE IS MISAO!
SHE WENT HOME HOURS AGO.
WHAT'S WRONG WITH HIM...?
HUH?
THEY WERE TALKING TRASH ABOUT LADY MISAO?
THWOK
I NEVER SAID THAT!
It wasn't me...
...who said that!
LORD KYO...
I WOULD KILL THEM.
SHUT UP!
YOU WOULDN'T STAND BY AND DO NOTHING IF SOMEONE WAS MAKING EROTIC COMMENTS ABOUT AYAME, WOULD YOU?
THAT'S A GOOD IDEA.
BUT FIRST...
BOOK OF EVIL
I WAS JUST DISCUSSING IT WITH ZENKI AND THE OTHERS...
LADY MISAO'S SCENT...

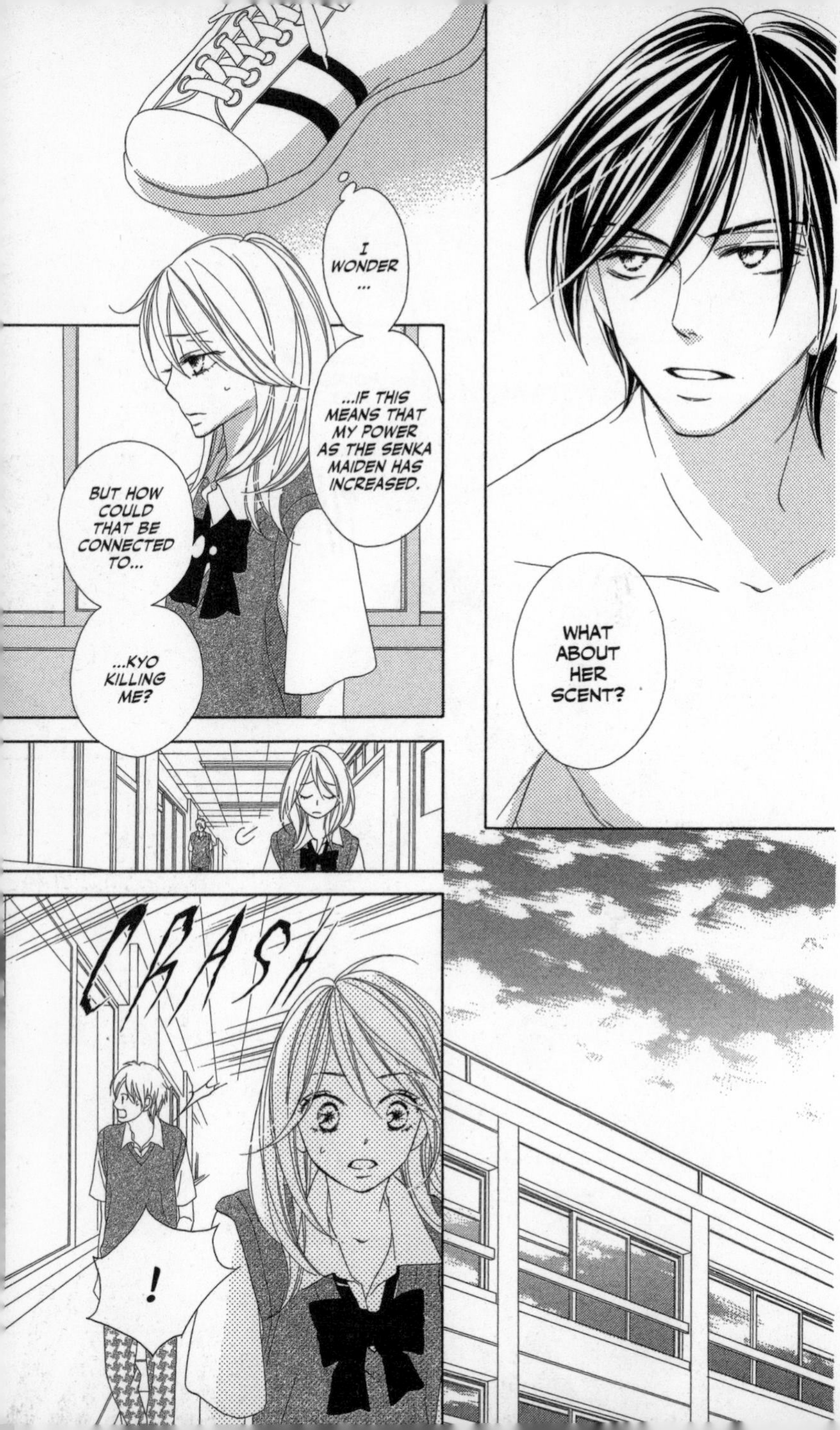

WHAT ABOUT HER SCENT?
I WONDER...
...IF THIS MEANS THAT MY POWER AS THE SENKA MAIDEN HAS INCREASED.
BUT HOW COULD THAT BE CONNECTED TO...
...KYO KILLING ME?
CRASH
!

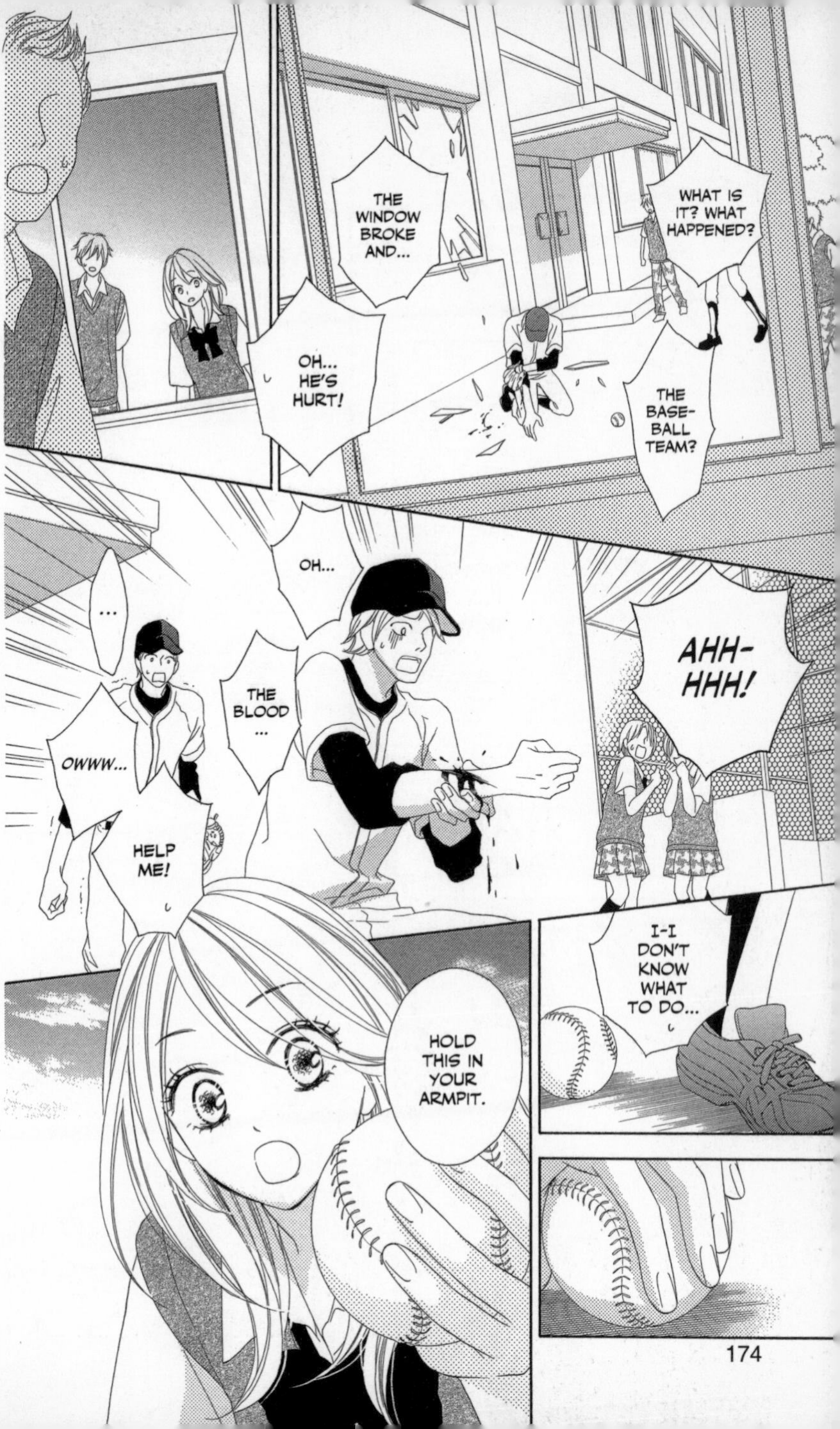
WHAT IS IT? WHAT HAPPENED?
THE WINDOW BROKE AND...
THE BASE-BALL TEAM?
OH... HE'S HURT!
AHH-HHH!
OH...
...
THE BLOOD ...
OWWW...
HELP ME!
I-I DON'T KNOW WHAT TO DO...
HOLD THIS IN YOUR ARMPIT.

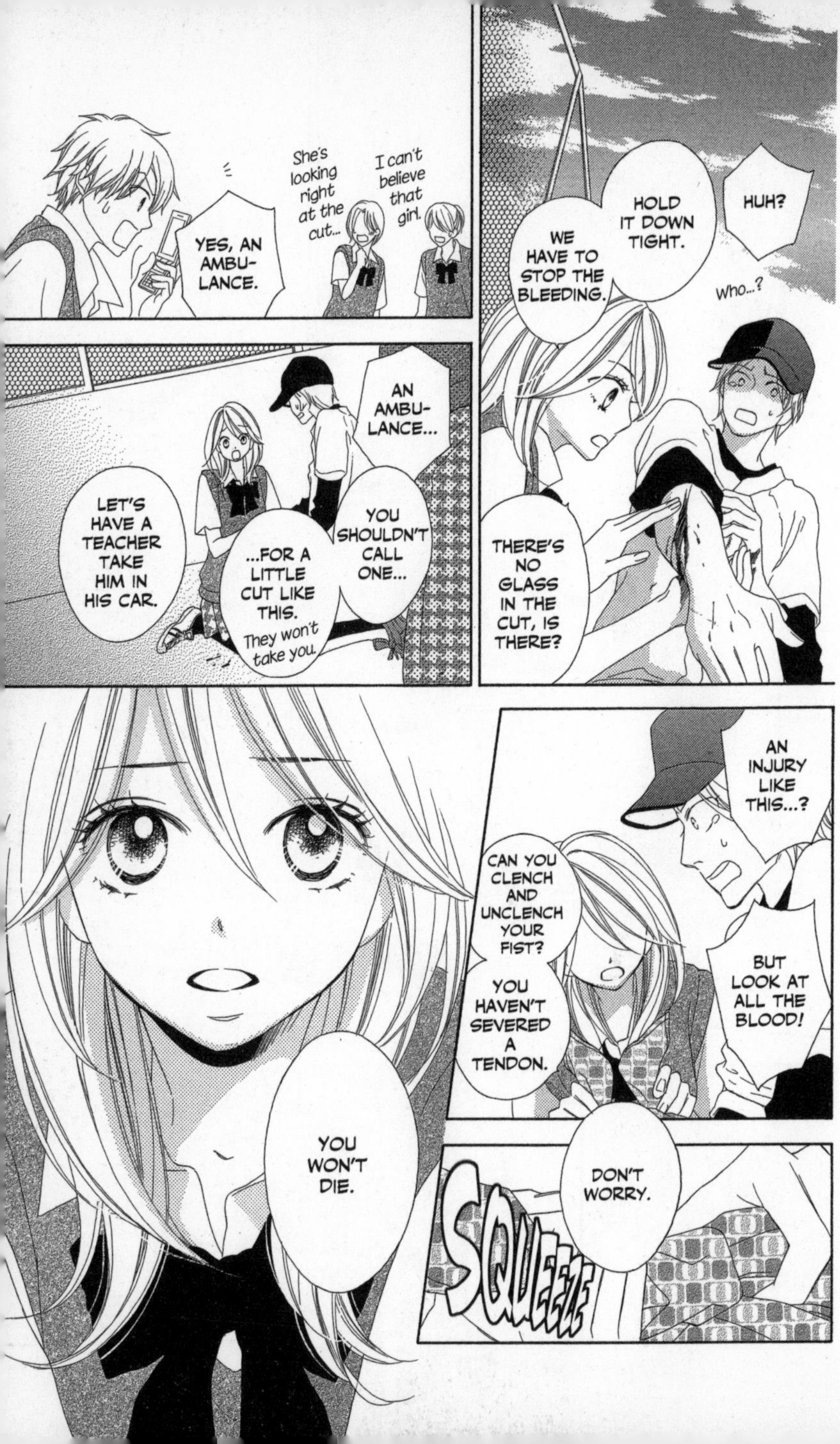
HUH?
HOLD IT DOWN TIGHT.
WE HAVE TO STOP THE BLEEDING.
Who...?
THERE'S NO GLASS IN THE CUT, IS THERE?
I can't believe that girl.
She's looking right at the cut...
YES, AN AMBULANCE.
AN AMBULANCE...
YOU SHOULDN'T CALL ONE...
...FOR A LITTLE CUT LIKE THIS.
They won't take you.
LET'S HAVE A TEACHER TAKE HIM IN HIS CAR.
AN INJURY LIKE THIS...?
CAN YOU CLENCH AND UNCLENCH YOUR FIST?
BUT LOOK AT ALL THE BLOOD!
YOU HAVEN'T SEVERED A TENDON.
DON'T WORRY.
SQUEEZE
YOU WON'T DIE.

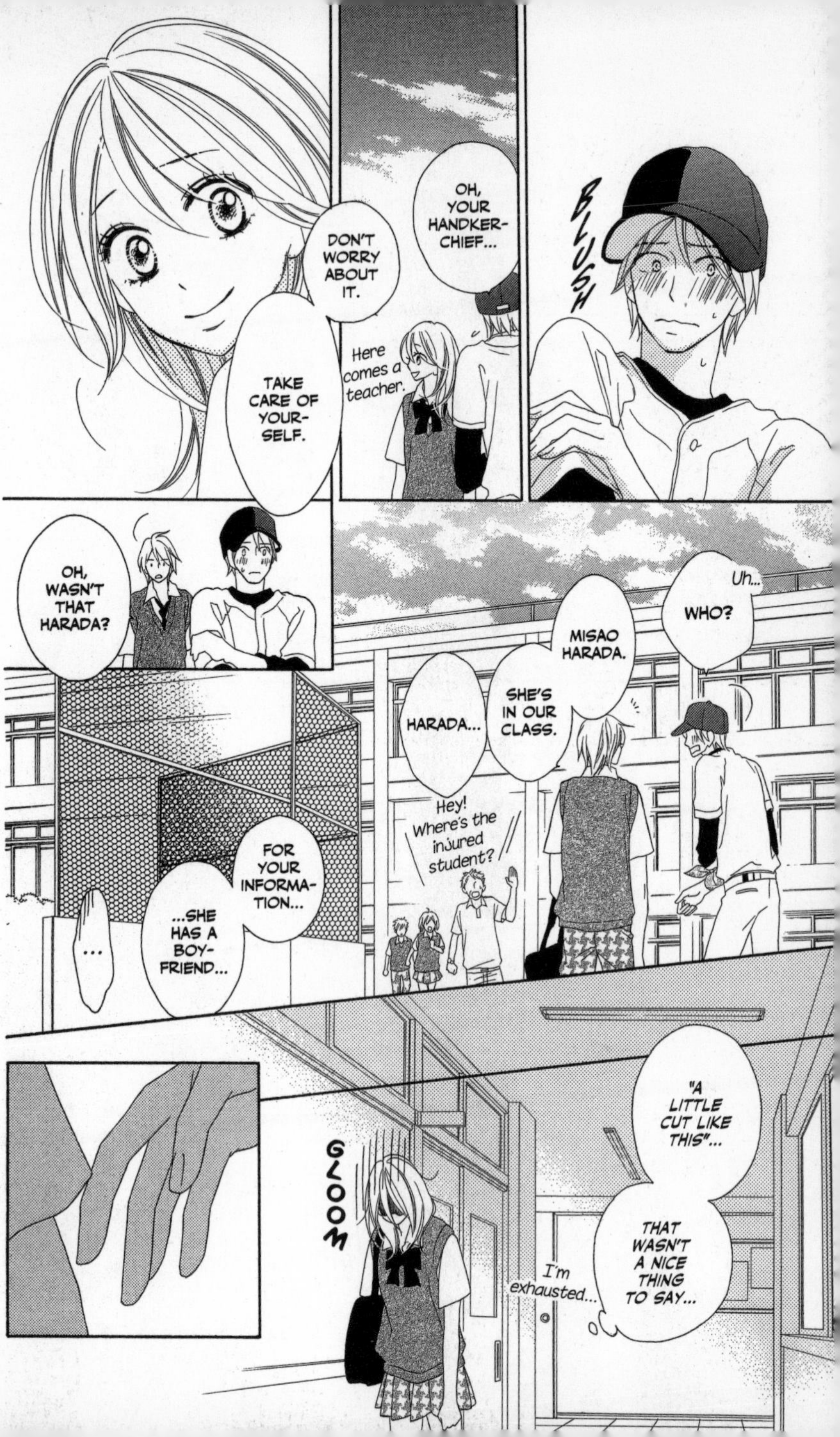
BLUSH
OH, YOUR HANDKER-CHIEF...
DON'T WORRY ABOUT IT.
Here comes a teacher.
TAKE CARE OF YOUR-SELF.
Uh...
WHO?
MISAO HARADA.
SHE'S IN OUR CLASS.
HARADA...
Hey! Where's the injured student?
OH, WASN'T THAT HARADA?
FOR YOUR INFORMATION...
...SHE HAS A BOY-FRIEND...
...
"A LITTLE CUT LIKE THIS"...
THAT WASN'T A NICE THING TO SAY...
I'm exhausted...
GLOOM

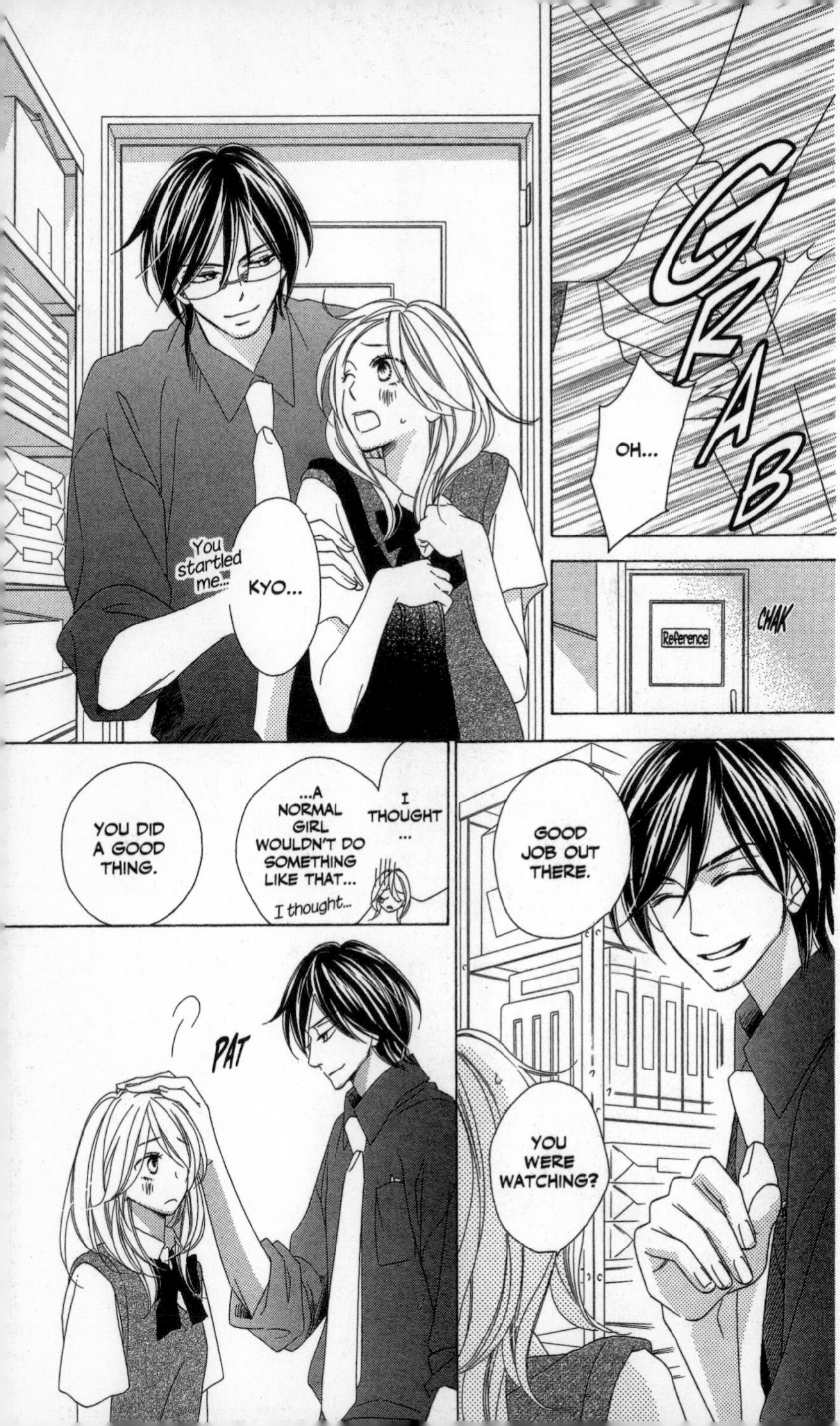
GRAB
OH...
CHAK
Reference
KYO...
You startled me...
GOOD JOB OUT THERE.
YOU WERE WATCHING?
I THOUGHT ...
...A NORMAL GIRL WOULDN'T DO SOMETHING LIKE THAT...
I thought...
YOU DID A GOOD THING.
PAT
?

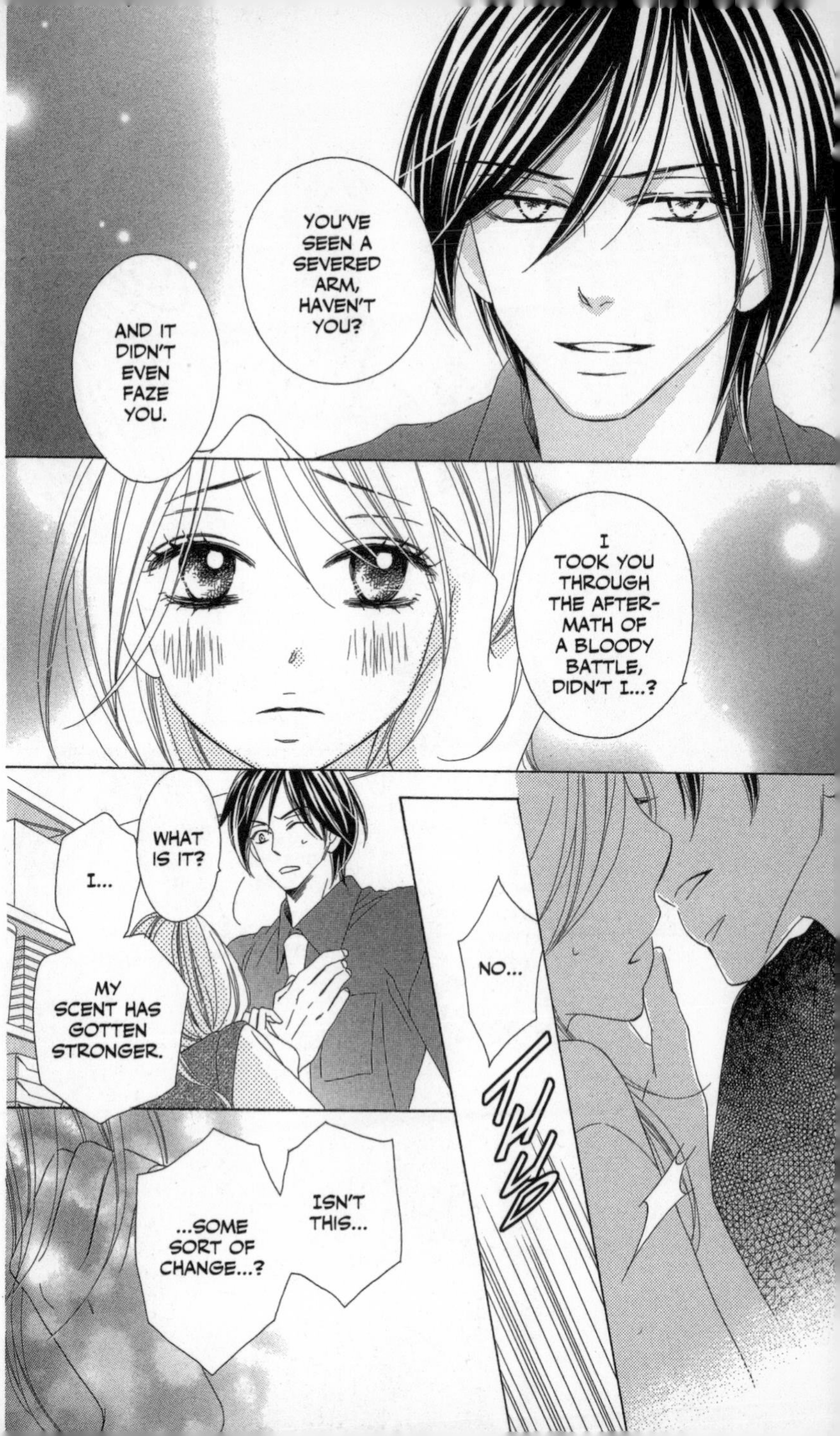
YOU'VE SEEN A SEVERED ARM, HAVEN'T YOU?
AND IT DIDN'T EVEN FAZE YOU.
I TOOK YOU THROUGH THE AFTER-MATH OF A BLOODY BATTLE, DIDN'T I...?
NO...
WHAT IS IT?
I...
MY SCENT HAS GOTTEN STRONGER.
ISN'T THIS...
...SOME SORT OF CHANGE...?

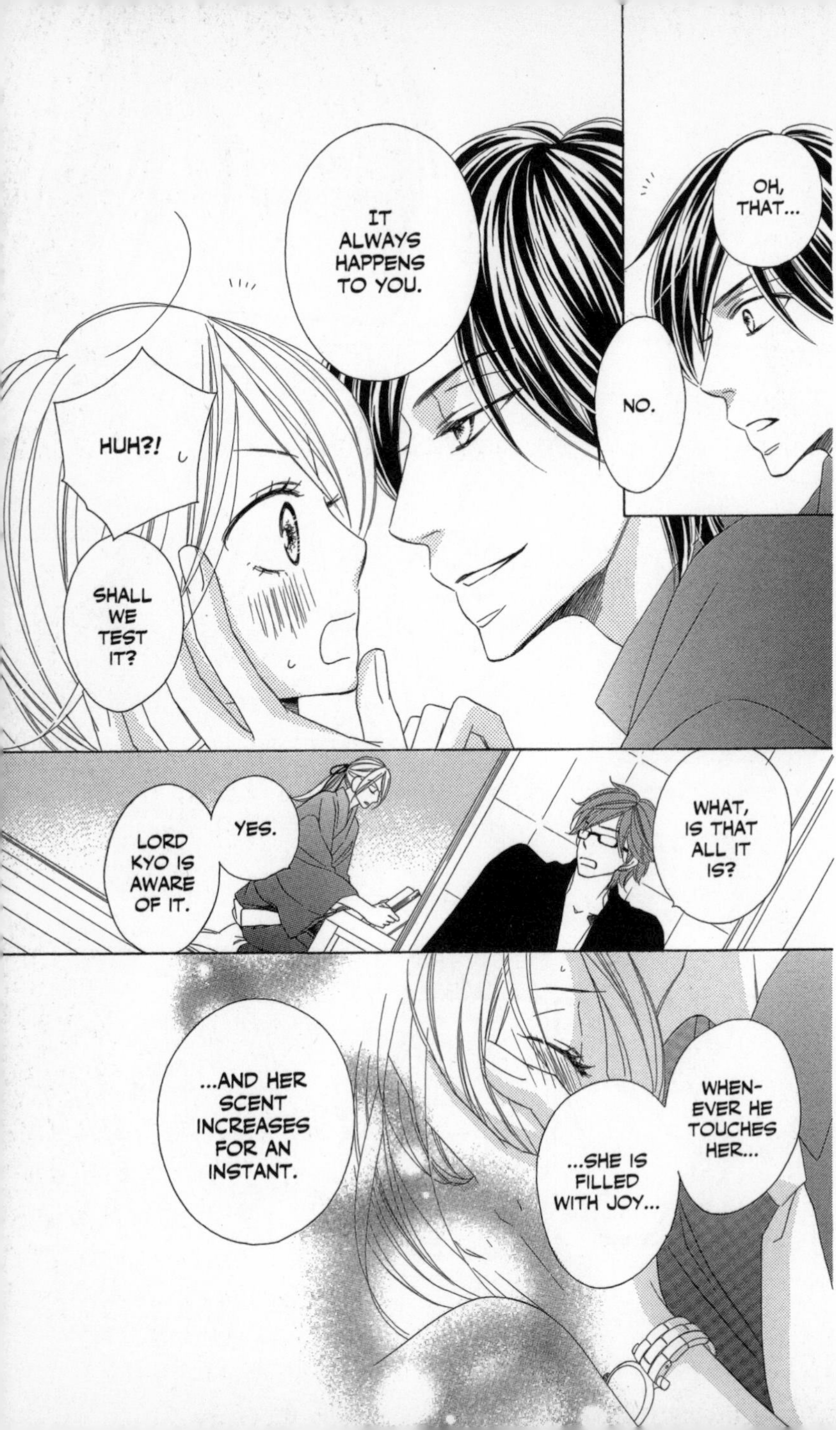
OH, THAT...
NO.
IT ALWAYS HAPPENS TO YOU.
HUH?!
SHALL WE TEST IT?
WHAT, IS THAT ALL IT IS?
YES.
LORD KYO IS AWARE OF IT.
WHEN-EVER HE TOUCHES HER...
...SHE IS FILLED WITH JOY...
...AND HER SCENT INCREASES FOR AN INSTANT.

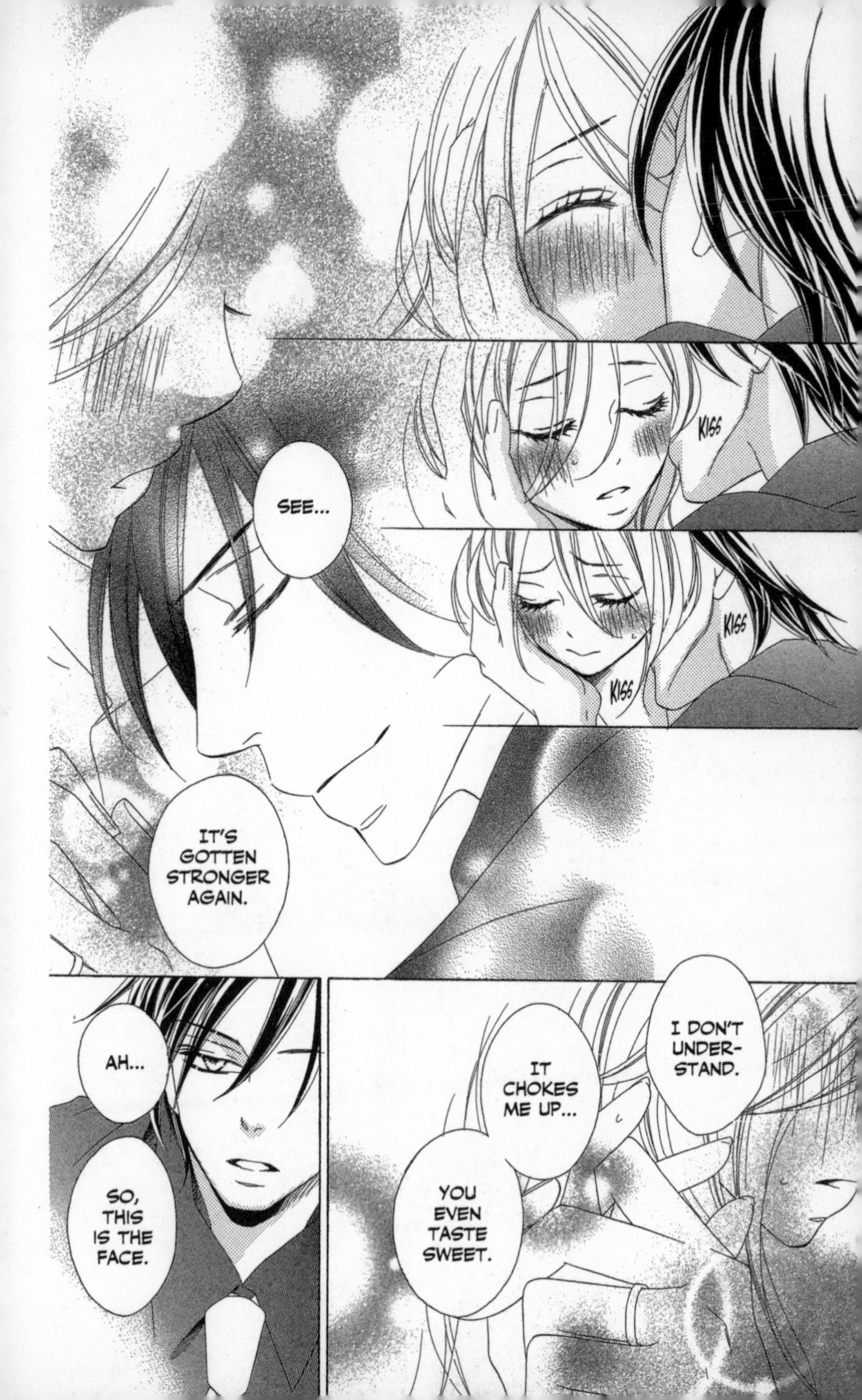
KISS
KISS
KISS
SEE...
IT'S GOTTEN STRONGER AGAIN.
I DON'T UNDER-STAND.
IT CHOKES ME UP...
YOU EVEN TASTE SWEET.
AH...
SO, THIS IS THE FACE.

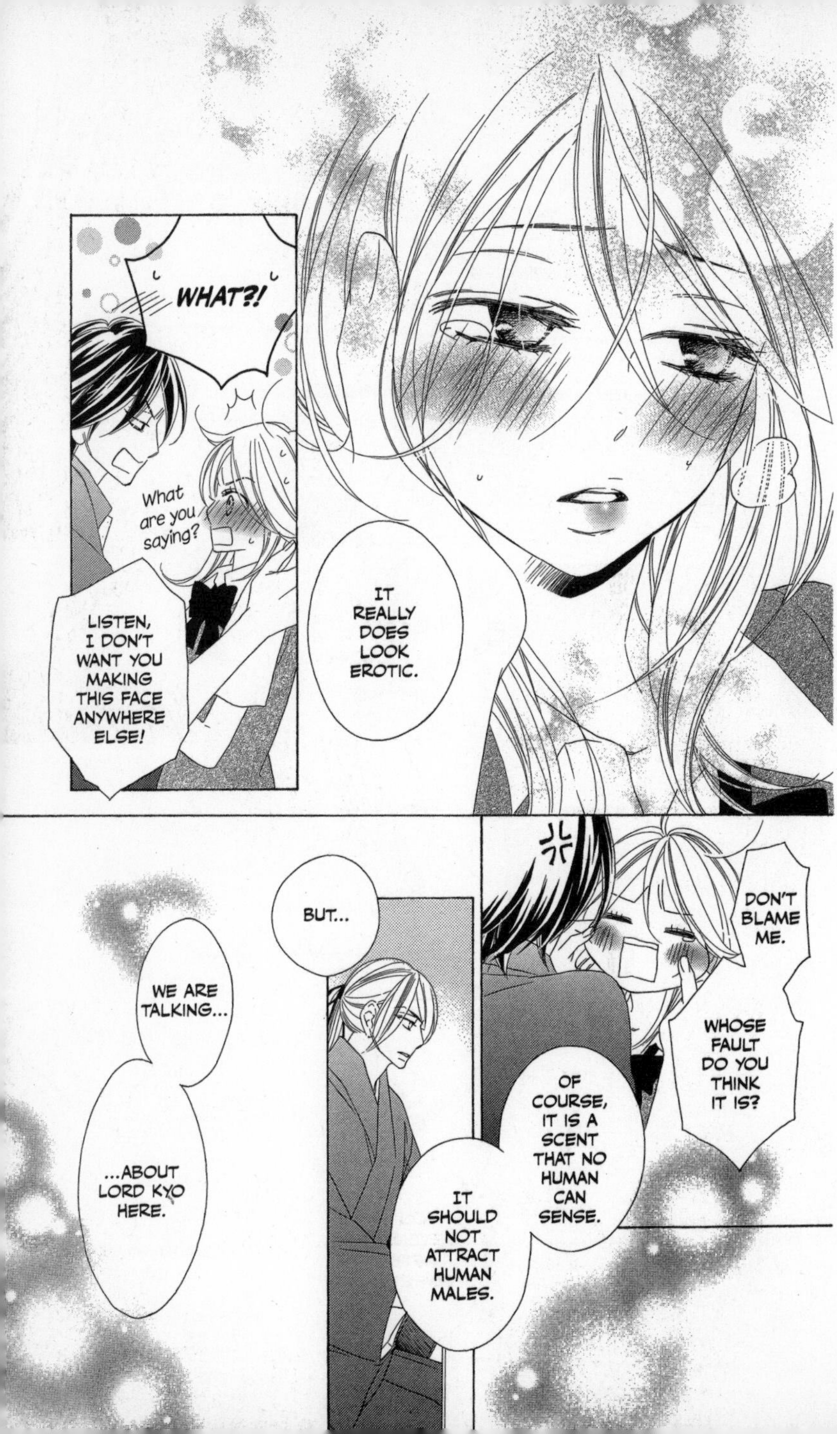
IT REALLY DOES LOOK EROTIC.
WHAT?!
What are you saying?
LISTEN, I DON'T WANT YOU MAKING THIS FACE ANYWHERE ELSE!
DON'T BLAME ME.
WHOSE FAULT DO YOU THINK IT IS?
OF COURSE, IT IS A SCENT THAT NO HUMAN CAN SENSE.
IT SHOULD NOT ATTRACT HUMAN MALES.
BUT...
WE ARE TALKING...
...ABOUT LORD KYO HERE.

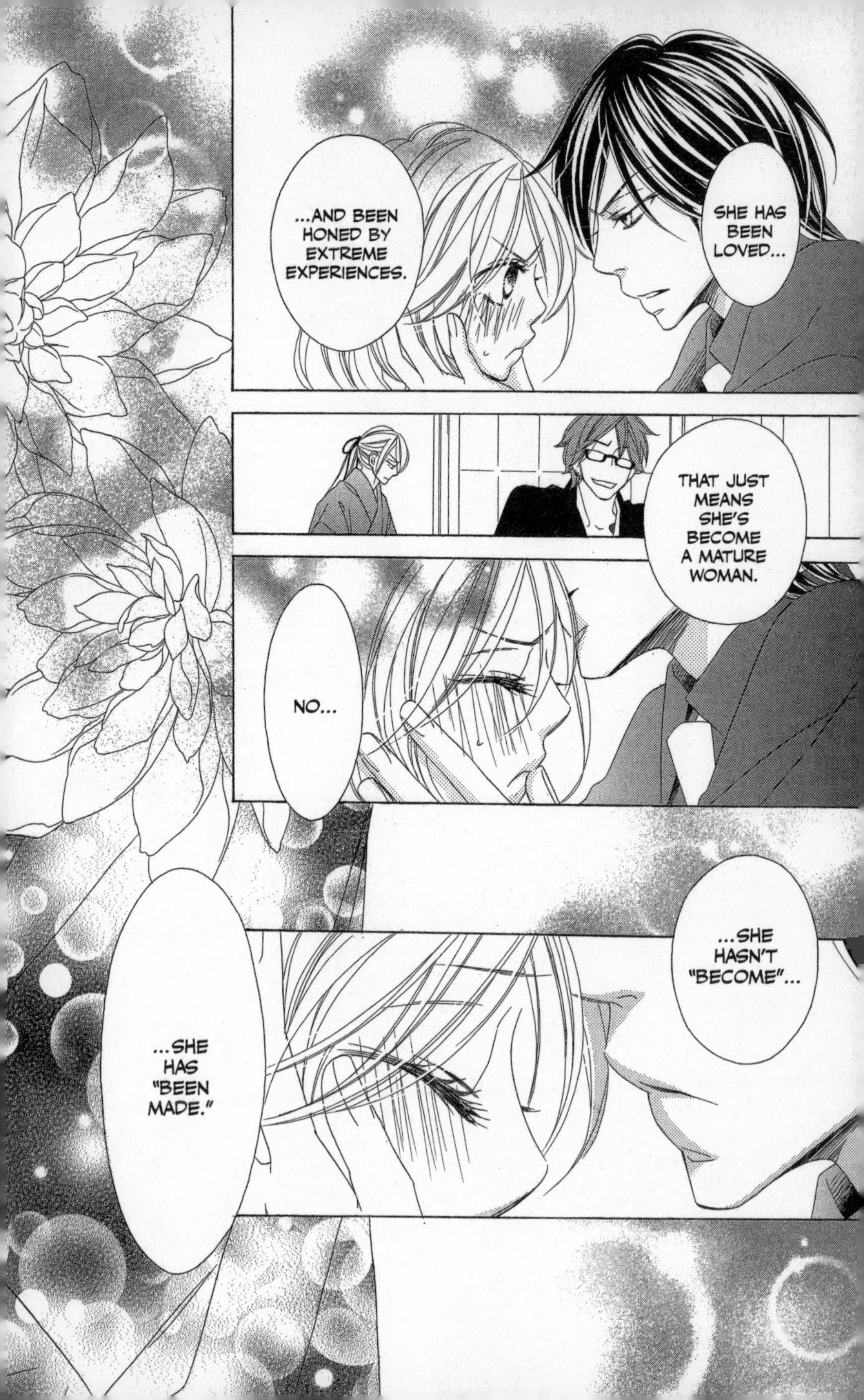
SHE HAS BEEN LOVED...
...AND BEEN HONED BY EXTREME EXPERIENCES.
THAT JUST MEANS SHE'S BECOME A MATURE WOMAN.
NO...
...SHE HASN'T "BECOME"...
...SHE HAS "BEEN MADE."

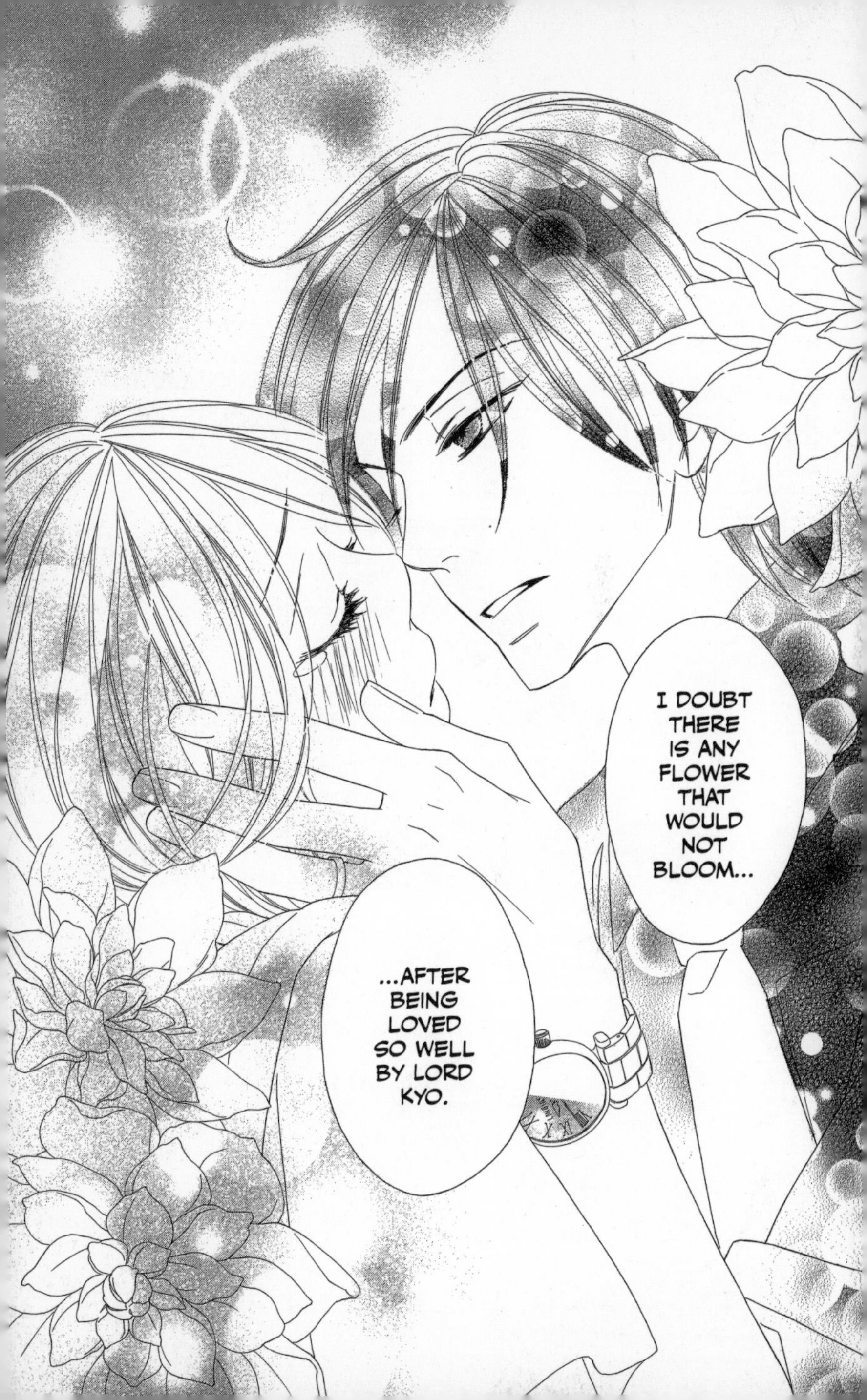
I DOUBT THERE IS ANY FLOWER THAT WOULD NOT BLOOM...
...AFTER BEING LOVED SO WELL BY LORD KYO.

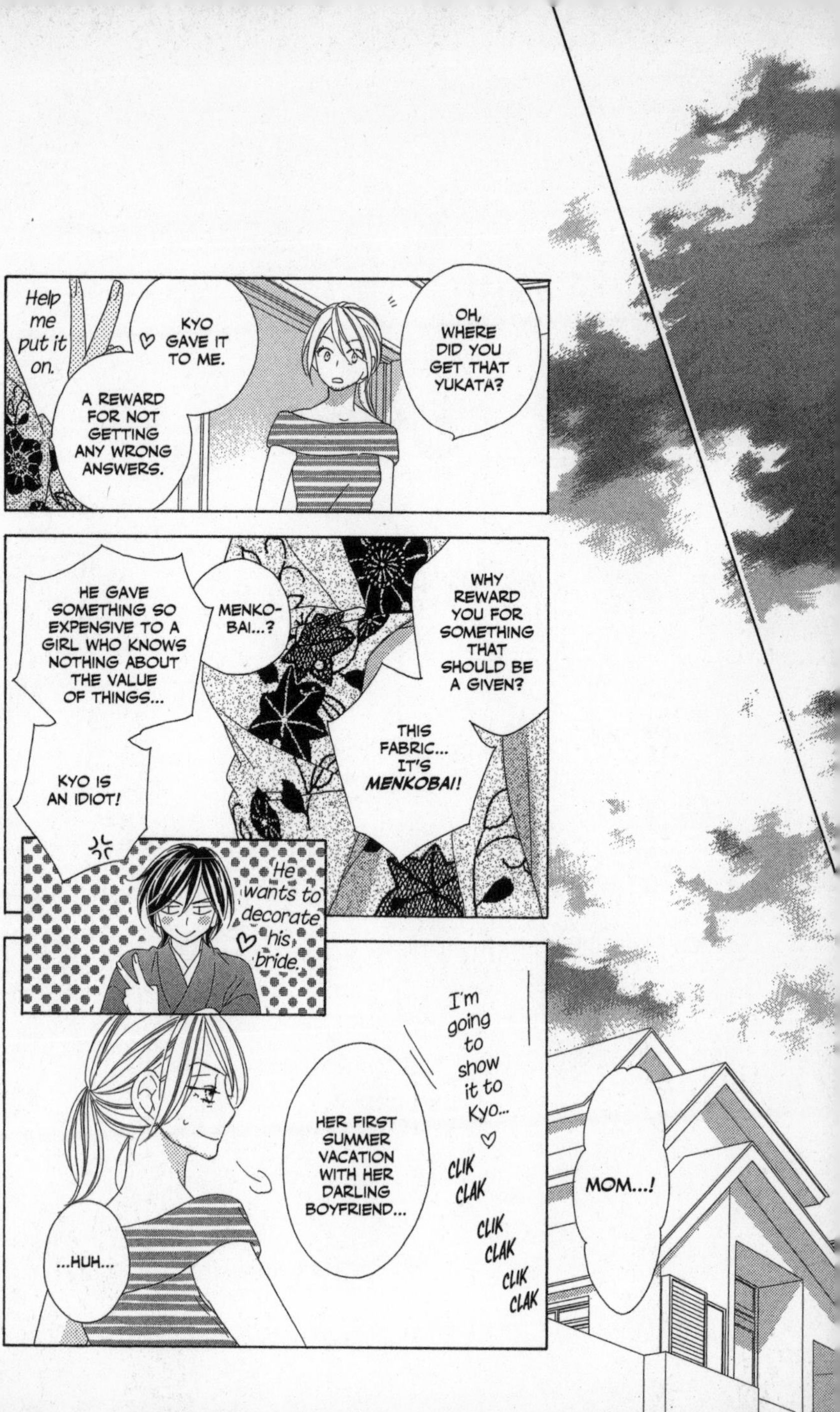
OH, WHERE DID YOU GET THAT YUKATA?
KYO ♡ GAVE IT TO ME.
A REWARD FOR NOT GETTING ANY WRONG ANSWERS.
Help me put it on.
WHY REWARD YOU FOR SOMETHING THAT SHOULD BE A GIVEN?
THIS FABRIC... IT'S *MENKOBAI!*
MENKO-BAI...?
HE GAVE SOMETHING SO EXPENSIVE TO A GIRL WHO KNOWS NOTHING ABOUT THE VALUE OF THINGS...
KYO IS AN IDIOT!
He wants to decorate ♡ his bride.
MOM...!
I'm going to show it to Kyo... ♡
CLIK CLAK
CLIK CLAK
CLIK CLAK
HER FIRST SUMMER VACATION WITH HER DARLING BOYFRIEND...
...HUH...

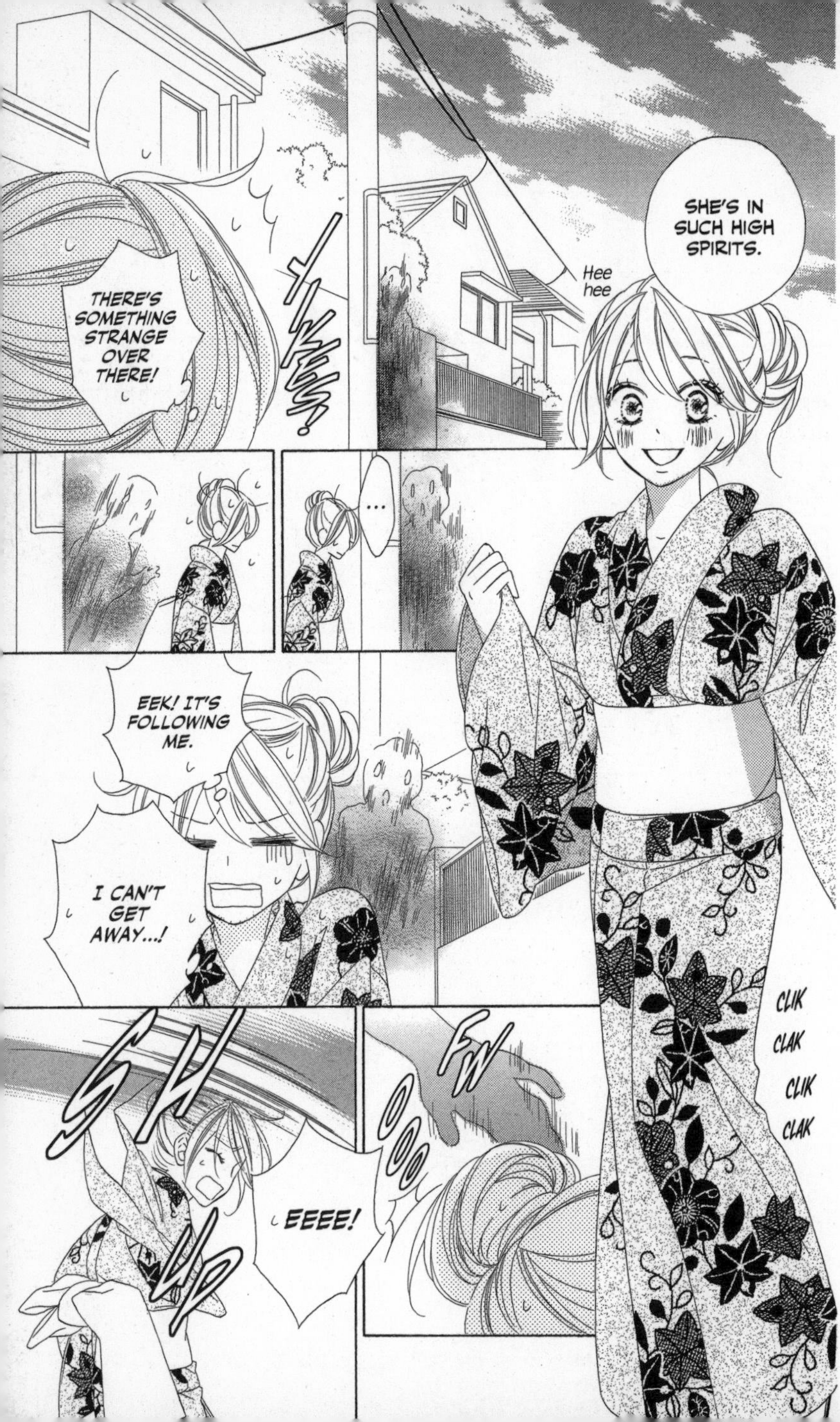
SHE'S IN SUCH HIGH SPIRITS.
Hee hee
CLIK
CLAK
CLIK
CLAK
THERE'S SOMETHING STRANGE OVER THERE!
...
EEK! IT'S FOLLOWING ME.
I CAN'T GET AWAY...!
FW
EEEE!

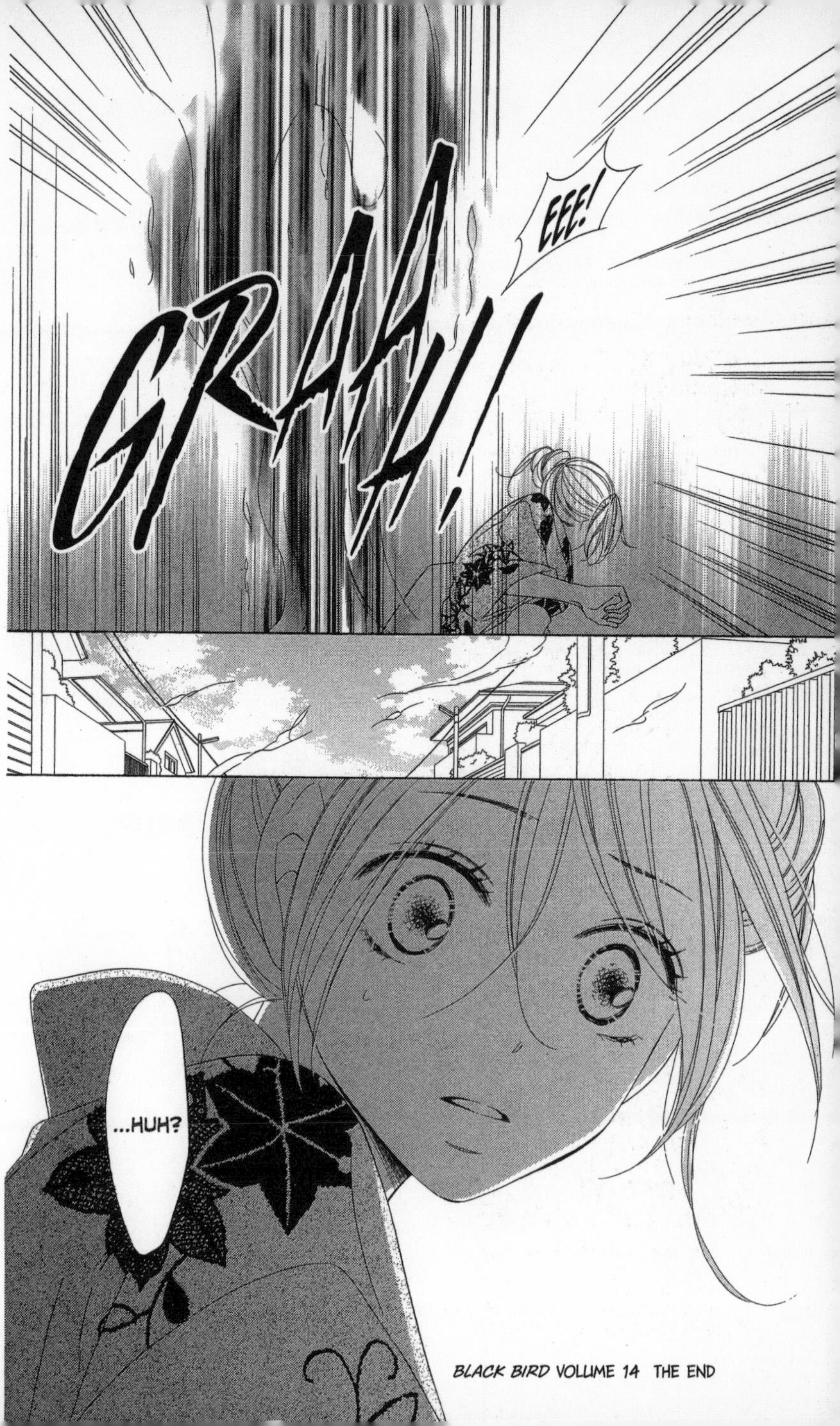
EEE!
GRAAH!
...HUH?

BLACK BIRD VOLUME 14 THE END

Tell Us, Mr. Usui! Part 2

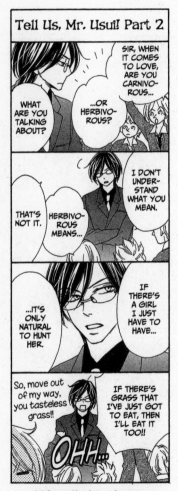

SIR, WHEN IT COMES TO LOVE, ARE YOU CARNIVOROUS...
...OR HERBIVOROUS?
WHAT ARE YOU TALKING ABOUT?
I DON'T UNDERSTAND WHAT YOU MEAN.
HERBIVOROUS MEANS...
THAT'S NOT IT.
IF THERE'S A GIRL I JUST HAVE TO HAVE...
...IT'S ONLY NATURAL TO HUNT HER.
IF THERE'S GRASS THAT I'VE JUST GOT TO EAT, THEN I'LL EAT IT TOO!!
So, move out of my way, you tasteless grass!!
OHH...

Well, now Kyo is carnivorous.

There seems to be a lot of "grass," both male and female, that will not move. Written with self-discipline.

Tell Us, Mr. Usui! Part 3

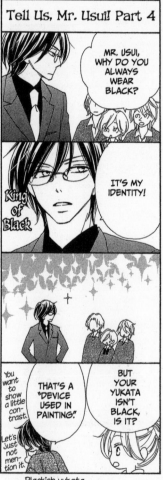

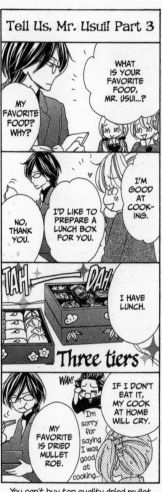

WHAT IS YOUR FAVORITE FOOD, MR. USUI...?
MY FAVORITE FOOD? WHY?
I'M GOOD AT COOK-ING.
I'D LIKE TO PREPARE A LUNCH BOX FOR YOU.
NO, THANK YOU.
TAH
DAH
I HAVE LUNCH.
Three tiers
IF I DON'T EAT IT, MY COOK AT HOME WILL CRY.
WAH!
I'm sorry for saying I was good at cooking...
MY FAVORITE IS DRIED MULLET ROE.

You can't buy top quality dried mullet roe for less than 10,000 yen (although I did say you could in the special feature in the previous volume).

Tell Us, Mr. Usui! Part 4

MR. USUI, WHY DO YOU ALWAYS WEAR BLACK?
IT'S MY IDENTITY!
King of Black
BUT YOUR YUKATA ISN'T BLACK, IS IT?
THAT'S A "DEVICE USED IN PAINTING."
You want to show a little con-trast.
Let's just not men-tion it.

Blackish yukata

Thank you very much for reading volume 14! I have relied on my editor for much more than what is mentioned in the comic strip to the right. This editor, Ms. S., always wears such sexy outfits (the one in the third frame is for real). Her reaction to the scene where Misao and Kyo first made love was, "I'm all hot!" Toward the end, she praised (not just those scenes, but) the whole thing as "erotic." She's the one who saw me through the serialization of *Black Bird* from chapter 2, but she's been transferred now. Thank you very much for everything! ♥

Incidentally, the person who was there for the birth of this series, who came up with the ultimate subtitle (*Imayou Tengu Kitan*, or *Modern Tengu Story*), and who left us soon after the manuscript for the first chapter was completed, was Mr. Y.

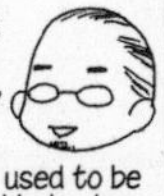

I used to be able to draw a better likeness of him...

My new editor is the editor I worked with when I first started out! I hope to be able to show some improvement! I hope...

Black Bird is finally in its final stretch. I hope you will continue to support me!

An auspicious day, July 2011

桜小路 かのこ ♥

Kanako Sakurakouji

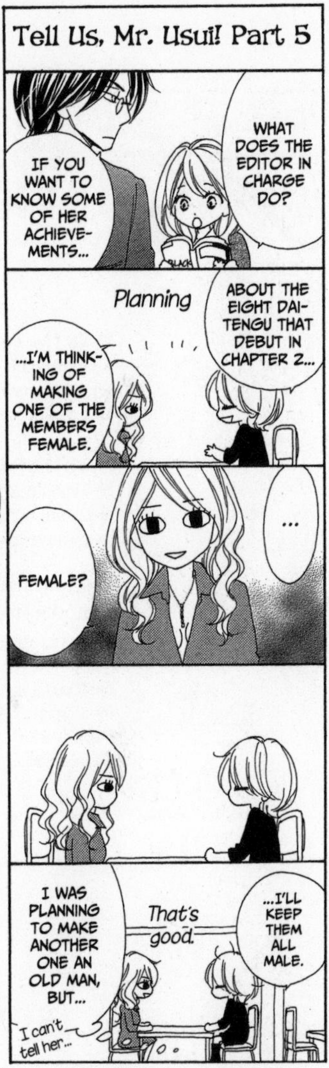
Tell Us, Mr. Usui! Part 5
WHAT DOES THE EDITOR IN CHARGE DO?
IF YOU WANT TO KNOW SOME OF HER ACHIEVEMENTS...
ABOUT THE EIGHT DAI-TENGU THAT DEBUT IN CHAPTER 2...
Planning
...I'M THINKING OF MAKING ONE OF THE MEMBERS FEMALE.
...
FEMALE?
...I'LL KEEP THEM ALL MALE.
That's good.
I WAS PLANNING TO MAKE ANOTHER ONE AN OLD MAN, BUT...
I can't tell her...

I won't say who the female and old man were going to be.

GLOSSARY

PAGE 134, PANEL 3: HOST CLUB
A host club is a social club that
employs primarily male staff
and caters to female patrons.

PAGE 184, PANEL 2: YUKATA
The *yukata* is a garment that is worn in
the summertime in Japan, especially
to outdoor festivals and events.

**PAGE 187, PANEL 1: CARNIVOROUS
AND HERBIVOROUS**
In Japan, "carnivorous" has recently
come to refer to people who actively
seek out a romantic relationship.
By contrast, "herbivorous" refers to
people who are passive about or have
no interest in romantic relationships.

Kanoko Sakurakouji was born in downtown
Tokyo, and her hobbies include reading,
watching plays, traveling and shopping. Her
debut title, *Raibu ga Hanetara*, ran in *Bessatsu
Shojo Comic* (currently called *Bestucomi*) in
2000, and her 2004 *Bestucomi* title *Backstage
Prince* was serialized in VIZ Media's
Shojo Beat magazine. She won the 54th
Shogakukan Manga Award for *Black Bird*.

BLACK BIRD

VOL. 14
Shojo Beat Edition

Story and Art by KANOKO SAKURAKOUJI

© 2007 Kanoko SAKURAKOUJI/Shogakukan
All rights reserved.
Original Japanese edition "BLACK BIRD" published by SHOGAKUKAN Inc.

TRANSLATION JN Productions
TOUCH-UP ART & LETTERING Gia Cam Luc
DESIGN Amy Martin
EDITOR Pancha Diaz

Printed in the U.S.A.

Published by VIZ Media, LLC
P.O. Box 77010
San Francisco, CA 94107

10 9 8 7 6 5 4 3 2 1
First printing, June 2012

www.shojobeat.com   www.viz.com